Higher Education and the Creative Economy

Since the DCMS Creative Industries Mapping Document highlighted the key role played by creative activities in the UK economy and society, the creative industries agenda has expanded across Europe and internationally. It has the support of local authorities, regional development agencies, research councils, arts and cultural agencies and other sector organisations. Within this framework, higher education institutions have also engaged in the creative agenda but have struggled to define their role in this growing sphere of activities.

Higher Education and the Creative Economy critically engages with the complex interconnections between higher education, geography, cultural policy and the creative economy. This book is organised into four sections which articulate the range of dynamics that can emerge between higher education and the creative economy: partnership and collaboration across higher education institutions and the creative and cultural industries; the development of creative human capital; connections between arts schools and local art scenes; and links with broader policy directions and work. While it has a strong UK component, it also includes international perspectives, specifically from Australia, Singapore, Europe and the USA. This authoritative collection challenges the boundaries of creative and cultural industry development by bringing together international experts from a range of subject areas, presenting researchers with a unique multi-disciplinary approach to the topic.

This edited collection will be of interest to researchers and policy-makers working in the area of creative and cultural industries development.

Roberta Comunian is Lecturer in Cultural and Creative Industries at the Department for Culture, Media and Creative Industries at King's College London, UK.

Abigail Gilmore is Director of the Centre for Arts Management and Cultural Policy at the University of Manchester, UK.

Regions and Cities

Series Editor in Chief
Susan M. Christopherson, *Cornell University, USA*

Editors
Maryann Feldman, *University of Georgia, USA*
Gernot Grabher, *HafenCity University Hamburg, Germany*
Ron Martin, *University of Cambridge, UK*
Martin Perry, *Massey University, New Zealand*
Kieran P. Donaghy, *Cornell University, USA*

In today's globalised, knowledge-driven and networked world, regions and cities have assumed heightened significance as the interconnected nodes of economic, social and cultural production, and as sites of new modes of economic and territorial governance and policy experimentation. This book series brings together incisive and critically engaged international and interdisciplinary research on this resurgence of regions and cities, and should be of interest to geographers, economists, sociologists, political scientists and cultural scholars, as well as to policy-makers involved in regional and urban development.

For more information on the Regional Studies Association visit www. regionalstudies.org

There is a **30% discount** available to RSA members on books in the *Regions and Cities* series, and other subject related Taylor & Francis books and e-books including Routledge titles. To order just e-mail alex.robinson@tandf.co.uk, or phone on +44 (0) 20 7017 6924 and declare your RSA membership. You can also visit www.routledge.com

and use the discount code: **RSA0901**

Higher Education and the Creative Economy

Beyond the campus

**Edited by Roberta Comunian
and Abigail Gilmore**

Routledge
Taylor & Francis Group

LONDON AND NEW YORK

First published 2016
by Routledge
2 Park Square, Milton Park, Abingdon, Oxon OX14 4RN

and by Routledge
711 Third Avenue, New York, NY 10017

Routledge is an imprint of the Taylor & Francis Group, an informa business

British Library Cataloguing in Publication Data
A catalogue record for this book is available from the British Library

Library of Congress Cataloging in Publication Data
Names: Comunian, Roberta, editor. | Gilmore, Abigail, editor.
Title: Higher education and the creative economy : beyond the campus /
edited by Roberta Comunian and Abigail Gilmore.
Description: Abingdon, Oxon ; New York, NY : Routledge is an imprint
of the Taylor & Francis Group, an Informa Business, [2016] | Includes
bibliographical references.
Identifiers: LCCN 2015039769| ISBN 9781138918733 (hbk) | ISBN
9781315688305 (ebk)
Subjects: LCSH: Cultural industries–Economic aspects. | Arts–Study and
teaching (Higher)–Economic aspects. | Culture–Study and teaching
(Higher)–Economic aspects. | Creation (Literary, artistic, etc.)–Economic
aspects.
Classification: LCC HD9999.C9472 H54 2016 | DDC 338.4/7700711–dc23
LC record available at http://lccn.loc.gov/2015039769

ISBN: 978-1-138-91873-3 (hbk)
ISBN: 978-1-315-68830-5 (ebk)

Typeset in Times New Roman
by Cenveo Publisher Services

Printed and bound by CPI Group (UK) Ltd, Croydon, CR0 4YY

Contents

Figures

Tables

Contributors

Daniel Ashton is Lecturer in Global Media Management within the Winchester School of Art at the University of Southampton. Before this he completed his PhD at Lancaster University and was a Senior Lecturer and Director of the Media Futures Research Centre at Bath Spa University. He is the co-editor of *Cultural Work and Higher Education* and has authored several journal articles exploring career pathways in the creative industries.

Dawn Bennett is John Curtin Distinguished Professor with Curtin University in Australia. Her research is focused on developing employability within higher education learning and teaching, including identity development and graduate work. A Principal Fellow of the Higher Education Academy and an Australian Learning and Teaching Fellow, Dawn is a regular reviewer and speaker. She serves as a director with the International Society for Music Education and Music Australia.

Paul Benneworth is a senior researcher at the Centre for Higher Education Policy Studies (CHEPS) at the University of Twente in the Netherlands. Paul's research concerns the nature of the relationship between universities and society in the context of the emerging knowledge economy. His particular focus is on the ways in which university activities, knowledge and interventions can lead to changes in societal structures, and exploring how that in turn relates to universities' complex organisational forms.

Scott Brook is Assistant Professor at the Centre for Creative and Cultural Research, University of Canberra. He is currently Chief Investigator on the Australia Research Council Discovery Project 'Working the Field: Creative Graduates in Australia and China'. This is a three-year research project that applies Bourdieu's model of the cultural field to investigate graduate work in the cultural sectors of Melbourne and Shanghai.

Pamela Burnard is Professor of Arts, Creativities and Education at the Faculty of Education, University of Cambridge, UK. She holds degrees in Music Performance, Music Education, Education and Philosophy. Her primary interest is diverse creativities research, including creative teaching and learning, for which she is internationally recognised. She is convenor of the

Creativities in Intercultural Arts Network (CIAN) and the British Education Research Association Creativity in Education SIG.

Roberta Comunian is Lecturer in Creative and Cultural Industries at the Department of Culture, Media and Creative Industries at King's College London. Her work focuses on the relationship between arts, cultural regeneration projects and the cultural and creative industries. She has recently worked on the connections between Higher Education and the Creative Economy and has published extensively on the career opportunities and patterns of creative graduates in UK

Lauren England is an MA student in the Department of Culture, Media and Creative Industries at King's College London. Her work focuses on creative graduates and higher education practices in creative pathways with a specific focus on craft. Her work is inspired by previous study in Glass and Ceramics and she has recently worked on the role of professional networks in the career development of glass-makers.

Alessandra Faggian is Professor at the Ohio State University, AED Economics Department and co-editor of Papers in Regional Science. Her research interests lie in the field of Regional and Urban Economics, Demography, Labour Economics and Economics of Education. Her publications cover a wide range of topics including migration, human capital, labour markets, creativity and local innovation and growth.

Alexandre Frenette is a Postdoctoral Scholar at Arizona State University's Herberger Institute for Design and the Arts. He specialises in the study of work, creative industries and youth labour markets. Using the music industry as a case study, he is currently working on a monograph about the challenges and promise of internships as part of higher education, tentatively titled *The Intern Economy: Laboring to Learn in the Music Industry*.

Abigail Gilmore is a Senior Lecturer in Arts Management and Cultural Policy at the Institute for Cultural Practices, University of Manchester. Her research concerns local cultural policy, management and participation and involves collaboration with cultural partners to inform teaching, knowledge exchange and public engagement. She is the Co-investigator on the AHRC Research Network Beyond the Campus: Higher Education and the Creative Economy, and the AHRC large-grant project 'Understanding Everyday Participation'.

David Gledhill is a Senior Lecturer in Fine Art at the University of Bolton and a PhD candidate at MIRIAD, Manchester. He has exhibited widely both in the UK and abroad. In addition to his activity as an artist David has contributed writing and reviews to numerous art projects and publications. He is co-administrator of Rogue Artists' Studios, the largest artists' studios in the North of England.

Silvie Jacobi is a Joint PhD candidate at the Department of Culture, Media and Creative Industries at King's College London and the Geographisches Institut at Humboldt University Berlin. Trained as visual artist, she holds an MSc in Creative Cities from King's and currently works as an independent consultant at the intersection between social science and cultural practice.

Sarah Jewell is Lecturer in Economics at the University of Reading, UK. Her research interests lie in the fields of labour economics, the economics of higher education, the graduate and time use. She has published on a range of topics including human capital, creative graduates in the UK, life satisfaction, executive pay and performance, and unpaid work.

Sebastian Olma is Professor for Autonomy in Art and Design at St Joost Art Academy and Avans University of Applied Sciences in Breda, the Netherlands. He was trained as a philosopher and organisational economist in Germany, New York and London. At the University of Amsterdam he co-founded the Creative Industries Research Centre and was research fellow at the Institute of Network Culture. He is also director of Amsterdam's Serendipity Lab.

Andy C. Pratt is a Fellow of the Royal Society of Arts, a Fellow of the Royal Geographical Society and an Academician of the Academy of Social Sciences. He has previously held academic appointments at Coventry University, Staffordshire University, University College London, London School of Economics and King's College London. He joined City University London in 2013 as the deputy head of the Department of Culture and Creative Industries.

Venka Purushothaman is an art writer, academic and cultural worker. His research interest centres on festival cultures, artist networks and cultural policy. He is currently Provost at Lasalle College of the Arts, Singapore.

Ivan Rajković is an Andrew W. Mellon Postdoc Fellow at the School of Slavonic and East European Studies, University College London. He specialises in social anthropology of work and (un)employment, particularly in relation to 'unproductive' jobs, the welfare state and moral registers of professions under the pressure of structural reforms, from factory labour to volunteering and art.

Annick Schramme is Professor at the University of Antwerp (Faculty of Applied Economics). She is also Academic Director of the Competence Centre Creative Industries at the Antwerp Management School. She researches creative industries, fashion management, cultural entrepreneurship, arts policy, international cultural policy and local cultural policy. She is a member of several boards of cultural organisations and president of ENCATC, International Network on Cultural Management and Policy Education.

Steven J. Tepper is the Dean of the Herberger Institute for Design and the Arts at Arizona State University, USA, the nation's largest, comprehensive design and arts school at a research university. Tepper is a leading writer and speaker on US cultural policy and his work has fostered national discussions around topics of cultural engagement, everyday creativity and the transformative possibilities of a twenty-first-century creative campus.

Tarek E. Virani is the Post-doctoral Research Assistant on the Place Work Knowledge research project for Creativeworks London, based at Queen Mary, University of London. His research includes examining the role of knowledge within artistic communities, examining formal versus informal learning in artistic communities of practice, musical practice, creative industries research, knowledge exchange policy and work in the cultural economy. He is also a musician and music producer.

Foreword

The chapters in this book provide a wealth of insights for those studying and promoting the engagement of universities with civil society in the round, both locally and globally. The book is a timely contribution to the debate around the economic role of higher education in response to the question: 'What are universities for?'. The response generally breaks down into inputs into business through research and to skills through teaching. These contributions are often seen as quite separate from the role of universities in society more broadly defined in what is commonly referred to as a third (and by definition inferior) mission. The chapters in this book show that a far more nuanced dialogue is required.

More specifically, and taken together, the contributions challenge the dominant science and technology commercialisation model that universities and their funders espouse as a justification for continuing public funding of research (with teaching in the UK funded through the marketplace). This challenge is important because, far from being confined to this sector, the patterns of collaboration between universities and creative enterprises based on trust, co-production of knowledge, networking and a deep linkage between teaching and research is arguably coming to characterise other sectors, particularly where small enterprises are important and open innovation is becoming the norm. Such convergence is driven by digitisation and the growing recognition that new ways of working or social innovations are essential if new products and services are to be widely adopted. And in relation to the public service activities of universities – manifested in venues such as museums, theatres and art galleries – several of the case studies demonstrate that these have a wider role as hubs in the creative economy. In short, if universities in the round are to play a broadly based civic role they will need to follow the lead of their arts and humanities departments in breaking down the distinctions between teaching, research and engagement, and reappraise the role of the research and industrial liaison offices still fixated with spin-outs, technology transfer, patents and licenses.

As the contributions make clear, new ways of working between universities and the creative sector are most manifest within cities. They clearly demonstrate the role of universities as key urban 'anchor institutions'. The Work Foundation (2010) defines anchor institutions as large locally embedded institutions – typically non-governmental public sector, cultural or other civic institutions – that are of significant importance to the economy and the wider community life of the cities in which they are based. They are important because they generate positive externalities and relationships that can support or 'anchor' wider economic activity in the locality.

> Anchor institutions do not have a democratic mandate and their primary missions do not involve regeneration or local economic development. Nonetheless their scale, local rootedness and community links are such that they can play a key role in local development and economic growth representing the 'sticky capital' around which economic growth strategies can be built.
>
> (Work Foundation 2010: 3)

While the role of higher education in the local creative economy is vital to this anchoring role there are threats to its long-term viability not least in the context of the turbulent financial environment confronting higher education and the cultural sector, particularly in the UK but also further afield, as is the focus of several contributions here. This can be coupled to fundamental changes in territorial governance with devolution running in parallel with massive cuts in local authority funding. With increasing competition in the higher education sector, this will inevitably produce winners and losers and have implications for cultural partnerships in different places. In the case of universities, when the bottom line is under threat the questions will be: Who will fund local engagement with the cultural sector when the immediate returns to the institution may be opaque? Will students faced with debt and uncertain local job prospects in the creative sector remain in the regions or will even more so than at present migrate to London? Or more fundamentally not sign up for courses in the creative arts outside of the capital? Will local government increasingly withdraw funding for the arts while the Arts Council expects universities to take on responsibility for arts venues? What weight will local enterprise partnerships give to the creative economy in their business support strategies?

Set against this pessimistic scenario is the possibility that some universities will recognise the insights in this volume and step up to the plate as anchor civic institutions through support of their links with the local creative economy. They could justify this not only as a way of making visible their public good role but also enhancing the attractiveness of their university and city to creative people and indirectly to recruitment to degree programmes outside the arts and humanities. More fundamentally, convergence between creative and digital sectors and the increasing weight given by research funders to engaging civil society in the co-production of research could highlight the importance of links with the creative sector for disciplines outside of the arts and humanities. On the teaching front the experiential learning model well established in arts department partnerships with the creative sector could be used in other degree programmes to enhance the employability of graduates. In short, in this model of civic engagement, the separate spheres of research teaching and engagement exhibit stronger overlap and in this regard university links with the creative sector could be leading the way.

But for this optimistic scenario to prevail the dialogue between those responsible for higher education, the arts and city development will also need to be stepped up. All too often there is a failure for each to understand the others' drivers. More boundary spanners who have knowledge of the creative sector, higher education and city development are required. The essays in this volume will help such people develop this understanding.

John Goddard
Emeritus Professor of Regional Development Studies
Formerly Deputy Vice-Chancellor
Newcastle University

Reference

Work Foundation (2010) *Anchoring Growth: The Role of Anchor Institutions in the Regeneration of UK Cities*, January. London: Work Foundation.

Acknowledgements

The book brings together discussions and ideas emerging from a two-year research network project funded by the Arts and Humanities Research Council (AHRC) in the UK entitled 'Beyond the Campus: Connecting Knowledge and Creative Practice Communities Across Higher Education and the Creative Economy'. The research network was created to provide a platform for academics, practitioners, artists, cultural organisations, business development managers and other university directors to exchange knowledge, make connections and discuss collaboration between higher education and the creative economy. The network enabled us to gather data from interviews and workshop presentations, including international examples of and perspectives on the 'creative campus' (via a research visit to Australia and the invited research papers of international speakers). Many papers were presented at the workshops which formed the main opportunity for 'live' engagement. The key outputs and findings remain available at http://www.creative-campus.org.uk. A policy report was also published in July 2015 aiming to translate some of the key issues in a guide for academics and creative practitioners, in collaboration with designer Adria Davidson.

We acknowledge – alongside the main AHRC Research Network Grant (AH/J005800/1) – the additional funding received from the AHRC to take part in the AHRC Creative Economy Showcase 2014 which enabled us to produce 'Love Story', a creative engagement project working with artist Alys Scott Hawkins and designer Robin Bini Schneider which resulted in a short film and a series of graphic design elements visualising the network's engagement over social media.

In developing the network activities and its outputs, we have benefited from conversations with many colleagues and experts. We would also like to acknowledge the support of our Advisory Committee which provided valuable guidance on the project development and opportunities for further dissemination, specifically: Kion Ahadi (Creative Skillset), Richard Russell (Arts Council England), Pablo Rossello (British Council), Anamaria Wills (CIDA), Jeremy Davenport (Creative Industries KTN, now Lancaster University), Hasan Bakhshi (Nesta) and Sara Selwood (independent cultural analyst).

Many thanks to all the colleagues and practitioners that contributed to the discussion and seminar series of the network and in particular (in alphabetical order): Maria Balshaw, Paul Benneworth, Robin Bini Schneider, Katherine Bond,

Scott Brook, Deborah Bull, Cheryl Butler, Adria Davidson, Lauren England, Alessandra Faggian, John Goddard, Silvie Jacobi, Paul Long, Simon Moreton, George Morgan, Sebastian Olma, Can Seng Ooi, Annick Schramme, Alys Scott Hawkins, Bruno Verbegt, Emma Wakelin, Jack Welsh and Kim Yasuda.

Abbreviations

AAWP	Australian Association of Writing Programs
ACCA	Advisory Council on Culture and the Arts
ACE	Arts Council England
ACUADS	Australian Council of University Arts and Design Schools
ADM	[School of] Art, Design and Media
AFTRS	Australian Film and Radio School
AHRC	Arts and Humanities Research Council
ARC	Australia Research Council
BERR	Department for Business, Enterprise and Regulatory Reform
BIS	Department for Business and Innovation
CAE	College of Advanced Education
CCI	Creative and Cultural Industries
CETL	Centre for Excellence in Teaching and Learning
CI	Creative Industries
CIC	Creative Industries Council
CTEC	Commonwealth Tertiary Education Commission
CUBA	Cultural Utility Building Ancoats
CURDS	Centre for Urban and Regional Development Studies
CVAM	Contemporary Visual Arts Manchester
CWL	Creativeworks London
DCMS	Department for Culture, Media and Sport
DEET	Department of Employment, Education, and Training
DLHE	Destinations of Leavers from Higher Education
EFTSL	Equivalent Full-Time Student Load
EFTSU	Equivalent Full-Time Student Units
ERC	Economic Review Committee Report
GNP	Gross National Product
GSAS	Glasgow School of Art Singapore
HE	Higher Education
HECS	Higher Education Contribution Scheme
HEFCE	Higher Education Funding Council for England
HEI	Higher Education Institution
HESA	Higher Education Statistical Agency

HGB	Hochschule für Grafik und Buchkunst
HMC	Helsinki Music Centre
IB	International Baccalaureate
IBCP	International Baccalaureate Career-related Diploma
IBDP	International Baccalaureate Diploma
IP	Intellectual Property
IPP	Institutions, People and Place
IRO	Independent Research Organisation
ITE	Institutes of Technical Education
JACS	Joint Academic Coding System
KE	Knowledge Exchange
KPI	Key Performance Index
KT	Knowledge Transfer
LASALLE	Lasalle College of the Arts
LDLHE	Longitudinal Destinations of Leavers from Higher Education
LHU	Liverpool Hope University
LPO	Liverpool Philharmonic Orchestra
MASA	Manchester Artists' Studios Association
MICA	Ministry of Information, Communications and the Arts
MMU	Manchester Metropolitan University
MOE	Ministry of Education
NACTMUS	National Council of Heads of Tertiary Music Schools
NAFA	Nanyang Academy of Fine Arts
NGC	National Glass Centre
NIDA	National Institute for the Dramatic Arts
NLS	New Leipzig School
NSSE	National Survey of Student Engagement
NUS	National University of Singapore
OECD	Organisation for Economic Cooperation and Development
QUT	Queensland University of Technology
R&D	Research and Development
RCP	Renaissance City Plan
REF	Research Excellence Framework
ROCC	Rebalancing Our Cultural Capital
SERCARC	Senate Environment, Recreation Communications and the Arts References Committee
SIC	Standard Industrial Classification
SIGMA	Sculptors in Greater Manchester Association
SMEs	Small and Medium-sized Enterprises
SMMEs	Small, Medium and Micro-sized Enterprises
SNAAP	Strategic National Arts Alumni Project
SOC	Standard Occupational Classification
SOTA	School of the Arts
STEM	Science, Technology, Engineering and Mathematics
TAFEs	Institute for Technical and Further Education

TLO	Technology Licensing Office
TTO	Technology Transfer Office
TUM	German Institute of Science and Technology
UNDP	United Nations Development Programme
UNESCO	United Nations Educational, Scientific and Cultural Organisation
UoS	University of Sunderland
UWE	University of the West of England
VAi	Flemish Architecture Institute
VET	Vocational Education and Training
WAC	Weekend Arts College
WECC	West Everton Community Council
YLE	Finnish National Broadcasting Co.

Introduction

1 Higher education and the creative economy

Introduction to a new academic and policy field

Roberta Comunian and Abigail Gilmore

This book brings together critically a series of academic reflections and research connected with a two-year research network project funded by the Arts and Humanities Research Council (AHRC) in the UK entitled 'Beyond the Campus: Connecting Knowledge and Creative Practice Communities Across Higher Education and the Creative Economy' (AH/J005800/1). The research network enabled the creation of a platform for academics, practitioners, artists, cultural organisations, business development managers and other university directors to exchange knowledge, make connections and discuss collaboration between higher education (HE) and the creative economy. Recognising the lack of research in this area, the network provided a point of reference for academics working in this area to reflect on the current state of research and consider future priorities. We recognise, therefore, that the opportunity to bring these findings together in an edited volume is particularly valuable. The network enabled us to gather data from a range of countries, going through different economic and cultural phases, which added value to our research and the range of chapters included here.

Through these activities, we were able to identify some key issues, recent changes and challenges faced by HE in establishing valuable connections with the creative economy. In this book, we explore in particular: the dynamics and inter-mediaries in partnership and collaboration across higher education institutions (HEIs) and the creative and cultural industries; the role of HE in developing creative human capital and its connection with careers and geography; the importance of arts schools and art courses in creating local art scenes; and, finally, the connection between HE policy and the creative economy in shaping future dynamics of regeneration, engagement and education.

The book addresses these key issues from a truly multidisciplinary perspective: we have chapters from geography and urban and regional studies alongside contributions from business studies academics as well as experts in cultural studies. As this field involves a complex level of analysis from the individual (artist or academic) to the organisational or business structure and its connection with places and regions, as well as broader national policy perspectives, we have welcomed the range of approaches and scales included and believe they offer an opportunity for an in-depth understanding that is not limited to one predominant disciplinary framework. It is also a very international effort. While the book has a strong UK component – and the network and debate started in the UK – it also includes international reflection, specifically from Australia, Singapore, Europe (Belgium, the Netherlands and Germany) and the USA.

In this introduction, we acknowledge that before starting on the collection of academic reflections, it is important to identify the actors and protagonists as well as define the terminology that is used throughout the book. It is also important to chart a brief history of the development of ideas that the book explores. After this overview, we then introduce the structure of the book and outline its components. Finally, we highlight the emergent nature of this new area of research and the need for more funding and publications that explore this agenda, both in Europe and further afield.

Genealogy and terminology of a new research agenda: higher education and the creative economy

When bringing together chapters from an international context, frameworks and terminology can sometimes differ. However, we believe that clarifying the range of actors and players is helpful to create a baseline, so we provide an overview (see Figure 1.1), specifically defining the terms 'higher education', 'communities', 'creative economy' and 'public policy' in relation to this research area (Comunian and Gilmore 2015).

In the UK and many other countries, the HE sector comprises mainly publicly funded HEIs that are driven by different measures in their teaching or research missions. While we acknowledge that in many countries there is also a growing private base for provision, the chapters in this book predominantly focus on publicly funded institutions, albeit to different degrees. In many countries there is a distinction between the agenda and activities of the *research-intensive universities* (in the UK these are often identified with the term 'Russell Group'), which view research (and research-informed teaching) as their main focus and who receive significant funding (from the public sector as well as other sources) to fulfil these goals, and *other universities* that tend to place more emphasis on teaching and training and have, therefore, also placed more emphasis on their contribution to local development and local skills (Goddard and Vallance 2013).

The role of HE is often identified by two main areas of activity: the development of human capital (Faggian and McCann, 2009; Karlsson and Zhang, 2001) and the development of new knowledge and R&D (Agrawal 2001; Löfsten and Lindelöf 2005). In relation to human capital in this book, we specifically address the development of *creative human capital*. Every year graduates enter the labour market (Comunian and Faggian 2014) with the relevant knowledge and critical thinking to contribute to the creative and cultural economy, as well as other sectors. The importance of this contribution is often underestimated and questioned in relation to the weak career outcomes of many creative graduates in the UK (Comunian *et al.* 2011). The role of creative human capital is discussed in greater detail in the chapters included in Parts II and III of the book.

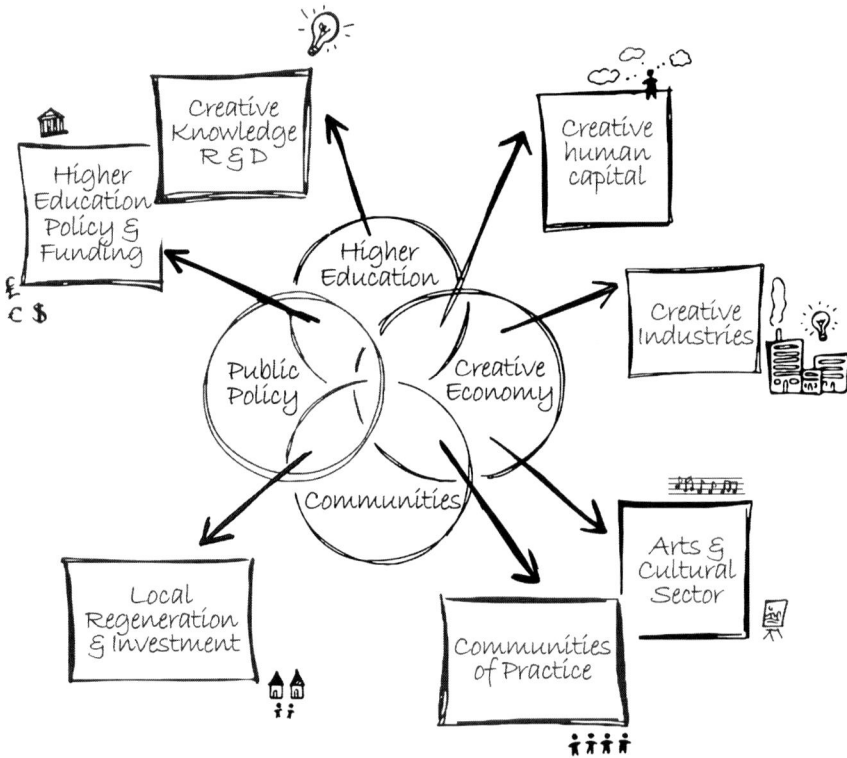

Figure 1.1 Terminology and key players in the relationship between higher education and the creative economy

Source: Comunian and Gilmore (2015: 8). Design courtesy of Adria Davidson.

However, in the book, we also address the importance of knowledge generation, and specifically *creative knowledge and R&D*, as being fundamental to the development of an innovative and competitive creative economy. Some have questioned the role played by HEIs in these sectors (Cunningham *et al.* 2004). In fact, while in science and technology knowledge transfer between academia and industry is a common occurrence, this does not seem as developed and takes less direct routes within the creative disciplines (Crossick 2006), a distinction which needs better understanding and support.

Many of the chapters in this book look at the connection between HE and the creative economy with reference to the role of communities. Comprehending the meaning of *communities* in this agenda can sometimes be oversimplified: they tend to be the people surrounding (spatially) the organisations under discussion. However, as many authors highlight, the new role played by digital technologies means that sometimes their location (and definition) should not be taken for granted (Pratt *et al.* 2007; Uricchio 2004). Communities can be very diverse, (sometimes) even remote stakeholders or audiences. Further considerations also lie in relation to *communities of practice or interest* (Wenger 1998). These are a special kind of community in which the bond is the shared interest in a specific subject or topic. Communities of practice are specifically relevant for the creative industries, as they build networks of knowledge and support among practitioners in specialised fields (Comunian 2012). These ideas are discussed in Chapters 1, 2 and 7, as well as in the chapters in Part III.

As per the definition of HE, the definition of what constitutes the *creative economy* (UNCTAD 2008) is also considered by many as an evolving concept with very different geographical connotations. Here, we can define the creative economy as an umbrella term that aims to capture a set of interrelated activities based around the production, distribution and consumption of creative and cultural goods (and ideas) which generate cultural, social and economic impact. In the UK, as well as internationally, there is an acknowledgement that there are two core (and interrelated) components of the creative economy: on one side the (mostly but not always) commercial *creative industries*, often promoted for their economic growth and potential for job creation (DCMS 1998), and the (often publicly funded) *arts and cultural sector* (Fisher 2012), recognised for its contribution to the socio- and cultural well-being of places. Most of the chapters in the book clarify their standpoint but it is useful to highlight the wide range of components as they have an important but different role in their work with HE and their relation to place.

In particular, the *creative industries* are defined as 'those industries which have their origin in individual creativity, skill and talent and which have a potential for wealth and job creation through the generation and exploitation of intellectual property' (DCMS 1998: 2) and include a range of sectors: advertising; architecture; arts and antique markets; crafts; design and designer fashion; film, video, and photography; software, computer games and electronic publishing; music and the visual and performing arts; publishing; television; and radio. While they have made headlines for the past decade for their speed of economic growth and development, they are also recognised in the literature for being mainly comprised of small and micro enterprises that rely on social networks and local clusters for their development. This dimension and its implications are discussed in a few chapters of the book, including Chapter 2, 3 and 8.

The *arts and cultural sector* is often identified with the publicly funded or not-for-profit art sector as a key partner of HEIs (Dawson and Gilmore 2009). It is commonly forgotten that HEIs are themselves often directly involved in the provision of arts and cultural activities to a range of audiences via their museums, theatres and concert halls, as Chapters 3 and 7 highlight.

Finally, the role of *public policy* is often underestimated, but pivotal in the interaction between HE and the creative economy. Public policy, both at national and regional or local level, is broadly concerned with communities, education and cultural policy, so in this respect, it is a key component of every intervention and relationship that is developed. However, in relation to our area of focus, two key aspects are particularly relevant: the *HE policy and funding framework* – this is often determined at the national level – and public policy intervention in relation to *local regeneration interventions* that are often developed in urban and regional contexts. Part IV of the book specifically addresses the role of policy.

The *HE policy and funding framework* has changed drastically in the last few years, with the move towards a more neoliberal HE system (Canaan and Shumar 2008; Slaughter and Rhoades 2004). This has seen the introduction of tuition fees across all subjects and a new market driven approach to teaching provision. From a research perspective, it has also highlighted the importance of demonstrating the impact of public funding, not only in STEM (science, technology, engineering and mathematics) subjects, but also within arts and humanities disciplines (Belfiore and Upchurch 2013; Preston and Hammond 2006). Emphasis on collaborative frameworks (across academia and external partners) and funding (such as the AHRC Creative Economy Hubs) has encouraged a new understanding of the role of research in the creative economy (AHRC 2011; Bakhshi *et al.* 2008; Hughes *et al.* 2011; Taylor 2005). *Local regeneration interventions* have been another key concern of public policy, beyond the HE and creative economy remits. With the changing landscape from industrial to post-industrial economies and changing patterns of employment and skills, many of the local regeneration interventions across the UK have seen the contribution of universities in reshaping old to new knowledge (Chatterton 1999; Noble and Barry 2008; Powell 2007).

Of course beyond introducing the key players in this area of research, it is important also to trace their history and while the focus of the book is on emerging dynamics and future challenges, it is also important to map out this history and current interconnections as they have evolved in past decades. The framework (Figure 1.2) aims to clarify some of the key dynamics and concepts within the growing literature

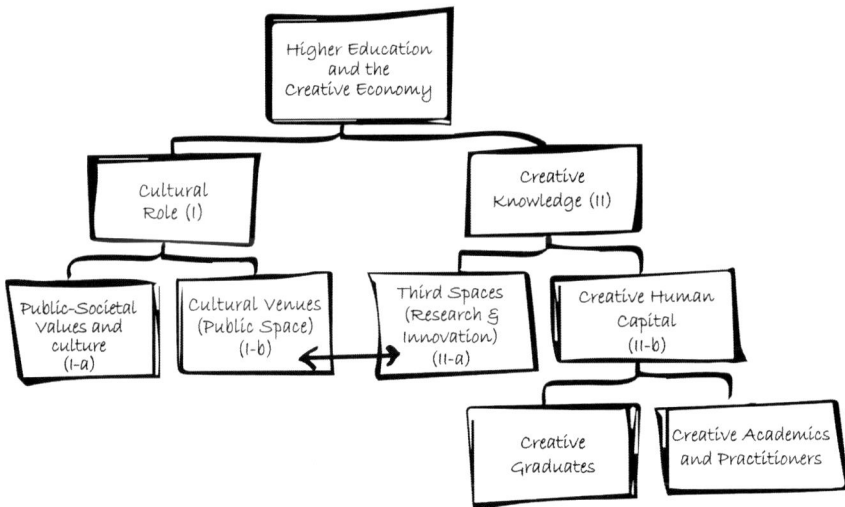

Figure 1.2 A framework to explore the relationship between higher education and the creative economy

Source: Comunian and Gilmore (2015: 10). Design courtesy of Adria Davidson.

surrounding the creative economy, to better understand the multiplicity and complexity of the interactions that connect the sector to HEIs (Comunian and Gilmore 2014).

Historically, universities have long been key cultural players in cities and communities. Many universities have been beacons of cultural production and preservation through the establishment of art collections, museums and galleries. This continues today with the hosting of performing arts spaces on campus and the undertaking of academic research on arts and cultural activities (Chatterton 1999; Comunian *et al*. 2014b). However, latterly, there has been a growing pressure from policy to understand and demonstrate the impact of HEIs in relation to the arts sector and the creative economy (Hughes *et al*. 2011; Universities UK 2010). A key objective is, therefore, to further facilitate these relationships and add to their potential value. This relates to a general level of interaction corresponding to the 'Cultural Role' (I) played by universities in the creative economy. Interactions are linked to the impact of the presence of the university and its public-societal agenda (I-a) (Chatterton and Goddard 2000; Goddard and Vallance 2013) and also in terms of the presence of venues, facilities and cultural spaces (I-b).

Alongside this cultural role, there is a much richer knowledge impact, as 'Creative Knowledge' (II) is generated within and on the boundaries between academia and the creative economy (Comunian *et al*. 2015; Comunian *et al*. 2014b). The concept of knowledge transfer (often labelled knowledge exchange or external engagement) has become increasingly important in making the argument that arts and humanities departments have a positive impact on society and provide good value for money (Crossick 2006). Some authors have seen this new pressure for knowledge transfer and exchange as an imposition of a 'techno-economic' paradigm on arts and humanities in academia (Bullen *et al*. 2004), but most HEIs have embraced this new perspective, seeing it as an opportunity to add value to their work (Lingo and Tepper 2010; Tepper 2006). The knowledge connections which universities develop with the creative economy are considered particularly important as measures of impact and engagement, increasingly embedded within research assessment exercise (Comunian *et al*. 2014b). Although the evidence gathered is currently mostly anecdotal, there is an increasing pressure within policy circles to show the value of these dynamics through robust measures (Bakhshi *et al*. 2009). Initially, relationships between HE and the creative economy have been characterised by the assumption that knowledge sitting within academia can benefit the work and practice of creative practitioners and organisations, with a strong emphasis on entrepreneurship (DCMS 2006). These values have been framed explicitly in relation to entrepreneurialism and the creative economy and more recently in relation to social responsibility, community engagement and development – where the injection of academic, specialist knowledge in history, classics, languages, literatures and cultures is seen to provide the basis for improvement and connection with those on the outside. New models for research and other collaborations are emerging – some analysed in the chapters of this book – which attempt to demonstrate how academic research can engage in other ways with the creative economy, establishing new principles for the ways in which these sectors can come together, producing shared outputs and the potential for genuine co-production and collaboration. This is in part due to the increased pressure on research funding councils (Belfiore 2015) to demonstrate the social and economic returns on investment, leveraging new programmes of funding that are deliberately targeting opportunities for knowledge exchange and collaboration with creative practitioners and communities. However, it is also partially in response to broader issues in HE policy, such as new financial barriers for access to knowledge and education, and an increasing interest in the civic university, as well as in taking down the walls of the institution in order to reconfigure the ways in which knowledge and knowledge-making practices move in and out (Goddard and Vallance 2013).

Within 'Creative Knowledge' (II) two important elements can be identified: one is the 'creative human capital' involved (II-b); the other is the role played by 'third spaces' in creating opportunities for shared research and innovation (II-a). The growing role played by creative human capital (Comunian *et al*. 2014a) and shared third spaces corresponds to the emergence of bilateral and more organic models of engagement, where new knowledge can be co-created and developed across and beyond academia (Olma 2012). The book builds on this complex landscape and history to chart the changing dynamics and drivers of the different relationships between universities and the creative economy as well as their interconnected communities.

The chapters

This book is the first attempt to identify key issues and emerging research questions. It draws from case studies and examples from the UK, Europe and further afield, specifically Australia, Singapore and the USA. The chapters are organised into four parts: Beyond the Campus: Partnership and Collaboration Across Higher Education Institutions and the Creative and Cultural Industries; Higher Education and Creative Human Capital; Connecting the Dots: Arts Schools and Local Art Scenes; and Higher Education Policy and the Creative Economy.

Part I Beyond the Campus: Partnership and Collaboration Across Higher Education Institutions and the Creative and Cultural Industries

In the first part of the book, we focus specifically on the partnerships and interconnections between HEIs and creative and cultural industries. Here, we look at the different forms that these partnerships and collaboration can take. In the first chapter by Ashton, we look at how collaboration happens through a creative hub – 'Artswork Media' – that enables students to work within creative clusters, whereas in the second chapter by Virani and Pratt, the focus is specifically on collaboration with small and medium size organisations in the creative industries. The last chapter by Schramme features a case study of the arts campus 'deSingel' in Antwerp (Belgium), where the collaboration is between a specialised arts institution and a large arts centre. This first part, therefore, highlights the range of organisations that are involved in collaborations and exchanges between HE and the creative economy. Of course, the creative economy is an umbrella term that encompasses a range of very different organisations, from private corporations to public sector organisations and not-for-profit activities. It is multi-faceted not only in relation to its needs and practices, but also in relation to the wide range of organisations of varying size that can be involved with universities: from large private global conglomerates and large public national institutions, to smaller creative charities and individual creative sole traders. It is important therefore to pay specific attention to the differences and avoid generalisation about practices in so diverse a sector, as the authors in this part highlight.

In the first chapter, Ashton describes the opportunities that might derive from new forms of workplace learning in the context of Artswork Media, a creative digital agency run by media professionals and third-year students on the BA Creative Media Practice of Bath Spa University. Ashton highlights how Artswork Media, embedded in a creative cluster called 'Paintworks' and surrounded by other creative and cultural industries, provides students with an opportunity not only to learn and test their skills, but to experience project-based learning and the nature of work in this sector. This potentially could facilitate their transition from students to workers in the creative economy. Artswork Media can be seen as a hybrid space that retains HE objectives while engaging in creative production practices with patterns which are more closely connected (and authentic) to the nature and practice of creative workplaces. One of the key elements of this hybridity – which Comunian and Gilmore (2015) would define as a third space in the context of HE and the creative economy – is the opportunity for students to establish networks and connections that bridge across learning and working practices.

In the second chapter in this part, Virani and Pratt look specifically at the role of intermediaries in bridging the relationship between HE and the creative and cultural industries (CCIs). They consider the work of Creativeworks London and their 'creative vouchers' scheme, which aims to partner CCIs with academic researchers to support new collaborations and knowledge exchange. While the overall project – supported by the Arts and Humanities Research Council in the UK – has a strong policy drive and offers a range of opportunities to London-based academics and CCIs, they focus specifically on the emerging role of intermediaries. They identify the role they play as brokers of new relations, translators across sectors and builders of networks and opportunities. Their findings also indicate that collaborations benefit significantly from active and engaged intermediaries who not only facilitate, but also embed themselves within the collaboration they support. Their conclusions highlight the role of trust reputation, and the informal maintenance and support for those processes and networks.

In contrast with the previous reflections, focusing on CCIs and small work-based enterprise activities, the third chapter of the part by Schramme considers what happens when partnerships are established between educational institutions and large cultural organisations. She looks specifically at the collaboration between the Royal Conservatory of Antwerp in Belgium and deSingel, the largest international arts centre in Flanders – however, she also includes international benchmarking of this case study with the Barbican Centre/Guildhall School of Music and Theatre (in London) and the Helsinki Music Centre (in Finland). The focus of the chapter is on how this kind of external collaboration or partnership triggers organisational change and provides encounters for new management practice. Schramme highlights that while many objectives and values are shared between educational and cultural institutions, there are also different approaches and motivations that can sometimes cause friction and misunderstandings. She also highlights that these kinds of collaboration need to be continually evaluated in relation to value and practices, not only from the perspective of the organisations themselves (their artists or teachers) but also from the perspective of their users (students and audiences) to retain the significance of the collaboration for those involved.

Part II Higher Education and Creative Human Capital

Creative human capital refers to the ways in which people are engaged, developed and applied as resources within the fields of the creative economy. By referring to people as 'capital', there is an explicit assumption that we are referring to the skills and attributes appropriate for work, labour and economic production. The focus of the second part of the book is, therefore, on graduates and their development and transformation through HE and training into creative workers. The creative workforce has been the centre of attention of in recent policy work and, understandably, the contribution that HE can make in developing this workforce, and in embedding creative human capital within economic development, is an important area for further research. There is a growing body of academic research that explores the impact of 'creative human capital' on specific places in the form of creative graduates (Comunian and Faggian 2014). The contributions in Part II take this debate further, firstly providing an international perspective, specifically on data from the USA. Secondly, they provide an in-depth analysis of what skills and capabilities are developed – discussed in Bennett and Burnard's chapter – and show how they relate also to geography, migration and place in Comunian *et al.*'s contribution.

Frenette and Tepper's contribution offers an insight into the employment patterns and longitudinal career outcomes of arts graduates in the USA. With US institutions graduating close to 130,000 visual and performing artists a year, it is of course very important to consider their destinations as well as their career satisfaction. The chapter draws on data from the Strategic National Arts Alumni Project (SNAAP), a survey of more than 92,000 arts alumni from over 140 institutions across North America started in 2011. The findings and reflections highlight that, despite unstable careers and employment patterns, arts graduates place great value on and are overall satisfied with their degree and careers. They also highlight issues of debt and inequality as challenges for institutions of higher education and arts graduates. One interesting table (Table 4.3) also shows how over time there is an increased (although still limited) provision of more business and entrepreneurial skills by HE, underlining the importance of HE responding to context and skills changes in this sector.

Similarly to Frenette and Tepper, Chapter 6 by Comunian, Faggian and Jewell explores via quantitative data the career patterns of creative graduates in the UK; however, their focus is on the mobility and migration strategies of these graduates. The chapter highlights that, influenced by the creative class theory (Florida 2002), we take for granted that creative graduates are highly mobile, but in fact they are no more mobile than other graduates and present interesting spatial strategies in response to career challenges. The most common migration pattern of creative graduates is 'return migration' and is often associated with the lowest salary level. This seems to be a coping strategy for recent graduates as they try and develop a portfolio and might resort to family support to enable them to start their career. However, the second most common migration path, 'repeat migration', is associated with the highest salary. Individuals who risk moving to follow opportunities seem to be able to get better rewards for it. These findings highlight that alongside geographical and sector differences, looking at migration patterns can help explain career outcomes and the trajectories of creative graduates.

In contrast with the previous quantitative works, Bennett and Burnard's chapter offers an in-depth qualitative reflection on the role of HE in developing 'human capital creativities' that enable graduates to enter creative work. They find that for creative workers, community capital, career-positioning capital, inspiration-forming capital and bestowed capital are essential forms of capital that graduates require to enter and establish themselves in the sector. They also consider the role of habitus in understanding creative workers' professional learning culture and work practices. They conclude by highlighting that while creative work is receiving increasing attention from researchers, the social practices through which different creativities are recognised and communicated remain under-researched.

Part III Connecting the Dots: Arts Schools and Local Art Scenes

The third part considers HE and local creative economies through the complex sets of relations between specialist education and the practices and communities which make up the nodes of 'soft infrastructures' of production and consumption – the art schools, scenes and 'dots' of the title. These interactions and their consequences are often neglected, and require particular qualitative research approaches to draw out the historical background and to further explore the issues, relationships and practices raised by quantitative research in this area.

England and Comunian consider the case of small businesses and sole traders in the creative industries and their interactions with HEIs through a study of regional craft production in the North East, specifically through exploring the testimonies of glass-makers based in and around Sunderland. They identify the range of interdependencies between HE and the local producers, which include the important provision of hard infrastructure, such as exhibition and studio space, and (expensive) production facilities afforded by continuing links with HE. They also point to the importance of soft infrastructure, the development of networks, the incubation mechanisms and market development, and the neglected role of HE in local governance as a potentially neutral intermediary and champion of local economic development, situated between policy and industry. In the case of glass-making in Sunderland, they find evidence that the neoliberal imperative for student recruitment has potentially led to oversupply and a weakened local market, due to the unfair competitive advantages provided by links to HEIs. They also note the absence of support for sustainable professional and business development, which would counterbalance the additional threat of shifting priorities within the local 'triple helix' (Etzkowitz and Leydesdorff 1997) of industry, policy and HE.

Taking a similar approach, Gilmore *et al.* consider the relationships between local economies and infrastructures for professional development and the skills and knowledge learnt at art school through the lived experiences and aspirations of artists working within a large studio complex in Manchester. Through qualitative interviews with a small sample of artists, they explore their trajectories since graduating against the backdrop of the city's history of involvement and support for contemporary visual arts markets and networks, in the current context of concerns about a regional deficit of opportunity 'to make it' as an artist without moving away. In contrast to recent complaints about the lack of local public support for exhibition and representation, they find a strong DIY culture has evolved in part through the connections and knowledge sharing available through co-location in studio groups, but also a sense of individual determination, both of which arguably have arisen as a direct result of lack of alternatives. Furthermore, they highlight how factors such as cheaper accommodation and studio space are favourable for artistic production, i.e. for making art, even if the gallery connections and networks that might launch or consolidate an artist's career may reside elsewhere (in the UK, still overwhelmingly in London). They conclude by suggesting that HEIs would better support artist professional development and, crucially, improve graduate retention in local creative economies if they worked more closely with local studio groups and other components of visual arts' soft infrastructures.

This theme is picked up and continued by Jacobi through a case study of Leipzig in Germany, based on qualitative interviews with visual artists and protagonists in professional development. She finds that the particular characteristics of urban fabric and housing stock in the city have supported the growth of a 'creative class' (Florida 2002), which is remarkable in the prevalence of artist-led, volunteer and bottom-up initiatives that contribute significantly to the health of the creative economy. The city's burgeoning reputation as the new 'old Berlin', or 'Hypezig', taken up in city branding, is proving controversial: it is resisted by those at the heart of the relationship with local HE, the visual arts movement 'New Leipzig School' (with close links to the major art school), who strive to protect their authenticity and autonomy from the 'hype' of commercialism. The research reveals the investments made by artists into the cultural and built fabric of their local art scenes, and comments on how the freedom to innovate and to make new work and living spaces while retaining links to formal institutional frameworks, has been facilitated by the strong sense of collectivism and artist community formation. In turn, Jacobi argues, these resilient 'communities of prac-tice' (Wenger, 1998) owe their basis in the pedagogic practices and networks formed at art school.

The final chapter in this section by Purushothaman examines the development of and influences on art schools in Singapore, in the context of its reinvention as a creative city-state, locating the arts within an instrumentalised agenda as a driver of local economic growth as well as of nation-building and civic well-being. He argues that this account rests on the history of colonialism, which saw the early development of arts school in British India in the 1800s, alongside the institution of the English language, as places of technical education in craft skills and the formation of aesthetic taste. The history of art schools in Singapore followed suit in the early nineteenth century, but drew also on the influences of Chinese art movements and the tensions between nationalism and anti-colonial regionalism in South East Asia. Tracing this history up to the present day, Purushothaman incorporates the broader history of policy-making and cultural infrastructure development in Singapore, to show how the current context of investment in creative tertiary education is anchored to the STEM (science, tech-nology, engineering and mathematics) agenda. The foremost art schools in Singapore, he argues, maintain their independence and distinction from this agenda through their allegiance to the preservation of traditional art forms, as well as their role in protecting a space for criticality and process-oriented practice.

Part IV Higher Education Policy and the Creative Economy

The final section examines the dynamic relations between policy and HE at both national and regional levels from three different but equally critical perspectives. HEIs contribute to local socio-cultural and economic regeneration processes, initiatives and projects that involve cultural and creative elements or strategies. They are also part of wider programmes of economic development and growth based on skills retention, development and supply. The examples featured here suggest these relations are influenced by the vested interests and hoped-for instru-mental outcomes of creative education; the authors are unified by their desire to find new ways for universities to make societal impacts through critical creative education, to engage with external communities and to provide the impetus for social innovation while honouring their unique role in knowledge-making and intellectual progress.

Benneworth's chapter focuses on the ways in which tensions and potential negative impacts can arise through the interventions universities make within creative economies as they enter into negotiation with the wider complex sphere of social and physical regeneration and community development by building 'creative campuses'. Benneworth argues that public value failures exist at the heart of these attempts, primarily through difficulties in balancing social compacts between HE and the wider society with the forms of societal benefits that can be realised by universities' more conventional purpose of intellectual development and knowledge-making. Looking at the case of Liverpool Hope University's

'Cornerstone' creative campus in Everton, he argues that even with the best intentions such developments involve the risk of public value failure, since they necessarily involve engagement with local political economies prevailing within surrounding communities. Within these relations, surrounding residential communities can become marginalised as stakeholders, a position which is further conflated when set against the needs and demands of other less marginalised, more powerful stakeholders (which may include 'creative types') who have discrete financial interests and gains from the decision-making processes within regeneration. Benneworth intentionally highlights these issues to counterbalance celebratory claims that creative campus developments are risk-free, and to warn that they should not serve as distractions from the core business of universities: delivering higher education.

Brook takes up further the moral concerns for creative higher education in his account of the perceived 'creative turn' in Australian HE over the last decade. Focusing his lens on the institutional context of the problems and criticisms associated with the growth in creative industries focused programmes (including oversupply to precarious industries, skills development issues and the loss of critical thinking from the curriculum), he argues that these changes have a longer history with roots in the earlier mass restructuring of the university sector, rather than as a branch of targeted cultural and economic policy *per se*. Creative arts education, he maintains, was an unanticipated outcome of the radical remaking of universities and their business models, which revealed these problems most acutely in the 'contact point' (Foucault 1997) between demand for new forms of creative HE and labour market outcomes. It is here that the issue of 'employability' is most prominent, alongside the metrics by which successful creative industries curricula are assessed, with distinct implications for arts education and for the boundaries and definitions of creativity, creative industries and the relative value of the skills they demand. Brook concludes by arguing that to address the criticisms of creative HE, we need to further uncouple advocacy based on the economic value of the sector from programme and curriculum design, and, at the same time, re-emphasise the more plausible arguments about the cognitive skills that creative education produces, which have a broader societal impact than in the misaligned area of enterprise.

In the final chapter, Olma follows Brook's lead, albeit from a more polemical and philosophical position, to address the structural determinism of university's contribution to creative education that, he argues, is constrained by disciplinary boundaries and confounded by managerial confusion. He considers the models for HE that can equip society with creative citizens rather than precarious workers, and argues that the fundamental concepts of sagacity, virtuosity and serendipity should be brought into play to design a new form of university that affords the 'Übungsraum' to promote social innovation among its graduates. Drawing on the philosophy of Serres (2000, 2012), Sennett (2008) and others, he argues that universities can transform themselves, not only through the use of digital technologies that are already changing the forms of knowledge transmission, storage and access to knowledge-making for broader society, but also by encouraging conditions for collaboration, exchange and serendipitous encounters across disciplines and boundaries with virtuous intent.

Each contribution has its own individual merit; when brought together in these four parts, we believe they provide a powerful set of reflections on the changing landscape of higher education and the creative economy in relation to place. It is hoped that this will instigate further research and discussion, not only looking at the creative economy as a sector where our higher education knowledge and research can be applied, but also as a sector that can shape the impact and value of higher education itself. In the concluding remarks, we highlight further steps to strengthen this research and policy area.

References

Agrawal, A. (2001) 'University-to-industry knowledge transfer: literature review and unanswered questions', *International Journal of Management Reviews*, 3 (4): 285–302.

AHRC (2011) 'AHRC announces £16m boost for arts and humanities researchers and the UK creative economy', Swindon. Online at: http://www.ahrc.ac.uk/News-and-Events/News/Pages/AHRC-announces-pound;16m-boost-for-Arts-and-Humanities-researchers-and-the-UK-Creative-Economy.aspx.

Bakhshi, H., Schneider, P. and Walker, C. (2008) Arts and Humanities Research and Innovation. Bristol and London: AHRC and NESTA.

Bakhshi, H., Schneider, P. and Walker, C. (2009) 'Arts and humanities research in the innovation system: the UK example', *Cultural Science*, 2 (1): 1–23.

Belfiore, E. (2015) '"Impact", "value" and "bad economics": making sense of the problem of value in the arts and humanities', *Arts and Humanities in Higher Education*, 14 (1): 95–110.

Belfiore, E. and Upchurch, A. (2013) *Humanities in the Twenty-first Century: Beyond Utility and Markets*. Palgrave Macmillan.

Bullen, E., Robb, S. and Kenway, J. (2004) '"Creative destruction": knowledge economy policy and the future of the arts and humanities in the academy', *Journal of Education Policy*, 19 (1): 3–22.

Canaan, J. E. and Shumar, W. (2008) *Structure and Agency in the Neoliberal University*. London: Routledge.

Chatterton, P. (1999) 'The cultural role of universities in the community: reivisiting the university–community debate', *Environment and Planning A*, 32: 165–81.

Chatterton, P. and Goddard, J. (2000) 'The response of higher education institutions to regional needs', *European Journal of Education*, 35 (4): 475–96.

Comunian, R. (2012) 'Exploring the role of networks in the creative economy of North East England: economic and cultural dynamics', in B. Warf (ed.), *Encounters and Engagement Between Economic Cultural Geography*. Netherlands: Springer, pp. 143–57.

Comunian, R. and Faggian, A. (2014) 'Creative graduates and creative cities: exploring the geography of creative education in the UK', *International Journal of Cultural and Creative Industries*, 1 (2): 19–34.

Comunian, R. and Gilmore, A. (2014) 'From knowledge sharing to co-creation: paths and spaces for engagement between higher education and the creative and cultural industries', in Annick Schramme, Rene Kooyman and G. Hagoort (eds), *Beyond Frames: Dynamics*

Between the Creative Industries, Knowledge Institutions and the Urban Context. Delft: Eburon Academic Press, pp. 174–85.

Comunian, R. and Gilmore, A. (2015) *Beyond the Creative Campus: Reflections on the Evolving Relationship Between Higher Education and the Creative Economy*. London: King's College London. Available at: http://www.creative-campus.org.uk.

Comunian, R., Faggian, A. and Jewell, S. (2011) 'Winning and losing in the creative industries: an analysis of creative graduates' career opportunities across creative disciplines', *Cultural Trends*, 20 (3/4): 291–308.

Comunian, R., Faggian, A. and Jewell, S. (2014a) 'Embedding arts and humanities in the creative economy: the role of graduates in the UK', *Environment and Planning C: Government and Policy*, 32 (3): 426–50.

Comunian, R., Gilmore, A. and Jacobi, S. (2015) 'Higher education and the creative economy: creative graduates, knowledge transfer and regional impact debates', *Geography Compass*, 9 (7): 371–83.

Comunian, R., Taylor, C. and Smith, D. N. (2014b) 'The role of universities in the regional creative economies of the UK: hidden protagonists and the challenge of knowledge transfer', *European Planning Studies*, 22 (12): 2456–76.

Crossick, G. (2006) *Knowledge Transfer Without Widgets: The Challenge of the Creative Economy*. Paper presented at the Lecture, Royal Society of Arts, Goldsmiths University of London.

Cunningham, S., Cutler, T., Hearn, G., Ryan, M. and Keane, M. (2004) 'An innovation agenda for the creative industries: where is the randd?', *Media International Australia: Incorporating Culture and Policy*, 112: 174–85.

Dawson, J. and Gilmore, A. (2009) *Shared Interest: Developing Collaboration, Partnerships and Research Relationships Between Higher Education, Museums, Galleries and Visual Arts Organisations in the North West*, a Joint Consultancy Research Project commissioned by Renaissance North West, Arts Council England North West and the North West Universities Association.

DCMS (1998) *Creative Industries Mapping Document*. London: Department for Culture, Media and Sport.

DCMS (2006) *Making the Case for Public Investment: Developing Entrepreneurship for the Creative Industries – The Role of Higher Education*. London: DCMS.

Etzkowitz, H. and Leydesdorff, L. (eds) (1997) *Universities and the Global Knowledge Economy: A Triple Helix of University-Industry-Government Relations*. London: Pinter.

Faggian, A. and McCann, P. (2009) 'Universities, agglomerations and graduate human capital mobility', *Journal of Economic and Social Geography (TESG)*, 100 (2): 210–23.

Fisher, S. (2012) *The Cultural Knowledge Ecology. A Discussion Paper on Partnerships Between HEIs and Cultural Organisations*. Working Paper. London: Arts Council England.

Florida, R. (2002) *The Rise of the Creative Class*. New York: Basic Books.

Foucault, M. ([1980] 1997) 'Subjectivity and truth', in S. Lotringer (ed.), *The Politics of Truth*. New York: Semiotext(e)

Goddard, J. and Vallance, P. (2013) *The University and the City*. Abingdon: Routledge.

Hughes, A., Kitson, M., Probert, J., Bullock, A. and Milner, I. (2011) *Hidden Connections: Knowledge Exchange Between the Arts and Humanities and the Private, Public and Third Sectors*. London: Arts and Humanities Research Council (AHRC) and Centre for Business Research (CBR) at the University of Cambridge.

Karlsson, C. and Zhang, W.-B. (2001) 'The role of universities in regional development: endogenous human capital and growth in a two-region model', *Annals of Regional Science*, 35 (2): 179–97.

Lingo, E. L. and Tepper, S. J. (2010) 'The creative campus: time for a "c" change', *Chronicle of Higher Education*, 15 October. Available at: http://chronicle.com/article/The-Creative-Campus-Time-for/124860/ (last accessed 7 December 2015).

Löfsten, H. and Lindelöf, P. (2005) 'Randd networks and product innovation patterns – academic and non-academic new technology-based firms on science parks', *Technovation*, 25 (9): 1025–37.

Noble, M. and Barry, T. (2008) *Supporting Regional Regeneration and Workforce Development: Establishing a New University Centre in Folkestone.* Paper presented at the UVAC Annual Conference Higher Education – Skills in the Workplace: Delivering Employer-led Higher Level Work-Based Learning, Royal York Hotel, York.

Olma, S. (2012) 'The serendipity machine', *A Disruptive Business Model for Society*, 3.

Powell, J. (2007) 'Creative universities and their creative city-regions', *Industry and Higher Education*, 21 (6): 323–35.

Pratt, A. C., Gill, R. and Spelthann, V. (2007) 'Work and the city in the e-society: a critical investigation of the sociospatially situated character of economic production in the digital content industries in the UK', *Information, Communication and Society*, 10 (6): 922–42.

Preston, J. and Hammond, C. (2006) *The Economic Impact of UK Higher Education Institutions.* London: Universities UK.

Sennett, R. (2008) *The Craftsman.* London: Allen Lane.

Serres, M. (2000) *The Birth of Physics*, trans. Jack Hawkes. Manchester: Clinamen Press.

Serres, M. (2012) *Petite Poucette.* Paris: Éditions Le Pommier.

Slaughter, S. and Rhoades, G. (2004) *Academic Capitalism and the New Economy: Markets, State, and Higher Education.* Baltimore, MD: JHU Press.

Taylor, J. (2005) *Unweaving the Rainbow: Research, Innovation and Risk in a Creative Economy*, AHRC Discussion Paper. London: AHRC.

Tepper, S. (2006). Taking the measure of the creative campus. *peerReview, Spring 2006.* Available at: https://www.aacu.org/publications-research/periodicals/taking-measure-creative-campus (last accessed 7 December 2015).

UNCTAD (2008) *Creative Economy Report.* Geneva: UNCTAD.

Universities UK (2010) *Creating Prosperity: The Role of Higher Education in Driving the UK's Creative Economy.* London: Universities UK.

Uricchio, W. (2004) 'Beyond the great divide: collaborative networks and the challenge to dominant conceptions of creative industries', *International Journal of Cultural Studies*, 7 (1): 79–90.

Wenger, E. (1998) *Communities of Practice: Learning, Meaning, and Identity.* Cambridge: Cambridge University Press.

Part I

Beyond the campus

Partnership and collaboration across higher education institutions and the creative and cultural industries

2 From campus to creative quarter

Constructing industry identities in creative places

Daniel Ashton

Introduction

In 2006, the first phase in the conversion of a former paintworks into the 'Paintworks' creative quarter in Bristol was completed. Paintworks is owned by Verve Properties – a limited company with the stated aim to 'reposition property into higher value markets' (Verve Properties n.d.). The mix of studio/offices, live/ work and residential spaces were presented to allow 'occupiers full rein to fulfil their needs and fantasies' (Paintworks 2015a). Developing in phases over time, the Paintworks creative quarter has become the home to a diverse range of businesses including: architecture, advertising agency, web design, film production, hospitality designers, a dental surgery and a distributor of epoxy resins (Paintworks 2015b, 2015c). As would be anticipated with the creative quarter framing, the majority of businesses self-define themselves in relation to creative, cultural and media activities. There are also clear instances where businesses that form part of a related production process come together. For example, the Paintworks website (2015b) includes details of MCMC SUPPLY who provide 'essentials to the replication and model-making industry' and ScaryCat Studio who provide 'modelmaking and design services within the film, television & advertising industries' – all industries located at Paintworks and within the Bristol area more widely, for example at Spike Island. Given this range of commercial operations, Paintworks was selected by Bath Spa University as the site for Artswork Media – a creative digital agency run by media professionals and third-year students on the BA Creative Media Practice course.

This chapter examines Artswork Media as a creative industries simulated work-based learning environment operated by a higher education institution within a creative quarter. Artswork Media presents a crossover environment in which credit-bearing and assessed higher education study takes place within the framework of a creative agency workplace. For the entirety of their third year/level 6 studies, students have exclusive access on a full-time basis. While an undergraduate degree framework of three modules with learning outcomes provides a structure of assessments and credit weightings, the focus is on facilitating industry ways of working. Contact time is not organised around timetabled sessions, but instead a flexible working week is encouraged with 'weekly team meetings' and bespoke workshops on technical training and professional practice.

This chapter examines the specifics of training for cultural workers as it takes place within creative industries spaces. Drawing on previous research (Ashton 2011, 2013), this discussion critically explores notions of identity and authenticity in how students articulate the emergence of their professional identities with(in) this environment. This chapter is structured in four parts. The first part outlines existing research on work-based learning and the importance of dedicated authentic spaces in developing career-focused experiences for higher education students. The second part introduces Artswork Media as the focus of the chapter and outlines the empirical research drawn on. Research on enterprise initiatives in higher education is set out before outlining how Artswork Media operates within its creative quarter context. The third part focuses on students' experiences and explores the ways in which Artswork Media as a 'professional place' factors in how students develop their 'industry' identities. The fourth part returns to the concept introduced earlier of authenticity to critically address some of the challenges and tensions associated with Artswork Media and work-based learning. These include the depth of external exchanges and collaboration between Artswork Media and its creative quarter context, and the nature of work and forms of professional practice that students engage in.

Locating work-based learning

There is a considerable body of analysis examining the relationships between higher education and the city (Goddard and Vallance 2013), and specifically the role of universities in the creative economy (Comunian, Taylor and Smith 2014). More specifically, Comunian, Taylor and Smith (2014) identify three key dimensions for the role of institutions of higher education within a specific geographical context – human capital, knowledge and infrastructure. This chapter follows Comunian and Faggian (2013) as they identify a shift in focus from infrastructure and consumption to creative production and people. In a later study, Comunian, Faggian and Jewell (2014: 430) highlight research showing that

> [...] the primary role of the university system is to be a conduit for bringing potential high-quality undergraduate human capital into a region, and having a highly skilled labour pool far outweighs the benefits generated by knowledge spillovers. Hence, attracting and retaining higher human capital and creative individuals is a more effective long-term strategy for local economic development.

There are multiple points of entry for examining the connections between the universities and their regional context (Goddard 2011). By focusing on 'human capital' and specific pedagogical innovations and practices, this chapter makes the connection between *types* of learning experiences and spaces that are identified as productive for developing skilled graduates, and the *location* of these learning experiences and spaces.

The transition from being a higher education student into working in the creative industries has been examined across a range of national contexts (Ashton and Noonan 2013; Ball *et al*. Pollard and Stanley 2010; Bridgstock 2011; Comunian *et al*. 2011; Oakley, Sperry and Pratt 2008). A key priority within higher education employability approaches is orientating and facilitating teaching and learning so that students graduate prepared for industry. This priority has been reiterated most recently with the 'Wilson Review', prepared for the Department for Business, Innovation and Skills (BIS) (Wilson 2012). Despite this sustained commitment, students' and graduates' understandings of industry and their 'industry-ready' status have continued to be a cause of concern. The *Manifesto for the Creative Economy* (Bakhshi *et al*. 2013: 106) echoed previous policy statements on the connections between higher education and industry in emphasising that steps should be taken to 'address the disconnect between what UK creative businesses need from graduates and what universities are teaching them' (see also DCMS 2006; Creative Industries Council 2014). Bakhshi *et al*. (2013: 104) raise concerns around 'the ability of most UK universities to teach those practice-based skills related to craft knowledge, team working and entrepreneurialism' and identify organisational structures and institutional inertia as creating barriers to the 'wider adoption of work-based learning models in universities'. Bakhshi *et al*. (2013) then go on to briefly provide illustration of real-world applications through the example of the *Dare to be Digital* work-based simulation programme organised by the Abertay University at Dundee.

Literature on 'work-based learning' helps in conceptualising and evaluating the different types of industry engagement with which students can be involved. Roodhouse (2010) considers a number of perspectives and definitions to draw out the differences between work-based and work-related learning. Recognising the challenges of introducing clarity about work-based learning, Roodhouse (2010) refers to the University Vocational Council Awards' position that work-based learning is about learning (not teaching) and occurs in the workplace (rather than on campus). Alongside this 'off-campus' aspect, the common factor that links the many potential forms of work-based learning is that 'the individual would be doing a job of work, or would be undertaking a work role' (Little and ESECT 2004, cited in Roodhouse 2010: 22). With work-based learning, there is a distinctive set of contextual circumstances that see students taking on roles within a specific environment. Indeed, it is these very acts of undertaking roles and working within specific contexts that underpins the employability aspects, which helps to make the links between being a higher education student and being a graduate with the potential to contribute to the economy.

A similar perspective is offered by Billett (2009: 838) in his discussion of integrating work experiences when he describes authentic experiences 'in terms of the enactment of an occupation in particular work situations'. As Billett (2009: 827) outlines:

> [...] programs in higher education are increasingly becoming occupationally specific and universities are being seen as providers of 'higher vocational

education'. With this have come expectations that graduates from these programs will enjoy smooth transitions into professional practice. Aligned with these expectations is an educational emphasis on providing students with access to and engagement in authentic instances of practice, and an expectation that these will be effectively integrated within higher education programs.

Billett's (2009) account of authenticity and the facilitation of authentic practice are especially important in drawing out a rationale for why universities seek to physically position students more closely alongside creative industries businesses. As the following further considers, authenticity is a significant aspect of work-based learning initiatives.

In their discussion of situated learning, Brown *et al.* (1989: 34) suggests that authentic activities are those 'most simply defined as the ordinary practices of the culture' and these are important for learners as the 'only way they gain access to the standpoint that enables practitioners to act meaningfully and purposefully' (ibid.: 36). Students based within the studio form together as part of a 'community of practice' (Lave and Wenger 1992) characterised by a shared domain with joint activities and learning relationships, and a shared repertoire of resources that are in part structured by the industry professionals who run the studio and in part negotiated on an annual basis by each cohort. The contributions of Holmes (2001, 2013a, 2013b) on 'graduate identity' are helpful here for illustrating how students engage in professional practice learning contexts. Specifically, Holmes (2001: 117) suggests that '[learning] tasks should be used explicitly and intentionally in relation to the practices within the occupational arena and the positions typically occupied by graduates.' He goes on to give the example of preparing a report for an organisational case study and requiring students to write the report as if they were employed within that organisation.

With Artswork Media students are not typically taking on roles occupied by recent graduates (for more on this tension, see Ashton 2013). The tasks they undertake though are firmly within relevant occupational arenas, and students approach tasks within Artswork Media as an employee for a creative agency might. For Shreeve and Smith (2012), within the creative arts there is a range of ways of providing 'authentic' learning experiences, including industry practitioners setting briefs, students undertaking work placements and the replication of conditions of working in a studio or workshop structure. The context and environment for engaging with authentic activities is a notable dimension in generating an authentic experience

> […] archetypal school activity is very different from what we have in mind when we talk of authentic activity, because it is very different from what authentic practitioners do. When authentic activities are transferred to the classroom, their context is inevitably transmuted; they become classroom tasks and part of the school culture.
>
> (Brown *et al.* 1989: 34)

Artswork Media aims to maintain an authentic context for cultural work. The replication of working environments and the development of work-based learning opportunities aims to create a contiguous experience between higher education and working in the creative industries. Locating students both alongside and as a form of creative business is at the core of this effort to provide authentic practices.

The concept of authenticity is also particularly helpful in considering how students approach and engage with Artswork Media as part of their trajectory into creative careers. Holmes (2001: 115) sets up his position on graduate identity in stating that '[…] situated identities are associated with sets of practices that may be specified in varying degrees, and may change over time or between different contexts'. These comments help in keeping sight of students not just as 'human capital' and 'industry-ready' workers, but also as socially situated individuals engaged in complex forms of identity work. In discussing work and the authentic self, James (2015) suggests that, 'in a time of increasingly fragmented careers and short-term, episodic work, it becomes more necessary to create a meaningful narrative to link numerous and varied jobs to a core sense of self.' This issue of fragmented careers and episodic work will be addressed later; for now James' analysis of authenticity connects with this analysis of Artswork Media in terms of the meaningful narratives that students operationalise to make sense of their emerging professional identities (see also Ashton 2013).

The Artswork Media experience

In exploring students' narratives, this chapter draws on findings from a past research study in which empirical data was generated through a mix of semi-structured interviews, focus groups and filmed 'talking head' interviews with students. The sample comprises 42 participants across four academic years/cohorts between 2008 and 2012. Each of the 10–18 students based at the studio within an academic year participated in interviews and/or focus groups at some point during their time at the studio. Interviews and focus groups were contextualised through interviews with the studio's industry professionals, as well as a series of participant observations following production projects and observing briefing meetings and guest sessions with industry professionals.

A constructionist approach was taken in which statements were seen as a form of identity work (Taylor and Littleton 2008). Taylor and Littleton (2008: 279) outline how this approach can be used to 'focus on the meanings that prevail in the wider contexts of the speaker's life, for example, around possible life courses and available choices'. Taylor and Littleton (2008: 279) clarify how 'speakers are understood to be already positioned within larger social formations but also active in their identity work and are able, within constraints, to position themselves and negotiate new positionings.' The larger social formations evident here are industry and education, and students were active in positioning themselves variably as: keen, motivated and driven future workers; disgruntled student 'consumers' of higher education; and disillusioned, uncertain and anxious near graduates.

Furthermore, in her discussion of the problems and inconsistencies of biographical talk and using quotations in qualitative research, Taylor (2012: 390) crucially highlights 'the speaker as a more complex and fragmented subject, and possibly one whose self-knowledge is in question'. Students offered perspectives on how they viewed themselves and how they could forge identity positions in relation to the Artswork Media experience. In responding to the complex range of ways in which ways students would present themselves, this study stresses contingent identity positions and seeks to avoid reducing the fieldwork participants to 'students' or other fixed roles or positions.

In introducing the Artswork Media learning experience, a helpful steer comes from Maton and Wright (2002: 383) on the importance of locating 'educational practices and pedagogies within their specific socio-historical conditions and explain[ing] how they are related to those conditions'. Located in a creative quarter, Artswork Media is a work-based simulation of a small enterprise. As Pittaway and Cope (2006) outline, enterprise education has had a profound impact on higher education. It is an important part of the narrative in considering the format that work-based learning environments can take, and in relation to the creative and cultural industries has generated a growing amount of interest (Henry 2007; Naudin 2013; Nesta 2007; Oakley 2013). As Oakley (2013: 150) argues, 'the idea remains a resilient one, not simply in the relentless promotion of government agencies, but in the minds of many young cultural workers themselves.' The following firstly addresses how higher education links to enterprise and then, secondly, leads into a more detailed investigation of enterprise initiatives within specific geographical contexts.

Enterprising higher education

Goddard (2011: 18) examines how: 'Universities that are actively promoting and supporting entrepreneurship amongst students and graduates are supporting their local and regional economies in two key ways; firstly by adding to the pool of businesses in the economy; and secondly, by retaining high skilled individuals in the region.' This promotion and support can take many different forms. Similar to the list of activities identified above in relation to work-based learning, Pittaway and Cope (2006) outline studies exploring different activities in which students and entrepreneurs come together – mentoring, student consulting projects, and internships and placements. The retention of skilled individuals is an area that has been addressed in past research exploring the relationship that cultural entrepreneurs can have with the university from which they graduated. Banks (2006) draws comparison between the Manchester-based cultural entrepreneurs he and colleagues conducted research with (see Raffo *et al*., 2000), and the nomadic and desocialised new media entrepreneurs that Wittel researched (2001). In exploring affiliation and retention, Banks (2006) highlights an abundance of collective memories and shared memories based on growing up in the area and staying on after university. Banks' (2006: 463) research 'revealed explicit historical and contemporary links between cultural entrepreneurs and higher education institutions', and identified that 'around 70% of entrepreneurs interviewed had been through humanities/liberal arts and/or design-based courses or were working in university "spin-off" companies.' Specifically in relation to Bristol, Chatterton (2000) elaborates on such an interchange with reference to the University of the West of England (UWE):

> UWE functions as a resource for the media and animation sectors in Bristol and the Media Centre is heavily involved in developing the city's media and design infrastructure, especially in terms of training provision. Such links create a virtuous cycle of growth between UWE, the Faculty, the media and cultural sectors, and the graduates from UWE who are retained by the city's media firms.
>
> (Chatterton 2000: 172)

These perspectives from Raffo *et al.* (2000) and Chatterton (2000) indicate how the retention of individuals within a geographical area – two different cities in these cases – is intricately linked to the relationships and forms of exchange between the university and the city. In seeking to establish a small enterprise, extant placed-based relationships and affinities are of great significance.

Further to the retention of graduates, Goddard (2011: 18) also outlines 'three main thematic areas deployed by universities to support entrepreneurship among students and recent graduates: training in the skills of "being enterprising"; providing business experience through placements in local SMEs; and supporting them in the creation of new ventures and the exploration of new business opportunities.' This notion of 'being enterprising' is particularly relevant in following on from the earlier introduced notions of authenticity. Evaluating empirical research to date, as part of a systematic literature review, Pittaway and Cope (2006: 16) argue that 'entrepreneurship education can have an impact on the awareness and perceptions of students, where it engages them with '"real-life" opportunities to learn and involves them in experiential learning'. Likewise, in their discussion of 'situated business learning through "doing with others"', Raffo *et al.* (2000: 217) note the approaches of situated learning (Lave and Wenger 1992) and highlight from their research with micro/small businesses in the cultural industries the importance of business learning within the social, economic and cultural contexts of the real world.

Enterprise education, as with other models of work-based learning, places a premium on 'real-world', situated learning, and the formation of professional competencies and identities. Formulating work-based learning as a small enterprise, in which activities are structured around the provision of business services, is increasingly common across higher education in the United Kingdom. Jackson *et al.*'s (2014: 11) report into *Students and Knowledge Exchange in University Business Services* draws on survey data of 164 higher education institutions to report that 144 have 'easily identifiable business services of some sort' and 111 offer business services in the field of 'marketing, communication and the creative industries'. Given that a large proportion of the creative industries sector is made of small business (Creative Industries Council 2014), a small business format for a real-world, work-based learning environment is highly appropriate.

'It's not like a classroom'

Artswork Media emerged out of the Artswork Centre for Excellence in Teaching and Learning (CETL) based at Bath Spa University. In the UK, the CETLs undertook diverse pedagogic research into learning and teaching from 2005–6 to 2009–10 (HEFCE 2011: ii). Different CETLs took different approaches to the allocation of funding. Among other resource allocations, Artswork used 'capital spend to build and purchase state-of-the-art learning spaces and equipment for their students' (ibid.: 38). Specifically in relation to Artswork Media, this saw the leasing of space in the Art Deco Building at Paintworks from 2008 – two years into the Paintworks development. As Artswork Media emerges out of a specific funding context, so to can the development of Paintworks be connected to wider socio-historical conditions. Of specific relevance is the focus on the small business set out in New Labour's cultural policy. In their discussion of Nesta and New Labour's cultural policy, Oakley *et al.* (2014: 303) highlight how 'ideas of the knowledge economy were hugely influential not only on New Labour's economic policies, but also on its cultural policies, many of which were shaped by this vision of an economy driven by small business creativity.' They go on later in their discussion to point out critical questions on the degree to which New Labour policy actually favoured small-businesses. That said, New Labour's approach to small enterprises was a significant part of its 'creative industries narrative, influenced as it was by the so-called flex-spec or post-Fordist ideas about the benefits of small, interdependent, and geographically clustered firms' (ibid.: 306). As Chapain *et al.*'s 2010 Nesta report presents, the creative industries are distinctive in the ways in which they cluster. Engagement with a creative quarter cluster, such as Paintworks, was a pertinent step for any university attempting to show its creative industries' credentials and create opportunities for its students.

The most obvious way in which Artswork Media presents an 'in situ' and 'real world' learning experience is by locating off campus. The desire to move away from campus self-containment in fostering the professional and entrepreneurial capacities of its students is central to the Artswork Media approach. In two short videos created for a public audience, staff and students at Artswork Media present an accessible account of their experiences. For the Dean of the School in which the degree course and Artswork Media experience reside, there is a clear emphasis on a particular type of space: 'It's not like a classroom, it's not like a set of offices, it's a place that people can go and learn through play, through discovery, through interacting in a different environment' (Middleton, in Artswork Media 2011). The physical organisation of the layout at Artswork Media sees a multifunction space emerge in which there is a equipment store, green screen space, kitchen, meeting table, projector/presentation area and workstations around the room. There is no permanence to the layout and it is this flexibility that could be said to underpin Middleton's statement on Artswork Media as a 'different environment'. Through a student from the same video (Simmonds, in Artswork Media 2011), the specifics of the Paintworks location were emphasised: 'We're at the heart of the media industry in Bristol and that's really important because we bump into people – we can kind of network a little bit whilst we're here.' Although these accounts were provided for promotional purposes, they concisely highlight the two main drivers around the student experience – firstly, the organisation of Artswork Media as a 'real-world' space, and, secondly, Paintworks as a creative place in which to situate this.

Professional places for industry identities

The distinctive aspect of the Artswork Media case study under discussion for this chapter is the location of activities off campus and within a creative quarter. Guile (2010: 480) has argued that 'vocational practice, social capital and entrepreneurial expertise have to be developed in situ, that is, in conditions of work or through the provision of opportunities to gain access to networks and specialist advice, rather than through study or simulation.' Although there is certainly a simulation aspect to the Artswork Media experience in terms of the business service and remuneration arrangements with 'clients', there is also a strong 'in situ' aspect that facilitates students developing vocational practice, social capital and entrepreneurial expertise. A small enterprise located within a creative quarter presents a distinctive way of facilitating authentic learning for students and helping to promote the 'right skills and experiences' (Creative Industries Council 2014).

De Propis and Hypponen (2008) outline a number of elements of the creative cluster, including a 'community of "creative people"' and acting as a 'catalysing place where people, relationships, ideas, and talents can spark each other'. On these points, the links between Artswork Media and Paintworks are well founded and in evidence (Ashton 2013). Indeed, other perspectives on creative clusters further help to illustrate the substance of the exchange between Artswork Media and Paintworks.

In their discussion of regional creative industries policy-making, Lee *et al.* (2014) cite Iain Bennett (Sector Leader, Digital and Creative Industries, North West Development Agency, 2006–11) and his account of creative clusters as 'some kind of concentration of individuals who were involved in some industries.' While this viewpoint captures the vagueness around the concept of clusters, it does, however, resonate with the Paintworks set-up. For example, the public consultation materials presented by Verve outline how the

> […] first two phases of Paintworks have proved a popular location for a remarkable diversity of activities and a real stimulus to young and developing small businesses, designers, crafts people, studios performance spaces, health care clinics and many more all amongst a place people can work and also live, with places for a wide range of social activities and cultural events.
>
> (Paintworks 2015c)

Approaching Paintworks as a concentration of 'some industries' helps in seeing that much of the significance for students associated with Paintworks lies in it being an off-campus location where 'real-world' businesses conduct their every-day affairs. In addressing the development of cultural entrepreneurs, Raffo *et al.* (2000: 218) emphasise not just 'the formal knowledge transmitted by education', but also point to the relevance of cultural capital to suggest that development 'is about a way of acting, a way of understanding, a way of conceiving one's self-identity.' Further to comments on networking and linking with potential collaborators and employers, there is also the less industry-specific aspect around ways of acting and understanding. Returning to James' (2015) early comments on authenticity, locating students within a creative environment is both a contribution to the 'community of creative people' and a way of immersing students within an environment where they can explore their own self-identity as creative professionals.

One of the major findings from previous research into Artswork Media centres on the formulation of professional identities. In discussing non-formal learning and professional work, Eraut (2000: 122) suggests that 'knowledge of contexts and organisations is often acquired through a process of socialization through observation, induction, and increasing participation rather than formal inquiry'. Previous analysis of Artswork Media makes the case that 'the creative quarter environment provided the lifestyle context for creative work [and] the studio space provided the context for the in-depth actualisation of work' (Ashton 2013: 475). This change in environment, from the campus to the creative quarter, is of considerable relevance for how students move from temporary role-play to a more detailed exploration of their emerging professional identities.

The strengths of this richly realised, authentic learning experience can be readily linked to questions of how students understand the working environments and contexts they might go into. The ability of students to reflect on their experiences at Artswork Media, in terms of their professional development, was evident in the analysis of research undertaken with four different cohorts of students (Ashton 2011) and as illustrated in the following comments from two participants:

> You know you definitely need somewhere that's not a classroom, that's not the University. That's completely separate space that you can use as if you were a professional production company. It makes a big difference.
>
> Being in this environment – well it's a professional environment. I've been doing real commissions for real companies. I've been able to get out and get that real hands on experience, working with a company, doing real briefs, attending real meetings, with real clients […] I've managed to develop so many skills, professional skills, that I can use for the future.

As explored in the reflections from staff and students in previous studies (Ashton 2011, 2013), the Artswork Media experience has had identifiable impacts on the sense of professional identity that students hold. Notwithstanding the importance of how students reflect on their experiences, there remain potential tensions and alternative possibilities associated with Artswork Media that this chapter examines for the first time.

Authentic places and practices?

Authenticity rated high for students in terms of their experiences and their perceived understandings of working in the creative industries. Nevertheless, there remain questions around this authenticity in terms of how the initiative operates. Firstly, the relationship of Artswork Media to its wider 'creative quarter' social milieu can be evaluated in terms of the external exchange and the depth of collaboration. Secondly, there is a need for sustained appraisal of the nature of work and the forms of professional practice that students are engaging in at Artswork Media.

Engaging in the creative quarter milieu

The nature of students' Artswork Media experience is shaped by the choice to locate the initiative within a creative quarter (rather than running the business service from campus) and, more specifically, within Paintworks. The importance of this wider creative milieu has been discussed in terms of how students understand vocational practice. The ways in which the Artswork Media experience is able to address emerging forms of industry practice will, however, continue to be a challenge. In his overview of project-based working in the creative industries, Watson (2012: 617) engages with Grabher's wider analysis of project-based working (2002) to suggest that 'the integrity of the firm as the basic analytical unit of the economic process is being increasingly undercut by organisational practices that are built around projects involving a multiplicity of organisational and personal networks.' With Artswork Media, the creative agency/firm is the organisational unit, and students work within their group in response to client briefs. This form of group work is valuable for students' development and employability (Luckman 2013), and there have also been instances in which students worked with industry freelancers on specific projects. In the main though, recurrent collaboration is unlikely as students work on client projects for academic credits and this limits how a project team might be constituted. In short, a framework of project collaboration that is largely restricted to students on the course is in place.

This disjuncture between emerging trends in project work and students working on client projects only within a creative agency leads into a more far reaching issue of the kinds of relationships Artswork Media is able to enter into with other creative organisations and workers. Firstly, and in relation to contributions to Paintworks, Artswork Media is not in a position to make the kinds of contributions to creative place-making that Markusen and Gadwa (2010) identify, such as creating jobs. This is equally the case in relation to spillovers, 'where the knowledge activities of one firm or industry result in economic benefits for another one that the former is not able to fully capture' (De Propis and Hypponen, 2008: 24).

As touched on earlier, there are common areas of activity that see businesses locate together at Paintworks. Although the relevance and appropriateness of Artswork Media as a creative agency makes the fit with Paintworks obvious, the relationships, collaborations and spillover aspects come less easily and obviously. Pratt (2015: 7) argues that

> […] for clustering to be meaningful it has to be more than a simple co-location of activities; rather a careful curating of inter-related activities whose sum will be more than its parts; activities that will gain from collective resources as a result of returns to scale.

This 'careful curating' is harder for Artswork Media to achieve, given its status as a work-based learning environment, not a company operating in the same ways as its neighbours. Indeed, the flow of benefit may be more obvious in the ways in which the creative quarter is leveraged in the promotion of the degree course. In *Spaces of Vernacular Creativity*, Edensor *et al*. (2010: 2) highlight Scott's (1999) suggestions that 'the temporal and spatial qualities associated with particular places are grafted onto the products produced in them and that these goods come to define their places of origin.' These comments could be translated to consider the educational 'product' of Artswork Media, as it situated within Paintworks. The qualities associated with Paintworks can be 'grafted' into the Artswork Media experience, but the more substantial clustering elements are harder to get a handle on. This is not to detract from the earlier discussion in this chapter around 'human capital', as businesses within the Paintworks area are able to benefit from direct access to graduates who have benefitted from an immersive, work-based learning environment. Overall though, the frame of authenticity raises questions on the scale and type of integration, and the interaction possible between a work-based learning environment operating out of a university context for students and the creative quarter that hosts it.

An extension of this issue of product and authenticity is to see how the qualities and kudos attached to Artswork Media are communicated not only to prospective students, but also to potential clients who would engage with the business service. This is a concern that has already been raised by Goddard (2011: 18) in his discussion of connecting universities to regional growth:

> It is important to ensure a close cooperation between the universities, the private sector and authorities responsible for delivering regional strategies to ensure there is coordination. Otherwise there can be resentment and tensions if graduate businesses are seen to displace or distort existing businesses and markets.

For potential clients, this is a distinctive opportunity to engage with an organisation that, through the involvement of experienced industry professionals as tutors, is able to respond to their business needs. As such, the issue emerges around the extent to which forms of supply and demand with local competitors are displaced or distorted. In their evaluation of business services provided by university-based units, Jackson *et al.* (2014: 21) point to issues of costs and the limited resources of many small business (e.g. potential clients) and suggest that 'the result is that there is demand for "free" advice in the form of student projects and this is an attraction for businesses.' In the case of Artswork Media, relationships have been developed with local businesses, through, for example, co-hosting end-of-year showcase exhibitions with organisations such as Creative Bath and the Royal Television Society. This has allowed the 'human capital' aspect identified by Comunian, Faggian and Jewell (2014) to be developed, as students may be retained in the area through securing employment, contracts or networks in the region. Nevertheless, for other businesses there can remain tensions with an initiative in which students complete projects for clients that might have worked with them. This is an issue that emerges also in England's chapter in relation to the University of Sunderland, the National Glass Centre and the local glass-making community. There is a further, related set of tensions in which the studio's work with clients might shape the employment and project opportunities of former students now competing in this market.

The issue of distortion may also be considered in assessing where and how a university has chosen to contribute. It may be too artificial to conceive of different circumstances in which universities might or might not introduce and develop initiatives such as Artswork Media. Nor does it seem possible – or desirable – to try and conceive of speculative futures for a place with or without higher education involvement, or to try and retrospectively unpick how involvement may have been different. Due attention should, however, be given to some of the related areas of concern raised by Edensor *et al.* (2010) and Luckman (2012) around the kinds of cultural work initiatives that are emphasised in policy and that receive support. For Edensor *et al.* (2010: 14), there is a concern to find out the implications of clusters:

> The deployment of clusters serves to establish boundaries around creativity, marking out 'creative spaces' in distinction to other, 'ordinary' spaces, and ignoring creative geographies that are socially produced activity across a range of sites and spaces in ways that are more rhizomatic or viral.

Similarly, Luckman (2012: 7) indicates how 'the non-urban and non-city experience remains under-explored in studies of cultural work'. Luckman (2012) points to the contributions of Bell and Jayne (2010) in marking out the need for research into rural creative industries. There is scholarship that takes this focus (Skoglund and Jonsson, 2012), and the aim within this chapter can only be to feed into a future conversation around the role of higher education in relation to urban and rural creative economies. It would not seem a stretch to argue that the cumulative impact of initiatives, such as Artswork Media, from different universities across the UK could shape the kinds of priorities and relationships that emerge between higher education and the wider creative economy.

Professional practices

Critically assessing how a university might contribute to shaping directions for the creative industries and specific places leads into a second area of reflection and evaluation concerning the forms of professional practice that might be facilitated. Beyond the rich body of reflections and comments from four cohorts of students articulating how the Artswork Media experience contributed to their professional development (Ashton 2011, 2013), there remain inevitable questions that come with this being a higher education work-based learning experience. Earlier analysis (Ashton 2013) critically addressed tensions between the opportunities provided through the studio and the 'humdrum' activities that could be associated with cultural work. In that article, it was argued that students would gain partial, and perhaps privileged, ways of experiencing cultural work. Here, the underlying argument is that any notion of authenticity needs to be critically evaluated as socially contingent. While students encounter *some* professional practices through their time at Artswork Media, this does not mean that these contexts are *the* professional practice. As MacIntyre (1983: 181, cited in Kemmis 2009: 22) argues: 'Practices must not be confused with institutions. Chess, physics, and medicine are practices; chess clubs, laboratories, universities, and hospitals are institutions.' In one respect this is obvious – there will inevitably be a diversity of arrangements and formats within the media industries with differences in how work is organised within and across sectors. That said, there is a query here around the sustained currency of 'work-based' learning.

In examining the tensions between the global and the local in higher education approaches to cultural work, Luckman (2013: 70) raises the question of how to realistically prepare students when 'much policy discourse and practical advice around cultural work presumes national, if not global, mobility, on the part of creative workers.' From this perspective, some significant questions emerge around continuing changes in conditions of working in the creative industries, and the extent to which global mobility must be emphasised over/alongside placed-based simulated learning. This is not to undermine the continued relevance of the creative quarter. Indeed, the movement to phase three of the Paintworks development at the time of writing points to a vibrant future for this specific creative quarter. This question instead hangs over the ways of working specific to Artswork Media and 'placed-based' experiential learning. Principally, to what extent are students able to develop a global dimension to learning? As Luckman (2013: 81) points out, 'with culturally diverse task groups likely to become increasingly prevalent in industry, even if they are not planning to relocate, cultural work graduates require the capacity to act globally, across time, space, language, and cultures.' Following these insights, a further line of investigation centres on how a place-rooted local experience might be augmented and refined, in terms of intercultural awareness and transnational collaboration.

Further to this point on the global and the local as different experiences that are difficult to combine 'authentically' within the Artswork Media work-based learning environment, a second area for evaluation concerns co-located and isolated ways of working. Exploring professional identity and the media industries, Deuze and Lewis (2013: 169) suggest that:

> Cultural work takes place in relative isolation – especially in the digital realm of software development and games design, but also in all kinds of other sectors of the creative industries (one could think of film post-production, audio mixing, clothing design, freelance reporting, video production, so on and so forth).

The Artswork Media experience emphasises students working in teams and, as such, the isolation that Deuze and Lewis (2013) suggest typifies cultural work is not evident. The emphasis on students collaborating and co-locating is entirely appropriate given the importance of group working for creative careers (Ball *et al.* 2010; Luckman 2013). A tension perhaps arises though, if this is not the kind of 'authentic' portfolio career that students will likely move into. Luckman (2013: 76) argues that 'much university-level training for cultural work seems to assume students will be moving into ongoing, full-time creative positions in large organizations.' As Artswork Media is aligned with a full-time education over an academic year, the students' participation necessarily and inevitably sits more closely to a full-time position within an organisation. Luckman (2013) further elaborates on the likelihood of students working as sole traders operating from contract to contract. Similarly, with the Artswork Media experience students do not face the uncertainty of seeking out and moving from contract to contract. Authentic activities (working on live briefs for external clients) situated within an authentic environment (the creative quarter) combine to create an immersive learning environment through which students are able to explore cultural worker identities. That said, an enduring distance remains between the student experience and the cultural worker experience. As discussed elsewhere (Ashton 2013), students would not experience the challenges of finding work and establishing a living wage, or other aspects of precariousness examined in extant literature (Gill and Pratt 2008). As the concluding discussion now addresses, perhaps there are elements of this distance to maintain and draw out.

Conclusion

Echoing James' (2015) closing remarks on authenticity as providing a purpose and a strategy for working through career questions, this conclusion looks to the potential in the gap between the drive for immersive, industry-ready vocational learning and the higher education context within which this activity remains located.

In noting the kinds of fragmented and episodic work that has been identified as common to the creative and cultural industries, James (2015) turns to Sennett's (1998) notion of 'drift'. James (2015) suggests that 'to counter this, individuals must create a convincing story that provides a rationale for career changes and can thereby "form their characters into sustained narratives" (Sennett 1998: 31).'

Rather than seeing Artswork Media presenting students with 'inauthentic' experiences of stability and close-knit collaboration, there is much to be said for a context and learning experience through which students can start to develop narratives for making sense of their careers. This means there are the possibilities not just for presenting students with a 'model' of what working in the creative and cultural industries looks like so they can better perform it. There is also the possibility to use the hybrid Artswork Media space to emphasise some of the aspects that are 'authentic' to higher education. While moving to the creative quarter, there remain openings for aspects of the campus experience to be continued and extended. As Holmes (2013b: 1045) suggests, 'the positions, roles, identities available to persons, is viewed as a negotiated outcome of constant interaction, within which any stabilized or structured arrangements are always and essentially temporary, subject to possible contestation and change.' The impetus may then be in wider creative industries practice to emphasise and strive for some of the dimensions and practices developed with students within their higher education learning environments.

An immediate opening here might be the ways of working. In response to well-established concerns around isolated and individualised cultural workers, comments by Deuze and Lewis (2013: 169) on building connections, are a helpful point of reference:

> As individuals in the workforce increasingly either choose to or are forced to build their own support structures, they must do so within the context of a peer group and some kind of organization, creating connections between the individual and the organization that are short term, contingent and rootless.

A similar agenda is put forth by Naudin (2013: 123) in relation to enterprise: 'While it is noted that networks can exclude as well as include, collaboration and creating a support network can counteract the difficulties faced by entrepreneurial media workers' (ibid.: 124). In these accounts there is a different direction in which the 'authenticity' of dominant conditions and practices can be connected with alternative visions. In emphasising collaboration and the formation of networks, Artswork Media is not 'inauthentic' as one line of enquiry might pursue. Rather, it is a different approach that, perhaps also, provides an invitation to work towards two-way negotiation and exchange in the co-construction of higher education and creative economy hybrid practices.

With Chatterton (2000: 177), the priorities of human capital and the possibilities of the university experience sit together: 'Universities have a role to play in the cultural development of the community and the wider region: they are seedbeds for new talent; they are one of the few remaining places where artistic experimentation and integrity is financially viable, especially in an era of local authority art-budget cuts.' While the changing pressures placed on universities must be recognised, Chatterton's comments on the diverse roles of the university may be a helpful reminder of the need for higher education to develop forms of authentic industry-relevant education and support the articulation of different visions.

References

Artswork Media (2011) 'Why is being at Artswork Media not like being at university?' Retrieved from: https://vimeo.com/10770921.

Ashton, D. (2011) 'Media work and the creative industries: identity work, professionalism and employability', *Education and Training*, 53 (6): 546–60.

Ashton, D. (2013) 'Cultural workers in-the-making', *European Journal of Cultural Studies*, 16 (4): 468–88.

Ashton, D. and Noonan, C. (2013) *Cultural Work and Higher Education*. Basingstoke: Palgrave Macmillan.

Bakhshi, H., Hargreaves, I. and Mateos-Garcia, J. (2013) *A Manifesto for the Creative Economy*. Nesta. Retrieved from: http://www.nesta.org.uk/sites/default/files/a-manifesto-for-the-creative-economy-april13.pdf (accessed 30 March 2015).

Ball, L., Pollard, E. and Stanley, N. (2010) *Creative Graduates Creative Futures*. Brighton: Creative Graduates Creative Futures Higher Education Partnership and the Institute for Employment Studies.

Banks, M. (2006) 'Moral economy and cultural work', *Sociology*, 40 (3): 455–72.

Bell, D. and Jayne, M. (2010) 'The creative countryside: policy and practice in the UK rural cultural economy', *Journal of Rural Studies*, 26 (3): 209–18.

Billett, S. (2009) 'Realising the educational worth of integrating work experiences in higher education', *Studies in Higher Education*, 34 (7): 827–43.

Bridgstock, R. (2011) 'Making it creatively: building sustainable careers in the arts and creative industries', *Australian Career Practitioner Magazine*, 22 (2): 11–13.

Brown, J. S., Collins, A. and Duguid, P. (1989) 'Situated cognition and the culture of learning', *Educational Researcher*, 18 (1): 32–42.

Chapain, C., Cooke, P., De Propris, L., McNeill, S. and Mateos-Garcia, J. (2010) *Creative Clusters and Innovation Putting Creativity on the Map*, Nesta Research Report. Retrieved from: http://www.nesta.org.uk/publications/creative-clusters-and-innovation-report (accessed 18 December 2013).

Chatterton, P. (2000) 'The cultural role of universities in the community: revisiting the university–community debate', *Environment and Planning A*, 32: 165–81.

Comunian, R. and Faggian, A. (2013) 'Higher education and the creative city', in D. E. Andersson, A. E. Andersson and C. Mellander (eds), *Handbook of Creative Cities*. Cheltenham: Edward Elgar, pp. 187–210.

Comunian, R., Faggian, A. and Jewell, S. (2011) 'Winning and losing in the creative industries: an analysis of creative graduates' career opportunities across creative disciplines', *Cultural Trends*, 20 (3/4): 291–308.

Comunian, R., Faggian, A. and Jewell, S. (2014) 'Embedding arts and humanities in the creative economy: the role of graduates in the UK', *Environment and Planning C: Government and Policy*, 32: 426–50.

Comunian, R., Taylor, C. F. and Smith, D. N. (2014) 'The role of universities in the regional creative economies of the UK: hidden protagonists and the challenge of knowledge transfer', *European Planning Studies*, 22 (12): 2456–76.

Creative Industries Council (2014) *Create UK*. Retrieved from: http://www.thecreativeindustries.co.uk/media/243587/cic_report_final-hi-res-.pdf (accessed 30 March 2015).

De Propris, L. and Hypponen, L. (2008) 'Creative clusters and governance: the dominance of the Hollywood film cluster', in P. Cooke and L. Lazzeretti (eds), *Creative Cities, Cultural Clusters and Local Development*. Cheltenham: Edward Elgar, pp. 340–71.

Department of Culture, Media and Sport (DCMS) (2006) *Developing Entrepreneurship for the Creative Industries: The Role of Higher and Further Education*. Department of Culture, Media and Sport.

Deuze, M. and Lewis, N. (2013) 'Professional identity and media work', in M. Banks, R. Gill and S. Taylor (eds), *Theorizing Cultural Work: Labour, Continuity and Change in the Cultural and Creative Industries*. London: Routledge, pp. 161–74.

Edensor, T., Leslie, D. Millington, S. and Rantisi, N. (2010) 'Introduction: rethinking creativity: critiquing the creative class thesis', in T. Edensor, D. Leslie, S. Millington and N. Rantisi (eds), *Spaces of Vernacular Creativity: Rethinking the Cultural Economy*. London: Routledge, pp. 1–16.

Eraut, M. (2000) 'Non-formal learning and tacit knowledge in professional work', *British Journal of Educational Psychology*, 70: 113–36.

Gill, R. and Pratt, A. (2008) 'In the social factory? Immaterial labour, precariousness and cultural work', *Theory, Culture and Society*, 25 (1): 1–30.

Goddard, J. (2011) *European Union – Regional Policy: Connecting Universities to Regional Growth*. Retrieved from: http://ec.europa.eu/regional_policy/sources/docgener/presenta/universities2011/universities2011_en.pdf (accessed 30 March 2015).

Goddard, J. and Vallance, P. (2013) *The University and the City*. London: Routledge.

Grabher, G. (2002) 'Cool projects, boring institutions: temporary collaboration in social context', *Regional Studies*, 36: 205–14.

Guile, D. (2010) 'Learning to work in the creative and cultural sector: news spaces, pedagogies, and expertise', *Journal of Education Policy*, 25 (4): 465–84.

HEFCE (2011) *Summative Evaluation of the CETL Programme*. HEFCE. Retrieved from: http://www.hefce.ac.uk/media/hefce/content/pubs/.../RE...CETL/rd11_11.doc (accessed 30 March 2015).

Henry, C. (2007) *Entrepreneurship in the Creative Industries: An International Perspective*. Cheltenham: Edward Elgar.

Holmes, L. (2001) 'Reconsidering graduate employability: the "graduate identity" approach', *Quality in Higher Education*, 7 (2): 111–19.

Holmes, L. (2013a) 'Competing perspectives on graduate employability: possession, position or process?', *Studies in Higher Education*, 38 (4): 538–54.

Holmes, L. (2013b) 'Realist and relational perspectives on graduate identity and employability: a response to Hinchcliffe and Jolly', *British Educational Research Journal*, 39 (6): 1044–59.

Jackson, D., Molesworth, M. and Goode, G. (2014) *Students and Knowledge Exchange in University Business Services*. Bournemouth: Bournemouth University. Retrieved from: https://microsites.bournemouth.ac.uk/cmc/files/2014/07/BU-Students-and-knowledge-exchange-in-university-business-services.pdf (accessed 30 March 2015).

James, S. (2015) 'Finding your passion: work and the authentic self', *M/C Journal*, 18 (1). Retrieved from: http://journal.media-culture.org.au/index.php/mcjournal/article/viewArticle/954 (accessed 30 March 2015).

Kemmis, S. (2009) 'Understanding professional practice: a synoptic framework', in B. Green (ed.), *Understanding and Researching Professional Practice*. Rotterdam: Sense, pp. 19–38.

Lave, J. and Wenger, E. (1992) *Situated Learning: Legitimate Peripheral Participation*. Cambridge: Cambridge University Press.

Lee, D., Hesmondhalgh, D. and Nisbett, M. (2014) 'Regional creative industries policy-making under New Labour', *Cultural Trends*, 23 (4): 217–31.

Luckman, S. (2012) *Locating Cultural Work*. Basingstoke: Palgrave Macmillan.

Luckman, S. (2013) 'Precariously mobile: tensions between the local and the global in higher education approaches to cultural work', in D. Ashton and C. Noonan (eds), *Cultural Work and Higher Education*. Basingstoke: Palgrave Macmillan, pp. 68–86110–30.

Markusen, A. and Gadwa, A. (2010) *Creative Placemaking*. Retrieved from: http://kresge.org/sites/default/files/NEA-Creative-placemaking.pdf (accessed 30 March 2015).

Maton, K. and Wright, H. K. (2002) 'Returning cultural studies to education', *International Journal of Cultural Studies*, 5 (4): 379–92.

Naudin, A. (2013) 'Media enterprise in higher education: a laboratory for learning', in D. Ashton and C. Noonan (eds), *Cultural Work and Higher Education*. Basingstoke: Palgrave Macmillan, pp. 110–30.

Nesta (2007) *Creating Entrepreneurship: Entrepreneurship Education for the Creative Industries*. London: Nesta.

Oakley, K. (2013) 'Good work? Rethinking cultural entrepreneurship', in C. Bilton and S. Cummings (eds), *Handbook of Management and Creativity*. Cheltenham: Edward Elgar, pp. 145–59.

Oakley, K., Hesmondhalgh, D. and Nisbett, M. (2014) 'The national trust for talent? NESTA and New Labour's cultural policy', *British Politics*, 9: 297–317.

Oakley, K., Sperry, B. and Pratt, A. (2008) *The Art of Innovation: How Fine Art Graduates Contribute to Innovation*. London: Nesta.

Paintworks (2015a) Phases 1 and 2. Retrieved from: http://www.paintworksbristol.co.uk/index.php?id=18 (accessed 30 March 2015).

Paintworks (2015b) Who's working here. Retrieved from: http://www.paintworksbristol.co.uk/index.php?id=2 (accessed 30 March 2015).

Paintworks (2015c) Phase Three Public Consultation. Retrieved from: http://www.paintworksbristol.co.uk/fileadmin/user_upload/Phase3-PublicConsultation.pdf (accessed 30 March 2015).

Pittaway, L. and Cope, J. (2006) *Entrepreneurship Education: A Systematic Review of the Evidence*. London: National Council for Graduate Entrepreneurship.

Pratt, A. C. (2015) 'Resilience, locality and the cultural economy', *City, Culture and Society*, 6 (3): 61–7.

Raffo, C., O'Connor, J., Lovatt, A. and Banks, M. (2000) 'Attitudes to formal business training and learning among entrepreneurs in the cultural industries: situated business learning through "doing with others"', *Journal of Education and Work*, 13 (2): 215–30.

Roodhouse, S. (2010) 'Defining and theorizing university work-based learning', in S. Roodhouse and J. Mumford (eds), *Understanding Work-Based Learning*. Farnham: Gower, pp. 21–7.

Scott, A. J. (1999) 'The cultural economy: geography and the creative field', *Media, Culture and Society*, 21 (6): 807–17.

Sennett, R. (1998) *The Corrosion of Character: The Personal Consequences of Work in the New Capitalism*. New York: W. W. Norton.

Shreeve, A. and Smith, C. (2012) 'Multi-directional creative transfer between practice-based arts education and work', *British Educational Research Journal*, 38 (4): 539–56.

Skoglund, W. and Jonsson, G. (2012) 'The potential of cultural and creative industries in remote areas', *Nordisk Kulturpolitisk Tidskrift*, 15: 181–91.

Taylor, S. (2012) '"One participant said …": the implications of quotations from biographical talk', *Qualitative Research*, 12 (4): 388–401.

Taylor, S. and Littleton, K. (2008) 'Art work or money: conflicts in the construction of a creative identity', *Sociological Review*, 56 (2): 275–92.

Verve Properties (n.d.) Home page. Retrieved from: http://www.verve-properties.co.uk/ (accessed 30 March 2015).

Watson, A. (2012) 'Sociological perspectives on the economic geography of projects: the case of project-based working in the creative industries', *Sociology Compass*, 6 (10): 617–31.

Wilson, T. (2012) *Review of Business–University Collaboration*. London: Department for Business, Innovation and Skills.

Wittel, A. (2001) 'Towards a network sociality', *Theory, Culture and Society*, 18 (6): 51–76.

3 Intermediaries and the knowledge exchange process

The case of the creative industries and higher education

Tarek E. Virani and Andy C. Pratt[1]

Introduction

Research on university–industry collaborations is dominated by attention to one sector: hi tech (Bramwell and Wolfe, 2008; Kodama *et al.* 2008; Youtie and Shapira 2008; Yusuf 2008). Its main focus has been to measure the outcome of these collaborations in terms of patents developed or products developed from patents (Acworth 2008; Jong 2008). Put simply, the output is a material product or income stream. The material product is assumed to act as a proxy for knowledge exchange and/or knowledge transfer (KE/KT). The economic field of the cultural economy has some differences from high-technology in terms of the form of products/outputs and their materiality as well as their organisational forms. We argue that this should alert us to a different perspective of KE/KT that challenges the normative closed 'black box' of KE/KT, which allows an active process of transfer and a relational concept of knowledge where value is embedded in, and produced by, contexts. Consequently, we argue that an appreciation of collaboration and knowledge exchange (KE) in the creative economy needs a methodology that is sensitive to these differences of product, process and context.

This chapter explores the process of collaboration between higher education institutions (HEIs) and small, medium and micro-sized enterprises (SMMEs) in the creative and cultural industries (CCI)[2] within London carried out as part of Creativeworks London's (CWL) creative voucher scheme – the scheme will be explained in more detail later. In this chapter, we highlight the role of 'intermediaries' in the collaboration process. We call them 'intermediaries' here; however, other studies use different terminology in order to describe them and their role in different sectors. They play an important part in these collaborations because it is they who facilitate through mediation, as well as embed themselves within, these projects. We use the term referring to the function performed, namely mediation. This is not a trivial point. Normative innovation theory assumes diffusion and transmission. Normative work on the CCI, as well as business and management, often refer to them as 'boundary spanners' (Williams 2002). However, these are essentially passive fillers of 'structural holes' (Burt 1982) – they are under-theorised and static in their depiction. Our findings point to another way of understanding intermediaries and the mediation process; namely *as* practice and process rather than purely as object (Ibert 2007).

The methodology used for this research, which we will describe in more detail later, allowed us to understand mediation as a process as opposed to an input–output model. Thus the examination of CWL's creative voucher scheme revealed to us that intermediaries enable the process of collaboration between universities and SMMEs (especially micro-enterprises) in the creative sector by doing three things: they act as brokers in order to facilitate partnerships that can lead to collaborations between SMMEs and HEIs; they act as translators between academics and SMMEs within the funded project in order to make sure that all expectations are met; and they are engaged in network building, as well as offering up their own networks, in order to gain the trust of the collaborating parties and to include them within it. Critically, much of this work is done informally, and sometimes as an on-cost. Thus, from our point of view, the presence of intermediaries as primarily agents of mediation introduces an active and agentic process that has the potential to articulate, or simply enable, or simply block, a nominal lineage.

This chapter will look at the work that has been conducted on university–industry collaborations and then examine the literature on intermediaries in this context. Third, it will discuss the methods used, including a description of CWL's voucher scheme. Fourth, it will outline our key findings regarding the collaborations that have taken place to date. And fifth, it will conclude with a discussion of the implications of these findings.

University–industry collaborations

Existing scholarship on university–industry collaborations (Bishop *et al.* 2009; Bruneel *et al.* 2010; Cohen *et al.* 2002) has pinpointed that which promotes, or hinders, the collaborative process.[3] Much has been learned about the factors smoothing university–industry collaborations (Arundel and Geuna 2004; Bruneel *et al.* 2010; Laursen and Salter 2004; Meyer-Krahmer and Schmoch 1998; Tether 2002). The first is perhaps proximity. The logic of science park development was to facilitate 'spin-off' companies that would share in the senior, common-room like atmosphere. Co-location was seen as necessary, but not always sufficient. The majority of this work is very much based on sector-specific collaborations and focuses primarily on technology transfer and science-based collaborations with enterprises of all sizes although, as SMMEs are uncommon in this sector, they are ignored.[4] This is important to acknowledge, since SMMEs represent the largest net contributor to the economy in a number of sectors and in a number of countries (Charles 2006, 2007; Charles *et al.* 2014; Gertner *et al.* 2011; Hoffman *et al.* 1998; Quayle 2002), especially in the creative sector where they are a dominant force. With this caveat, normative findings have garnered significant insights into the ways that university–industry collaborations can work. Research thus far indicates that collaborative success depends on: first, a long-standing culture of co-operation and economic success through collaborations (Bruneel *et al.* 2010; Meyer-Krahmer and Schmoch 1998);[5] second, the types of firms being considered and how this relates to innovation practices (Bruneel *et al.* 2010; Tether 2002); and third, an acknowledgement that collaborative opportunities are actively looked for by specific types of firms, namely those who promote open search strategies and invest in research and development (Bruneel *et al.* 2010; Laursen and Salter 2004).

On the other hand, barriers exist that seem to hinder these types of collaboration, regardless of whether or not they are within the creative sector. Bruneel *et al.* (2010) have identified two general obstacles to university–industry collaborations, and we add a third in this paper. The first involves major differences in incentive structures within higher education versus within industry. For instance, where researchers would like to disseminate interesting ideas quickly in order to gain academic respect in their field, firms may want to stay quiet so as to not reveal pertinent information to their competition (ibid.). Added to this, there is a large variance between industries themselves, for instance pharmaceutical industries have to disseminate information quickly in order to apply for standardised approval (such as Federal Drug Administration approval in the United States).

The second barrier/obstacle concerns immaterial exchanges and is exemplified, but not exhausted by, conflicts over intellectual property (IP) and other types of commercially sensitive information (ibid.). It has been found that, in some instances, universities have attempted to cash in on the potential commercial success emanating from research, which has led to profound distributional conflicts between universities and their industrial partners (Florida 1999; Shane and Somaya 2007). This can be described as a clash of differing (as well as quickly evolving) IP cultures, essentially a clash between the traditional 'open innovation of universities' and the closed innovation of industry, which has reversed in recent years as industry has sought to save cost by outsourcing innovation and universities have sought to generate money by exploiting innovation.

The third barrier is in regard to the time allotted to specific collaborations by the different parties and within any sector. There is a cost of time that needs to be acknowledged, which seems to be valued by enterprise/industry – whereas university time appears to be free but is, in fact, not. Staff have full-time jobs, so collaborations with businesses are additional, an increased workload that can actually be a significant barrier to these types of collaborations. For instance, it may be more cost-effective for the academic to sit in the library writing a paper that will earn a good REF (Research Excellence Framework) score in the United Kingdom and bring in funding for their department rather than talking to an entrepreneur about their idea for free. The latter will implicitly damage their bottom line, which is the sustainability of their particular 'business' – the university. This being said, it might be argued that universities are funded by the state, hence they should make all research freely available. On the other hand, universities are also like businesses, they have to cover their costs. More significantly, it has long been argued that there was a useful division of labour with universities doing blue-skies research funded by the state and firms expending costs on applications. The complexity has occurred when the boundary between pure and applied research has closed. Universities are required to demonstrate value (impact), which pushes them to applied research. However, this leads to an undersupply of basic research. Again, the internal economic model of the university should be brought to the fore.

As a way to mitigate against these types of barriers, Bruneel *et al.* (2010) and Santoro and Saparito (2003) suggest that the development of trust between university and industry actors is essential. That said, such trust does not erase any asymmetries of power and resource between universities and the private sector (Comunian and Gilmore 2014). Nevertheless, it is important to establish in these types of collaborations, especially at the level of individual actors/collaborators.

In order for trust to be established, aspects like the aforementioned barriers to collaboration must be understood and negotiated, as well as compensated.[6] Higher trust between partners stimulates rich social and information exchanges, and encourages partners to exchange more valuable knowledge and information (Ring and Van de Ven 1992). It must also take into consideration the constraints and management of sensitive elements that contribute to a healthy working relationship, such as the difference between 'free' time and 'paid' time. Once this is established, trust-based relationships can facilitate the exchange of difficult-to-codify knowledge (or tacit knowledge) and information as well, which is by definition difficult to communicate (Kogut and Zander 1992) and endemic in these types of collaborative endeavours involving these specific types of organisations. This chapter extends this notion. Trust (or reputation) cannot exist in an asocial or non-embedded condition. We show the value of exploring this institutional embedding and the accompanying constituted, and/or constituting, processes.

The role of intermediaries

According to Yusuf (2008: 1167), achieving effective knowledge exchange between universities and businesses 'requires the midwifery of different kinds of intermediaries'. That said, the literature on intermediaries – and cultural intermediaries within the CCI in particular – is somewhat disjointed. The work on intermediaries in university–industry collaborations focuses mainly on technology transfer (ibid.), whereas the work on cultural intermediaries is embedded within a discourse that is dictated primarily through the lens of Pierre Bourdieu (1984). It is worth noting that these two literatures are seldom if ever considered together as they deal with different spheres. While sharing the same term – intermediaries – there are a number of important nuances between different usages. Both of these streams of work will be briefly examined, in order to carve a path for a third way of understanding intermediaries. This third way envisages them as actors embedded within university–industry collaborative projects in specifically the CCI, where their primary role is the facilitation of collaborations through the process of mediation. In this way, they might be better understood with regard to what they do and how they do it, as opposed to being under-theorised fillers of 'structural holes' that might exist within university–industry collaborations.

According to Yusuf (2008), the transition from the 'lab' to the commercial sphere is a tricky one, and developing a new technology can be fraught with risk. At the heart of the process is the diffusion of tacit forms of knowledge and information, as well as the ways in which university technology transfer offices (TTOs) work and having the experience and knowledge of how to deal with these entities. That said, due to a lack of knowledge in this arena, many ideas and findings (including patents) remain undeveloped in the university, where many researchers lack the know-how to access the business world (ibid.). In 2008, a special issue of the journal *Research Policy* on the role of intermediaries in university–industry collaborations argues that this is the reason that a role for intermediaries of 'many different stripes' exists (Yusuf 2008: 1170). These intermediaries are described as 'knowledge' intermediaries, whose primary role is the facilitation of knowledge exchange in order to bring universities and industry closer, 'by diagnosing needs and articulating the demand for certain kinds of innovation, by instituting a dynamic framework for change and working to achieve the change through financing and other means' (ibid.). According to the special issue, there are four types of these intermediaries as summarised in Table 3.1.

This way of viewing intermediaries is very much embedded in the language of technology transfer, as is quite obvious. Missing from the discourse are the links that tie notions of trust (which are inherently important to university–industry relations) with that of successful collaborative projects in this sphere, and perhaps outside of purely technology driven agendas. The human element seems to have been dispensed with in order to frame an understanding of intermediaries assisting with knowledge exchange in terms of, for instance, how to get the most patents from 'filed' to 'pending'. Moreover, this way of articulating the role of intermediaries misses crucial elements of collaborative behaviour and process within university–industry collaborations in the cultural economy, especially with regard to micro-enterprises, and therefore is critically important for CCIs.

Another strand of work examines what are termed 'cultural intermediaries'. Whereas normative notions of intermediaries in the innovation literature are the

Table 3.1 Typology of intermediaries according to Yusuf (2008: 1170)

Type of intermediary	Example/explanation
General purpose intermediary	Such as the university that produces and disseminates different forms of knowledge.
Specialised intermediary	Such as the university technology licensing/technology transfer office (TLO/TTO) which seeks out, helps codify via patenting and also helps to transfer knowledge to commercial users.
Financial intermediary	Such as a venture capitalist or an angel investor who supplies risk capital. This provider brings additional tacit knowledge in the form of managerial know-how, contacts, troubleshooting skills or risk assessment skills which can assist start-ups.
Institutional intermediary	Such as a public agency that offers incentives to encourage knowledge transfer and a variety of services to facilitate interaction among researchers and firms.

passive means of diffusion, in the sociological literature, the term includes an active process of transformation and translation. While Bourdieu's (1984) work does not specify the role of cultural intermediaries in collaborations between organisations, he does speak to their role as important in an 'economy of qualities' (Callon *et al.* 2002). In this way, these agents are tastemakers and 'needs merchants', but are also positioned in between the production and consumption of culture (Negus 2002; O'Connor 1998; Taylor 2013). This is important because it acknowledges the role of the agent and/or actor (which is missing in the technology-oriented discourse about intermediaries), and it also situates it within the cultural economy (Pratt 2008; Pratt and Jeffcutt 2009). According to Negus (2002), and relevant here, positioning cultural intermediaries in between production and consumption is an important aspect to come to terms with, because it acknowledges that the cultural economy does not have an assembly-line model of cultural production and consumption. Instead, in what Scott (1999) identifies as an economy of 'symbols,' the intermediary can occupy three roles at once: the producer, the intermediary and the consumer. Newer articulations of this notion use the term 'curation' as a way to speak to an increasingly fragmented economic landscape, giving value to cultural products within this landscape (Balzer 2014).

When it comes to the collaboration between university and industry specifically, the work on cultural intermediaries has very little to say. Theoretically, the notion of the cultural intermediary, in its Bourdieu-sian articulation, can identify those that are able to make decisions about how best to maintain and facilitate a collaboration between actors and agents who are not used to working with each other. Thus cultural intermediaries in this light might need to occupy a space in between producer and producer (or prosumer and prosumer), as opposed to producer and consumer.

It is here that a newer articulation of the intermediary concept might need to be endorsed, in this particular case, one that speaks to the issues that arise here such as:

- the articulation of the process of mediation;
- the cultural economy; the collaboration between organisations that do not traditionally have access to each other;
- the notion that agents as opposed to organisations are the primary facilitators;
- the notion that tacit knowledge is not only industrial knowledge but personal knowledge as well (Polanyi 1962); and
- the role of agency in activities, such as brokering relationships and enhancing trust in order to ensure industrial outcomes.

Methodology

Creativeworks London is an Arts and Humanities Research Council (AHRC) funded knowledge exchange hub. Its primary aim is to bring researchers, creative entrepreneurs and businesses together to explore the issues that impact on London's creative economy. It is therefore in line with current policy in the UK attempting to better articulate the value and impact of HE knowledge exchange within the creative economy (AHRC 2012).

The CWL creative voucher scheme was an initiative that enabled SMMEs in London's creative sector to develop unique and innovative short-term, collaborative research and development projects with CWL's academic partners within HEIs and independent research organisations (IROs). It is primarily designed to foster university–industry collaborations, albeit on a smaller scale then those seen in more tech-oriented schemes. The design of the CWL creative voucher scheme was based on 'innovation vouchers' that have been used widely in Europe since 1997 (Bakhshi *et al.* 2012). Creative vouchers – and innovation vouchers before them – are public sector-driven policy initiatives that seek to enable knowledge exchange (KE). Importantly, the notion is developed in a technology context (with assumptions as above) with the normative conception that KE failed due to 'blockages' in the diffusion, due to physical distance or lack of incentive, in the university. A point that has been further stressed by right-wing politicians is that, in principle, state funding of universities is inefficient and creates non-market incentives. Thus blockages of monetary or social incentive are solved by the marketisation (a pretend market) of the knowledge voucher. This seeks to mobilise a market exchange in knowledge. As noted above, this model was migrated to the creative sector (with no modification due to industry type, structure or output). The creative voucher scheme seems to be based on this logic, although – and this is another issue – no evaluation has been done of vouchers localised to cultural/creative contexts. A confounding factor in all innovation process is that there is a recursive and reflexive learning process. So, even if the policy does not work, participants may work out ways to make it work (in spite of) the policy. This highlights the intelligent and imminently creative innovative action of intermediaries – which is the topic of a later paper.

The CWL scheme started in mid-2012, ending in mid-2016. As of the time of writing this chapter, CWL has awarded 48 vouchers aimed at fostering collaborations between creative SMMEs and academics within partner HEIs. This involved matching these academics with creative SMMEs to deliver a collaborative project. There was a large variance of types of SMMEs from the creative sector that engaged in these collaborations such as designer-makers, software developers, architects, social enterprises, visual artists, musicians, dance enthusiasts and more. Similarly, there was a huge range of academic expertise available to draw from. Academics involved in these collaborations included art historians, cultural geographers, scholars of business, scholars of fashion, digital media professors and more. The collaborative projects ranged in topic and type from the development of new business models for mobile platforms, to the production of music software for disabled people to new ways of encouraging young people from deprived urban areas within greater London to participate in drama and theatre.[7] The sheer range of CWL collaborations funded by this scheme illustrated the interdisciplinary nature of the CCI in London, and therefore highlighted some of the challenges associated with facilitating this many collaborations from such a wide-ranging group of subsectors, which will be expanded upon later. The scheme was designed to provide a flexible, easy mechanism for small businesses in the

CCI to access the knowledge, expertise and skills of partner knowledge providers, like HEIs and IROs. The maximum sum offered was £15,000, of which a maximum of £5,000 was used for SMME costs.

Importantly, since the vouchers were funded by the AHRC, the project had to have a research component to it, which the SMMEs were made aware of prior to applying. That said, there was no discernible tension within the projects that came from this. A researcher–participant relationship did inevitably develop in many of the projects. However, this was not hierarchical, nor was it one-sided, since in many of the projects the learning was reciprocal. For instance, in one project, the SMME needed help with copyright issues regarding converting music into woven fabric. She collaborated with an academic working in the legal field. However, the academic had never looked into this particular issue before, since it was such a unique query. The process of learning what constituted copyright infringement, in this context, was a learning curve that they both undertook simultaneously, hence the reciprocity of this collaboration. The process of knowledge exchange, for most collaborations, was primarily a two-way street. Although, in one case, misunderstandings regarding IP, as well as what the academic was going to bring to the table for the SMME regarding unrealistic expectations of commercialisation, did cause some tension.

Interviews were used to gather data about the collaborations – 26 interviews based on the voucher collaborations were conducted at the time of writing this chapter. Interviews were recorded then subsequently transcribed for analysis. The interviews were conducted separately between the partner academic and the SMME, which meant that 13 voucher collaborations out of 48 underwent an interview. Each interview lasted from 30 minutes to an hour and was conducted with consent. The purpose of using interviews was to build a picture of the nature of these collaborations. These interviews were open-ended in nature with a few probing questions. Interviews were also conducted with two members of CWL's knowledge exchange team who helped facilitate some of these collaborations. This brings the total number of interviews for this chapter to 28. The knowledge exchange team are five individuals who have experience in: network creating/building strategy development; the curation of spaces and places that bring together researchers with cultural/creative sector practitioners; arts policy development; creative collaborations; organisational development; and a detailed knowledge of the CCI in London.

Importantly, the methodology allowed us a snapshot of the process of collaboration, rather than seeing it as a black-box, input–output model. The interviews covered a range of topics and issues such as the nature of these collaborations, the challenges, what was achieved and how this was done. However, a strong focus that emerged was the role of intermediaries. Therefore, in this chapter, we specifically explore the emerging findings on intermediaries in university–industry collaborations in the CCI.

Findings

Three overarching findings appear that all challenge the singular normative notion of the intermediary. Instead, we begin to see their role as multiple or various.

We also point out the role of specificity in the CCI, the role of SMMEs and complexities there in. Finally, we begin to explore the socially embedded nature of mediation in KE – not as codified and atomised but as a living, breathing knowledge whose texture and grain, in part, depend on the conditions of exchange and the values inherent in both parties.

There were two types of intermediaries in regard to these collaborations: the first were part of CWL's knowledge exchange team and the second was either an academic or an SMME within the collaboration who had prior experience with, and/or knowledge of, these types of projects. Moreover, intermediation was needed most with collaborations where those involved had not worked with each other in the past and where no previous experience existed in these types of partnerships. Intermediaries played an important part with respect to these collaborative projects where they acted as three things: broker, translator and network builder.

Intermediary as broker

Our research identified that there were a number of brokering activities that took place before and during these collaborations. We observed that this was conducted primarily by CWL's knowledge exchange team. Critically, knowledge brokerage in this instance meant more than simply the allocation of funds or match-making at events. It required a specific and sensitive interaction, which might be conceptually similar to that of curation (Balzer 2014). Two collaborations examined here had approximately four phases of brokerage: the first was at an introduction event sponsored by CWL, where the academic and the SMME meet and networking is brokered by the knowledge exchange team. Brokerage here meant that there is a managing of expectations and compatibilities that takes place before a project is embarked upon. Potential partners are introduced and put in a setting with each other based on the KE team's intimate knowledge of their wider network; a provision of linkages is hence offered up.

The second phase (or moment – as in the mechanical analogy of a moment, the resolution of forces at a place and time) is after a partnership, or willingness to work with each other, between the SMME and the academic has been struck. This is the stage in the process when the application is put together, and the potential voucher recipients attend an all-day workshop that is also run by the KE team. Interestingly, this stage is important according to one of the KE team members, who termed it the 'demystifying stage'. According to the KE team member:

> Surprisingly a lot of SMEs are actually intimidated by the word 'research'. It sounds like someone is going to watch you and then try and figure you out. But then they'd ask why would someone be interested in what they do, I call this the demystifying stage. One of my most challenging activities was actually telling SMEs [*sic*] that they have intrinsic value and that, of course, academics are interested in what they do … and in a good way.
>
> (Interview, KE team member)

At the application stage there seemed to be quite a bit of hand-holding, which was particularly necessary for those who had not entered into these types of contractual agreements in the past. Although hand-holding might suggest a certain level of naivety and/or anxiety at this stage, it would not be wrong to think of it in this way. Many serious concerns over the prospect of these collaborations are identified and dealt with at this stage. Anxiety levels are high here, but they are mediated and essentially 'demystified'.

The third phase of brokerage happens within the actual collaboration where expectations have to be configured and outputs discussed and managed. For instance, it is at this stage where the partners will iron out the specifics of what it is that they can contribute – hence, a need to make sure that the project is actually deliverable and not too ambitious. It is also about which compromise they will mutually agree upon in order to achieve a new 'collective goal'.

The fourth phase, in this particular case, has to do with matching or recognising difference in the levels of experience between the academic and the SMME. In one case, the academic had far more experience in these types of collaborations then the SMME. In another case, it was a director of the SMME who, in fact, had more experience and thus brokered their collaboration through a management of expectations and what was, in fact, deliverable. In some cases, there were two or more individuals embarking on brokering and, in some cases, micro-brokering expectations. In most collaborations, there is a significant amount of learning that takes place and the less experienced party gains new knowledge from the collaboration generally. So brokering is primarily about self-knowledge and humility, and not just 'banging heads together'.

Importantly, as trust and familiarity increase, the level of brokering is reduced. Importantly, those that had more than three phases of brokerage also had previous experience in university–industry collaborations and had also secured a positive outcome – which, in this case, was defined as the desire to continue to work with each other. However, those recipients that had worked together before are not guaranteed a positive outcome, which may mean that brokering may need to increase, even if levels of trust and familiarity increase. This notion needs more research.

It is also important to stress the context that the process of brokering happens in. It is one of mutual respect, trust and understanding that is often problematic, as the ideology of vouchers to technology transfer is embedded in distinct power relations that assume asymmetries of absolute knowledge, rather than different combinations. Much of the broker's role (especially the CWL KE team) was about challenging this role and, in effect, subverting it – without this, it most likely would not have worked.

Intermediary as translator

To illustrate this point, we can refer to one particular case where the managing director of an SMME was in charge of representing a number of artists, who in effect made-up the small business. He is not an artist, but had the knowledge and the experience to understand what the collaboration entailed in terms of working with both academics and artists. He (consciously) 'translated' the rules of participation between them; in essence, he managed the exchange of knowledge by speaking both 'languages' while, at the same time, being one of the stakeholders. This example of translation (or a lack thereof) appeared in a number of collaborations. What came strongly to the fore here were three notions related to translation: the first had to do with the activities themselves; the second had to do with managing incentivisation structures; and the third was the importance of being able to speak multiple languages. This again stresses the contrast with a market exchange model, where simple price agreement produces exchange. In this case, all of the value systems and trust had to be aligned.

Regarding the three aforementioned findings, by far this multiple language/concept ability is a critical resource in this process, and is one not recognised, nor evenly distributed, among networks. One project involved an SMME that had a wider network of businesses than it worked with. This business is a design consultancy that aims to build teams (usually in the design or tech area) to work on commissioned projects. They build teams in the areas of visual communication, system design, music tech and Open Product concepts. This means that the director/founder (of which there are two) must speak different languages within the field of design, and translate these concepts into a language that is understood by those who become collaborative partners as well as internal partners. In this particular project, the academic was a professor of fine art who wanted to capture the historical narrative of locals who live in a quickly gentrifying urban neighbourhood in South London. The combination of these two 'disciplines', one based on design and the other based on narrative analysis and history, required a certain level of translation in order to work. The academic had to be made aware of what was feasible as well as what was affordable, while the SMME was made aware of the need for academic outputs as well as material ones. It turns out that one of the directors spoke both of these 'languages' because of her extensive experience working with academics. What was produced was a mobile digital platform for the dissemination of community-generated narratives, but also a challenging introduction to methodologies that took fine art researchers out of their comfort zones:

> As a result of [said university's] involvement in this project, our Fine Art researchers have been privy to a number of new research practices. Interviewing the public about their own memories, and connections to the sites at which particular memories are routed, was deemed an exciting and inspiring process. The researchers have produced a range of audio-visual materials that reflect the idiosyncratic nature of the many 'community-generated narratives' documented.
>
> (Interview, professor of fine art)

Of course, there were also examples where translation was not as clear as it could have been. One particular case saw real tensions arise with regard to a prototype that was being developed and researched through the project. The main point of contention was that the SMME would have liked to get their ideas and their prototype out to market quickly using the university's resources. The researcher involved was more concerned with research outputs, but also maintained that the university's role was primarily for knowledge generation and not commercial interests. In an interview, the academic stated:

> I think there should be some promotion to the SMEs on what a university is … they don't understand why they've got to work with these dusty old teachers … they need to adjust their expectations of what these universities do … I mean, they're not the route to cheap labour … students and interns are not cheap labour … I think there should be a collaboration manifesto.
>
> (Interview, professor of design)

In this case, the SMME thought that they would be able to use students and expertise in the design department to make their prototype more commercially viable. The lead academic, on the other hand, did not see her role as one that was conjoined with the commercial viability of the SMME's prototype. Clearly, this collaboration could have probably benefited from more translation in order to manage the expectations that existed for both organisations. Nevertheless, many other cases indicated the importance of the role of translator; however, in order to translate these, intermediaries needed to be multi-lingual. When asked about the space that they believe they occupied with regard to the work that they do, one member of the KE team stated that:

> When I think of my career path and development – I mean, I've worked in the arts, at the Arts Council, I understand cultural policy development, funding. I've done placements at the House of Commons, so understand the legislative process and policy development for the creative and cultural industries. So, I bring all of these skills to bear in this role. I think of myself as a generalist, and usually one might think this as a disadvantage; but […] in this particular role, I speak the language of many constituencies and this I find is very advantageous. We are the antidote to a silo mentality and work in a very cross cutting way.
>
> (Interview, KE team member)

The notion of the generalist is an important one to conceptualise when thinking about the intermediary role, since the translation process requires working knowledge of a number of these 'constituencies'. Strategically, a generalist approach to these types of collaborations allows for a nuanced understanding of where to place policy and, hence, elevates the intermediary's position through their experience. Of course, this needs more research, but it also begs the question of who intermediates between the intermediaries. A generalist approach might be perfectly placed to do just that.

Intermediary as network builder

At the heart of the knowledge exchange programme is the issue of network provision and network building. It was, and still is, seen that in order for businesses in the creative sector to do well, they need to be connected to or within networks that will be able to facilitate transactional opportunities. In this regard, network building (and maintenance) was an important aspect of the mediation process. According to a KE team member, there are certain logistics that need to be in place for the successful building of networks, one of which is the building of a space for networking. According to the KE team member, 'My job was 90% making the space and 10% making the connections. Unless the space is there, the collaboration won't happen' (interview, KE team member).

This was especially true during the conceiving of the introduction events, where the academic and the SMMEs would initially meet. The space needed to be accessible, open, friendly and welcoming. In order for networks to be built, it was felt that a thematic component was important so as to tie those that attended these events with others who had similar interests. Hence, a network could be created around themes of interest as opposed to just funding. This stresses the social shaping of the social environment where a concept was developed in order to ensure that an ecosystem was physically built first (base building) before being populated by 'the network'. This enabled the organisation and the building of connections that joined agents/actors within the network.

This was especially effective when it came to bringing academics into the fold. They are defined by their disciplinary boundaries and, hence, working up a potential collaboration with an SMME in their area of interest was seen as beneficial, although there was still much hand-holding that had to be done in order to maintain these networks. As one KE team member said:

> Some academics and some SMEs needed more hand-holding than others. More often then not, it was the partners that did not know each other that needed the most hand-holding. Some were very hands off, because you know their work and you know that they know each other.
>
> (Interview, KE team member)

Another important aspect, with regard to network building, was incorporating partners that already had extensive networks into the scheme, so as to increase the network provision for SMMEs in the creative sector. For instance, one collaborating academic commented on the voucher scheme and his SMME partner:

> These opportunities are fantastic because of the breadth of what we're talking about. I've met the people at ——, the people that work with —— are excellent. —— is a special person, her breadth of knowledge is staggering.
>
> (Interview, professor of creative arts)

The SMME partner that the above quote mentions has multiple networks in different sectors. She has a working knowledge of the project's intended research subject as well as how to conduct research in this area. She adopts the intermediary role with respect to this particular collaboration. Importantly, many of these actors know that they are working in the interstices between art, industry and higher education, and thus realise that building and maintaining networks is pivotal to success in such a precarious and interdisciplinary environment. This is done through the legitimisation of expertise and its role in increasing network, as well as networking, capacity. The building and maintaining of networks, in this case, is a potential strategic role that emerges due to the configuration of the systems and imbalances of knowledge that have to be navigated. The creation of a knowledge exchange ecosystem is the 'infrastructure' upon which the 'cars and trains' of knowledge are able to flow.

Conclusions

Most of the work that has been conducted on university–industry collaborations examines knowledge exchange in the field of high technology. As has been shown, its main focus has been to conceptualise the process of knowledge exchange as a black box, and to measure the outcome of these collaborations in terms of material outputs such as patents developed or products developed from patents.

By examining the case of the creative voucher scheme run by CWL, we were not seeking to evaluate the scheme; instead, we sought to develop an understanding of the process of collaboration that the scheme might have enabled. That said, the extant conceptions of knowledge exchange, as understood by the voucher concept, were developed in relation to high-technology collaborations with universities (or other knowledge-based providers) and relied upon variants of diffusion to 'account for' the exchange of knowledge. Seeking to apply this to the CCI, we were forced to ask critical questions of the nature of the assumed relationship of knowledge exchange, substituting the existing passive model with a more active one. In normative approaches, knowledge exchange is conceived as output driven and sequential, where the greatest threat to any exchange is 'distance decay' and a lack of incentives (money). The latter factor is addressed in voucher schemes: a premium is added to both parties to engage with each other. We found this may be necessary, but certainly not sufficient. Additional parties, and in some cases additional experience and expertise, were needed to achieve knowledge exchange, notably mediation through intermediaries.

In normative literature, intermediaries are akin to bridges that forge a transfer gap; we found intermediaries to play a far more active and transformative role as translators. Normative studies assumed that organisational forms had symmetry or were irrelevant to exchange (again a market model). We found that a divergence in organisational form and scale, between micro enterprises and universities, was a barrier to engagement on both sides; intermediaries had to do more than bridge a gap, they had to construct a term of engagement (institution building and trust building). This is because intermediaries have an interest in being useful in the immediate term and as part of a future network. However, the trust relationship and reputational capital exceeds that of simply 'network supply'. The relationship is commonly a learning relationship for all participants. Intermediaries gain skill and market advantage through successful brokerage and mediation, and these benefits are sold forward, or given forward, as part of participation. In this sense, we hypothesise that intermediaries (through successful mediation) are the key conduits and nourishment of a creative ecosystem. Such ecosystems are characterised by a multiplicity of micro and project-based enterprises that suffer from a 'missing middle' organisationally and long-term sustainability. Strong intermediaries contribute resilience to a creative ecosystem.

Finally, we noted the non-normative forms of creative businesses, where the balance between economic value and cultural value was different to (say) high technology, where the scale and form of businesses (from freelance, project-based companies to a handful of employees) led to different working conditions and critical dependence on a wider ecosystem of skill and expertise. In summary, in the case of the CCI at least, a more active and transformative model of knowledge exchange was discovered, one that is overlooked – or underestimated – by black-box models of innovation.

Notes

1. The authors acknowledge the support of AHRC/Creativeworks London which funded this research (Grant No.: AH/J005142/1).
2. This work interconnects with and complements Chapter 8 in this book by England and Comunian, which focuses specifically on individual makers and sole traders in the craft sectors in the North East of England.
3. This includes the huge literature on science parks (Link and Scott 2003, 2006, 2007), technology transfer (see Sazali and Raduan 2011 for a comprehensive review) and knowledge transfer (see Ankrah 2007 for a comprehensive review regarding university–technology collaborations).
4. The fact that the CCI is mostly comprised of SMMEs illustrates that the size of organisations in this sector is different and, therefore, facilitating collaboration might take a different route, even though the general principles of these types of activities might remain the same. That said, there are a number of issues that have to be dealt with in order to facilitate collaborations of this size. See Virani (2015) for a discussion of some of these.
5. Importantly, long-standing relationships can sometimes have limiting effects regarding important collaborative aspects, like innovation, as has been pointed out by Meyer-Krahmer and Schmoch (1998), due to a lock-in effect of knowledge based on an entrusted organisational network.
6. Another related challenge here is that trust may exist between an SMME and a researcher, but then the contract is with the SMME and the university – where no trust has been established.
7. A breakdown of CWL Creative Voucher projects is available at: http://www.creativeworkslondon.org.uk/creative-voucher-scheme/.

References

Acworth, E. B. (2008) 'University–industry engagement: the formation of the Knowledge Integration Community (KIC) model at the Cambridge-MIT Institute', *Research Policy*, 37 (8): 1241–54.

AHRC (Arts and Humanities Research Council) (2012) *KE Hubs for the Creative Economy*. Retrieved from: http://www.ahrc.ac.uk/innovation/knowledgeexchange/hubsforthecreativeeconomy/.

Ankrah, S. N. (2007) *University–Industry Interorganisational Relationships for Technology/Knowledge Transfer: A Systematic Literature Review*, Leeds University Business School Working Paper Series. Retrieved from: http://business.leeds.ac.uk/fileadmin/webfiles/research/WPS/ANKRAH1.pdf.

Arundel, A. and Geuna, A. (2004) 'Proximity and the use of public science by innovative European firms', *Economics of Innovation and New Technologies*, 13: 559–80.

Bakhshi, H., Edwards, J. S., Roper, S., Scully, J., Shaw, D., Morley, L. and Rathbone, N. (2012) 'An experimental approach to industrial policy evaluation: the case of Creative Credits', *Enterprise Research Centre*, 4.

Balconi, M. and Laboranti, A. (2006) 'University–industry interactions in applied research: the case of microelectronics', *Research Policy*, 35 (10): 1616–30.

Balconi, M., Breschi, S. and Lissoni, F. (2004) 'Networks of inventors and the role of academia: an exploration of Italian patent data', *Research Policy*, 33 (1): 127–45.

Balzer, D. (2014) *Curationism: How Curating Took Over the Art World and Everything Else*. London: Pluto Press.

Bishop, K., D'Este, P. and Neely, A. (2011) 'Gaining from interactions with universities: multiple methods for nurturing absorptive capacity', *Research Policy*, 40 (1): 30–40.

Blumenthal, D., Gluck, M., Louis, K. S., Stoto, M.A. and Wise, D. (1986) 'University–industry research relationships in biotechnology: implications for the university', *Science*, 232 (4756): 1361–6.

Bourdieu, P. (1984) *Distinction: A Social Critique of the Judgement of Taste*. London: Routledge.

Bramwell, A. and Wolfe, D. A. (2008) 'Universities and regional economic development: the entrepreneurial University of Waterloo', *Research Policy*, 37 (8): 1175–87.

Brown, J. S. and Duguid, P. (2000) *The Social Life of Information*. Boston: Harvard Business School Press.

Brown, J. S. and Duguid, P. (2001) 'Knowledge and organization: a social-practice perspective', *Organization Science*, 12 (2): 198–213.

Bruneel, J., D'Este, P. and Salter, A. (2010) 'Investigating the factors that diminish the barriers to university–industry collaboration', *Research Policy*, 39 (7): 858–68.

Burt, R. S. (1982) *Toward a Structural Theory of Action: Network Models of Social Structure, Perception, and Action*. New York and London: Academic Press.

Callon, M., Méadel, C. and Rabeharisoa, V. (2002) 'The economy of qualities', *Economy and Society*, 31 (2): 194–217.

Charles, D. (2006) 'Universities as key knowledge infrastructures in regional innovation systems', *Innovation*, 19 (1): 117–30.

Charles, D. (2007) 'Regional development, universities and strategies for cluster promotion', in A. Harding, A. Scott, S. Laske and C. Burtscher (eds), *Bright Satanic Mills: Universities, Regional Development and the Knowledge Economy*. Burlington, VT and Aldershot, Hants: Ashgate, pp. 53–68.

Charles, D., Kitagawa, F. and Uyarra, E. (2014) 'Universities in crisis? New challenges and strategies in two English city-regions', *Cambridge Journal of Regions, Economy and Society*, 7: 327–48.

Clarysse, B., Wright, M., Lockett, A., Mustar, P. and Knockaert, M. (2007) 'Academic spinoffs, formal technology transfer and capital raising', *Industrial and Corporate Change*, 16: 609–40.

Cohen, W. M., Nelson, R. R. and Walsh, J. P. (2002) Links and impacts: the influence of public research on industrial R&D', *Management Science*, 48 (1): 1–23.

Comunian, R. and Gilmore, A. (2014) 'From knowledge sharing to co-creation: paths and spaces for engagement between higher education and the creative and cultural industries', in A. Schramme, R. Kooyman and G. Hagoort (eds), *Beyond Frames: Dynamics Between the Creative Industries, Knowledge Institutions and the Urban Context*. Delft: Eburon Academic Press, pp. 174–85.

D'Este, P. and Patel, P. (2007) 'University–industry linkages in the UK: what are the factors underlying the variety of interactions with industry?', *Research Policy*, 36: 1295–313.

Etzkowitz, H. and Leydesdorff, L. (2000) 'The dynamics of innovation: from national systems and "Mode 2" to triple helix of university-industry-government relations', *Research Policy*, 29: 109–23.

Florida, R. (1999) 'The role of the university: leveraging talent, not technology', *Issues on Science and Technology*, XV: 67–73.

Gertner, D., Roberts, J. and Charles, D. (2011) 'University–industry collaboration: a CoPs approach to KTPs', *Journal of Knowledge Management*, 15 (4).

Heckman, J. J. (2000) 'Causal parameters and policy analysis in economics: a twentieth century retrospective', *Quarterly Journal of Economics*, 115: 145–97.

Hoffman, K., Parejo, M., Bessant, J. and Perren, L. (1998) 'Small firms, R&D, technology and innovation in the UK: a literature review', *Technovation*, 18 (1): 39–55.

Ibert, O. (2007) 'Towards a geography of knowledge creation: the ambivalences between "knowledge as an object" and "knowing in practice"', *Regional Studies*, 41 (1): 103–14.

Jong, S. (2008) 'Academic organizations and new industrial fields: Berkeley and Stanford after the rise of biotechnology', *Research Policy*, 37 (8): 1267–82.

Kodama, F., Yusuf, S. and Nabeshima, K. (2008) 'Introduction to special section on university–industry linkages: the significance of tacit knowledge and the role of intermediaries', *Research Policy*, 37 (8): 1165–6.

Kodama, T. (2008) 'The role of intermediation and absorptive capacity in facilitating university–industry linkages – an empirical study of TAMA in Japan', *Research Policy*, 37 (8): 1224–40.

Kogut, B. and Zander, U. (1992) 'Knowledge of the firm, combinative capabilities, and the replication of technology', *Organization Science*, 3: 383–97.

Laursen, K. and Salter, A. (2004) 'Searching low and high: what types of firms use universities as a source of innovation', *Research Policy*, 33: 1201–15.

Link, A. N. and Scott, J. T. (2003) 'US science parks: the diffusion of an innovation and its effects on the academic missions of universities', *International Journal of Industrial Organization*, 21 (9): 1323–56.

Link, A. N. and Scott, J. T. (2006) 'US university research parks', *Journal of Productivity Analysis*, 25 (1–2): 43–55.

Link, A. N. and Scott, J. T. (2007) 'The economics of university research parks', *Oxford Review of Economic Policy*, 23 (4): 661–74.

Meyer-Krahmer, F. and Schmoch, U. (1998) 'Science-based technologies: university–industry interactions in four fields', *Research Policy*, 27: 835–51.

Negus, K. (2002) 'The work of cultural intermediaries and the enduring distance between production and consumption', *Cultural Studies*, 16 (4): 501–15.

O'Connor, J. (1998) 'New cultural intermediaries and the entrepreneurial city', in T. Hall and P. Hubbard (eds), *The Entrepreneurial City: Geographies of Politics, Regime and Representation*. Chichester: John Wiley, pp. 225–40.

Polanyi, M. (1964) *Personal Knowledge: Towards a Post-critical Philosophy*. Chicago: University of Chicago Press.

Pratt, A. C. (1998) 'Science, technologie, innovation: ouvrir la boîte noire', in J. Cohen, J. D. Hart and J. Simmie (eds), *Recherche et développement: travaux Franco-Brittanique*. Paris: Publications de la Sorbonne.

Pratt, A. C. (2008) 'Innovation and creativity', in J. R. Short, P. Hubbard and T. Hall (eds), *The Sage Companion to the City*. London: Sage, pp. 266–97.

Pratt, A. C. and Jeffcutt, P. (2009) 'Creativity, innovation and the cultural economy: snake oil for the 21st century?', in A. C. Pratt and P. Jeffcutt (eds), *Creativity, Innovation in the Cultural Economy*. London: Routledge, pp. 1–20.

Quayle, M. (2002) 'E-commerce: the challenge for UK SMEs in the twenty-first century', *International Journal of Operations and Production Management*, 22: 1148–61.

Ring, P. S. and Van de Ven, A. H. (1992) 'Structuring cooperative relationships between organizations', *Strategic Management Journal*, 13: 483–98.

Santoro, M. and Gopalakrishnan, S. (2001) 'Relationship dynamics between university research centers and industrial firms: their impact on technology transfer activities', *Journal of Technology Transfer*, 26: 163–71.

Santoro, M. and Saparito, P. (2003) 'The firm's trust in its university partner as a key mediator in advancing knowledge and new technologies', *IEEE Transactions in Engineering Management*, 50: 362–73.

Sazali, A. W. and Raduan, C. R. (2011) *The Handbook of Inter Firm Technology Transfer – An Integrated Knowledge-Based View and Organizational Learning Perspective*. Germany: LAP LAMBERT Academic Publishing.

Scott, A. J. (1999) 'The cultural economy: geography and the creative field', *Media, Culture and Society*, 21: 807–17.

Shane, S. and Somaya, D. (2007) 'The effects of patent litigation on university licensing efforts', *Journal of Economic Behavior and Organization*, 63: 739–55.

Taylor, C. (2013) 'Between culture, policy and industry: modalities of intermediation in the creative economy', *Regional Studies*, 49 (3): 362–73.

Tether, B. S. (2002) 'Who co-operates for innovation, and why: an empirical analysis', *Research Policy*, 31: 947–67.

Virani, T. E. (2015) *Mechanisms of Collaboration Between Small, Medium and Micro-sized Enterprises and Higher Education Institutions: Reflections on the Creativeworks London Creative Voucher Scheme*, Creativeworks London Working Paper Series No. 4.

Williams, P. (2002) 'The competent boundary spanner', *Public Administration*, 80 (1): 103–24.

Wright, M., Clarysse, B., Lockett, A. and Knockaert, M. (2008) 'Mid-range universities' linkages with industry: knowledge types and the role of intermediaries', *Research Policy*, 37 (8): 1205–23.

Youtie, J. and Shapira, P. (2008) 'Building an innovation hub: a case study of the transformation of university roles in regional technological and economic development', *Research Policy*, 37 (8): 1188–204.

Yusuf, S. (2008) 'Intermediating knowledge exchange between universities and businesses', *Research Policy*, 37 (8): 1167–74.

4 Heading towards a sustainable collaboration on the Arts Campus 'deSingel' in the city of Antwerp, Belgium

Annick Schramme

In this world of networks, coalitions, and alliances, strategic partnerships are not an option but a necessity.

(Doz and Hamel 1998: ix)

Introduction

Collaboration in the cultural sector is not new. In recent years, however, this sector has changed more than ever before, as companies merge and experiment with new collaborative models. Collaboration between arts organisations has become an important part of their daily operations due to the uncertainties of public funding, the increased demand for outreach and the continuous search for new artistic content (Johansson and Jyrämä 2015). Such partnerships can take on many different forms, ranging from infrastructure sharing, co-productions and joint ventures to mergers and cooperative undertakings, and more informal, looser alliances such as networks, communities and temporary collaborative projects. Project-based collaboration is especially popular in the creative industries. Small, creative businesses create temporary alliances – usually for the duration of the project or as long as both parties stand to gain from it (Sarasvathy, 2001; Van Andel *et al.* 2014).

Another key driver to work together, or to encourage collaboration between sectors, is the belief that this can lead to innovation. The previous Flemish Minister for Innovation and Media, Ingrid Lieten (2009–14), emphasised the role of the creative industries in this regard. In 2012, the Minister launched a new call, named the 'CICI' Call (Call for Innovative, Cooperative Initiatives), aimed specifically at supporting collaborative projects between knowledge institutions and the creative industries. You could compare this call with the Creativeworks London initiative, illustrated by Virani and Pratt in Chapter 3 in this book. The Minister earmarked one million euros to this end, and 45 projects were ultimately selected.

In this chapter, our focus is not on the numerous project-based collaborations between knowledge institutions and creative enterprises (SMEs and also the very small or 'nano' companies), as in Chapters 2, 3 and 8 in this book. Instead, we zoom in on a cross-sectoral case involving an art academy, the Royal Conservatory of Antwerp, and the biggest international arts centre in Flanders, known as 'deSingel'. Both organisations share the same infrastructure and have been working together for some time through individual projects. Now, however, since the expansion of their joint infrastructure in 2010, they want to see how they can establish a more structured collaboration, in order to be able to realise greater added value for various stakeholders. To this end, a new name was launched: 'deSingel Arts Campus'. The factors that contribute to the development and implementation of this 'Arts Campus' are analysed and discussed in this article. We will also look at similar cooperation models abroad.

This investigation into the 'deSingel Arts Campus' is a case study with an exploratory nature (Yin 2013: 8; Mortelmans 2007: 97). The research assesses the critical success factors of this collaboration using qualitative (through semi-structured interviews) and quantitative (through a survey based on a structured questionnaire) techniques (Fux 2013; Yin 2013). A variety of data collection methods were used, such as interviews, participatory observation and document analysis. Eighteen qualitative in-depth interviews were undertaken by Nicole Fux,[1] and analysed with staff and management at both organisations, as well as with the artist-in-residence organisation 'Champ d'Action'. For the purpose of triangulation, another survey was conducted with middle management and other collaborators that was based upon the structured questionaire.

This chapter is structured as follow. First, we introduce a framework for investigating our case – here we consider the role of initial conditions, collaboration process, organisational structure and management, contingencies and constraints, and outcomes and accountabilities. Secondly, we examine two other international case studies, the Barbican Centre-Guildhall School of Music and Theatre (London) and the Helsinki Music Centre (Finland), to provide additional insights into the development of sustainable collaborations between an education institution and an art organisation. Finally, some relevant conclusions are made concerning cross-sectorial collaboration in general and our case in particular.

Theoretical framework

As previously stated, collaborations exist in all shapes and sizes, ranging from partnerships on a project basis to long-term integration. Collaboration can be horizontal or vertical, complementary or overlapping, formal or informal, full or partial. Increasingly, we see organisations joining forces in models that maintain their respective autonomy, usually referred to as alliances or networks. An alliance is described as 'a form of collaboration between two or more parties in specific domains [that] join forces in order to achieve better results' (Huizingh, 2011: 263–4; Schramme 2009). Kanter highlights the vulnerability of these relationships, which are often difficult to control and less stable (Kanter 2009, 1997). We can also observe an increasing number of new networks in the cultural sector. A network is 'a collaborative format involving at least three sovereign organisations that jointly achieve an outcome by linking or sharing information, resources, activities and skills, which they could not have achieved individually'(Provan and Kenis, 2008: 231). Our case of the 'Arts Campus' can be seen as an alliance between an art centre and an art college on the one hand, and as a network involving other artistic partners on a project basis on the other.

One of the main drivers to work together is to obtain synergy effects. Synergy can be reached in different ways (Huxham and Vangen 2013). In management literature, this phenomenon has received more attention over the last few years. Business experts like Porter (1987), Kanter (1997, 2009), Campbell and Luchs (1998), Ansoff (1965) and Prahalad and Doz (1992) have attempted to describe and explain the mechanisms of synergy through theories and practical examples. In economic terms, synergy means that the combination of different business units has more value than the individual business units together (Campbell and Luchs 1998). A distinction is made between synergies based on the effect they produce: a cost-saving synergy realises the same result with less resources while an additive synergy delivers better results by combining existing resources. Resources are interpreted in a very broad sense, from infrastructure and business and artistic expertise to knowledge and networks. Furthermore, synergies are also possible following the merger of two complementary, diversified organisations. The knowledge and experience from one organisation can be a source of ideas, insights, information and, even, innovation for the other. In times of financial crisis and shrinking government resources, the need for both types of synergies is even greater than before (Schramme 2009).

Although the usefulness and importance of collaborations is generally recognised, cross-sectoral collaboration is less common. Collaborations between organisations from different industries tends to occur mainly from two possible starting points: either an organisation is failing and can only achieve its goal through collaboration (Hudson *et al.* 1999) or there is an external pressure to do so. In the case of the latter, it is assumed that collaboration is 'the holy grail' of innovation. Governments, for example, attempt to stimulate collaborations from this perspective, although they do not know in advance whether the results will be good (Ostrower 2005). The central aim of the collaboration is to use complementary resources from other organisations. Where possible, organisations are striving to differentiate themselves from the competition based on organisation-specific, non-reproducible resources. Hence differences between organisations are crucial, whereby these differences are embedded in the organisational structure and are partially immaterial. These crucial differences also have a downside, however. Differences exist precisely because people work and think in different ways, leading to natural – and to a certain extent lasting – obstacles to achieve cross-over effects and, thus, benefit from collaborative partnerships (Nooteboom 1999). Organisational identity literature also recognises that people draw on various sources when forming their identities that may overlap and support each other, but which can also be in tension and unable to coexist (Collinson 2003).

Collaboration usually calls for common (or at least compatible) agreed goals as a starting point. In practice, however, it seems that the variety of organisational and individual agendas that are present in collaborative situations often hamper reaching a common agreement (Huxham and Vangen 2013). The reasons behind this clash are not always clear. When organisations work together, each player contributes different resources and expertise, which in turn leads to the *potential* for collaborative advantage. However, organisations have different reasons for their commitment and every organisation is also trying to achieve another output from this involvement. Conflicts of interest are not excluded in this regard. Stresses that can lead to collaborative inertia often arise because some organisations seek to influence and control the joint agenda, or because some organisations are reluctant to commit resources (Huxham and Vangen 2013). Collaboration with a view to innovation is a much discussed topic in the academic literature. Bryson *et al.* (2006) conducted an extensive literature review on this topic, which led to an inventory of key concepts (see Figure 4.1).

Initial conditions

The first category focuses on broad themes related to the overall environment in which partnerships are embedded and other specific and immediate conditions that affect the formation of partnerships. A cross-sectoral collaboration cannot be disso-ciated from the general environment in which it is embedded. A high complexity in the environment can produce a need to make connections in order to reduce uncertainty and increase stability. The complexity can come from different sides, whereby both competitive (competitors) as well as institutional pressure (such as changes in the normative environment or regulations) may play a role. Other factors that can influence the formation of partnerships include: the failure of an organisa-tion to survive alone in an industry, pressure or encouragement from legitimate 'sponsors' (such as governments or major industry players) and a problem of iden-tification between several independent players and pre-existing relationships between independent players (Bryson *et al.* 2006).

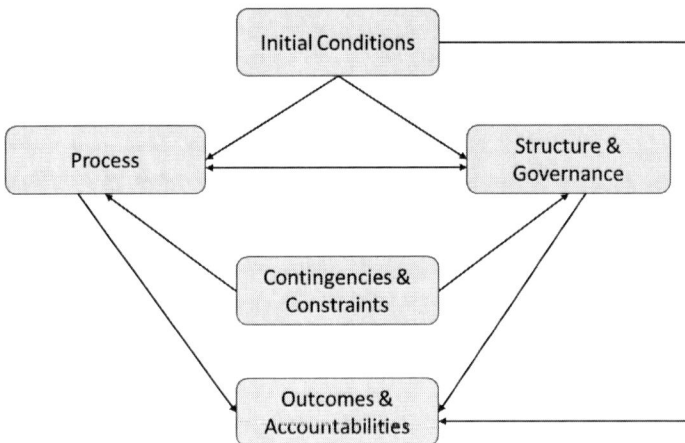

Figure 4.1 A framework for understanding cross-sector collaborations
Source: Adapted from Bryson *et al.* (2006).

Collaboration process

The collaboration process can be analysed, described and evaluated in many ways. Kaats and Opheij (2012) distinguish the following dimensions: the formulation of a common ambition, the mapping of several (conflicting) interests, the relationship between the relevant organisations and the development of the leadership role, the organisational structure designed and the management of the collaboration process. Bryson also adds safeguarding the legitimacy (both of the network as well as of the originators) and the importance of building trust and intervening in the case of conflicts (Bryson *et al.* 2006).

Contingencies and constraints

The collaboration process is also influenced by *contingencies and constraints*. An important factor is the influence of a possible power imbalance between partners which could lead to mistrust. This usually occurs when there is no clear agreement between the stated joint and individual goals of the collaboration. This is also the case in our example. In addition, internal and external events may occur during the collaboration process that can disrupt the relationship between partners. Another blocking factor is institutional reasoning, historically developed patterns at the macro level that determine the formal and informal rules of the game and provide their meaning (Thornton and Ocasio 1999). Such institutional reasoning provides justification of conscious and unconscious choices. When two or more partners from different industries come together, they bring their own conceptual framework that – if it is imposed from above – can cause misunderstanding and mistrust. Especially in our case – with education and culture collaborating – such reasoning can be prohibitive. Examination of boundaries also provides valuable insights on the processes of organisational identity construction, particularly in the context of inter-organisational collaboration (Hernes 2004).

Organisational structure and management

Another important success factor is the organisational structure. The way in which collaboration is organised greatly influences the development, sustainability and effectiveness of collaboration.

Outcomes and accountabilities

With respect to the results of cross-sector cooperation, we can distinguish effects on a first, second and third level. First-level effects are directly applicable results of a process of cooperation (e.g. the creation of social, intellectual and political capital, new agreements and commitments and new strategies). Second-level effects are more likely if the cooperation is more advanced and can also occur outside the boundaries of cooperation. Examples of this include new partnerships and/or new joint actions that go beyond the cooperation objectives that may entail changes in behaviors and perceptions. Finally, the third-level effects are results that are expressed only in the long term, such as a certain co-evolution between partners producing results in the market, new standards, etc. In our case, the cross-sector cooperation is still on the first level. Some of the common projects already surpass the boundaries of their cooperation, but there is an urgent need for a long-term vision on the cooperation.

Management literature shows that several authors try to understand the complexity of working together (Kanter 1997, 2009; Campell and Goold 1998; Child and Faulkner 1998; Huxham and Vangen 2013; Senge 2010). However, they do not apply similar classifications or principles; each author starts from a different paradigm. For example, Bell *et al*. (2006: 1611) conclude that 'the body of knowledge on the dynamics of cooperation developed so far is characterized by fragmentation, lack of coherence, and non-comparable research output'. Huxham and Vangen (2013) argue for reflection and acceptance of the complexities of the collaboration. The best practice is to identify the tensions inherent in collaboration and to deal with these rather than trying to solve them. Kaats and Opheij (2012) focus on complex collaboration issues, mainly in the non-profit sector. They give an updated overview and their research is classified into five themes: ambition, interests, relationships, organisation and process. These components also largely correspond to the factors mentioned by Bryson *et al*. (2006) and we will use them to further analyse our case.

Initial conditions

As stated above, an understanding of cross-sectoral collaboration cannot be separated from the context in which it is embedded. The first important fact is that the deSingel international art centre and the Conservatory of Antwerp share the same building. The design, by architect Léon Stynen, dates from the 1960s and was originally designed to house only the Conservatory. The building embodied the dream of the founder, the Flemish composer Peter Benoit, who at the end of the nineteenth century not only wanted a school for students, but also wanted to involve the entire population in international music and theatre through his institute. During the 1960s, with the democratisation of culture, the Flemish Minister of Culture decided to build a new conservatory that would reincarnate that dream, an educational institution that also has a connecting function with society. The Flemish Music Conservatory opened its doors in 1968 and is located on the outskirts of the city of Antwerp, away from the city centre and close to the motorway.

The plans for an arts centre in the same building were only launched in 1980. It was to become a place where different art forms could be presented with a view to achieving broad public participation. This led to an expansion of the building with two venues designed by the same architect, with a capacity of 850 and 1,000 seats each. In 1983, the autonomous arts organisation deSingel opened its doors and was, from the start, influenced by a widespread movement of innovation that was taking place in the Flemish art sector during at that time. A young generation of avant-garde artists, including Jan Fabre, Jan De Corte, Wim van de Keybus and Anne-Theresa de Keersmaeker, presented their productions in what were termed 'arts centres': new alternative venues that were not structurally subsidised by the government, but were operating on the sidelines and offering young talent a platform. The young deSingel art centre also played this reformist card, and the house quickly grew into an international arts centre with a strong reputation for quality and innovation. Only with the approval of the Performing Arts Decree by the Flemish Parliament in 1993 did art centres become recognised by the government, and were subsequently eligible to receive structural support (for four years). Since then, deSingel has gradually expanded its programming. This initially included music, while later dance, drama and architecture were added as well.

In the 1990s, the Conservatory also expanded. As of 1995, it became a single department as part of Antwerp University College. The Flemish architect Stéphane Beel was asked to examine the needs and possibilities of the building and to create a new extension. The inauguration of the renovated building took place in 2010. With an additional 12,000 m^2, the site now covers a total area of 46,000 m^2. Previously, the dance and drama departments of the Conservatory were scattered across the cities of Lier and Antwerp. When they moved to this site, all performing arts disciplines were gathered in one place. This move is undoubtedly one of the major challenges in the further exploration of interdisciplinary collaboration.

The expansion of the infrastructure also presented deSingel with the opportunity to further expand its core business. This included a new spacious cafe-restaurant, an exhibition space, a multimedia room and art shop, a theatre, a dance studio and rehearsal space for music ensembles:

> The new building allows deSingel to further grow into a dynamic 21st century Arts Campus, where in addition to showcasing different arts ('presenting'), the production of art ('making') and art education ('learning') interact as an organic whole. The Arts Campus idea has been launched and the trinity 'presenting-producing-learning' can be shaped in this new building.
>
> (deSingel, Policy Plan, 2006–10)

At that moment, DeSingel also launched its new name: 'Arts Campus'. It was a catalyst for new collaboration opportunities on the site. Spontaneously, pilot projects came about between the Conservatory and deSingel, which both organisations regarded as an added value. Most projects currently also involve other artistic partners that are located in the building, such as the international production house for contemporary music and multidisciplinary art projects 'Champ d'Action' and the non-profit organisation for the support of architectural culture in Flanders, the 'Flemish Architecture Institute' (VAi). In the next section, we examine what the concept 'Arts Campus' means for all partners.

Collaboration process

The concept of the Arts Campus

The Arts Campus concept is one that is about collaboration between an arts centre and an arts college, where synergy and innovation are pursued. As explained above, the concept is closely linked to the history of the building which has its origins in the 1960s with the construction of the conservatory.

The making of the policy plan in 2006–10 by deSingel was a pivotal moment in this development. For the first time, the term 'Arts Campus' appeared in deSingel's policy, 'the new building should provide opportunities to grow into an Arts Campus of the 21st century with substantive content, exemplary for the collaboration between culture and education' (deSingel 2006–10).

The Conservatory also had high expectations for the new opportunities offered by the new building. In 2008, *Forum*, the magazine of the Conservatory, made an appeal to consider the possibilities for collaboration at this new Arts Campus: 'dare to dream, because if we don't fill the new Arts Campus today with our imagination and our dreams, it will be reduced to just another construction project' (Dowit and Voets 2008). The authors see the 'Arts Campus' as a radical union of the academic and the artistic in one physical centre, a unique combination of performing arts in all its aspects.

In 2010, the year the new building was opened, a new name was officially introduced: the former 'arts centre' became the 'international Arts Campus deSingel'. The concept 'Arts Campus', however, remained confusing. DeSingel launched the concept without really assessing how this could effect the Conservatory. One example is the confusion it caused due to the word carrying several meanings: it contains both a partnership concept as well as an educational concept. It also refers to a part of deSingel's offering and is also part of deSingel's brand name. Based on the different definitions of the Arts Campus concept given by the respondents, Fux (2013) arrived at the following definition:

> The Arts Campus is a place where the best conditions are created for transmittance between the arts, education, and research. It is a catalyst for interaction between students, professionals, and the public; a place where synergies can be achieved between the different arts disciplines; a place where learning, making, and showing are one.
>
> (Fux 2013: 53)

The importance for arts graduates to engage with cultural work to access networks and opportunities is acknowledged in the literature (Comunian *et al.* 2014). Ashton's chapter in this book also highlights the importance of work-based learning in the context of media students. It is not dissimilar for music and performance students.

Respondents were also asked about the added value of the Arts Campus from their perspective. Within the many different answers that were given, four categories can be distinguished from the literature: positioning and market development, cost advantages, knowledge development and exchange, and external pressures. In terms of positioning and market development, because of their complementary nature, deSingel and the Conservatory have a stronger profile and position together. In addition to attracting potential new audiences, they can also differentiate their offerings. DeSingel, which was mainly a place for showing, now also wants to focus more on production, while the Conservatory gets the opportunity to establish new connections with the professional field. Both organisations can, thanks to the collaboration, also respond to new developments faster. Because of the contact between young talent and established artists, they can feel the pulse of the emerging generation of artists, allowing them to develop new markets and products. In terms of synergy effects, the savings effect is rather small (cost synergy), but the most added value can be gained from an exchange of services and resources (additive synergy). Although this cooperation was the initiative of the arts organisation deSingel (bottom up), the external pressure refers to the general appeal by the government to utilise resources rationally by working together. However, the most important added value of the Arts Campus is collaboration in the field of knowledge development and strengthening innovative capacity. This means opportunities to do original things such as innovate and experiment with the boundaries between art, education and research. As we can see, the motives for collaboration were numerous.

The collaboration process at the Arts Campus is a complex matter. Although the diversity of partners is one of the strengths of the collaboration that can lead to collaborative advantage, it is also this diversity that entails inevitable tensions.

Common ambitions?

Not only is there no consensus concerning the concept of 'Arts Campus', there is no consensus present on the common objectives. However, the mission statements of deSingel and the Conservatory contain common values, such as internationalism, interdisciplinarity, creativity, collaboration and reflection. These are interesting similarities but lack the clear umbrella of an explicit, common ambition. Some teachers, students and other cooperators state that they see the lack of a clear, common mission statement as a shortcoming:

> What I feel, regarding the Arts Campus, is that it is something coming from deSingel, and which was never discussed. Had we discussed it together, things would be very different. Everyone also knows that the building was the conservatory's in the beginning.
>
> (Staff member, Conservatory)

On the other hand, several pilot projects already exist that create added value for the collaboration partners, to everyone's satisfaction. In other words, they tried to put practice and experimentation ahead of future development ambitions. Huxham and Vangen (2013) also indicate the importance of having this kind of iterative processes which bridge planned development and practice. The advantage of this way of working is that trust can also grow at a secure pace. Any ambitions must also be attractive for stakeholders. The interviews show that not all stakeholders have grasped the Arts Campus concept yet. For example, the general public is not aware, and students are only slightly aware, of some of the advantages. For example, they rarely make use of the option to attend all performances for only five euros. In the boardrooms, collaboration within the framework of the Arts Campus is rarely discussed. The top management of both institutions, on the other hand, support the collaboration. The Arts Campus has a personal meaning for the management of both institutions; the personal involvement is also evident from the fact that many projects grow spontaneously from the individual initiative of several employees at different levels. In the survey, this aspect also received high marks. Another positive point is that the collaboration strategy is aligned with the strategy of all partners. After a long period of project-based collaboration, the time has come to formulate a more sustainable and shared ambition.

Organisational structure and management

Another important success factor is the organisational structure. The way in which collaboration is organised greatly influences the development, sustainability and effectiveness of that collaboration. At present, there is no specific collaborative structure. Projects grow spontaneously, following the initiative of some employees from the bottom up. Besides the operation of the common library, there are no formal arrangements for the management of the collaboration. A well-functioning collaboration structure has, however, existed since 2010 for the management of the building: the separate Management Committee. Both partners contribute proportionately towards the costs, but the Management Committee is only responsible for the management and maintenance of the building complex. Although the Management Committee is seen as a major asset in the collaboration, the Management Committee maintains its distance from a substantive alignment between the partners and limits its power to purely infrastructure-based issues.

The interviews also revealed that the complexity of the Arts Campus has increased since the new extension. Coordination tasks have become heavier, programming has extended, and the technical support has become more complex. The number of staff has grown, but not in relation to the work required. The collaboration also demands great flexibility on the part of the staff.

Contingencies and constraints

Conflicting interests?

Especially if the collaboration draws strength from the diversity and complementarity of the partners (collaborative advantage), an inherent aspect is that there are contradictions between the interests of those involved that can lead to collaborative inertia. For example, there is continuous tension between the various functions that the Arts Campus wants to cover, especially between learning (the conservatory), presenting and producing art (deSingel). From the conservatory's management perspective:

> The conservatory is experimenting all the time, there are as many projects that fail as well as succeed [...] For deSingel this is different: everything

depends on the quality of the presentation; which is not to say that there is no room for experimenting, but that nevertheless a real risk is taken that must be treated carefully.

(Manager, Conservatory)

DeSingel's management perspective on the Arts Campus label is as follows:

For example, I oppose the fact that underperforming students would be allowed in any of our Arts Campus-initiated activities, because I believe that this does not meet professional practice. In the professional phase, the harsh law of auditioning, selection, just being the best prevails. Those who are not good enough, drop off. Education does not work in the same way. Education actually provides opportunities to those who are less talented, hoping that maybe they will recover and perhaps, ultimately, reconnect. Education is also subsidized on a quantitative basis. We justify our subsidies on a qualitative basis, which is a substantial difference.

(Manager, DeSingel arts centre)

Thus several opposing or uncoordinated interests exist. Also on the regulatory level, there is a big difference: deSingel autonomously manages allocated budgets and is held accountable vis-à-vis the Flemish Ministry of Culture, whereas the Conservatory is part of an overall educational structure of university colleges and depends on the Ministry of Education. The challenge is to find solutions for these conflicting interests that may result in a win-win through joint funding, artistic talent and/or staff, as in the example of the orchestra academy:

With the Royal Philharmonic Orchestre ('deFilharmonie') and deSingel, we set up the orchestra academy a few years ago, where we have the following concept: the students in symphony occupy the large hall, stand on the stage, are coached by teachers and musicians from deFilharmonie, some of whom also play. All students are selected based on an audition […] this results in setting the bar higher for your own students because you need the best anyway […] in that context, it is fantastic to have two partners, we can do things we could otherwise never pay for.

(Staff member, Conservatory)

The interviews clearly show that each partner in this project contributes to their own capacity. DeSingel naturally intervenes more regarding financial aspects, while the Conservatory can sometimes deploy personnel or students more easily and does everything within its power to integrate activities in its structure, despite the more rigid educational system. However, there are some conflicts that generate lasting resentment. For example, a number of respondents mentioned the unilateral application by deSingel of the Arts Campus label to projects was a major issue. In particular, the teaching staff of the Conservatory would also like a say about the application of the 'quality' aspect. Also, they experience a lack of equality in the external communication of the Arts Campus projects. The conservatory feels a bit crushed by the strong marketing power of deSingel. In communicating with the public, there is also little clarity on the contribution of the Conservatory. Hence, a necessary condition for success is a good dialogue. The respondents have indicated, however, that communication is difficult between both organisations: 'One bottleneck is in fact communication: it is simply difficult, these remain autonomous organisations that have their own schedule, their own rhythm, and that does not always match' (staff members, Conservatory and deSingel).

The opportunity is not always present either: the workload is high and some staff organise activities without actually being in contact with the other partners. During the interviews, it was often stated that there is little transparent consultation. Concerning value creation, the survey showed that the partners truly believed in the added value of collaboration. In addition to the shared infrastructure, which everyone recognised as an added value, it is also important to explicitly state the artistic and organisational added value, as well as clarify the input and the return of both organisations regarding the collaboration. Right now, there is much confusion about this, because both institutions are also involved in other collaborative networks from which they also draw value.

Organisational culture

In the literature, trust, equality and diversity are crucial success factors for collaboration, particularly in the cultural sector. Diversity is reflected in the two different organisational cultures and identities. Although all the actors in the inter-organisational joint venture share a joint dream of the 'Arts Campus', they also emphasise their own established and distinctive organisational and professional identities. Although the ability to connect between both is very large, many people indicate that trust is not universally shared, caused by social and mental boundaries (Hernes 2004). Especially within the Conservatory, there is a lack of trust. This is linked to the imbalance of power between the two organisations and the lack of a formal and binding leadership. Formally, there is no agreement on a leading partner or a broker in the collaboration. Whoever has an idea takes the initiative and the associated processes unfold organically. Binding leadership is mostly indicated as a key success factor for collaboration, not only with regard to the relationship between people but also concerning the productivity of the organisations. The Arts Campus needs a leader/broker who can give a boost to group processes so mutual trust can grow. The kind of boundary broker needed is one that can be a member at various levels of the organisations and that can bridge the gaps in the social structure, as well as adding to the diversity of the organisations and contributing to the social capital (Burt 2005; Gilpin and Miller 2013; Johansson and Jyrämä 2015).

The contrast is also visible in organisational culture: the difference between the more horizontal, participatory (but sometimes also more bureaucratic) culture of the Conservatory and the efficiency-oriented and more top-down driven organisation of deSingel with a small team. This, of course, influences the capacity to take decisions within the partnership. Partly because of these cultural differences, there is a tension in the collaboration's decision-making process.

> This has always been their [the conservatory's] internal problem, it's always been that way. They work in a less structured manner than we do […]. Here at deSingel some things also go slow, but once a decision is made in-house, then everyone agrees and supports it, and all heads are turned in the same direction. In the conservatory, this is constantly changing.
>
> (Manager, deSingel)

The development of a common organisational culture based on equality would contribute to achieving synergy between the partners. One of the ways to do so is to create common meeting times. The new Grand Café would be the perfect place for such gatherings. However, many students have responded that the new Grand Café is too elitist for them and does not have the appeal of a friendly, democratic meeting area or co-working space.

Outcomes and accountabilities

The current collaboration grew organically and spontaneously in parallel with the development of the site's infrastructure. A phased plan was never considered or discussed. The Arts Campus operation is, in fact, still in an exploratory phase. Although the quality of projects is satisfactory, the structure is perceived as ineffective. An extension of the collaboration requires well-developed process management with attention to phasing and planning. A balance between content and processes, and a clear definition of roles and supervision, are part of the collaboration's management.

Comparison: models of cooperation

As described above, one of the best ways to explore the management practice of collaborating is to learn from other 'good practices' through benchmarking. Benchmarking is defined as

> [the] systematic investigation of performance and underlying processes and practices of one or more leading organisations in a particular area and the comparison of one's own performance and working methods to these best practices with the aim to determine a position and improve performance.
>
> (Camp 1989: 23–5)

However, because the Arts Campus concept is still being developed, performance indicators are not clearly known and cannot be readily measured. That's why we have assumed a more informal meaning of benchmarking, i.e. by studying the best practices to accelerate internal learning and change processes (Bogan and English 1994). The practices investigated for our case are all unique in their history, content and type of collaboration, combination of collaboration partners and structure. To this extent, they cannot be copied easily. Nevertheless, we can learn some lessons based on this comparative perspective. The selection of the cases was done based on our own definition of an arts campus and the corresponding characteristics. Five interesting cases emerged from a survey, but we will discuss only the two most relevant cases in this article: the Guildhall School of Drama and Music in collaboration with the Barbican Centre in London and the Helsinki Music Centre in Finland. A summary of the benchmarking is provided in Table 4.1.

The Barbican Centre and Guildhall School were neighbours in the same building complex for 30 years. The partnership was launched in 2007–8, driven by two new directors, and took place in various domains. A collaboration agreement with the London Symphony Orchestra is also in place and, in September 2013, a permanent collaboration regarding the shared use of the new building, Milton Court, was started. In the first phase, an administrative platform was created for the HR, finance, IT and infrastructure departments. In the second phase, the common division Creative Learning was launched, an amalgamation of the Barbican Creative Learning Division and Guildhall Connect. This collaboration unit operates under its own director and relies on resources from both the Barbican and Guildhall.

In the case of the Helsinki Music Centre (HMC), the three main actors in the Centre are the Sibelius Academy, the Radio Symphony Orchestra and the Helsinki City Orchestra. Established in 1882, the Sibelius Academy is the only university-level music institution in Finland. In the beginning of 2013, the Sibelius Academy became part of the University of the Arts Helsinki, together with the Theatre Academy and the Academy of Fine Arts. The Radio Symphony Orchestra, established in 1927, is part of the Finnish national broadcasting company (YLE) and aims to promote and develop Finnish music culture nationally and internationally. The Helsinki City Orchestra was established in 1883 and currently employs 102 musicians and an administrative staff of 11. The Helsinki City Orchestra is governed as a bureau of the city of Helsinki. The fourth actor, the service organisation of the Helsinki Music Centre Ltd, was established in 2010. It is a for-profit corporation installed by the city government and responsible for the maintenance of the Music Centre and IT contracts with various service providers, such as the restaurant, shop and users as well as the technical, security and cleaning services. In March 2012, the Helsinki Music Centre Ltd had 11 full-time employees.

What can we learn from these cases?

Initial conditions

The arts campuses in Helsinki and London have grown due to external pressure either following an explicit governmental instruction or due to a reduction of resources that imposed synergies (London). These collaborations thus clearly originated under external pressure. DeSingel launched the Arts Campus project

Table 4.1 Summary of the case studies analysed

	deSingel Antwerp	Barbican/Guildhall	Helsinki Music Centre
Initial conditions	Bottom up	External ressure (funding)	External pressure
Collaboration process	No common ambition or clear objectives. Production and presentation	Common ambition and the existence of clear objectives and framework. Education, learning, participation.	No common ambition or clear objectives Education; learning and participation
Organisational structure and governance	No integrated organisational structure: an additional management committee that only takes care of the infrastructure. Leadership: DeSingel is the sole trigger, but assumes no actual leadership in the practical collaboration.	Creative Learning Division: integrated organisational culture. Leadership: two new directors who both support the collaboration.	The service provider is a for-profit organisation, which is responsible for coordinating the outsourced activities (maintaining the building, marketing, technical services, and renting out spaces). Leadership: the first manager seemed to have a role as a (identity) broker but left the organisation too early.
Contingencies and constraints	Power imbalance Organisational culture: different institutional logics.	Power imbalance Organisational culture: slow and increasing process.	Power imbalance Organisational culture: two different identities.
Outcomes and accountabilities	A gradual approach, starting with an exploration phase. Need for a more systematic approach.	Long preparation, especially regarding the structural aspects of collaboration. The artistic aspect grew gradually, step by step.	Lack of established rules and procedures, and lack of comprehensive contracts. Constant renegotiation of the norms and practices.

itself to better express themselves, to stimulate innovation and to generate possible additional funds. Hence the Arts Campus idea was born from an artistic ambition and the strategic choice of deSingel itself.

Collaboration process

The formulation of a common ambition, and the existence of clear objectives and a clear framework, are experienced as a great asset by the Barbican. It allows targeted and strategic work and support of creativity within a clear framework. Our analysis showed that in our case a clear shared mission is missing. Also in the case of the HMC, even though the actors share the same dream and vision for the HMC as a vibrant community around music, this seems not to have materialised in shared goals and practices. It does not mean that through an iterative process between practice and the development of ambitions, a shared mission could not emerge. This way, trust could be supported gradually. We see that in the Barbican-Guildhall case, a similar process unfolded. For several years, the Creative Learning division operated based on the individual missions of the two parent organisations. Only later on did they reach agreement on a shared mission. This provided a boost to collaboration and created an opportunity to develop a strategic plan that was supported by an external coach and two administrators.

In London and Helsinki, learning/education is the common denominator of the partners. In both, education, participation and learning were already important parts of the mission of the arts centres involved. The government wanted to promote this educational and collaborative operation by providing additional funds for this purpose. On the contrary, deSingel is mainly focused on presentation and production and, for the time being, does not have any ambition in the field of education. It does not receive additional funds from the government to this end. The structural collaboration was also possible because the Guildhall and Barbican depend on the City of London. So it was quite easy, for example, to share staff given that the regulations and staff status were the same. For the Arts Campus in Antwerp, and for the Helsinki Music Centre as well, the situation is totally different. Each party (the Conservatory and deSingel) depends on different ministries, respectively the Flemish Minister of Education and the Flemish Minister of Culture. The local government is not even involved.

We already mentioned that a binding leadership and trust are necessary for successful collaboration, especially in a cross-sectoral collaboration. A collaboration unit is an incentive for creativity and innovative capacity, if the internal organisation is based on trust and support, flexibility and communication, as in the shared Creative Learning division of the Barbican-Guildhall. At the Barbican-Guildhall, two new directors were present who jointly decided to start the collaboration. DeSingel, on the other hand, is the sole trigger, but assumes no actual leadership in the practical collaboration. This creates a perception of inequality. This lack of leadership is also present in the Helsinki Music Centre. The first manager of the Helsinki Music Centre seemed to have a role as a (identity) broker who negotiated with different actors on the aims and joint plans.

However, the manager changed and the person's role was transformed to manage the services rather than building joint activities (Johansson and Jyrämä, 2015).

Organisational structure and management

At the Barbican, there is a common organisational structure and the partners can collaborate freely, at an artistic level, because a clear framework and a safe environment are present. With the Barbican-Guildhall, apparently the creation of a shared administrative service also boosted the artistic collaboration process. The shared structure, thus, provides a proper environment to achieve synergy. At the Barbican, the change in the organisational structure at each of the three phases gave a boost to substantive collaboration. The opportunities that arose were more numerous than expected.

Contingencies and constraints

In all the cases, there is also a power imbalance in terms of the artistic choices and decisions in the programming of the collaboration in favour of the arts organisation. We found that this power imbalance is apparently inherent in an arts campus of this kind (as opposed to collaboration with creative industries, whereby mostly the research institution is dominant – see Comunian and Gilmore 2014). Established values such as quality, after all, collide with the explorative nature of a learning process. DeSingel distinguishes itself as an arts centre precisely by serving quality and does not want to dilute this image by delivering productions at a 'student level'. This imbalance is also reflected in the discussions about identity, brand name and external communications and audiences. An interesting learning point for deSingel is also the permanent evaluation of projects and processes by the Barbican. The Barbican continuously gathers information from all stakeholders to gain insight into how the programming strikes the audience. This allows gradual adjustment and minimises the risks of joint productions.

In these cases, we can speak of a (partially) integrated organisational culture. This does not exist at deSingel because, up until now, the collaboration grew organically and, as both parties are housed at the same site, with less urgency. At the Barbican, a merger of two existing services took place and, thus, cost synergies applied. For deSingel and the Conservatory, to the contrary, it would mean an additional investment. The expansion of the tasks of the existing management committee could be an alternative. In the case of the Helsinki Music Centre, the key tension seemed to emerge between the artistic programming organisations and the service provider, a for-profit organisation, responsible for coordinating outsourced activities such as maintaining the building, providing technical services and renting out spaces. On the one hand, it is perceived as a key actor aiming to be in power and, on the other, an organisation serving the other actors in the HMC. However, its ability to understand the other actors and their audiences was questioned. There had been tensions escalating into conflicts, such as how, when and by whom to sell the concert tickets and whether to start charging for cloakroom services that used to be free (Johansson and Jyrämä 2015).

Outcomes and accountabilities

Regarding the Barbican, we learned that collaboration was accompanied by a master plan consisting of three major phases. This was preceded by a long preparation, especially regarding the structural aspects of collaboration. The artistic aspect grew gradually, step by step. DeSingel has also opted for a gradual approach, starting with an exploration phase. However, this should not prevent a more systematic approach. Advances in the development of the organisational structure can also boost substantive collaboration. The monitoring of process quality (Barbican) allows for dynamic adjustment of the creative processes and benefits the discussion on parties' interests with the involvement of stakeholders. Also, in the case of the HMC, the lack of established rules and procedures, and the lack of comprehensive contracts, have created a need to constantly renegotiate the norms and practices. The culture for continuous re-negotiation also questioned the power structures among the actors and enhanced the tensions in between (Johansson and Jyrämä 2015).

Conclusions

Based on our benchmark, we have learned that cross-sectoral collaborations between organisations mostly do not arise spontaneously, but are imposed by the government. If sufficient time is spent on developing an understanding of the partners involved and the complementarity of their operation as well as investing in additional resources and developing leadership and trust, the success rate is high. Usually there is a power imbalance between the cooperating partners, often in favour of the arts centres, but if good internal dialogue, a suitable management structure and a clear external communication are put in place, this can be overcome.

Our case study shows that there is a wealth of opportunities for creating sustainable added value at the deSingel Arts Campus. After five years of project operations and expansion of the infrastructure, the appropriate time has come for a more systematic and strategic approach. It is necessary that a strategic course is determined for the collaboration; otherwise, there is a risk that enthusiasm will decrease and dilute any spontaneous collaboration. Starting with the practical application is a good way to build trust, but this should be alternated with the development of ambition. The tasks of the Management Committee that is responsible for the infrastructure could be extended to the substantive domain, creating an overarching structure that is also willing to boost artistic cooperation. Regular evaluation of the process was also essential in our benchmark. In this regard, we refer to an evaluation of the collaboration by artists and teachers, but also by the public and the students in order to continuously remain in touch with the significance of the collaboration for those involved. A flexible response to this evaluation can gradually make the collaboration and trust evolve.

Unlike many partnerships between higher education institutions and creative industries in urban areas, this collaboration has no immediate impact on the local environment. First and foremost, this has to do with the location of the building. The campus is located on the outskirts of the city, surrounded by a highway with condominiums and commercial buildings. In the future, though, this may change. After all, the city is working on the design of a major plan to tackle the mobility situation in Antwerp. One of the scenarios garnering support from a large part of the population is known as 'Ringland' the aim of which is to cover the outer ring motorway with a large green area surrounding deSingel. This could also lead to a whole new direction for the site and the environment. Additionally, deSingel, as a major Flemish cultural institution, is mainly subsidised by the Flemish government. This results in the activities of deSingel having a supra-local presence in the first place. Nevertheless, several collaborations do exist with other cultural parties in the centre of town, but the big challenge over the coming years remains to strive for better integration in the city and its residents.

The new Arts Decree (2013) – that will regulate the arts grants on a Flemish level from 2016 – can be a lever to bridge existing differences. The new Arts Decree, indeed, focuses on the functions (such as creation, production, presentation, participation/education and reflection) that cultural institutions perform to qualify for funding. In its new policy plan (2017–21), which must be submitted by October 2015 to the Flemish government, deSingel could indicate that, in addition to presentation and production, it also wants to focus on participation and education. That way, it could integrate the various functions of the arts campus in the new policy plan.

At the start of this article, we mentioned the importance of cross-sectoral cooperation for innovation. In the case of the deSingel Arts Campus, the potential for innovation is certainly present. In particular, the opportunity to allow renowned artists to work together with young talent from the Conservatory can be a powerful strategy to further the development of the disciplines (and their interconnections) both at the level of training as well as within the professional scene. In the artistic field as well, crossovers are increasingly seen in practice and are a source of innovation. In the field of artistic research, many opportunities are still present. The Arts Campus indeed is a unique place to be a catalyst between art, education and research, as well as breaking down barriers and making new connections. This could be the realisation of the respondents' own indication of what an 'Arts Campus' could be, specifically 'a place where the best conditions are created for transmission between the arts, education and research; a catalyst for interaction between students, professionals and the public; a place where synergies can be achieved between the different arts disciplines; a place where learning, making and presenting are one' (staff members, Conservatory and deSingel).

Note

1. This chapter is mainly based on research that was executed by Nicole Fux, an MA in Cultural Management student at the University of Antwerp whom was supervised by Bruno Verbergt.

References

Aigner, G. (2011) *Leadership Beyond Good Intentions: What It Takes to Really Make a Difference*. Sidney: Allen & Unwin.

Ansoff, H. I. (1965) *Corporate Strategy*. New York: McGraw-Hill.

Barett, F., Fry, R. and Wittockx, H. (2011) *Appreciative Inquiry*. Tielt: Lannoocampus.

Barney, J. B. and Hesterly, W. S. (2010) *Strategic Management and Competitive Advantage: Concepts and Cases*, 3rd edn. Upper Saddle River, NJ: Pearson Education.

Bell, J., Van den Ouden, B. and Ziggers, G. W. (2006) 'Dynamics of cooperation: at the brink of irrelevance', *Journal of Management Studies*, 43 (7): 1607–19.

Bell, J., Kaats, E. and Opheij, W. (2013) 'Bridging disciplines in alliances and networks: in search for solutions for the managerial relevance gap', *International Journal of Strategic Business Alliances (IJSBA)*, 3 (1): 50–68.

Bogan, E. C. and English, M. J. (1994) *Benchmarking for Best Practices: Winning Through Innovative Adaptation*. New York: McGraw-Hill.

Bremekamp, R., Kaats, E. and Opheij, W. (2009) 'Een nieuw kijkglas voor een heldere blik op samenwerken', *Holland Management Review*, 127: 2–9.

Bremekamp, R., Kaats, E., Opheij, W. and Vermeulen, I. (2009) 'Succesvol samenwerken, een kompas en aanbevelingen voor betekenisvolle interactie', *Holland Management Review*, 130: 8–15.

Bryson, J. M., Crosby, B. C. and Stone, M. M. (2006) 'The design and implementation of cross-sector collaborations: propositions from the literature', *Public Administration Review*, 66: 44–55.

Burt, R. S. (2005) *Brokerage and Closure: An Introduction to Social Capital*. New York: Oxford University Press.

Camp, R. (1989) *Benchmarking: The Search for Industry Best Practices That Lead to Superior Performance*. Milwaukee, WI: Quality Press.

Campbell, A. and Goold, M. (1998) *Why Links Between Business Units Often Fall and How to Make Them Work*. London: Capstone.

Campbell, A. and Luchs, K. (1998) *Strategic Synergy*. London: International Business Press.

Chesbrough, H. (2003) *Open Innovation: The New Imperative for Creating and Profiting from Technology*. Boston: Harvard Business School Press.

Child, J. and Faulkner, D. (1998) *Strategies for Cooperation. Managing Alliances, Networks and Joint Ventures*. New York: Oxford University Press.

Collinson, D. L. (2003) 'Identities and insecurities: selves at work', *Organisation*, 10 (3): 527–47.

Comunian, R. and Gilmore, A. (2014) 'From knowledge sharing to co-creation: paths and spaces for engagement between higher education and the creative and cultural industries', in A. Schramme, R. Kooyman and G. Hagoort (eds), *Beyond Frames: Dynamics Between the Creative Industries, Knowledge Institutions and the Urban Context*. Delft: Eburon Academic, pp. 216–27.

Comunian, R., Faggian A. and Jewell, S. (2014) 'Exploring music careers: music graduates and early career trajectories in the UK', in N. Crossley, S. McAndrew and P. Widdop (eds), *Social Networks and Music Worlds*. Abingdon: Routledge Advances in Sociology, pp. 165–88.

DeSingel (2006–10) *Policy Plan*. Antwerp. Available at: http://www.desingel.bc.

Dowit, H. and Voets, K. (2008) 'The international Art Campus. Close encounters of the Third Kind?', *Forum: Journal of the Royal Conservatory Artesis University College*, No. 3.

Doz, I. M. and Hamel, G. (1998) *Alliances Advantage*. Boston: Harvard Business School Press.

Fux, N. (2013) *Koers zetten naar een duurzame samenwerking op de Kunstcampus deSingel. Een exploratief onderzoek naar de meerwaarde van een structurele samenwerking tussen de Internationale Kunstcampus deSingel en het Koninklijk Conservatorium Antwerpen.* Dissertation, MA in Cultural Management (2012–13), University of Antwerp.

Gilpin, D. R. and Miller, N. K. (2013) 'Identity brokerage and nonprofit community building', *Journal of Nonprofit and Public Sector Marketing*, 25: 354–73.

Hernes, T. (2004) 'Studying composite boundaries. A framework of analysis', *Human Relations*, 67 (1): 9–29.

Hudson, B., Hardy, B., Henwood, M. and Wistow, G. (1999) 'In pursuit of inter-agency collaboration in the public sector: what is the contribution of theory and research?', *Public Management*, 1 (2): 235–60.

Huizingh, E. (2011) *Innovatiemanagement*. Amsterdam: Pearson Education Benelux.

Huxham, C. and Vangen, S. (2013) *Managing to Collaborate: The Theory and Practice of Collaborative Advantage*. New York and London: Routledge.

Johansson, T. and Jyrämä, A. (2015) *Towards a Community Identity: Negotiating the Boundaries of Collaboration in the Helsinki Music Centre*. Paper presented at the AIMAC Conference 2015, Aix-en-Provence.

Kaats, E. and Opheij, W. (2008) *Bestuurders zijn van betekenis. Allianties en netwerken vanuit bestuurlijk perspectief*. Maarssen: Reed Business.

Kaats, E. and Opheij, W. (2012) *Leren samenwerken tussen organisaties. Allianties, netwerken, ketens, partnerships*. Deventer: Kluwer.

Kanter, R. M. (1997) *On the Frontiers of Management*. Boston: Harvard Business School Press.

Kanter, R. M. (2009) 'How to strike effective alliances and partnerships', *Harvard Business Review*, 13 April. Available at: https://hbr.org/2009/04/how-to-strike-effective-allian.html# (last accessed 7 December 2015).

Mortelmans, D. (2007) *Kwalitatieve onderzoeksmethoden*. Leuven: Acco.

Nooteboom, B. (1999) *Interfirm Alliances: International Analysis and Design*. London and New York: Routledge.

Ostrower, F. (2005) 'The reality underneath the buzz of partnerships', *Stanford Social Innovation Review*, Spring, pp. 34–41.

Porter, M. (1987) 'From competitive advantage to corporate strategy', *Harvard Business Review*, 65: 43–59.

Prahalad, C. K. and Doz, Y. L. (1992) 'Evaluating interdependencies across businesses', in A. Campbell and K. S. Luchs (eds), *Strategic Synergy*. Oxford: Butterworth-Heinemann, pp. 95–110.

Provan, K. G. and Kenis, P. N. (2008) 'Modes of network governance: structure, management, and effectiveness', *Journal of Public Administration Research and Theory*, 18: 229–52.

Raab, J., and Kenis, P. (2009) 'Heading toward a society of networks: empirical developments and theoretical challenges', *Journal of Management Inquiry*, 18 (3): 198–210.

Renshaw, P. (2011) *Working Together. An Inquiry into Creative Collaborative Learning Across the Barbican Campus*. London: Guildhall School Publications.

Sarasvathy, S. D. (2001) 'Causation and effectuation: toward a theoretical shift from economic inevitability to entrepreneurial contingency', *Academy of Management Review*, 26 (2): 243–63.

Schramme, A. (ed.) (2009) '1 + 1 = 3', *Over samenwerkingsverbanden in de culturele sector*. Louvain: Lannoocampus.

Schramme, A. (2011) *Cultural Management. The Rules of the Arts*. Louvain: Lannoocampus.

Schramme, A., Kooyman, R. and Haghoort, G. (2014) *Beyond Frames: Dynamics Between the Creative Industries, Knowledge Institutions and the Urban Context*. Delft: Eburon.

Senge, P. (2010) *The Necessary Revolution. How Individuals and Organizations Are Working Together to Create a Sustainable World*. London and Boston: Nicholas Brealey.

Thornton, P. H. and Ocasio, W. (1999) 'Institutional logics and the historical contingency of power in organizations: executive succession in the higher education publishing industry, 1958–1990', *American Journal of Sociology*, 105 (3): 801–43.

Van Andel, W., Schramme, A., Schrauwen, J. and Demol, M. (2014) *Evaluatie van het CICI programma. Evaluatie van het gehele traject en de procesbegeleiding*. Antwerp and Louvain: Antwerp Management School/Flanders District of Creativity.

Yin, R. K. (2013) *Case Study Research: Design and Methods*. London: Sage.

Part II

Higher education and creative human capital

5 What difference does it make? Assessing the effects of arts-based training on career pathways

Alexandre Frenette and Steven J. Tepper

Introduction

Richard Florida's (2002a) best-selling book, *The Rise of the Creative Class*, has perhaps served as a catalyst for policy-makers, researchers, and business leaders to debate how creativity serves as a critical resource to our economy and society. Florida (2002b) argues that the key to economic growth for cities lies not just in attracting creative people to the workforce, but more importantly in nurturing and connecting these individuals to maximize the chances for robust 'creative economic outcomes.'

Of course the exact drivers of creativity in cities are highly debatable – with critics of Richard Florida arguing that traditional human capital theories explain economic growth better than Florida's emphasis on more intangible aspects like tolerance, cultural amenities, and innovative organizational cultures (Glaeser 2005). Still others point out that Florida and the creative class advocates ignore rising issues of inequality (Donegan and Lowe 2008), the parallel growth of low-wage service jobs, urban gentrification, and the way in which corporate America has co-opted creativity romanticizing routine white-collar jobs and justifying endless consumerism (Frank 1997; Crawford 2009). Moreover, many of these creative jobs have shifted risk in the new economy from capital to workers, as workers must navigate contingent employment and precarious livelihoods (Ross 2010); meanwhile the romanticism of 'living like an artist' actually creates the conditions for artists to witness their own exploitation while providing the engine of the new post-industrial economy (Lloyd 2010).

While the exact drivers of a city's creative economy are still unknown, there is increasing acceptance that artists are part of the equation and are critical for 'creative place making' (Markusen and Gadwa 2010), community development (Markusen 2006; Ocejo 2014), tourism (Wynn 2011), and business incubation (Phillips 2004). And while artists do not have a monopoly on creativity, they bring a set of core creative competencies – risk-taking, dealing with ambiguity, idea generation, collaboration, pattern recognition, improvisation, inductive reasoning, and radical revision – to the work they do, both as artists and when applying their creative skills outside of the arts (Hearn *et al.* 2014; Tepper and Kuh 2011). As Jamie Bennett, executive director of ArtPlace – a US-based consortium of funders supporting artists and community development – remarked, 'There continues to be a growing understanding in this country that artists are the one asset that exists in every community and that artists have a unique value to add when they work alongside other citizens in shaping the futures of their communities' (Monroe 2015).

So, artists can be considered important components of a city's creative capital – the collection of knowledge, practices, and human ingenuity that drive innovation, solve problems, spur enterprise, and create the cultural environment that activates public life (Zukin 1995), create vibrant scenes (Lloyd and Clark 2001), and build community (Stern and Seifert 2010). The chapters by Jacobi and Gilmore in this book, using Manchester (UK) and Leipzig (Germany) as case studies, highlight the importance of place attachment and connections between arts graduates and localities. Universities and colleges are potentially important producers of a city's creative human capital – with US institutions graduating close to 130,000 visual and performing artists a year. This talent base, in principle, should be a furnace fuelling the creative economy.

However, some research and popular conceptions of artists call into question the value of an arts degree. These include notions of the self-taught artistic genius, stereotypes about the arts-educated barista, and a recent report (BFAMFAPhD 2014) claiming most professional artists in the United States do not attend art school. Yet what is the value of higher education for workers in creative fields? Do arts graduates contribute to the creative capital of cities and economies? A growing body of literature seeks to address these questions, notably by researchers in the UK and Australia (Ball *et al.* 2010; Bennett 2007; Brook 2013; Cunningham and Bridgstock 2012; Morgan and Ren 2012; Oakley *et al.* 2008). Building on these efforts, this chapter draws on data from the Strategic National Arts Alumni Project (SNAAP), a survey of more than 92,000 arts alumni from over 140 institutions across North America, in order to assess the effects of arts-based training on career pathways. While the data does not allow us to measure the impact of artists on local creative economies, we can extrapolate to draw informed hunches about how arts graduates contribute more broadly to creative economies and communities.

SNAAP is a comprehensive survey administered online to the arts[1] alumni of participating institutions. In 2011, 2012, and 2013, 92,113 arts alumni participated in the SNAAP survey from 153 institutions – 140 post-secondary institutions and 13 arts high schools. The average institutional response rate for 2011, 2012, and 2013 combined is 18 percent.[2] Table 5.1 provides selected respondent characteristics for those alumni who participated.

Among the participating educational institutions, 57 percent are public and 43 percent are in the private non-profit sector. The SNAAP sample represents a range of regions across the United States – the participating institutions are spread almost evenly across the country's four main regions: Northeast (22 percent), South (27 percent), Midwest (29 percent), and West (21 percent).

Below we present findings on how arts graduates assess the benefits of their education, how they deploy creative skills in various areas of life, and an analysis

Table 5.1 SNAAP 2011, 2012, and 2013 selected respondent characteristics

Characteristics	Percentage of respondents
Gender	
Male	39.8%
Female	60.1%
Transgender	0.2%
Cohort	
1983 and before	25.6%
1984–1993	17.4%
1994–1998	10.2%
1999–2003	12.6%
2004–2008	17.5%
2009–2013	16.6%
First-generation student	
Yes	34.8%
No	65.2%
Majors	
Architecture	6.6%
Art History	3.4%
Arts Administration	0.9%
Arts Education (Art, Music, Dance, Drama)	8.0%
Creative and Other Writing	1.9%
Dance	2.3%
Design	12.1%
Fine and Studio Arts (including Photography)	28.5%
Media Arts	10.5%
Music History, Composition, and Theory	1.7%
Music Performance	13.2%
Theater	9.3%
Other Arts	1.5%

of challenges for higher education institutions and graduates (inequality, debt, and skill gaps). The chapter concludes by expanding current definitions of creative human capital to incorporate how competencies developed during arts education are deployed in various sectors.

How arts graduates assess their education and current employment

Existing data on career outcomes for arts alumni provide two seemingly opposing views: on the one hand, arts graduates appear to fare very poorly on the job market (BFAMFAPhD 2014; Carnevale *et al.* 2011; Comunian *et al.* 2011), yet other data suggest such graduates are among the happiest professionals within the United States workforce (Bille *et al.* 2013; Ivey and Kingsbury 2008; Lindemann and Tepper 2014; Steiner and Schneider 2013; Tepper *et al.* 2014). In this section we address this contradiction by analysing how arts graduates assess their education and current employment. Below, we provide SNAAP data on arts alumni self-assessments along three measures: satisfaction with their education, skill development during school, and current job satisfaction.

Satisfaction with education

To a surprising extent, alumni reported being overwhelmingly satisfied with their arts education. When asked to assess their experience while at their institution, the vast majority (91.6 percent) of graduates rated their overall educational experience as 'good' or 'excellent' and, if they needed to start over, most (76.1 percent) indicated they would definitely or probably attend the same institution again.[3] When asked if they would recommend their school to another, similar student ('like you') nearly nine out of ten (87.8 percent) answered positively.

Perhaps what is most striking about these results is their relative consistency across graduates' income level and employment status. Alumni who earn more annual income tend to rate their overall educational experience more positively than lower earners, but the difference is minimal: over 93 percent of graduates earning more than $40,000 per year (individual income) rated their experience positively, compared to 88.6 percent for alumni who reported earning $20,000 or less per year. These answers were consistently positive (over 90 percent) no matter what percentage of the graduates' income was earned from working as an artist – therefore graduates working as artists and non-artists are similarly positive in their assessments of their schooling. Moreover, as Table 5.2 shows, even the majority of unemployed graduates answered the above questions positively, albeit to a lesser extent.

Overall, these findings confirm previous arts alumni data, which suggest that such graduates do not assess the value of their education solely based on their current economic situation[4] (Lindemann *et al.* 2012). Although the above

Table 5.2 Measures of alumni assessing their educational experience, by current employment status

Current employment status	Percentage rating their overall educational experience 'good' or 'excellent'	Percentage indicating they 'definitely' or 'probably' would attend same institution again if they had to start over	Percentage who would recommend institution to a student like them
Full-time	92.4%	77.6%	88.8%
Part-time	90.9%	73.4%	86.0%
Unemployed	83.9%	63.7%	76.6%
In school	90.8%	80.9%	88.2%
Caring for family	92.3%	74.2%	87.3%
Retired	95.6%	82.8%	92.4%

confirms that arts graduates do not employ a predominantly economic lens for such assessments, the less positive answers by unemployed graduates suggest there are limits to such an outlook. Similarly, alumni who indicated that debt incurred from attending art school had a 'major impact' on their career or educational decisions were less likely (65.6 percent) to indicate they would attend the same institution again were they to start over, compared to those for whom debt had only 'some' (77 percent) or 'no' (79.5 percent) impact. Nonetheless, as a whole these results suggest arts graduates are generally very satisfied with their education, and these assessments appear to be only slightly informed by their current economic standing. There is some evidence from previous research that educational satisfaction is correlated with a perception that one's schooling is strongly related to work. We present evidence below that confirms that satisfaction is linked to perceived relevance of one's education. And, importantly, as we show below, one critical source of satisfaction and relevance is the extent to which graduates feel that training helped them develop creative skills – from creative thinking to collaboration, revision, and artistic technique.

Assessing skills

SNAAP asked graduates to what extent their institution helped them acquire or develop a series of skills, including artistic technique, project management, and communication skills (persuasive speaking and clear writing). Alumni indicated whether they felt their institution helped them acquire or develop these skills or abilities 'not at all,' 'very little,' 'some,' or 'very much.' The results across all cohorts (i.e. historical averages) in Table 5.3 suggest that arts schools are particularly effective places to acquire or develop the following skills: creative thinking and problem-solving, how to improve work based on feedback from others, artistic technique, broad knowledge, and critical thinking and analysis of arguments and information.

Most arts alumni also reported acquiring or developing a variety of other transferrable skills, including how to work collaboratively, research skills, and clear writing. Notably, when comparing recent graduates (alumni who last attended their institution sometime between 2009 and 2013) to historical averages, it appears as though the perceived quality of training has improved for a variety of skills, such as project management skills (+10.6 percent), networking and relationship building (+10.3 percent), and leadership skills (+8 percent).

Lastly, despite some apparent improvements among recent alumni, graduates were considerably more likely to indicate that their institution helped them acquire certain skills 'very little' or 'none at all': teaching skills, entrepreneurial skills, as well as financial and business management skills. It is unclear whether these skills, particularly financial and business skills, are not taught because they are assumed to be acquired on the job, or whether they are seen as inconsistent with the focus on non-monetary rewards within arts training institutions (Oakley 2009). We will revisit these cases later in the chapter, but, despite these exceptions,

Table 5.3 How much (by percentage) alumni indicate that institutions have helped them acquire identified skills ('some' or 'very much'), comparing historical average (all cohorts) to recent graduates (graduated from institution between 2009 and 2013)

Skill/ability that institution helped alumni acquire	All cohorts	Recent graduates only (2009–13)	Percent difference
Creative thinking and problem-solving	92.9%	93.9%	1.0%
Improved work based on feedback from others	92.1%	92.8%	0.8%
Artistic technique	90.7%	88.5%	–2.2%
Broad knowledge and education	90.0%	90.0%	0.0%
Critical thinking and analysis of arguments and information	89.3%	91.7%	2.4%
Interpersonal relations and work collaboratively	78.7%	81.7%	3.0%
Research skills	74.9%	79.3%	4.4%
Clear writing	71.5%	76.1%	4.6%
Project management skills	68.0%	78.6%	10.6%
Technological skills	67.6%	73.1%	5.5%
Leadership skills	67.4%	75.4%	8.0%
Persuasive speaking	64.1%	70.8%	6.7%
Networking and relationship building	61.6%	71.9%	10.3%
Teaching skills	58.4%	60.9%	2.5%
Entrepreneurial skills	26.1%	32.5%	6.4%
Financial and business management skills	22.5%	27.7%	5.2%

SNAAP data show that most arts graduates are equipped with a broad range of skills, many directly related to core creative competencies.

Job satisfaction

In addition to being satisfied with their educational institution and reporting positively about their skill development, arts alumni are mostly very pleased with their current job. SNAAP asked alumni to indicate whether they were 'very dissatisfied,' 'somewhat dissatisfied,' 'somewhat satisfied,' or 'very satisfied' with their current work on a variety of measures including opportunity to be creative, income, and job security.[5] As Table 5.4 shows, arts graduates are generally satisfied with their work.

At least four out of five respondents indicated that: they were satisfied with their job overall (87.3 percent); their work reflects their personality, interests, and values (84.2 percent); their job affords them the opportunity to be creative (83.1 percent); and they are satisfied with their opportunity to contribute to the greater good (81.7 percent). While only 65.8 percent of respondents report being satisfied with their income, only one in eight (12.5 percent) said they were 'very dissatisfied' on that measure.

Table 5.4 Percentage of currently employed alumni who indicated they are 'somewhat' or 'very' satisfied with identified aspects of their current work.

Aspects of job satisfaction for arts alumni	Percentage who indicated being 'somewhat' or 'very' satisfied
Overall job satisfaction	87.3%
Work that reflects my personality, interests, and values	84.2%
Opportunity to be creative	83.1%
Opportunity to contribute to greater good	81.7%
Job security	79.5%
Balance between work and non-work life	76.1%
Opportunity for career advancement	70.4%
Income	65.8%

Taken together, arts alumni self-assessments regarding satisfaction with their education, skill development during school, and current job satisfaction all support the view that arts graduates are extremely happy with their training and work.[6] Importantly, graduates are finding work that allows them to be creative and for which they are personally motivated (i.e. reflects their interests and personality). This explains the high satisfaction rates overall, as researchers have found that when people are creative in their work and self-motivated, they are happier (Amabile 1996). If arts graduates were largely unemployed, unhappy, and disconnected from creative work, we might expect them to have a negligible impact on the overall creative human capital of a city. But, they are positive about their education and work, mostly employed (see below), and, according to the above statistics, in jobs where they are satisfied with their ability to be creative. While this does not empirically confirm the size or impact of their contribution to a creative economy and milieu, it does suggest that they are probable suspects in stimulating, supporting, and contributing to the creative human capital of a place. Below we look more closely at exactly what their careers look like, how arts graduates fare on the job market, and what proportion find work in artistic fields.

Deploying creative skills in various areas of life

Below we consider the array of ways arts alumni deploy their creative skills after graduation and answer a series of questions:

- What proportion of arts graduates found work in a closely related field?
- How relevant do alumni consider their education for their current position?
- How else, apart from paid employment, do arts graduates deploy their creative skills and participate in the arts?

Overall, the evidence below supports expanding current definitions of creative human capital – and strengthening conversations about what it means to be an artist – to incorporate how competencies developed during arts education are deployed in various sectors.

Careers of arts graduates

Despite the myth of the 'starving artist' and concerns for the art graduate's supposedly limited career opportunities, SNAAP data indicate that the majority of arts alumni deploy their creative skills in the arts or a related sector. Most respondents reported that they are currently or used to be professional artists (74.5 percent).[7] However, not all graduates indicated that they began their studies with the intention of working as an artist. The majority (84.3 percent) of arts graduates report that they intended to work as artists after graduation, but this varies across majors: alumni in most arts majors are very likely to intend on becoming artists, such as design (91.8 percent), fine and studio arts (88.9 percent), dance (88.4 percent), architecture (87.9 percent), theatre (87 percent), and music performance (86.4 percent), whereas only a minority of arts administration (45.1 percent) and art history (37.1 percent) graduates report having such intentions. Among those graduates who indicated that they intended to become an artist, 80.8 percent are currently or have ever worked in an occupation as an artist. Even among those alumni who did not intend on becoming an artist, more than four in ten (43.8 percent) report having worked as an artist. Therefore, these data support the view that most arts graduates find work consistent with their training, although, as we discuss below, not necessarily under standard employment arrangements.

Consistent with other research, SNAAP data show that the careers of arts graduates are typically 'boundaryless' and extend beyond the context of one employer (Arthur and Rousseau 2001; Lindemann *et al.* 2012; Throsby and Hollister 2003; Throsby and Zednik 2011). Rather, when surveyed, 39.4 percent of employed arts graduates were currently working more than one job; three-quarters (75.1 percent) of arts alumni had at some point in their careers either been self-employed, an independent contractor, or a freelancer; and 16.1 percent of SNAAP respondents had founded a non- or for-profit enterprise at some point in their lives. These data suggest that arts graduates must be extremely entrepreneurial and nimble to build and sustain careers. To the extent that creative economies are increasingly 'gig' economies, arts graduates are well versed in holding multiple jobs, working as independent contractors, working across sectors and ultimately doing whatever it takes – despite potential costs in well-being and heightened precariousness – to flexibly deploy their talents to create and seize opportunities to make a living, make art, and make careers.

Table 5.5 shows the current jobs in which employed arts alumni spend the majority of their work time; most employed respondents (61.8 percent) spend the majority of their work time in an arts-related occupation.

Notwithstanding the durable stereotype of artists working at restaurants and cafes, only 1 percent of arts graduates indicated that they currently spend the

Table 5.5 Current jobs in which employed arts alumni spend the majority of their work time

Jobs associated with the arts	Percentage of respondents	Jobs outside of the arts	Percentage of respondents
Graphic designer, illustrator, or art director	7.9%	Education, training, and library	5.1%
Higher education arts educator	7.2%	Other occupations outside of the arts	4.2%
K-12 arts educator	7.0%	Communications	3.2%
Fine artist	4.8%	Management	2.9%
Other arts occupation	4.5%	Office and administrative support	2.7%
Musician	4.1%	Sales	2.4%
Architect	3.8%	Computer and mathematics	1.8%
Other designer	3.4%	Healthcare	1.6%
Arts administrator or manager	3.0%	Financial and other business services	1.3%
Film, TV, video artist	2.4%	Legal	1.1%
Private teacher of the arts	2.1%	Food preparation related	1.0%
Writer, author, editor	1.8%	Social services	1.0%
Photographer	1.4%	Services and personal care	0.6%
Museum or gallery worker	1.4%	Engineering and science	0.6%
Web designer	1.2%	Construction	0.5%
Interior designer	1.2%	Building, maintenance, installation, and repair	0.4%
Other arts educator	1.2%	Human resources	0.4%
Craft artist	1.1%	Manufacturing	0.3%
Actor	0.8%	Military and protective services	0.3%
Multimedia artist or animator	0.5%	Transportation and material moving	0.2%
Theater and stage director or producer	0.4%	Farming, fishing, and forestry	0.1%
Engineer or technician	0.3%	Other	6.7%
Dancer or choreographer	0.3%	**Total**	**38.2%**
Total	**61.8%**		

majority of their time working in a food-related job. Moreover, although a bit less than one in six (16.3 percent) respondents spend the majority of their work time as a teacher of the arts (classroom setting or private lessons), 56.8 percent of arts alumni indicated that they had worked in such a position (either full- or part-time) at some point in their career; thus, arts teaching is considered by many as part of a portfolio career in the arts (Huddy and Stevens 2011).[8] Similarly, another notable type of work among arts alumni not captured by a 'current job' snapshot is employment managing or administering in the arts: a high percentage of graduates (37.8 percent) indicated that they have worked, either full- or part-time, managing or administering programmes or people for an arts or arts-related entity at some point in their career. These results suggest the importance of capturing artistic workers' employment by pairing questions about current employment (akin to the US Census) with data on their job patterns over time. When we look over time, the pattern that emerges shows arts graduates to be working across the interstices of the creative economy – teaching and developing creative skills in others, working as artists, and, importantly as we discuss below, deploying their creativity even in non-arts jobs (Higgs *et al.* 2008).

Perceived relevance of training

While most arts graduates find work that appears to be in some way related to their education, do arts alumni perceive their first job experience as related to their education? Do they perceive their arts training as relevant for their current job?

According to a survey conducted by CareerBuilder (2013) of 2,134 US workers who graduated from college, almost half (47 percent) of these workers claim their first job after college was unrelated to their field of study. Conversely, 59.3 percent of SNAAP graduates say their first job or work experience was closely related to their training; more broadly, only 18.8 percent of respondents said their first job or work experience was not related to their training. However, as Table 5.6 illustrates, there is some variation by major. Graduates from majors

Table 5.6 How related was your first job/work experience to your training, by major

Major	Closely related	Somewhat related	Not related
Architecture	74.2%	19.8%	5.9%
Arts education (art, music, dance, drama)	83.6%	9.1%	7.3%
Design	73.1%	19.4%	7.5%
Media arts	58.2%	26.3%	15.6%
Arts administration	59.8%	22.1%	18.0%
Other arts	57.8%	23.1%	19.1%
Dance	65.1%	15.5%	19.4%
Music performance	64.7%	15.5%	19.8%
Music history, composition, and theory	54.1%	22.4%	23.5%
Theater	59.8%	16.5%	23.7%
Fine and studio arts (including photography)	44.0%	29.2%	26.8%
Creative and other writing	34.1%	32.7%	33.2%
Art history	39.0%	22.6%	38.4%
Total	**59.3%**	**21.9%**	**18.8%**

with more formalized paths to employment (such as architecture, arts education, and design) describe having a first job that is closely related to their training, whereas alumni from other majors (writing, fine and studio arts, etc.) may need to contend with less formal pathways to find career-oriented employment. These differences by major suggest the need for more research that considers differences among subgroups of arts graduates.

After their first job, arts graduates continue to see their education and main occupation as relatively well aligned. As a whole, 87.2 percent of SNAAP respondents described their arts training as somewhat to very relevant[9] to their current work. Perceived relevance of training varies slightly between graduates who report primarily working within versus outside of the arts. The vast majority (97.6 percent) of arts alumni who intended to become artists and report currently working in a job associated with the arts described their training as somewhat to very relevant. Although in lower numbers, most (70.1 percent) arts graduates who intended to become artists, but are currently primarily working outside of the arts, still find their training somewhat to very relevant to their occupation. Furthermore, as Bennett and Burnard highlight elsewhere in this volume, graduates need to engage with a broader range of 'professional capital creativities' as they enter a range of career options.

Other forms of artistic participation

In addition to deploying their creative skills through an array of occupations, arts alumni continue their artistic engagement after graduation in other ways. Notably, SNAAP data show that arts graduates generally remain active in the arts, at least avocationally, and are strong supporters of their artistic community.

Even though about six out of ten arts graduates work primarily in an arts-related occupation, about three-quarters (75.2 percent) of all respondents indicated that they make or perform art in their personal (not work-related) time. When asked how often they practice art in their personal time, 88.5 percent responded 'several times a month' or more often. The majority of arts graduates (70.1 percent) also indicated that they perform or exhibit their art in public, and slightly more than half (54.8 percent) of respondents do so at least once per year. The creative human capital of a city, arguably, is supported by thriving scenes (Lloyd and Clark 2001), street-level culture (Florida 2002a), and a healthy cultural ecology. Importantly, the 130,000 arts graduates every year in America are finding ways to contribute to strong arts ecologies – making and presenting art even when not being paid for this work. These quantitative findings seem to connect strongly with some of the qualitative research included in the book from case studies in Manchester (UK) and Leipzig (Germany).

Artists contribute to community development in a variety of ways (Markusen and Schrock 2008), not least by supporting its artistic vibrancy. According to a survey by the Independent Sector (2001), only 2 percent of Americans volunteer for an arts, cultural, or humanities organization; conversely, 27.2 percent of SNAAP respondents report volunteering at an arts organization in the past 12 months.

What is more, in the past 12 months, arts alumni indicated having done the following: 14.5 percent reported serving on the board of an arts organization; 19.6 percent volunteered to teach the arts; 43.6 percent donated money to an arts organization or artist; and 86.1 percent attended an arts event (including exhibits, concerts, and performances). As a whole, 90.8 percent of SNAAP respondents said they had supported the arts in some form in the 12 months before filling out the survey.

Therefore, arts graduates deploy their creative skills in a considerable range of artistic and non-artistic occupations, they perceive their arts training as relevant to these efforts, and also contribute to the wider community through many forms of artistic engagement. Also, as previously discussed, arts alumni assess their education very positively, report developing several crucial (and employable) skills, and are highly satisfied with their occupational standing. Taken together, the above paints a positive and promising picture of arts education in the US, particularly in its assessment of the effects of arts-based training on career pathways (from the perspective of the individual arts graduate, as well as the larger community). Nonetheless, a data-driven assessment of the value of arts education serves partly as an opportunity to more clearly elucidate the challenges faced by higher education and the creative economy. Below we build on the insights above to analyse two major challenges: the intertwined problems of debt and inequality, as well as 'skill gaps' between pedagogical outcomes and professional needs.

Challenges

While the evidence above contradicts the literature and common wisdom that says one should not pursue the arts because it is a hard (or nearly impossible) and unfulfilling path, institutions of higher education and arts graduates nonetheless face considerable challenges. The arts are not immune to the educational and professional inequities found in other sectors. There are concerns that the high cost of arts education limits access to this form of training and creates an uneven playing field (Oakley and Banks 2015). Moreover, data suggest that graduates lack certain forms of preparation to be even more nimble within the fast-changing creative economy.

Inequality and debt

Not all groups are equally likely to work as artists. Whites (74.9 percent) are more likely than Black (70.7 percent) and Hispanic/Latino (70.9 percent) arts alumni to report having ever worked as a professional artist; as expected from research on gender and creative labour (Conor *et al*. 2015) the discrepancy is even larger in terms of gender, with eight out of ten men (80.3 percent) saying they have ever worked as a professional artist compared to seven out of ten women (70.6 percent). Surprisingly, there are no differences between first-generation and non-first-generation college graduates in this regard.

Table 5.7 Reasons SNAAP respondents stopped working as artists or chose not to pursue work as artists, by racial/ethnic category

Racial/ethnic category	Barrier to artistic career			
	Higher pay/steadier income in other fields	Change in interests	Lack of access to important networks and people	Debt (including student loans)
White	57.3%	29.3%	21.8%	23.8%
Black	52.2%	22.6%	35.4%	33.9%
Hispanic	57.9%	24.4%	29.2%	37.9%
Asian	57.1%	31.7%	28.3%	19.9%

Differences in career outcomes are partly linked to gaps in early professional experiences. For example, SNAAP data show that women, Black, Hispanic/Latino, and first-generation college graduate arts alumni all appear to have held a disproportionate number of unpaid internships, which are tied to significantly weaker career payoffs than paid internships (Frenette 2013; Frenette *et al.* 2015).

Moreover, SNAAP respondents who had worked as professional artists in the past but not currently, or who had never worked as professional artists but intended to when they began at their institutions, were asked to identify reasons why they were not working in the arts. As summarized in Table 5.7, the results based on racial patterns were striking: in comparison to White arts alumni, Black and Hispanic/Latino respondents were much more likely to cite debt (including student loan debt) and lack of access to professional networks as barriers to artistic careers.

Despite inclinations towards non-monetary rewards (Menger 1999; Oakley 2009), economic matters nonetheless inform the careers of arts alumni; a high proportion of people say they have left the arts because of debt and/or in order to pursue higher paid employment. Also, the above results are important because, as we have known for some time, professional networks are exceedingly crucial in navigating the art world (Becker 1982). Moreover, there is evidence that the rising cost of higher education – not least arts education – and the related ascent in student loan debt have impacted career decisions of groups at a historical economical disadvantage, such as women, Blacks, and Hispanics/Latinos.

Overall, debt is increasingly challenging for arts graduates, and from our analysis we see that it has differential effects based on race/ethnicity. SNAAP asked arts alumni how much of an impact debt incurred from attending art school had on their career or educational decisions. Among graduates who have taken on debt, only 28.9 percent of Whites claimed the debt had a 'major impact' on their decisions, compared to 40.4 percent for Black and 43.6 percent for Hispanic/Latino arts alumni. Perhaps of considerable concern, arts graduates are increasingly taking on several tens of thousands of dollars in student loan debt

Table 5.8 Student loan debt, comparing recent (within five years) and non-recent graduates

Student loan debt	Recent graduates	Non-recent graduates
More than $60,000	14%	4%
$50,001 to $60,000	5%	2%
$40,001 to $50,000	6%	3%
$30,001 to $40,000	8%	5%
$20,001 to $30,000	13%	8%
$10,001 to $20,000	10%	12%
$10,000 or less	7%	15%
None	31%	46%
Not applicable	5%	5%

(see Table 5.8). About one quarter of recent graduates (graduated within five years of filling out the survey) had accumulated over $40,000 in student loan debt, compared to less than 10 percent for previous cohorts.

Therefore, to ensure equitable access to arts education and arts-related occupations, the years ahead will require close attention to be paid to ways to facilitate access and minimize the economic burden for all potential arts alumni. Importantly, scholars have found that diversity (intellectual, cultural, and demographic) is a critical ingredient that spurs innovation and creative human capital across time and place (Hall 2000; Simonton 2000). To the extent that inequalities persist in the ability of graduates from diverse backgrounds to successfully forge careers as creative workers and artists, then cities are not maximizing the diversity of their creative workforce and, ultimately, their stock of creative human capital.

Skills mismatch

While arts graduates develop many valuable skills during their studies, such as creative and critical thinking skills, answers by SNAAP respondents (see Table 5.9) suggest there are some gaps between what they are learning during school and what they need to navigate the creative economy after graduation.

As mentioned above, more than one in three (37.8 percent) graduates have worked, either full- or part-time, managing or administering programmes or people for an arts or arts-related entity at some point in their career: 16.1 percent of arts graduates have founded a non- or for-profit enterprise at some point in their lives; and more than half (56.8 percent) of arts alumni have been a teacher of the arts (classroom setting or private lessons). Yet there are considerable 'skills mismatches' regarding financial and business management skills (58.7 percent), entrepreneurial skills (45.1 percent), and teaching skills (18.6 percent). While we do not advocate attempting to 'vocationalize' higher education – or, put otherwise, matching skill development to current existing jobs – it would be a disservice to future graduates to ignore these gaps.

Table 5.9 Skills mismatch: how much (by percentage) alumni indicate that institutions have helped them acquire identified skills ('some' or 'very much'), compared to how much (by percentage) alumni indicate these identified skills are important to their professional or work life ('some' or 'very much')

Skill/ability that institution helped alumni acquire	Percent of alumni indicating institution helped 'some' or 'very much' to develop skill/ability	Percent of alumni indicating skill/ability is 'very' or 'somewhat' important to profession or work life	Skill gap
Financial and business management skills	22.5%	81.2%	58.7%
Entrepreneurial skills	26.1%	71.2%	45.1%
Networking and relationship building	61.6%	94.4%	32.8%
Persuasive speaking	64.1%	91.9%	27.8%
Project management skills	68.0%	94.7%	26.7%
Leadership skills	67.4%	93.4%	26.0%
Technological skills	67.6%	93.3%	25.7%
Clear writing	71.5%	90.8%	19.3%
Teaching skills	58.4%	77.0%	18.6%
Interpersonal relations and work collaboratively	78.7%	96.8%	18.1%
Research skills	74.9%	89.3%	14.4%
Critical thinking and analysis of arguments and information	89.3%	95.8%	6.5%
Broad knowledge and education	90.0%	96.4%	6.4%
Creative thinking and problem-solving	92.9%	98.5%	5.6%
Improved work based on feedback from others	92.1%	96.0%	3.9%
Artistic technique	90.7%	80.1%	−10.6%

Conclusion

This chapter summarizes findings from the Strategic National Arts Alumni Project survey of arts alumni ($N = 92,113$) to provide an assessment of the effects of arts-based training on career pathways. The results are mostly quite positive: arts alumni are extremely satisfied with their educational experience, regardless of their current income; most graduates say they are equipped with a range of valuable skills; arts graduates are extremely satisfied with their work; most alumni find work in the arts and find their training to be relevant to their current occupation; and arts graduates contribute to the arts ecology (within and beyond their paid employment) and thereby enhance the vitality of cities and communities. However, there are limits to the arts graduates' happiness with non-monetary rewards; unemployed graduates rate their educational experience less positively than their employed peers. The issues of debt, inequality, and some forms of skills mismatch form challenges for institutions of higher education and arts graduates.

The above results should inform our understandings of the ways arts graduates deploy creative human capital. About four out of five arts students who aim to become professional artists will succeed at doing so at least for some part of their careers, but they will also most likely deploy their creative thinking, critical thinking, and other skills in a variety of sectors. This expanded view of creative human capital goes hand in hand with conceptualizing or appreciating an expanded definition of 'success' for arts graduates – not everyone can become a professional musician or actor, but this does not preclude satisfaction in other occupations. Understanding the deployment of creative human capital also requires maintaining a long-term view; within the rapidly changing creative economy, arts graduates frequently do project-based work, work multiple jobs at once, shift in and out of sectors (including in and out of the arts), and start non- or for-profit entities. Further research should explore how art students utilize and might expand their occupational imagination while at school and after graduation.

Finally, SNAAP data show that more than one-third (36.9 percent) of all postsecondary arts graduates remain or return to the city where they went to school.[10] These graduates are potentially important sources of creative capital – ready to start companies, work on projects, teach, perform, and contribute to a place's general vitality, both economic and cultural. This also reflects some of the findings discussed in Chapter 6 of this book showing how UK students also develop an attachment and tendency towards being 'university stayers.' Unfortunately, many graduates report that their schools did not do enough to help them learn basic business skills, or how to manage projects, or, most importantly, help them network. Therefore, graduates are often flying blind in the early years after graduation, learning how to navigate the world of work through trial and error and without proper support, mentoring, and professional development. If urban leaders want to take advantage of the skills, energy, and creativity of the thousands of young creative graduates who stick around after graduation, they must understand better what these graduates need in order to get a foothold in the creative economy. City leaders might spend less time trying to attract young creative class workers and more time nurturing, connecting, and supporting the local creative graduates who are ready to contribute and are already invested in the community.

Notes

1. SNAAP defines 'the arts,' 'art,' and 'artist' to include a broad range of creative activity, such as performance, design, architecture, creative writing, music composition, choreography, film, illustration, and fine art.
2. According to analyses by Lambert and Miller (2014), the demographic characteristics of SNAAP respondents are similar to those of graduating seniors in the National Survey of Student Engagement (NSSE).
3. Other options for overall rating of experience while at an institution also included 'poor' and 'fair'; other options for the 'starting over' question also included 'definitely no,' 'probably no,' and 'uncertain.'

4. It is also possible that these findings are linked to lower expectations of arts graduates towards achieving higher salaries and economic rewards.
5. Although arts graduates often hold several jobs simultaneously, respondents were asked to indicate their satisfaction with aspects of the job in which they spend the majority of their work time.
6. Nonetheless, these data do not include comparisons to graduates from other fields.
7. Among the 74.5 percent of respondents who have ever been a professional artist (either part- or full-time), 53.6 percent are currently artists and 20.9 percent were artists in the past, but not currently.
8. If we exclude Arts Education majors from the equation, since they would obviously be more prone to teaching, the figure is high nonetheless: 53.5 percent of all other arts graduates report having worked as a teacher in the arts.
9. Employed arts graduates were asked to identify whether their training while at a SNAAP institution was 'not at all relevant,' 'somewhat relevant,' 'relevant,' or 'very relevant' to the occupation in which they currently spend the majority of their time.
10. Alumni were asked the following yes/no question: 'Within the first five years after leaving [INSTITUTION], did you take up residency in the town/city where [INSTITUTION] is located to pursue your career?'

References

Amabile, T. M. (1996) *The Motivation for Creativity in Organizations*. Boston: Harvard Business School.

Arthur, M. B. and Rousseau, D. M. (2001) *The Boundaryless Career: A New Employment Principle for a New Organizational Era*. New York: Oxford University Press.

Ball, L., Pollard, E., and Stanley, N. (2010) *Creative Graduates, Creative Futures*. London: Creative Graduates Creative Futures Higher Education Partnership and the Institute for Employment Studies.

Becker, H. S. (1982) *Art Worlds*. Berkeley and Los Angeles, CA: University of California Press.

Bennett, D. (2007) 'Utopia for music performance graduates. Is it achievable, and how should it be defined?' *British Journal of Music Education*, 24 (2): 179–89.

BFAMFAPhD (2014) *Artists Report Back: A National Study on the Lives of Arts Graduates and Working Artists*. Retrieved from http://bfamfaphd.com/#artists-report-back.

Bille, T., Fjællegaard, C. B., Frey, B. S., and Steiner, L. (2013) 'Happiness in the arts – international evidence on artists' job satisfaction,' *Economics Letters*, 121 (1): 15–18.

Brook, S. (2013) 'Social inertia and the field of creative labour,' *Journal of Sociology*, 49: 309–24.

CareerBuilder (2013) *One-third of College-educated Workers Do Not Work in Occupations Related to Their College Major: Thirty-six Percent Wish They Majored in Something Different*. Retrieved from http://www.careerbuilder.com/share/aboutus/pressreleasesdetail. aspx?sd=11%2F14%2F2013andid=pr790anded=12%2F31%2F2013.

Carnevale, A. P., Cheah, B., and Strohl, J. (2011) *Hard Times: Not All College Degrees Are Created Equal*. Washington, DC: Georgetown Center on Education and the Workforce.

Comunian, R., Faggian, A., and Jewell, S. (2011) 'Winning and losing in the creative industries: an analysis of creative graduates' career opportunities across creative disciplines,' *Cultural Trends*, 20: 291–308.

Conor, B., Gill, R., and Taylor, S. (2015) Gender and creative labour,' *Sociological Review*, 63 (S1): 1–22.

Crawford, M. (2009) *Shop Class as Soulcraft: An Inquiry into the Value of Work*. New York: Penguin Press.

Cunningham, S. D. and Bridgstock, R. S. (2012) 'Say goodbye to the fries: graduate careers in media, cultural and communication studies,' *Media International Australia Incorporating Culture and Policy*, 145: 6–17.

Donegan, M. and Lowe, N. (2008) 'Inequality in the creative city: is there still a place for "old-fashioned" institutions?' *Economic Development Quarterly*, 22 (1): 46–62.

Florida, R. (2002a) *The Rise of the Creative Class*. New York: Basic Books.

Florida, R. (2002b) 'The rise of the creative class,' *Washington Monthly* [online]. Retrieved from http://www.washingtonmonthly.com/features/2001/0205.florida.html.

Frank, T. (1997) *Conquest of Cool: Business Culture, Counterculture, and the Rise of Hip Consumerism*. Chicago: University of Chicago Press.

Frenette, A. (2013) Making the intern economy: Role and career challenges of the music industry intern. *Work and Occupations*, 40(4), 364–397.

Frenette, A., Dumford, A. D., Miller, A. L., and Tepper, S. J. (2015) *The Internship Divide: The Promise and Challenges of Internships in the Arts*. Bloomington, IN: Indiana University and Arizona State University, Strategic National Arts Alumni Project.

Glaeser, E. L. (2005) 'Review of Richard Florida's *The Rise of The Creative Class*,' *Regional Science and Urban Economics*, 35 (5): 593–6.

Hall, P. (2000) 'Creative cities and economic development,' *Urban Studies*, 37 (4): 639–49.

Hearn, G., Bridgstock, R., Goldsmith, B., and Rodgers, J. (eds) (2014) *Creative Work Beyond the Creative Industries: Innovation, Employment and Education*. Northampton, MA: Edward Elgar.

Higgs, P. L., Cunningham, S. D., and Bakhshi, H. (2008) *Beyond the Creative Industries: Mapping the Creative Economy in the United Kingdom*. London: Nesta.

Huddy, A. and Stevens, K. (2011) 'The teaching artist: a model for university dance teacher training,' *Research in Dance Education*, 12 (2): 157–71.

Independent Sector (2001) *Giving and Volunteering in the United States: Findings from a National Survey*. Washington, DC: Author.

Ivey, B. and Kingsbury, P. (2008) *The Pocantico Gathering: Happiness and a High Quality of Life: The Role of Art and Art Making*. Nashville, TN: Curb Center for Art, Enterprise, and Public Policy at Vanderbilt University.

Lambert, A. D. and Miller, A. L. (2014) 'Lower response rates on alumni surveys might not mean lower response representativeness,' *Educational Research Quarterly*, 37 (3): 38–51.

Lindeman, D. J. and Tepper, S. J. (2014) 'Perspectives: For the money? For the Love? Reconsidering the "worth" of a college major,' *Change: The Magazine of Higher Learning*, 46 (2): 20–3.

Lindemann, D. J., Tepper, S. J., Gaskill, S., Jones, S. J., Kuh, G. D., Lambert, A. D., and Vanderwerp, L. (2012) *Painting with Broader Strokes: Reassessing the Value of an Arts Education*, SNAAP Special Report No. 1. Bloomington, IN: Indiana University and Vanderbilt University, Strategic National Arts Alumni Project.

Lloyd, R. (2010) *Neo-Bohemia: Art and Commerce in the Postindustrial City*. New York: Routledge.

Lloyd, R. and Clark, T. N. (2001) 'The city as an entertainment machine,' *Critical Perspectives on Urban Redevelopment*, 6 (3): 357–78.

Markusen, A. (2006) 'Urban development and the politics of a creative class: evidence from a study of artists,' *Environment and Planning A*, 38 (10): 1921–40.

Markusen, A. and Gadwa, A. (2010) *Creative Placemaking*. Washington, DC: National Endowment for the Arts.

Markusen, A. and Schrock, G. (2008) *Creative Communities: Artist Data User Guide. Leveraging Investments in Creativity (LINC)*. Retrieved from http://www.hhh.umn.edu/projects/prie/pdf/419LINCArtistDataUserGuide2008.pdf.

Menger, P. M. (1999) 'Artistic labor markets and careers,' *Annual Review of Sociology*, 25: 541–74.

Monroe, K. (2015) 'The complex funder pushing creative placemaking with millions in new grants,' *Inside Philanthropy*. Retrieved from http://www.insidephilanthropy.com/arts-education/2015/7/13/the-complex-funder-pushing-creative-placemaking-with-million.html.

Morgan, G. and Ren, X. (2012) 'The creative underclass: culture, subculture, and urban renewal,' *Journal of Urban Affairs*, 34 (2): 127–30.

Oakley, K. (2009) 'From Bohemian to Britart – art students over 50 years,' *Cultural Trends*, 18: 281–94.

Oakley, K. and Banks, M. (2015) 'The dance goes on forever? Art schools, class and UK higher education,' *International Journal of Cultural Policy* (in press.)

Oakley, K., Sperry, B., Pratt, A., and Bakhshi, H. (2008) *The Art of Innovation: How Fine Arts Graduates Contribute to Innovation*. London: National Endowment for Science, Technology and the Arts.

Ocejo, R. E. (2014) *Upscaling Downtown: From Bowery Saloons to Cocktail Bars in New York City*. Princeton, NJ: Princeton University Press.

Phillips, R. (2004) 'Artful business: using the arts for community economic development,' *Community Development Journal*, 39 (2): 112–22.

Ross, A. (2010) *Nice Work If You Can Get It: Life and Labor in Precarious Times*. New York: New York University Press.

Simonton, D. K. (2000) 'Creativity: cognitive, personal, developmental, and social aspects,' *American Psychologist*, 55 (1): 151–8.

Steiner, L., and Schneider, L. (2013) The happy artist: An empirical application of the work-preference model. *Journal of Cultural Economics*, 37 (2): 225–246.

Stern, M. J. and Seifert, S. C. (2010) 'Cultural clusters: the implications of cultural assets agglomeration for neighborhood revitalization,' *Journal of Planning Education and Research*, 29 (3): 262–79.

Tepper, S. J. and Kuh, G. D. (2011) 'Let's get serious about cultivating creativity,' *Chronicle of Higher Education*. Retrieved from http://chronicle.com/article/Lets-Get-Serious-About/128843/#disqus_thread.

Tepper, S. J., Sisk, B., Johnson, R., Vanderwerp, L., Gale, G., and Gao, M. (2014) *Artful Living: Examining the Relationship Between Artistic Practice and Subjective Wellbeing Across Three National Surveys*. Nashville, TN: Curb Center for Art, Enterprise, and Public Policy at Vanderbilt University. Retrieved from http://arts.gov/sites/default/files/Research-Art-Works-Vanderbilt.pdf.

Throsby, D. and Hollister, H. (2003) *Don't Give Up Your Day Job: An Economic Study of Professional Artists in Australia*. Sydney: Australia Council.

Throsby, D. and Zednik, A. (2011) 'Multiple job-holding and artistic careers: some empirical evidence,' *Cultural Trends*, 20: 9–24.

Wynn, J. R. (2011) *The Tour Guide: Walking and Talking New York*. Chicago: University of Chicago Press.

Zukin, S. (1995) *The Cultures of Cities*. Malden, MA: Blackwell.

6 Talent on the move

Creative human capital migration patterns in the UK

*Roberta Comunian, Alessandra Faggian
and Sarah Jewell*

Introduction

The last decade has seen an increasing number of contributions, from both academics and policy-makers, focusing on the role of higher education in developing human capital (Charles 2003; Cramphorn and Woodlhouse 1999; Preston and Hammond 2006) and hence contributing to local and regional growth (Faggian and McCann 2006; Mathur 1999; Moretti 2004). Within this broader literature, the role played by more 'scientific' types of human capital, such as STEM (science, technology, engineering and mathematics) graduates and science parks (Bozeman, Dietz, and Gaughan 2001; Linderlöf and Löfsten 2004; Löfsten and Lindelöf 2005), has also been explored. Little attention has been paid so far to the role played by more 'creative' types[1] of human capital. This chapter aims at filling this gap, in light of the central role that the term 'creative' took in policy and academic discourses in the UK (Comunian and Faggian 2011; Comunian and Gilmore 2015; DCMS 2006; Powell 2007; Universities UK 2010). From a policy perspective, the focus on creative human capital has been the result of the legacy of policy interventions and promotional discourses surrounding the creative industries (DCMS 2001, 2006), and a general emphasis on creative careers as being a new area of growth in the post-industrial economy (DCMS and BERR 2008). From an academic perspective, research has highlighted the struggles and unstable career patterns of creative human capital (Blair 2003; Comunian, Faggian *et al*. 2010; Towse 2006), but also their value within local systems of production and the creative city literature (Comunian and Faggian 2011).

Nonetheless, every year higher education institutions (HEIs) in the UK train an increasing number of graduates across a range of creative disciplines. Data from the Higher Education Statistical Agency (HESA) show that after a slight decrease in enrolment in 'Creative Arts and Design' disciplines between 2012 and 2013 (probably related to the introduction of full fees), enrolment is up again (with an overall growth of 5 per cent in the last seven years).[2]

The literature on human capital and regional economic development has become increasingly interested in the role of the 'creative occupations' in economic growth (Comunian *et al*. 2015; Lee and Drever 2013). Attracting quality human capital and cultivating creative industries have been given an unprecedented level of significance in regional policies. As a result of this, understanding the factors determining the migration behaviour of graduates – and especially graduates in creative disciplines – has become more crucial for policy-makers. In addressing these issues and advancing our understanding of the relationship between creativity and mobility of human capital, this study provides the first empirical analysis of the role played by creative graduates' subject background in influencing their migration choices in the UK.

However, we know that the geography of where students train is very different from the geography of opportunities for creative work and a creative career (Comunian and Faggian 2011; Faggian *et al*. 2012). The chapter takes a closer look at the migration patterns and movements of recent creative graduates in the UK and considers the pattern of interregional migration and geographical strategies to either enter a creative career or seek support towards establishing one. Using micro-data from the HESA, graduates are classified into five migration categories (going from the most migratory group, i.e. repeat migrants, to the least migratory, i.e. non-migrants) based on their migration choices from domicile to university and then on to workplace. Using the data, we explore the distribution of graduate jobs, creative jobs and salary levels in relation to the creative graduates' migration. It is found that different subdisciplines in the creative field have different migration patterns and these also relate to their ability to obtain better-paid creative jobs.

The chapter is articulated in four parts. Firstly, we explore the existing literature on human capital and migration and the more focused research on creative work, talent and mobility. We then explain the methodology and definitions adopted for the data analysis, followed by our results. Finally, conclusions are drawn about the impact of our results for higher education policy and local development.

Human capital, mobility and economic development

The role of human capital and mobility (Faggian and McCann 2009) in the development of regions and knowledge economies has been the subject of increasing research. What the broader literature does not differentiate on is the 'type' of human capital required for local development. Graduates are considered equally important for economic development, irrespective of the subject they studied. More recently, some questions arose about this point. Does *creative human capital*, i.e. the human capital specifically developed via education and advanced training in creative and artistic subjects (Comunian and Faggian 2014), play the same role as, say, more scientific-oriented human capital in fostering local development?

The importance of human capital and specialised knowledge for local and regional economic growth has long been acknowledged in the literature. The link between human capital and growth was formalised by Lucas in 1988, but most theoretical models overlooked the role played by the migration and mobility of highly skilled individuals. There is an increased recognition that international and internal migration impact regions in fundamental ways (Beine *et al.* 2008; DaVanzo 1976; DaVanzo and Morrison 1981; Sjaastad 1962) because of the very nature of regions which are open systems that continuously exchange material goods, ideas and individuals. The success of a region is highly dependent on the balance of the trade of these goods and individuals. Therefore, in this literature it is argued that a better understanding of the factors determining the migration behaviours of people, especially those highly skilled or educated, is vital.

Studying the migration behaviour of highly skilled individuals is not an easy task. Until recently, sophisticated micro-data on highly skilled and educated individuals were not available. Nevertheless, thanks to the availability of detailed micro-individual data for certain countries, recent works have appeared on graduate mobility (Faggian and McCann 2006 and 2009 for Great Britain; Venhorst *et al.* 2010 and 2011 for the Netherlands; Bjerke 2012 for Sweden; and Corcoran *et al.* 2010 for Australia). Faggian (2005) shows that the most mobile group of graduates, i.e. repeat migrants, have an average salary advantage of about 4.5 per cent when entering the labour market, but no university subject/major breakdown is reported. She also shows that graduates from the Arts and Humanities faculty are more likely to migrate back home after graduation (i.e. being 'return migrants' à la DaVanzo 1976), rather than move on towards a different job location (confirmed also by Faggian *et al.* 2014). It is unclear, though, whether return migration represents a 'corrective' movement or a rational behaviour, which allows these graduates to maximise their salaries and find a better job.

Jewell and Faggian (2014) also compared the migration behaviour of creative graduates to STEM graduates and found that creative graduates were more likely to enter the labour market either in the location where they studied and graduated (i.e. being what we call 'university stayers') or back home (i.e. being 'return migrants') than STEM graduates. Creative graduates had, on average, a lower 'migration premium' than STEM graduates and were therefore less likely to engage in repeat migration.

The focus on the mobility and attraction of human capital has received even more attention among academics and policy-makers following the popularity of the 'creative class' concept (Florida 2002). While Florida saw the 'creative class' as an alternative – and better – way of defining the skills and talents of workers than the outdated 'human capital' measured by education, some researchers saw little or no value in this new concept. Economists such as Glaeser (2005) prefer the traditional 'human capital' concept over the new notion of the creative class and point out that regional growth is the outcome of a very highly educated workforce rather than a 'creative' one in the Floridian sense. Many others acknowledged that the term 'creative class' does not correspond to either cultural or creative workers (Markusen 2006). However, the work of Comunian, Faggian *et al.* (2010) in trying to clarify the relationship between human capital and the creative class helps us define a more coherent subgroup of human capital, i.e. the 'creative human capital', which connects the human capital literature (because of the higher level of education) and the creative economy (UNESCO 2013) and creative industries (DCMS 2015) literature (because of the subject studied). Furthermore, the acknowledgement of policy and research that workers in the creative industries in the UK are a 'highly educated' sector (NESTA 2003)[3] proves a strong overlap between (high) human capital and creative occupations within the broader literature on creative industries and creative work (Banks and Hesmondhalgh 2009) which is the focus of our next section.

Creative talent, mobility and work

After discussing the general role played by human capital and mobility, we now focus on the (limited) literature available on the relationship between mobility and creative human capital. While the literature on the mobility of artists and creative workers is relatively developed, only a few contributions are specifically focused on the mobility of core creative workers à la Florida.

Recent work on the nature and practice of artists and creative workers has often highlighted the instability and mobility of their careers. There is general recognition that 'artists, musicians and writers have always been great travellers' (Addison 2008: 1). Historical research shows the tendency of visual artists and composers to cluster (O'Hagan and Hellmanzik 2008; O'Hagan and Borowiecki 2010), so that migration patterns of creative workers are not only determined by amenities but also by certain locations (mainly cities) being known worldwide as creative milieus (Hall 1998). Acheson and Maule (1994), analysing the development of cultural industries, consider the important role played by international trade and investment, as well as the transfer of key workers and technical staff. Furthermore, with the development of the creative and cultural industries as a globally recognised economic sector (UNESCO 2013), there has been increased emphasis on the international market for creative work and talent (Solimano 2006). Following the uneven distribution of creative industries and their tendency to cluster (Comunian, Chapain *et al.* 2010), it is become clear that mobility within countries and across borders plays an important role interlinking new global hubs with disperse satellite sites (Vang and Chaminade 2007). Addison (2008) highlights how this might have effects on the uneven distribution of talent to the disadvantage 'of poorer countries, which can lose talent to the richer world'.

In relation to Florida's work (2002) and its policy emphasis on the retention and attraction of creative individuals (specifically artists, also referred to in his theory as 'Bohemians'), there seems to be an assumption that creative people are highly mobile and that locations with certain characteristics can attract them. However, while most of the contributions focus on the debate of whether labour market characteristics or amenities are more important in attracting them (e.g. Scott 2010), only a handful of contributions question the fundamental assumption that creative people are in fact highly mobile. Hansen and Niedomysl (2009), studying the case of Sweden, find that highly educated people are as mobile as the rest of the population. Martin-Brelot *et al.* (2010) question the mobility of the 'creative class' in the European context as they argue that soft location factors, such as amenities, the open-minded and tolerant character of the city and the diversity of its atmosphere, play only a marginal role in attracting the creative class to a city, although they are more important in retaining them after they settle there. Lawton *et al.* (2013) highlight how too much emphasis has been placed on the importance of soft factors to attract the creative class to specific cities while often key classic location factors, such as housing cost and travel-time to place of employment, are underestimated.

Similarly, Borén and Young (2013: 207), studying specifically the case of artists in Sweden, question the assumption of the high mobility of creative workers. They point out that networks are vital for artists and that once artists are 'embedded in their networks … it [is] more difficult for them to migrate'. They also caution about reducing the migration histories of artists to a 'simplistic set of assumptions' (ibid.), as the migration dynamics of creative occupations are very heterogeneous. Bennett (2010), also studying the migration of artists for the case of Western Australia, finds that employment opportunities do play a role in attracting them (in accordance with the findings of Hansen and Niedomysl 2009 for Sweden). However, she also finds that the move is 'rarely the result of securing a position' (ibid.: 125), making migration very risky financially. Comunian and Faggian (2011) show the importance of location for creative graduates and the importance that locating in a 'creative city' might have in providing opportunities to enter creative occupations. However, as with Borén and Young (2013), they caution against a one-size-fits-all approach when studying artists' migration, showing that in some cases artists can be attracted to more rural locations, such as her case study, Launceston in Tasmania, where the 'small scale is perceived as a safe haven to escape the rat race of the city' (ibid.: 139).

Recent research (Comunian, Faggian *et al.* 2010; Markusen *et al.* 2008) has proved the need to consider that the subsectors of the 'creative class' – such as the 'Bohemian' subgroup – might have very different jobs, migration behaviour and geographical patterns. Lawton *et al.* (2013) stress the importance of considering the evolving life cycle of cultural workers. Although there is a tendency to identify creative workers with young and highly mobile individuals, some of them are older and have family commitments whose influence might offset their professional reasons for moving. While there is a tendency for younger creative workers to prefer city-centre locations, older workers prefer to live in suburban areas (Lawton *et al.* 2013).

While most of the studies cited focus on creative workers, not enough attention has been given to the earlier stage of creative careers. As highlighted also by Frenette and Tepper's chapter in this book, we still have limited knowledge about the transition of arts graduates from academia into work. In this essay, we use the term 'creative human capital' to capture the development of research within this field. We specifically focus on 'creative graduates', a subgroup of the highly educated individuals who are specialised in artistic, creative and cultural disciplines, and who are most likely to enter creative occupations both within and beyond the creative industries (Comunian, Chapain *et al.* 2010; Comunian *et al.* 2011; Faggian *et al.* 2012).

Methodology and data

The chapter builds on an extensive number of papers that have recently explored the career patterns of creative graduates in the UK (Comunian and Faggian 2014;

Comunian, Faggian and Jewell 2011; Comunian, Faggian and Jewell 2014a, 2014b; Faggian *et al.* 2013; Faggian *et al.* 2014). It adopts a methodology and research framework consistent with previous contributions, but expands on them by looking more specifically at the migration behaviour of subgroups of creative graduates never explored before.

Our main sources of data are the 'Students in Higher Education' and the 'Destinations of Leavers from Higher Education' (DLHE) surveys, both collected by the UK Higher Education Statistical Agency (HESA). The former contains data on all students enrolled in UK HEIs, while the latter, generally targeted at British-domiciled students, is a survey undertaken every year by each institution on behalf of HESA to collect information about graduates' employment activities six months after graduation. Since we are interested in migration, we focus on British-domiciled students (both part-time and full-time) for which we have full location information (postcode information for pre-university, university and job location). In particular, we focus on the cohort of students who graduated in 2005 (with a DLHE return referring to their employment situation in January 2006). Second, in line with the literature on the topic (Abreu *et al.* 2012) and due to the lower response rate of postgraduates (who we also do not know if they migrated for their first degree) and other undergraduates (those below first-degree level) to the DLHE survey, we focus on first-degree undergraduates[4] who represent 61 per cent of the full 'Students in Higher Education' sample. As we are interested in employment patterns, these two years are particularly good as they refer to the pre-recession period. The recession which took place following the 2007 credit crunch in the UK had a negative effect on graduate employment in general (Shattock 2010), but it might have impacted graduates from different disciplines differently hence biasing our results.

The 'Students in Higher Education' data contain individual student record data with information on a series of variables including: personal characteristics (such as gender, age and ethnicity), subject of study (at the four-digit Joint Academic Coding System (JACS[5]) code), mode (full-time vs. part-time), degree results and institution attended. The DLHE survey, which is matched to the student record data, includes information on the graduate's employment, in particular: salary level, employer sector code (four-digit SIC code), job occupational code (four-digit SOC code), and location of employment (postcode). For the 2005 cohort of graduates, the student dataset includes 268,143 records of British-domiciled finalists (who are all eligible for a DLHE return) from 164 HEIs. The DLHE data has information on 202,947 British-domiciled graduates, which equates to an overall 75.7 per cent response rate. Once restricted to those employed and with full location information (original domicile, institution and job location), our sample reduces to 137,256 valid observations. Seventy-three per cent of the respondents to the DLHE survey were in employment at six months with 14 per cent in further study only, 6 per cent unemployed and 6 per cent doing something else. Of our employed valid cases, 81 per cent are in full-time paid employment, 14 per cent are part-time employed, 3 per cent are self-employed (or working freelance) and 1 per cent are employed in voluntary work or other unpaid work.

Our definition of 'creative human capital' comes from Comunian, Faggian *et al.* (2010). 'Bohemian' (or creative) graduates include students in creative arts and design subjects (all JACS codes starting with W), creative media graduates (all JACS codes starting with P) and other creative graduates: subjects mainly linked to technology-based creative subjects and architecture (for the list of JACS codes used in the category of 'Bohemian' graduates, refer to Comunian *et al.* 2011). This categorisation is helpful to first compare creative graduates in general to all the graduates in other disciplines (see also Comunian, Faggian *et al.* 2010). However, as already explained, it is also crucial to understand the different trends and patterns between the different subgroups within the creative graduates group.

We are interested not only in comparing the general human capital (graduates from non-creative disciplines who make up 85 per cent of our valid sample) with creative graduates (15 per cent of our valid sample), but also different subgroups of creative graduates. To that effect, we divide creative graduates into eight subgroups in line with Comunian *et al.* (2011) (we combined crafts with design, due to the small cell size and advertising with writing and publishing) namely: Architecture, Design and Craft, Film and Television, Fine Art, Music, Performing Arts, Technology, and Advertising, Writing and Publishing. As Table 6.1 shows 21,074 (15.35 per cent) of our sample are graduates from creative disciplines. The larger subdisciplinary groups are in the fields of Design and Crafts (4.6 per cent of our sample), Film and Television (2.9 per cent), Performing Arts (1.84 per cent) and Fine Art (1.62). Advertising, Writing and Publishing, Music, and Technology students represented each just over 1 per cent of our sample, while students in Architecture represented just below 1 per cent of our sample. This first glance at our sample highlights already the difficulties in defining 'creative human capital' as it is a very heterogeneous group with some disciplines being more prominent and some representing just a smaller niche.

Using a creative job definition à la Cunningham *et al.* (2004), we consider both creative careers within the creative industries but also creative occupations in other

Table 6.1 The sample of HESA data used in the analysis

	Freq.	*%*
All other graduates	116,182	84.65
Creative graduates	21,074	15.35
Architecture	1,178	0.86
Design & Crafts	6,310	4.60
Film & TV	3,979	2.90
Fine Art	2,219	1.62
Music	1,507	1.10
Performing Arts	2,531	1.84
Technology	1,532	1.12
Advertising, Writing & Publishing	1,818	1.32
Total	137,256	100

non-creative industries. Our definition of a creative job is based on the initial DCMS definition based on four-digit SIC codes. However, we supplement this definition with the inclusion of other creative workers (based on occupations using four-digit SOC codes that are defined as creative) based in industries outside the creative industries as identified by DCMS (2010b) (see also Comunian *et al.* 2010b for detailed SOC and SIC codes). This chapter also builds on the work of Faggian *et al.* (2014), which highlights the different patterns of migration of 'Bohemian' graduates in the UK compared with non-'Bohemian' graduates. The findings from Faggian *et al.* (2014) show that graduates from disciplines such as business/management and more importantly engineering/technology are more migratory, more likely to be repeat migrants and land higher paid jobs than graduates from the creative arts, education or law. This chapter expands on this last finding, looking at the sequential migration behaviour of graduates in creative subdisciplines. In the three-year period from entering university to graduation (and subsequently entering the labour market), students are faced with two distinct migration decisions. The first is whether to study locally or migrate to study in a different area. The second is whether to work locally (i.e. in the university's immediate region) or make another move to enter the labour market in a different location. By combining these two choices, it is possible to identify five different migration paths (Figure 6.1): repeat migrants, return migrants, university stayers, late migrants and non-migrants. The first three migration categories include students who all migrated to study, but they differ in regard to the second migration (following graduation). Repeat migrants are those who move to work in an area different from both their original pre-university domicile and the university region. Return migrants also move out of their university region to work, but only to go back to their original domicile. When analysing migration to study and migration to work separately, these two categories are undistinguishable, as both repeat and return migrants are in fact migrating twice. Nevertheless, differentiating between repeat and return migrants is vital because the two groups have different characteristics (DaVanzo and Morrison 1981; Newbold 1997). Repeat migrants are generally individuals who, encouraged by a successful first migration, venture upon a new migration, while return migrants are likely to be people who found the first migration to be a failure (DaVanzo 1976; Faggian 2005) and return home to a familiar surrounding where the network of acquaintances can help them enter the labour market. The third category, university stayers, includes all students who migrate to study, but then find a job near their university. The last two categories, late migrants and non-migrants, include graduates with the lowest migration propensity. Late migrants study near home and only migrate once they graduate. Non-migrants, as the name suggests, are those who study and then work in the same area as their original domicile. Figure 6.1 illustrates the five categories.

Starting from this broad sample of creative graduates and their migration patterns, in this essay we explore three key aspects:

1. Creative graduates' location choices, both in reference to location to study and location where they find, or migrate to, for employment.

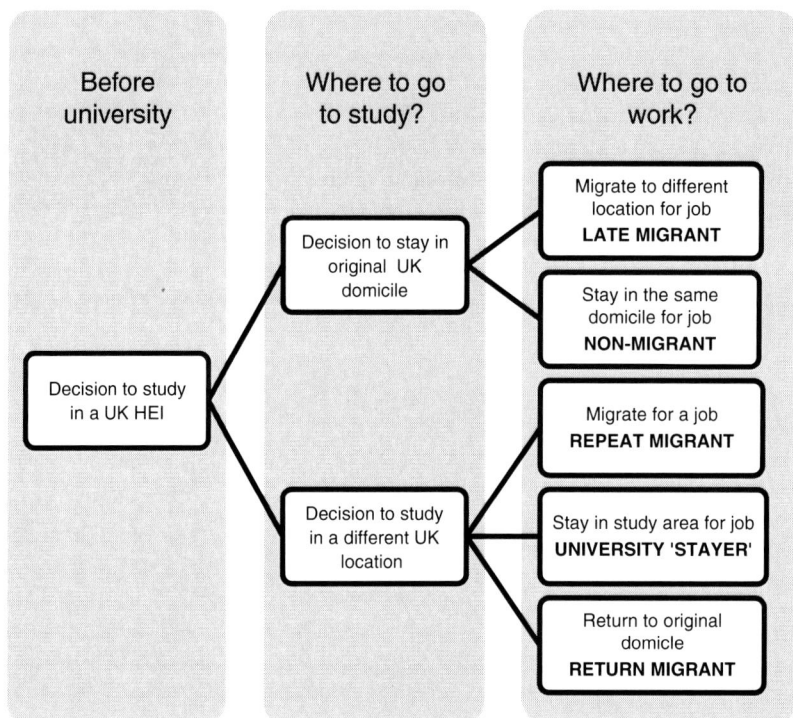

Figure 6.1 Graduate migration categories (as defined by Faggian 2005)

2. Creative graduates and the different migration behaviours they follow across the subdisciplinary groups identified.
3. The relationship between the migration patterns and the impact on creative career outcomes, such as the ability to secure a graduate-level job, a creative job and a higher salary level. This question is particularly important in the light of what others (including various contributions in this book) have found in terms of job insecurity among creative graduates.

Creative graduates' location: study and employment

The initial descriptive statistics of study location by UK countries shows that 86.16 per cent of the creative graduates in our sample have studied in England, which is more as a percentage than the overall graduate population (Table 6.2). England also has the highest retention rate of creative graduates (97.86 per cent), followed by Northern Ireland and Scotland, while Wales only retains 53.18 per cent of creative graduates (and a slightly higher percentage of non-creative).

Table 6.2 Creative and non-creative (in brackets) graduates' location choices: country to study and work

Country of study	Country of employment (%)				Country of study (%) (total)
	England	Scotland	Wales	N. Ireland	
England	97.86 (97.41)	0.73 (0.8)	1.21 (1.46)	0.2 (0.34)	86.16 (80.69)
Scotland	11.2 (12.32)	87.11 (85.9)	0.24 (0.22)	1.45 (1.56)	5.89 (10.56)
Wales	46.01 (37.9)	0.52 (0.43)	53.18 (61.5)	0.3 (0.18)	6.42 (5.8)
Northern Ireland	2.16 (2.45)	0.87 (0.62)	0.09 (0)	96.59 (97.22)	1.54 (2.95)
Country of employment (Total)	87.96 (82.17)	5.8 (9.76)	4.47 (4.77)	1.77 (3.3)	100 (100)

Table 6.3 highlights the regional dimension of these migration patterns. The regions in England that are able to retain more students are London (74.01 per cent) and the North West (65.83 per cent). The role of London as place to study and work is acknowledged in the literature (Lee and Drever 2013). Similarly, we can see the strength of the North West, which, despite losing many creative graduates, is in second place for retention. This supports some of the concerns and dynamics explored via qualitative interviews with artists in Manchester in the Gilmore *et al.* chapter in this book. Although just after the graduation of our cohort of analysis, the North West has also benefitted from increased investment and attention towards the creative economy, with Liverpool winning the role of European Capital of Culture in 2008 but also with the move of the BBC to Salford (near Manchester) in 2009–10. The regions with the lowest retention rate of creative graduates are the East Midlands, Yorkshire and the Humber, and the South East. Yorkshire and the Humber see 12.67 per cent of graduates moving to the North West, a relative short-distance migration, and 12.29 per cent moving to London. The 'London effect' is also clear for the East Midlands, the East of England and the South East with 15.6 per cent, 30.75 per cent and 28.63 per cent of their creative graduates migrating to London to work.

Creative graduates and different migration behaviours across disciplines

Sequential migration patterns (as defined in Figure 6.1) differ quite substantially by creative subdisciplines, as shown in Table 6.4. Architecture graduates are the most mobile, with 38.37 per cent of them falling in the 'repeat migrants' category. 'Design and Craft' graduates are equally split into repeat and return migrants (30.63 per cent and 30.78 per cent respectively). If we think of return migration

Table 6.3 Creative graduates' location choices: region to study and work (percentage)

Region of study (%)	Region of employment (%)												
	NE	NW	YOR	EM	WM	EE	LON	SE	SW	WAL	Scot	NI	All
North East	**58.08**	6.04	9.62	2.71	1.85	2.71	9.12	3.21	1.48	0.25	4.44	0.49	3.85
North West	1.55	**65.83**	6.12	2.89	4.52	2.71	7.54	3.45	1.64	1.77	1.59	0.39	11.01
Yorkshire & Humber	2.81	<u>12.67</u>	**48.79**	7.38	4.05	4.57	<u>12.29</u>	4.19	1.95	0.52	0.48	0.29	9.96
East Midlands	1.17	5	10.3	**34.78**	9.26	10.59	<u>15.6</u>	9.09	2.59	0.83	0.54	0.25	11.39
West Midlands	0.31	5.18	3.01	5.87	**62.6**	3.79	8.66	5.26	3.32	1.39	0.46	0.15	6.14
East of England	0.3	1.79	1.64	2.69	1.94	**50.3**	30.75	8.06	1.49	0.75	0	0.3	3.18
London	0.32	1.11	0.77	1.37	1.51	5.28	**74.01**	12.02	2.69	0.66	0.18	0.08	17.97
South East	0.32	0.93	0.57	1.98	2.19	6.86	<u>28.63</u>	**49.21**	7.79	1.19	0.29	0.04	13.21
South West	0.2	1.81	1.1	1.6	4.81	3.06	16.25	13.94	**53.06**	3.26	0.75	0.15	9.46
Wales	0.3	4.81	0.74	2.07	7.1	2.74	7.25	7.91	13.09	**53.18**	0.52	0.3	6.42
Scotland	0.73	1.13	0.97	0.56	0.73	0.56	4.83	0.81	0.89	0.24	**87.11**	1.45	5.89
Northern Ireland	0	0.31	0	0	0	0.31	1.23	0	0.31	0	0.62	**97.22**	1.54
Total	**3.03**	**10.56**	**7.73**	**6.39**	**7.45**	**6.25**	**25.07**	**13.07**	**8.41**	**4.47**	**5.8**	**1.77**	**100**

Table 6.4 Migration type by subject studied (percentage)

	Non-migrant	Late migrant	University stayer	Return migrant	Repeat migrant
All other graduates	18.09	5.73	17.01	29.44	29.72
Creative graduates	15.63	4.47	20.25	30.85	28.80
Architecture	13.92	5.43	20.46	21.82	**38.37**
Design & Crafts	16.04	5.25	17.31	**30.63**	30.78
Film & TV	15.61	3.82	20.18	**33.83**	26.56
Fine Art	19.06	3.11	25.60	**31.37**	20.87
Music	11.88	3.19	**29.13**	28.33	27.47
Performing Arts	12.21	3.75	21.81	**33.07**	29.16
Technology	21.41	7.90	16.32	**26.37**	28.00
Advertising, Writing & Publishing	14.19	3.36	17.71	**33.11**	**31.63**
Total	17.84	5.58	17.72	29.31	29.55

as a possible corrective move, this finding might highlight the difficulties encountered by some who decide to revert to their area of origin to build up a portfolio with the support of family and/or their original network. The percentage of 'return migrants' is even higher for Film and TV graduates, Performing Arts graduates, Fine Art graduates and Advertising, Writing and Publishing graduates (33.83 per cent, 31.37 per cent, 33.07 per cent and 33.11 per cent respectively). Overall, this is consistent with Comunian, Faggian *et al.* (2010) highlighting the more difficult and undefined career patterns of creative disciplines where non-graduate, temporary and multiple jobs are not uncommon, as well as the findings of Frenette and Tepper's chapter in relation to arts graduates in the USA. Return migration is often associated with a higher reliance on family and friends and is therefore a coping mechanism to deal with job insecurity while building a portfolio and establishing a career.

Finally, it is worth noticing the large number of 'university stayers' among music graduates – possibly linked to the role of networks and local connections (to work and perform) established for music graduates in the place of study (see also Comunian *et al.* 2014b). This is also true – although less so – for Fine Art, Performing Arts, and Film and TV graduates.

Technology graduates are an interesting case, as an almost equal percentage of them are return migrants (a prospect with potential low rewards) and repeat migrants (on the contrary, a pattern usually associated with high levels of economic rewards). This seems to support the findings of Comunian *et al.* (2015) that show some contradictions emerging in their job market, as digital technology graduates enjoy both higher economic rewards in the labour markets (compared to creative arts and design graduates) but also higher level of initial unemployment (9.26 per cent versus 8.36 of creative arts and design graduates).

'Late migrants' are also fewer in creative disciplines than 'other subjects' (with the exception of Technology graduates). This seems to confirm the attachment of creative workers to specific locations where they have developed networks. It also confirms what Chapain and Comunian (2010) found interviewing creative workers in Birmingham and Newcastle-Gateshead, i.e. that creative workers have a strong sense of pride and belonging stemming from being 'born and bred' in a specific context.

While it is interesting to look at migration patterns per se, the ultimate goal of migration for many of these creative graduates is to improve upon their future career. In this light, the next section explores more closely the impact of migration on future career opportunities.

Migration patterns and impact on career outcomes

Confirming the findings of Comunian *et al.* (2011), Table 6.5 shows creative graduates are more likely than non-creative graduates to find jobs that are classified as 'non-graduate' (in other words, for which a degree is not deemed necessary). Interestingly, return migration and non-migration are universally linked to higher levels of non-graduate jobs (Faggian *et al.* 2014). However, the difference between creative and non-creative graduates is that the former also settle for non-graduate jobs if they stay in the university area after graduation (i.e. they are classified as 'university stayer'). This could be a short-term effect, as creative graduates might not feel ready straight away to leave the 'university life' (including friends and established networks). What is fascinating is that, as Faggian *et al.* (2014) point out, migration after graduation (either in the form of late migration or repeat migration)

Table 6.5 Percentage of graduates in *non-graduate jobs* by migration type and degree subject

	Non-migrant	Late migrant	University stayer	Return migrant	Repeat migrant	Total
All other graduates	**39.5**	24.6	37.0	**44.6**	24.1	35.1
Creative graduates	**47.9**	35.3	**47.6**	**55.9**	35.3	46.1
Architecture	**14.6**	9.4	7.5	**19.1**	6.2	10.6
Design & Crafts	46.9	33.9	**48.8**	**53.1**	31.3	43.6
Film & TV	**59.4**	48.7	52.4	**63.0**	44.4	54.8
Fine Art	46.3	46.4	**56.2**	**58.5**	51.6	53.8
Music	41.3	29.2	**48.1**	**50.5**	38.4	44.7
Performing Arts	49.8	40.0	**50.7**	**65.2**	46.1	53.6
Technology	45.0	27.3	41.4	**49.1**	25.2	38.5
Advertising, Writing & Publishing	**53.5**	37.7	45.7	**56.8**	33.6	46.4
Total	40.6	25.9	38.9	**46.4**	25.8	36.8

plays a key role in securing a graduate-level position, and this applies equally to both creative and non-creative graduates.

Notwithstanding this general finding, some differences do emerge across subdisciplines. For Design and Craft, Fine Art, Music and Performing Arts graduates, staying in the area of study (university stayers) puts them in a worse position (high level of non-graduate jobs) than non-migration. Again, this seems to suggest that while universities might be a great place to build networks for further employment, this might not provide enough negotiation power or motivation to find permanent and high-quality jobs after graduation. Some graduates might get 'trapped' in a non-graduate job found before graduation and prefer the security of a low salary while looking for new opportunities and building their portfolio rather than tempt fate with a migration movement (speculative migration).

Aside from the 'level' of employment (graduate vs. non-graduate job), we are also interested in the chances of creative graduates to get into a creative occupation (i.e. 'field' matching). Table 6.6 shows the relationship between migration trajectory and the ability of graduates to secure a creative job.

Overall, Table 6.6 confirms that migrating after graduation (late or repeat migration) facilitates the matching between creative skills and job requirements (creative occupation). This holds for most of the subdisciplines, but there are some exceptions worth noting. Architecture graduates have the highest chances of entering a creative job (89.21 per cent) if they stay around the university area after graduation. Maybe surprisingly – as it contradicts the general trend – 'non-migration' gives Fine Art graduates the best chances of entering the creative sector (34.28 per cent). While networks are important for both groups, architects rely more on formal career pathways (such as internships) that might be provided

Table 6.6 Percentage of graduates in *creative jobs* by migration type and degree subject

	Non-migrant	Late migrant	University stayer	Return migrant	Repeat migrant	Total
All other graduates	8.47	11.73	10.74	8.84	14.31	10.89
Creative graduates	36.46	**47.82**	40.68	30.27	**51.91**	40.36
Architecture	80.49	87.50	**89.21**	78.21	**87.83**	84.97
Design & Crafts	39.92	**49.24**	42.95	33.32	**57.42**	44.29
Film & TV	30.92	**39.47**	36.61	26.97	**47.30**	35.41
Fine Art	**34.28**	27.54	30.99	25.86	**31.53**	30.01
Music	31.28	**33.33**	**36.45**	21.55	29.47	29.60
Performing Arts	31.72	**36.84**	34.60	19.83	**43.36**	32.00
Technology	29.57	**57.85**	43.60	36.39	**61.31**	44.78
Advertising, Writing & Publishing	29.84	**50.82**	37.89	29.07	**50.09**	38.12
Total	12.26	16.20	16.05	12.27	**19.93**	15.41

by university connections, while Fine Art graduates contend with less defined and institutionalised paths for which more informal networks (e.g. through family and friends) are more relevant.

Lastly, we look at the role of migration on creative graduates' salaries (Table 6.7).

As for the chances of getting a graduate type job, the highest salaries are linked to late migration and repeat migration for both creative and non-creative graduates. Similar results have been found by Jewell and Faggian (2014).

As for graduate jobs, some differences exist in terms of salaries across the creative subdisciplines. Surprisingly, non-migration is associated with the highest salaries for Architecture graduates and the second highest for Film and TV graduates. For these graduates, it seems that the ability to build stronger, long-term connections comes with a salary premium. However, it must be noted that Architecture and Film and TV graduates are also highly clustered in the London area, so this might explain part of their higher returns.

Table 6.7 Mean and median (in brackets) *salaries* by subject and migration type (GBP £*)

	Non-migrant	Late migrant	Universi-ty stayer	Return migrant	Repeat migrant	All
All other	18,193	**19,526**	17,902	17,016	**19,791**	18,392
graduates	(18,000)	(19,000)	(17,000)	(16,000)	(19,000)	(18,000)
Creative	14,928	**15,733**	14,112	13,612	**15,607**	14,653
graduates	(14,000)	(15,000)	(14,000)	(13,000)	(15,000)	(14,000)
Architecture	**17,631**	**17,313**	15,722	16,580	16,512	16,593
	(17,500)	(17,000)	(15,000)	(15,000)	(16,000)	(16,000)
Design &	14,145	**15,246**	13,821	13,258	**15,420**	14,381
Crafts	(13,000)	(15,000)	(13,150)	(13,000)	(15,000)	(14,000)
Film & TV	14,547	**14,699**	14,029	13,496	**15,091**	14,272
	(14,000)	(15,000)	(14,000)	(13,250)	(15,000)	(14,000)
Fine Art	12,797	**13,986**	12,775	12,751	**14,639**	13,216
	(12,255)	(12,000)	(12,000)	(12,000)	(14,000)	(13,000)
Music	**15,538**	13,065	13,543	13,275	**14,414**	13,917
	(14,000)	(11,606)	(13,000)	(13,000)	(15,000)	(14,000)
Performing	13,378	**14,887**	13,759	13,116	**14,798**	13,870
Arts	(13,000)	(14,000)	(13,000)	(13,000)	(15,000)	(14,000)
Technology	18,321	**18,550**	16,432	15,422	**18,994**	17,579
	(17,000)	(17,500)	(16,000)	(15,000)	(19,000)	(17,000)
Advertising,	15,633	**16,409**	14,968	13,885	**16,074**	15,158
Writing &	(15,000)	(15,000)	(14,000)	(14,000)	(15,000)	(15,000)
Publishing						
Total	17,851	19,129	17,362	16,603	19,271	17,936
	(17,000)	(19,000)	(16,000)	(15,000)	(19,000)	(17,000)

*We exclude salary values equal to and above £100,000 due to the possibility these high values represent miscoding as a result of an extra 0 being typed or they may reflect extreme outliers.

Conclusions, implications and future research

This chapter has argued that, in order to understand the relation between creative human capital and geographical locations, it is important to have a better understanding of the factors determining the migration behaviours of people. In particular, as we explore the transition period from university education to employment of creative graduates, this helps us understand how mobility (non-mobility) can be seen as an outcome (for example, the outcome of a job offer/opportunity), but also used a strategy to reinforce existing networks or explore specific potential opportunities in the short and long term. Some of our results confirm the trends already explored in the literature for creative graduates. Looking at the geographical distribution and migration dynamics of creative graduates in the UK, we can confirm further the role of London as a hub for talent (Knell and Oakley 2007), but also as a magnet (Comunian and Faggian 2014) attracting creative students from all over the UK and retaining almost 75 per cent of them.

As consistent with previous literature, creative graduates have lower salaries and a higher percentage of non-graduate jobs (Comunian *et al*. 2010; Abreu e*t al*. 2012). However, the chapter has highlighted that migration could mitigate some of their difficulties allowing them to find a better occupation more fitted to their skills. The most common migration pattern of creative graduates, i.e. return migration, is the one associated with the lowest mean (and median) salary, which is just above £13,000. The fact that return migration is the most common choice of creative graduates suggest that networks and peer-to-peer support are crucial just after graduation (Comunian 2012). Networks are helpful in developing trust to respond to the risky nature of the creative economy (Banks *et al*. 2000), but also the importance of family support is recognised in the literature on creative work/careers (Ball *et al*. 2010; Nesta 2008) and is key for creative graduates (Faggian *et al*. 2014).

The second most common migration path, i.e. 'repeat migration' (28.80 per cent), is associated with the highest salary (£15,000). Alongside these general trends, we identified some specific subgroup trends. In particular, music graduates show a stronger tendency towards being 'university stayers'. While this gives them lower salaries and a higher probability of being in a non-graduate job, it also coincides with a higher ability for this group to secure a creative job. Considering that creative jobs in music are associated with low salaries and a high level of instability (Comunian *et al*. 2014b), the fact that music graduates can at least enter a creative career seems a positive outcome. It also confirms some early findings by Comunian *et al*. (2014b) that university networks play a crucial role in helping music graduates to eventually secure successful careers.

In general, aside from music graduates, 'university stayers' do not benefit from high rewards in choosing to stay in the area where they studied. While this strategy allows them to build on local knowledge and networks, it also means that graduates settle for non-graduate jobs (maybe the same ones they held while studying) to support themselves while they establish their career or portfolio, rather than moving on to graduate-level jobs straightaway.

In summary, the findings from this chapter highlight that while the mobility of highly skilled labour is key to a better understanding of career patterns and opportunities, a more refined understanding of the different types and characteristics of creative graduates is needed.

However, the data also highlight some limitations common to this type of analysis in relation to the creative economy. If graduates are asked to only identify a main current occupation, this may underrepresent those who might not be in a creative occupation but might, nonetheless, undertake creative activities (Throsby and Zednik 2011). Finally, alongside income measures, other measures of success and fulfilment – as highlighted also in Frenette and Tepper's chapter – might be required as, for example, 'university stayers' might not achieve a higher income but might benefit from the support and well-being (Bille *et al.* 2013) derived from stronger support networks in a specific locality. Finally, the interconnection between the resilience of urban spaces and the career of creative graduates and practitioners needs to receive further attention (Comunian and Jacobi 2015), as migration patterns could also be the result of the processes of gentrification or relocation determined by the context and not only by the creative workers themselves. The data also are not able to account for the importance of networks and connected migration patterns among the mobility dynamics which could be researched with more qualitative frameworks (like the ones adopted by Jacobi and Gilmore *et al.* in their respective chapters in this book).

Building on the initial findings of this chapter, several avenues for further research can be identified. The new 'Longitudinal Destinations of Leavers from Higher Education' (LDLHE) survey, which captures graduates up to three and a half years after graduation, provides data to study the migration behaviour and employment circumstances of graduates over a longer time span. This is particularly important for creative graduates, whose careers often take longer to take off. This would also allow for a better understanding of the role of the 'return migration' and the 'university stayer' strategies, e.g. whether they are temporary coping strategies rather than long-term trajectories. Longitudinal data might also help shed some light on how often creative graduates have to change jobs before settling into more permanent (and better fitting) ones.

As mentioned in respect to the limitation of the data, the fundamental role of networks for creative careers has been widely acknowledged (Borén and Young 2013) and a follow-up study of a more qualitative nature, focusing on how the networks developed in a specific locality are the main reason for staying rather than moving, would be really noteworthy. A more qualitative study would also help in understanding the phenomenon of multiple jobs held simultaneously, which is often lost in more quantitative, large datasets such as the one used in our study. Finally, one point worth mentioning is that our findings show that assuming that individuals with high human capital (i.e. graduates) are highly mobile is misleading. There are obvious differences based on the subject studied (and subsequent career), and our contribution has only scratched the surface of what could be an interesting and prosperous line of research.

Notes

1. We use the word 'creative' in the chapter not to generically qualify students or courses (we would happily argue that all students and academic disciplines have a creative component), but to refer to students and courses that align with the definition of the creative industries in the UK (for the latest definition see DCMS 2015). So it is possible to argue that all 'human capital' is creative, but in this essay we use the term 'creative human capital' to specifically define individuals with high levels of knowledge and specialisation (a degree) in creative industries-related disciplines.
2. See HESA press release 221 (12 February 2015) available at: https://www.hesa.ac.uk/pr211.
3. With 43 per cent of the employees having a tertiary degree qualification or higher – compared to an average of 16 per cent for the workforce as a whole (Nesta 2003).
4. The response rate to the DLHE survey for the 2005 cohort was 77 per cent for undergraduates, 62 per cent for postgraduates and 58 per cent for undergraduates below first-degree level.
5. For more information on the Joint Academic Coding System (JACS) see http://www.hesa.ac.uk/index.php?option=com_content&task=view&id=158&Itemid=233.

References

Abreu, M., Faggian, A., Comunian, R. and McCann, P. (2012) '"Life is short, art is long": the persistent wage gap between bohemian and non-bohemian graduates', *Annals of Regional Science*, 49 (2): 305–21.

Acheson, K. and Maule, C. J. (1994) 'International regimes for trade, investment, and labour mobility in the cultural industries', *Canadian Journal of Communication*, 19(3). Available at: http://cjc-online.ca/index.php/journal/article/view/826/732 (accessed 7 December 2015).

Addison. T. (2008) 'The international mobility of cultural talent', in A. Solimano (ed.), *The International Mobility of Talent: Types, Causes, and Development Impact*. Oxford: Oxford Scholarship Online, pp. 236–63.

Ball, L., Pollard, E. and Stanley, N. (2010) *Creative Graduates, Creative Futures*. Available at: http://www.creativegraduates.com (last accessed May 2010). London: Creative Graduates Creative Futures Higher Education Partnership and the Institute for Employment Studies.

Banks, M. and Hesmondhalgh, D. (2009) 'Looking for work in the creative industries policy', *International Journal of Cultural Policy*, 15 (4): 415–30.

Banks, M., Lovatt, A., O'Connor, J. and Raffo, C. (2000) 'Risk and trust in the cultural industries', *Geoforum*, 31: 453–64.

Beine, M., Docquier, F. and Rapoport, H. (2008) 'Brain drain and human capital formation in developing countries: winners and losers', *Economic Journal*, 118 (528): 631–52.

Bennett, D. (2010) 'Creative migration: a Western Australian case study of creative artists', *Australian Geographer*, 41 (1): 117–28.

Bille, T., Fjællegaard, C. B., Frey, B. S. and Steiner, L. (2013) 'Happiness in the arts – international evidence on artists' job satisfaction', *Economics Letters*, 121 (1): 15–18.

Bjerke, L. (2012) 'Knowledge Flows Across Space and Firms'. PhD thesis, Jönköping University, Jönköping (Sweden).

Blair, H. (2003) 'Winning and losing in flexible labour markets: the formation and operation of networks of interdependence in the UK film industry', *Sociology*, 37 (4): 677–94.

Borén, T. and Young, C. (2013) 'The migration dynamics of the "creative class": evidence from a study of artists in Stockholm, Sweden', *Annals of the Association of American Geographers*, 103 (1): 195–210.

Bozeman, B., Dietz, J. S. and Gaughan, M. (2001) 'Scientific and technical human capital: an alternative model for research evaluation', *International Journal of Technology Management*, 22 (7): 716–40.

Chapain, C. A. and Comunian, R. (2010) 'Enabling and inhibiting the creative economy: the role of the local and regional dimensions in England. *Regional Studies*, 43 (6): 717–34.

Charles, D. (2003) 'Universities and territorial development: reshaping the regional role of English universities', *Local Economy*, 18 (1): 7–20.

Comunian, R. (2012) 'Exploring the role of networks in the creative economy of North East England: economic and cultural dynamics', in B. Warf (ed.), *Encounters and Engagement Between Economic Cultural Geography*. The Netherlands: Springer, pp. 143–57.

Comunian, R. and Faggian, A. (2011) 'Higher education and the creative city', in C. Mellander, A. Andersson and D. Andersson (eds), *Handbook on Cities and Creativity*. London and New York: Edward Elgar, pp. 187–207.

Comunian, R. and Faggian, A. (2014) 'Creative graduates and creative cities: exploring the geography of creative education in the UK', *International Journal of Cultural and Creative Industries*, 1 (2): 19–34.

Comunian, R. and Gilmore, A. (2015) *Beyond the Creative Campus: Reflections on the Evolving Relationship Between Higher Education and the Creative Economy*. London: King's College. Available at: http://www.creative-campus.org.uk.

Comunian, R. and Jacobi, S. (2015) 'Resilience, creative careers and creative spaces: bridging vulnerable artist's livelihoods and adaptive urban change', in H. Pinto (ed.), *Resilient Territories: Innovation and Creativity for New Modes of Regional Development*. Cambridge: Cambridge Scholars, pp. 151–66.

Comunian, R., Chapain, C. and Clifton, N. (2010) 'Location, location, location: exploring the complex relationship between creative industries and place', *Creative Industries Journal*, 3 (1): 5–10.

Comunian, R., Faggian, A. and Jewell, S. (2011) 'Winning and losing in the creative industries: an analysis of creative graduates' career opportunities across creative disciplines', *Cultural Trends*, 20 (3/4): 291–308.

Comunian, R., Faggian, A. and Jewell, S. (2014a) 'Embedding arts and humanities in the creative economy: the role of graduates in the UK', *Environment and Planning C: Government and Policy*, 32 (3): 426–50.

Comunian, R., Faggian, A. and Jewell, S. (2014b) 'Exploring music careers: music graduates and early career trajectories in the UK', in N. Crossley, S. McAndrew and P. Widdop (eds), *Social Networks and Music Worlds*. Abingdon: Routledge, pp. 165–88.

Comunian, R., Faggian, A. and Jewell, S. (2015) 'Digital technology and creative arts career patterns in the UK creative economy', *Journal of Education and Work*, 28 (4): 346–68.

Comunian, R., Faggian, A. and Li, Q. C. (2010) 'Unrewarded careers in the creative class: the strange case of bohemian graduates', *Papers in Regional Science*, 89 (2): 389–410.

Comunian, R., Gilmore, A. and Jacobi, S. (2015) 'Higher education and the creative economy: creative graduates, knowledge transfer and regional impact debates', *Geography Compass*, 9 (7): 371–83.

Corcoran, J., Faggian, A. and McCann, P. (2010) 'Human capital in remote and rural Australia: the role of graduate migration', *Growth and Change*, 41 (2). 192–210.

Cramphorn, J. and Woodlhouse, J. (1999) 'The role of education in economic development', *Industry and Higher Education*, 13 (3): 169–75.

Cunningham, S., Cutler, T., Hearn, G., Ryan, M. and Keane, M. (2004) 'An innovation agenda for the creative industries: where is the randd?', *Media International Australia: Incorporating Culture and Policy*, 112: 174–85.

DaVanzo, J. (1976) 'Differences between return and non-return migration: an econometric analysis', *International Migration Review*, 10 (1): 13–27.

DaVanzo, J. and Morrison, P. (1981) 'Return and other sequences of migration in the United States', *Demography*, 18(1): 85–101.

DCMS (2001) *Creative Industries Mapping Document*. London: Department for Culture, Media and Sport.

DCMS (2006) *Making the Case for Public Investment: Developing Entrepreneuriship for the Creative Industries – The Role of Higher Education*. London: DCMS.

DCMS (2015) *Creative Industries Economic Estimates*. London: DCMS.

DCMS and BERR (2008) *Creative Britain – New Talents for the Economy*. London: DCMS.

Faggian, A. (2005) *Human Capital, Migration and Local Labour Markets: The Role of the Higher Education System in Great Britain*. University of Reading, Reading.

Faggian, A. and McCann, P. (2006) 'Human capital flows and regional knowledge assets: a simultaneous equation approach', *Oxford Economic Papers*, 58 (3): 475–500.

Faggian, A. and McCann, P. (2009) 'Universities, agglomerations and graduate human capital mobility', *Journal of Economic and Social Geography (TESG)*, 100 (2): 210–23.

Faggian, A., Comunian, R. and Li, Q. C. (2014) 'Interregional migration of human creative capital: the case of "bohemian graduates"', *Geoforum*, 55: 33–42.

Faggian, A., Comunian, R., Jewell, S. and Kelly, U. (2013) 'Bohemian graduates in the UK: disciplines and location determinants of creative careers', *Regional Studies*, 47 (2): 183–200.

Faggian, A., Comunian, R., Jewell, S. and Kelly, U. (2013) 'Bohemian graduates in the UK: disciplines and location determinants of creative careers', *Regional Studies*, 47 (2): 183–200.

Florida, R. (2002) *The Rise of the Creative Class*. New York: Basic Books.

Glaeser, E. L. (2005) 'Review of Richard Florida's "the rise of the creative class"', *Regional Science and Urban Economics*, 35: 593–6.

Hall, P. (1998) *Cities in Civilization: Culture, Innovation and Urban Order*. London: Weidenfeld & Wishart.

Hansen, H. K. and Niedomysl, T. (2009) 'Migration of the creative class: evidence from Sweden', *Journal of Economic Geography*, 9: 191–206.

Jewell, S. and Faggian, A. (2014) 'Interregional migration wage premia: the case of creative and stem graduates in the UK', in K. Kourtit, P. Nijkamp and R. Stimson (eds), *Applied Modeling of Regional Growth and Innovation Systems*. The Netherlands: Springer, pp. 197–216.

Knell, J. and Oakley, K. (2007) *London's Creative Economy: An Accidental Success?* London: Work Foundation.

Lawton, P., Murphy, E. and Redmond, D. (2013) 'Residential preferences of the "creative class"?', *Cities*, 31: 47–56.

Lee, N. and Drever, E. (2013) 'The creative industries, creative occupations and innovation in London', *European Planning Studies*, 21 (12): 1977–97.

Linderlöf, P. and Löfsten, H. (2004) 'Proximity as a resource base for competitive advantage: university–industry links for technology transfer', *Journal of Technology Transfer*, 29: 311–26.

Löfsten, H. and Lindelöf, P. (2005) 'Randd networks and product innovation patterns – academic and non-academic new technology-based firms on science parks', *Technovation*, 25 (9): 1025–37.

Markusen, A. (2006) 'Urban development and the politics of a creative class: evidence from the case study of artists', *Environment and Planning A*, 38 (10): 1921–40.

Markusen, A., Wassall, G. H., DeNatale, D. and Cohen, R. (2008) 'Defining the creative economy: industry and occupational approaches', *Economic Development Quarterly*, 22 (1): 24–45.

Martin-Brelot, H., Grossetti, M., Eckert, D., Gritsai, O. and Kovacs, Z. (2010) 'The spatial mobility of the "creative class": a European perspective', *International Journal of Urban and Regional Research*, 34 (4): 854–70.

Mathur, V. K. (1999) 'Human capital-based strategy for regional economic development', *Economic Development Quarterly*, 13 (3): 203–16.

Moretti, E. (2004) 'Human capital externalities in cities', *Handbook of Regional and Urban Economics*, 4: 2243–91.

Nesta (2003) *Forward Thinking – New Solutions to Old Problems: Investing in the Creative Industries*. London: Nesta.

Nesta (2008) *The Art of Innovation: How Fine Arts Graduates Contribute to Innovation*. London: Nesta.

Newbold, K. B. (1997) 'Primary, return and onward migration in the U.S. and Canada: is there a difference?', *Papers in Regional Science*, 76 (2): 175–98.

O'Hagan, J. and Borowiecki, K. J. (2010) 'Birth location, migration, and clustering of important composers: historical patterns', *Historical Methods*, 43 (2): 81–90.

O'Hagan, J. and Hellmanzik, C. (2008) 'Clustering and migration of important visual artists: broad historical evidence', *Historical Methods: A Journal of Quantitative and Interdisciplinary History*, 41 (3): 121–36.

Powell, J. (2007) 'Creative universities and their creative city-regions', *Industry and Higher Education*, 21 (6): 323–35.

Preston, J. and Hammond, C. (2006) *The Economic Impact of UK Higher Education Institutions*. London: Universities UK.

Scott, A. J. (2010) 'Jobs or amenities? Destination choices of migrant engineers in the USA', *Papers in Regional Science*, 89 (1): 43–63.

Shattock, M. (2010) 'Managing mass higher education in a period of austerity', *Arts and Humanities in Higher Education*, 9 (1): 22–30.

Sjaastad, L. A. (1962) 'The costs and returns of human migration', *Journal of Political Economy*, 70 (5): 80–93.

Solimano, A. (2006) *The International Mobility of Talent and Its Impact on Global Development: An Overview*, Vol. 52. Santiago, Chile: United Nations Publications.

Throsby, D. and Zednik, A. (2011) 'Multiple job-holding and artistic careers: some empirical evidence', *Cultural Trends*, 20 (1): 9–24.

Towse, R. (2006) 'Human capital and artists' labour markets', *Handbook of the Economics of Art and Culture*, 1: 865–94.

UNESCO and UNDP (2013) *Creative Economy Report 2013 Special Edition: Widening Local Development Pathways*. New York and Paris: United Nations Development Programme and the United Nations Educational, Scientific and Cultural Organization).

Universities UK (2010) *Creating Prosperity: The Role of Higher Education in Driving the UK's Creative Economy*. London: Universities UK.

Vang, J. and Chaminade, C. (2007) 'Cultural clusters, global–local linkages and spillovers: theoretical and empirical insights from an exploratory study of Toronto's film cluster', *Industry and Innovation*, 14 (4): 401–20.

Venhorst, V., Van Dijk, J. and Van Wissen, L. (2010) 'Do the best graduates leave the peripheral areas of the Netherlands?', *Tijdschrift voor Economische en Sociale Geografie*, 101 (5): 521–37.

Venhorst, V., Van Dijk, J. and Van Wissen, L. (2011) 'An analysis of trends in spatial mobility of Dutch graduates', *Spatial Economic Analysis*, 6 (1): 57–82.

7 Human capital career creativities for creative industries work

Lessons underpinned by Bourdieu's tools for thinking

Dawn Bennett and Pamela Burnard

Introduction

Graduates need to develop multiple human capital career creativities if they are to create and sustain careers in the creative industries. This is because creative work is characterised by multiple concurrent roles within portfolio careers that are commonly protean and boundaryless: the former emphasising capital expansion as an output of human capital career creativities where the facilitative skills practices transcend those of a portfolio career; and the latter emphasising work that transcends fields, digital boundaries, economic sector and employment type.

Understanding graduate work in the creative industries

Our claim that multiple human capital career creativities are crucial to higher education graduate learning and development is by necessity based on empirical evidence, because large-scale data collections are insufficiently refined to capture the complexity in the workforce (Bennett *et al.* 2014). Both census and graduate destinations are scrutinised by measurements that largely rely on rates of full-time employment and, despite the growing trend of non-linear careers across the labour market (Commonwealth of Australia 2013), these data have become 'easily measurable proxies for graduate employability' (Bennett and Bridgstock 2015: 5). Given that employability (more usefully defined as 'work readiness') is likely to be driven and maintained at the individual level, we have turned to Bourdieu to help shed light on the development and impact of human capital career creativities on higher education graduates.

Human capital career creativities

A growing number of scholars have contributed to understanding the practices of creative workers, including their work and professional learning cultures (for example, see Peck 2005; Smith and McKinlay 2009; Oakley 2009; Cunningham 2013; Bennett *et al.* 2014). However, the social practices, through which different types of artistic creativities are recognised and communicated (understood within professional learning cultures), remain under-researched. Our research responds by exploring the interaction between the 'habitus', 'fields' and 'capitals' in which creative workers' practices are generated. In so doing we probe:

- the taken-for-granted, internalised dispositions that operate in the personal histories (*habitus*) of creative workers and the social spaces (*fields of action such as the field of music*) in which creative workers participate. Here, we recognise that each field of action operates in relation to many other fields and that agents can occupy more than one field at a time (Thomson 2008);
- *professional capital career creativities*, meaning the appropriation of field-specific strategies, which take on a new significance or career advantage. We thematise those strategies which link to the Bourdieusian discourse on human *capital* (i.e. social, cultural, symbolic, economic) in the careers of creative workers (Burnard 2012, 2014; Burnard and Haddon 2015); and
- the plurality of *practices*, the forms and ways of doing that are not simply the outcome of individual actions but also of wider structural factors, as put forward in Bourdieu's theory of practice. These provide the conditions necessary for relevance to market positioning.

The complexity of creative work suggests that higher education graduates require multiple human capital career creativities to transition from study to work. Professional capital creativities are, therefore, keys that mediate professional learning cultures and the potential of graduates to negotiate their careers. Thus, in this chapter and in line with the current volume, we focus on the specifics of professional capital creativities in the creation of *human capital* in general.

Higher education institutions (HEIs) are fields of engagement in which students, teachers, administrators and policy-makers are players. They allow for the distribution and acquisition of educational capital (in the forms of knowledge and practices), along with ownership of human capital. Within HEIs, capable people use and develop distinctive practices and use diverse forms of capitals in interaction with others. According to Bourdieu (1986), cultural capital exists in three forms: (1) *embodied* through physical and psychological states; (2) *institutionalised* through social and cultural recognition such as degrees or other marks of success; and (3) *objectified* by means of external goods such as books or the media.

In terms of education, *symbolic capital* (Bourdieu 1986) is most evident in the form of academic legitimation. *Professional capital* is seen as the exercise of *social capital* in the workplace along with the shared practice, judgement and values found at the interface of culture and commerce. These capitals are socially recognised and remunerated. The central principle here, for creative workers, is that of *practice*: that which is deliberately pursued and necessary for high performance and that which helps develop *professional capital career creativities* to a high level. With this in mind we explore some of the strategic practices that constitute and enable employability (or work readiness), career success and sustainability.

Approach and theoretical framework

The economic and social background of creative workers equips them with a range of cultural and social capitals which need to be effectively applied in different cultural contexts, in varying roles and in diverse environments. With Bourdieu's conceptual tools in mind, particularly when understanding the relationship between experiences, dispositions, human capitals and the particularities and enabling conditions needed for graduates to successfully enter the creative workforce, we describe what constitutes human capital career creativities and how strategic practices are changing.

Our research is informed by a Bourdieusian lens which focuses on the capacities and resources necessary for creative graduates to build careers. As such, our two main questions were:

1. How can Bourdieu's tools (field, habitus, practice and capitals) be used to enhance our understanding and identification of career *creativities* necessary for creative graduates to build careers? and
2. How can Bourdieu's tools extend our understanding of the strategies that enhance the *career creativities* of higher education creative graduates?

In order to put to use Bourdieu's trilogy of 'thinking tools' – habitus, capital and field – as understood through the practices constituted by the social and cultural actions of the participants, we employed two distinct forms of data collection. First, three in-depth interviews gave us the opportunity to explore human creative capitals in detail. To understand how these capitals might play out in broader terms, we then turned to a detailed questionnaire. Combined, this gave us 184 cases for analysis.

The semi-structured interviews involved three creative workers (two male) who were purposefully selected because of the diversity of their practice in music. The first, Simon, was a DJ whose work in nightclubs took him to multiple countries. The second, Roshi, was a freelance singer, songwriter and workshop leader who worked across multiple genres and contexts. Kenneth, the third participant, was a company-based video games audio designer responsible for the audio experience in games. The participants were aged between 22 and 62 years. The sampling criteria included: (1) working as professionals in corporate settings or cultural or higher degree institutions; (2) having gained acceptance and recognition in their respective fields; and (3) negotiating multiple selves that shifted between creator, presenter and musician.

The second data collection involved an in-depth questionnaire that elicited responses from 181 creative workers (Bennett *et al*. 2014). Participants were recruited through arts networks and represented a broad spectrum of creative occupations and employment types. Participants were aged from 18 to 80 years and 60 per cent were female. The survey included closed and open questions. Section 1 amassed data about location, engagement, motivation and identity. Section 2 explored the characteristics of work. Section 3 addressed the distribution of time. Section 4 focused on formal and informal learning. Section 5 recorded demographic information, after which respondents were invited to write freely about their creative work.

Our analysis began with analytic induction to enhance data by examining similarities and differences, and developing new concepts and ideas (Ragin 1994). Therefore all initial themes were derived from the data and interrogated in light of other participants' responses to determine essential characteristics. Next, we undertook pattern analysis with multiple readings of each complete 'case'. From this, we identified the notions of 'community', 'career', 'inspiration' and 'bestowed' strategies that constituted human capital career creativities. We acknowledge the presence of Bourdieu's four different types of capital in the data, but, in this chapter, we thematise four related career creativities that add value to the activities of the field and of field-specific capitals identified as being at the centre of learning and negotiating creative careers:

1. *Community-building creativity* represents professional networks and communities of practice.
2. *Inspiration-forming creativity* includes role models, inspirational figures and supporters.
3. *Career-positioning creativity* represents the creation of capacity through interest, recognition, new markets (including market 'engagement') and professional learning.
4. *Bestowed gift-giving creativity* refers to capital that is 'given away' in forms such as mentorship and pro-bono work.

Findings and discussion

Identifying career creativities

The participants in this study reported a diversity of professional dispositions within specific fields and field practices. These creative workers maximised their potential by drawing on institutional specialisation and employing a potent mix of human capitals as artists, authors, entrepreneurs, managers, designers, cultural producers, researchers, culture bearers, academics and teachers. They also made use of their positional status and referred to distinctive, yet overlapping, networks within which creative work and product is created, communicated and recorded. The data created an empirical picture of different forms of capitals and strategies employed as career creativities.

Bourdieu's tools in the study of graduate career trajectories

In this chapter, we are focused on the strategic practices *through which creative workers learn*, in other words through learning cultures (James *et al.* 2007). To facilitate this enquiry, we follow Bourdieu's argument that practice can only be understood through the application of the three thinking tools. These three are taken to be intrinsically interlinked, so that *practice* = [(*habitus*) (*capital*)] + *field* (Bourdieu 1979: 101). Each tool has an integral role to play in understanding the practices of learning at play in initial and life-wide education; each tool must be 'put to use' in order to elicit new understandings of practice.

In each case study, we first deploy two domains of practice – habitus and field – to understand and critique how the creative industries are navigated. We then turn to the focus of this volume, human creative capitals, and highlight where these capitals are essential for graduates to create and sustain careers in and beyond the creative industries. In particular, we outline the creativities and professional practices that become spaces of position and specific positioning.

Field as a conceptual tool

Field can be understood as 'a particular social setting where class dynamics take place, for example, a classroom or a workplace, but it can also refer to more abstract and broader concerns like the field of politics or the legal field, or the field of higher education' (Reay *et al.* 2005: 27); one's habitus interacts with the fields of action in which we are embedded. In earlier views and understandings of the concept of field as argued by Bourdieu, a more 'relational configuration' was argued: for example, Bourdieu and Wacquant (1992: 89) described field not as a single entity but rather as 'a relational configuration endowed with a specific gravity which it imposes on all the objects and agents which enter in it'. This is another way of presenting what we have argued thus far, that is that fields of action engage creative workers with the need for accumulating different skills as useful types of human capital that can mobilise the resources necessary for creative graduates to build careers.

It is not difficult to see how research analyses of creative work, and the practices of individuals within and across fields of action, can also benefit from understanding both the habitus of and/or around creative workers, as well as the fields that act upon them and through which they act. What we argue is how creative workers with well-defined habitus in particular fields who generate meaningful and well-defined practices and products (taste) constitute precisely the capacity to unsettle the weight that one's habitus and field place upon an individual or community. Key in this process is the notion of influence, as argued above, as it is linked to how we see our own condition, as well as how we are able to envision our futures.

Various studies (see Burnard and Haddon 2015; Burnard *et al.* 2015) locate the sociology of music education and creativities' conceptual expansion within the empirical examination of relationships between classifiable practices and classificatory judgements in fields that encompass creative work. These studies describe access to the cultural field of production as being mediated by habitus and multiple fields of action. These are likely to shape the key factors in generating professional capital creativities and reproducing patterns of all fields, understood as the complex set of social, cultural, aesthetic, spatial and economic factors. As argued by Bourdieu and Wacquant (1992: 44), these can 'be the product of the embodiment of the immanent necessity of the field' (or of a hierarchy of intersecting fields).

We contend that creative workers navigate careers and exercise professional capitals differently and that professional capitals work differently for different creative industries groups. The disjuncture between habitus and fields occur for

Bourdieu when individuals with a well-developed habitus find themselves in different fields or different parts of the same social field, or when there are social changes affecting a field. Feeling like a 'fish in water' (knowing how to act in particular situations) or a 'fish out of water' describes processes of disjuncture, particularly when creative workers act in entrepreneurial ways to generate change, reformulate or reinterpret rules, or mobilise alternative forms of capital in a particular field of action as 'designated bundles of relations' where there is often struggle within a domain of power (Bourdieu and Wacquant 1992: 16).

Clearly articulated in these quotes is the plurality of fields of action as sites of endless change, 'where agents and institutions constantly struggle according to the regularities and the rules constitutive of this space of play … and where there exists a set of "logics" particular to that field' (Bourdieu and Wacquant 1992: 102). The array of professional capital creativities featured in this chapter varies according to the fields of action in which products are set and move into the marketplace (see Figure 7.1). Creative workers working in the rap industry, for example, may work across territorial spaces as fields of action where representation of the ghetto as habitus is geographically determined (Schmidt 2015) and where the peddling of power is exercised as the accumulation of forms of capital that challenge the notion of value creation by making a distinction between human and physical forms of capital (Bowman and Swart 2007). Reay (2015) has recently sketched out the conceptualisation of emotional capital, a new capital that expands the potential array of Bourdieu's lexicon of capitals, internalised and played out in practices across fields. As shown in Figure 7.1, this illustrates thematised strategic practices that contribute to professional capital career creativities developed by creative workers.

Seen in the following summaries, multiple fields of action emerge in the three interview cases. The musical field did not operate in isolation; rather, each field

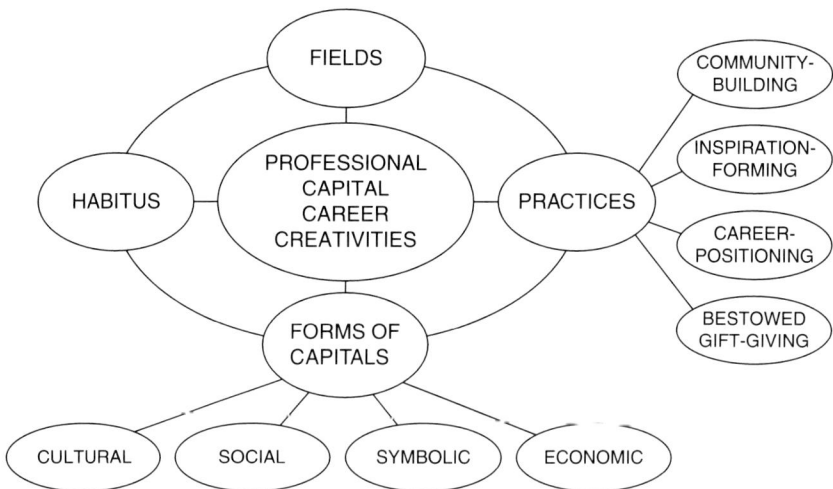

Figure 7.1 Creative workers' professional capital career creativities

operated in relation to other fields (Thomson 2008) as an arena of struggle over, and success in, the appropriation of career creativities.

Simon Lewicki (artist name DJ Groove Terminator) is an Australian electronic music artist. He lives in Los Angeles where he DJs and produces, and makes frequent tours as a guest international DJ at clubs in Europe, Australia and across the United States. From an early age, within a particular cultural setting and urban youth practices, he has learnt the production and practical operational knowledge required of a DJ. Simon's DJing is produced within a system of close-knit local networks, crossing between radio techniques and pioneering club disco work. He constantly repositions himself across multiple fields by broadening his remit and locating his work across different industries (creative, cultural, dance music, recording, fashion, Internet, recording, broadcasting, publishing). For Simon, the fields of commerce include merchandise, record companies, marketing and corporate media, and the fields of cultural production include clubs, arenas, festivals, corporate centres, awards and multimedia. His DJing involves aesthetic and cultural 'structured spaces' that are geographic and territorial, which build upon hierarchical forms of capital. His practice of DJing and VJing (using video) are products of the conditions of a place, venue, time, scene, production style and act. The rules of the field are defined in terms of the heroes and creators of dance scenes, technological advancement, expert reputations in production and knowledge of musical styles, genres and subgenres. He understands very well the rules that govern how the game is played. The rules concern the creative sense of 'interaction with the crowd', but also global and local market forces. By importing ready-made material, Simon positions the publishing and copyright industries as powerful institutional forces.

Roshi trained as a classical musician. Familial, educational and ethnic habitus plays a significant role in her decision-making and these three aspects are key influences that operate synergistically with her musical background. Roshi started playing the piano when she was nine years old. She has had many years of formal music education and training, including the completion of an undergraduate music performance degree. She is a self-managed, portfolio careerist, that is she self-manages her career and practises as a singer, songwriter and music workshop leader. Roshi's work as a freelance and session singer-songwriter requires knowledge of multiple industries, including the musical, recording, digital and cultural. Roshi aspires to traditional pathways, such as being signed by a record label, but she also prioritises the cultural layers and politics of Iranian ethnic minority groups that influence her creative voice. The field of industries overlaps the creative and cultural, recording and broadcasting, copyright and advertising.

Sound engineer Kenneth describes an interconnecting network of intersecting fields which he navigates to position his company's products to influence the fields of digital media, games industry, and software and hardware industries associated with video games development, and to create 'breakthrough' software and hardware. Kenneth was born in Scotland and lives in London where, as the lead audio designer at Media Molecule, he is responsible for the audio experience in the games they make, most recently the PlayStation 3 title *LittleBigPlanet* and its sequel *LittleBigPlanet2*. A strong sense of personal efficacy has had positive consequences for his career. His personal history stresses over and over again the importance of education and, at the same time, the need to understand and negotiate the hierarchical forms of capital that dominate in the gaming world.

These cases highlight diverse professional and strategic practices, fields of action, human capitals and musical habitus. While participants possess *capitals*, the game that occurs in these fields is always competitive, and the accumulation of capitals (and status) is at stake. Whether economic, social or educational, each field has distinctions that are symbolically valued. The point being made here is not about *who* becomes a creative musician, whether that be a popular DJ, an intercultural songwriter and community musician or a corporate gaming sound designer, but rather *how* musicians position their own career creativities within the fields of action in and across what they practice. Bourdieu's tools for thinking facilitate and show how these tools take many shapes in offering a foundation for the analysis of musicians' habitus, their career creativities and their aspirations.

Habitus as a conceptual tool

Habitus can be defined as modes of thought, opinion and behaviour that are the internalisation of experience built up over a lifetime. Habitus allows for agency and choice, and also recognises that choices are restricted by socio-economic positioning. Similarly, habitus predisposes individuals towards certain ways of behaving. Bourdieu and Wacquant (1992: 127) explain the relationship between habitus and field in two directions:

> On one side, it is a relation of conditioning: the field structures the habitus, which is the product of the embodiment of the immanent necessity of a field (or of a set of intersecting fields, the extent of their intersection or discrepancy being at the root of the divided or even torn habitus). On the other side ... habitus contributes to constituting the field as a meaningful world, a world endowed with sense and value, in which it is worth investing one's energy.

Bourdieu intends habitus to be understood as internalised dispositions that operate in numerous social spheres. He uses the word to refer to what people think, do and prefer. Creative worker habitus can be expressed by the way it disposes people to play, present, create, make and produce in a particular way. Bourdieu calls this orientation a 'strategy,' which is a semi-conscious, but characteristic, way of doing things. For creative workers in social and collective authorship situations, habitus can be expressed in day-to-day practice as strategic *career creativity*.

Below, the three case-study musicians illustrate a fluid notion of habitus within the context of their practice.

- In Simon's words, the DJ habitus means: 'creating your own sound, your own vibe, identity, being able to read crowds, and inspire them to dance throughout the night. It is about self-marketing; seeing yourself as a creator, a creative individual and using technology and your technical prowess in deconstructing and reconstructing songs … you're seen as a celebrity' (Simon, DJ).
- A classically trained musician with enthusiasm for jazz, folk, traditional Iranian music and popular cultural forms, Roshi takes the musical traditions of Iran as the origins, heart and voice at the centre of her song habitus. Her capacity to realise her aspirations depends on creating reputation and differentiating herself from other songwriters. Roshi's life course, cultural experiences and skills are inscribed in her biography and in the social world.
- Kenneth's gaming career is endowed with highly capitalised cultural and creative value. The habitus of this designer and entrepreneur is characterised by judicious, long-term career choices, the building of a strong professional identity, clearly driven goals, creative aspirations and self-belief. Kenneth stresses the importance of education, risk-taking and innovating. Success, in the games industry, means pushing boundaries with the development of new digital technologies.

Although habitus affects how a person thinks and what a person thinks about, it delineates the parameters of thought and action without determining thought and action per se. As the product of history and experience, habitus is never fixed: it is changed by history and new experiences, and by the accrual of *capitals*.

Capitals as a conceptual tool

For Bourdieu, capital is what Grenfell and James (1998: 18) describe as 'the social products of field or system of relations through which individuals carry out social intercourse … not readily available to everyone on the same basis: scarcity of social resource is the lubricant of social systems.' Metaphorically expressed, capital 'is what makes the games of society … something other than simple games of chance offering at every moment the possibility of a miracle' (Bourdieu 1986: 46). In other words, some people will accrue more (and different) capital and will use this to play 'the games of society' differently. Capitals, then, are 'assets that bring social and cultural advantage or disadvantage' (Moore 2008: 104).

In this study, analysis of the questionnaire and interview data revealed the importance of capital for creative industries workers. Capital was seen in the individual skills and knowledge that creative workers apply in multiple contexts, and which they obtain and bestow in networked ways:

> Most of my work draws on my skills as an artist, e.g. as a journalist, I write and review for arts publications and produce feature articles for arts marketing distribution; for non-arts clients, I apply creative writing techniques to produce feature journalism; as an administrator, I work with arts companies or in a creative producer role … To a limited degree, my arts journalism feeds back into my creative work, as a result of contact with other artists and artistic projects.
>
> (Simone, writer)

> I had, over the years, worked within a variety of arts practices and had gathered a lot of the skills necessary to put on … [a festival]. It was great to be able to pass many of those skills on.
>
> (Mike, visual artist)

Typical of creative work, the practices of individuals within fields are guided by what Bourdieu calls a 'feel for the game'. The game analogy helps us understand the dialectical relationship between habitus, capital and field, in that the strategies of players operate in relation to the volume and structure of their capital. Even when practice appears as rational action to an impartial observer who possesses all the necessary information to reconstruct it as such, rational choice is not its principle.

As previously noted (Burnard 2012), a key aspect of creative industries work is the accumulation of different forms of capital. For a DJ, this might encompass participation in high-status activities: for instance, constructing a 'catalogue' of widely distributed, innovative albums; acquiring status through high-volume sales; successful world tours; and entrepreneurship in image building.

Accumulation, sharing and context

We next frame the accumulation, sharing and context of professional capital career creativities within the four thematised strategic practices that emerged from our data. We note, however, the close relationships between these four themes, taking particular account of Reay's (2015) addition of the psychosocial to Bourdieu's work. As Reay asserts, this psychosocial dimension concerns 'inquiry into the mutual constitution of the individual and the social relations within which they are enmeshed' (ibid.: 10). As such, our four themes cannot be abstracted as exclusive strategic practices that are separate from one another; rather, they illustrate dimensions of career creativities within collective industry practices of creative workers.

In this study, the key aspect of creative workers' habitus was the way it disposed people to explore, create and communicate their practice in a particular way. In the following example, habitus explains how a creative worker (a magician) strategically found an audience and subsequently built on each opportunity as his professional capital career creativity increased:

> I disappeared a cigarette on board a flight back from Noumea … turned out the cigarette belonged to an advertising man who was opening Fisherman's Wharf on the Gold Coast [Australia]. I started my first paid job four days later and it lasted five years. This saw me explode onto the scene … within a couple of months, I was working on TV for a kids show, employed by the Crest Hotel in Brisbane, and corporate work was snowballing.
>
> (Mikael, magician)

In another example, a digital arts duo began by building a following in the night-club scene. Through this they then:

> Established more demand by networking with others in our field, getting a body of corporate clients who were happy to pay a good commercial rate. We also did a *Percent for Art* [PFA] scheme project using digital techniques … We used most of the money from the PFA to buy equipment, which now earns us more money and enables us to do bigger corporate events.
>
> (Kim and Lisa, digital artists)

The duo described strategically building on their success and reinvesting in their business. They then embraced new global opportunities using the Internet for live streaming and social media presence. According to Bourdieu (1993: 65), what this duo thought and did – their strategic practice – was to establish:

> The configuration, at the moment, and the various critical turning-points in each career, of the space of possibilities (in particular, the economic and symbolic hierarchy of the genres, schools, styles, manners, subjects, etc.), the social value attached to each of them, and also the meaning and values they received for the different agents, or classes of agents, in terms of the socially constituted categories of perception and appreciation they applied to them.

Bourdieu's 'field of cultural production' led him to analyse the relationship between ways of understanding the world, the principles behind creative works made in a particular place and time, and the meanings people attach to what he calls 'practices of distinction': the strategic practices evident in the examples above.

We next address the distinctive plurality of professional capital career creativities that are inscribed in the industry practices of creative workers, using the four types of career creativities that emerged as useful types of human capital for creative workers. These are: community-building creativity, career-positioning creativity, inspiration-forming creativity and bestowed creativity.

Community-building creativity

We use the term community-building creativity in relation to the creation of professional and social networks, including opportunities for peer learning, networked forms of obtaining work, and work that is undertaken with others. Of all the human capital career creativities, the 181 questionnaire narratives most commonly emphasised community capital and the community-building creativity through which it is developed.

The importance of community-building creativity for building and sustaining a career in the creative industries cannot be overestimated. For new graduates in particular, community building can be a major consideration in all decision-making. This can be seen in the form of creative workers taking unpaid work placements or work in cultural venues in order to be close to existing networks – or potential social capital – and activities. One new music graduate described this in action: 'Bartending provides an opportunity to expand my knowledge and network in the music industry as I work at a music venue' (Sam, musician). The results of this are seen in comments from a member of an established band: 'We have, through extremely consistent marketing activities over the years, developed a healthy network of contacts enabling us to win gigs at hotels, taverns, corporate events, dances, parties, concerts, etc.' (Duke, musician).

Even for established artists, networks shift according to opportunity and need. They also reflect changes in technology over time:

> YouTube, Facebook, Twitter, etc. make us feel connected with the VJ community worldwide … As a result we have a bigger following in Europe than we do locally.
>
> (Nat, video jockey)

> I have recently used the latest digital technology to bring major live performances to audiences that would otherwise never have experienced them.
>
> (Amin, producer)

Observed in greater detail within the three interviews, community-building creativity was described as the central and defining practice of all professional capital career creativities. It is also open to negotiation and is often renegotiated to realise new creative possibilities.

Simon described the professional networks of DJs as a 'crucial club'. He also talked of a 'guest DJ circuit' that took him 15 years to 'crack'. He learnt 'the logic' of DJ practice, the building of an identity, a celebrity DJ status and a certain DJ style for each scene, club and circuit by:

> Hanging around with other DJs, picking up tips, learning from my peers, like the rule of three which is play one they know, a new one and something they love, but not necessarily in that order … learning how to get to work the room from beginning to end means you've got to take the cues, read the crowd, and keep building specific community knowledge.
>
> (Simon, DJ)

Roshi emphasised the importance of community building when she noted that, 'Although, as a songwriter, its *my* project, meaning I'm bringing the material that we work with, what comes out of *all* the different musicians I work with are certain valuable voices … important additions to the song' (Roshi, musician). The songwriter becomes a function of connecting individuals, working with new and traditional sources, and the influence afforded by the community-building creativity, which helped gained Roshi her artistic recognition.

For sound designer Kenneth, working for a games company involves innovators who engage community members and attempt to influence them in order to build a prototype/model that will influence their actions. Kenneth started as an apprentice where he faced the demands of high-status projects, where the success or failure of new companies, corporate initiatives and projects was dependent on building community capitals. This is a distinctive characteristic of the gaming industry, and relates to learning how to successfully tap into and contribute to team collaboration in a company where teams rely on diverse skills and expertise throughout a project cycle.

For these creative workers, community-building creativity was accumulated by working in and across diverse community networks. Whether by peer learning as a DJ, collaborating in song performance or generating networked feedback for emerging game products, community positioning capital emerged as the most commonly realised of all career creativities.

Career-positioning creativity

Career-positioning creativity was reported in relation to developing knowledge, self and market. We have previously linked this concept with career creativities (Bennett 2013) and career literacies (Bennett and Robertson, forthcoming) through the lens of Cook's layered literacies. Through this work, we have argued that, in studenthood, the development of career-positioning creativity is a strategic practice that enables students to identify themselves as professionals and move away from the abstracted notion of success towards individually oriented aspirations and goals. Many students graduate without having begun this process and, as a result, they undergo a period of intense identity uncertainty as they seek to transition into work.

In practical terms, and as seen in the interview narratives, the development of knowledge, self and careers is often undertaken 'on the job' and in a networked form. This was evident from the survey narratives:

> It has taken 13 years so far and I do not think I am 'there yet'!!! And I have learnt that (for me), unlike commercial employment, an arts career is not something I can achieve on my own; all my shifts have been due to collective support. The journey has been expeditionary, and included many people, mainly my writing groups, but also community support through publications, grant funding, and an increasing and broadening recognition that the arts … are an essential component of our social wellbeing and cultural identity.
>
> (Prem, writer)

Table 7.1 Frequency of respondents' most important creative and business needs

Three most urgent creative needs (frequency)

Theme (total count 531)	Count	%
Human capital: peer expertise, assistance	223	42.0
Physical infrastructure: rehearsal, work or exhibition space	193	36.3
Materials and equipment	84	15.8
Time	22	4.1
Career capital: exhibitions, productions, publications	9	1.7

Three most urgent business needs (frequency)

Theme (total count 492)	Count	%
Human capital: administrative support, expertise (e.g. legal, financial and marketing advice), networking opportunities	334	67.9
Office space, materials and equipment	50	10.2
Additional skills in business	48	9.0
Loans and/or funding	39	7.9
Insurance	21	4.3

As part of the questionnaire, respondents identified their three most urgent creative and business needs (Table 7.1). These needs spanned all forms of capital that emerged from our analysis, but we pinpoint here the prevalence of human capital: some 54.5 per cent of all needs. These responses afford a rare insight into the types of learning sought by creative workers, and they have, of course, direct implications for the content of higher education provision in terms of knowing where and how to connect with sources of expertise, how to self-promote and how to access sources of funding.

Career-positioning creativity

The in-depth interviews with the DJ, songwriter and game designer enabled the theme of *career-positioning creativity* to be explored in terms of how it is operationalised within a creative worker's practice. Simon reflected that DJs see themselves as creators of their own unique career paths:

> Being at the top of the game and one of the biggest in the world means you're seen as a celebrity, and getting Grammy nominations is part of that mainstream game. I make my own sound and create my own sort of vibe and that's what I look for and what keeps me excited.
>
> (Simon, DJ)

Career-positioning creativity is also associated with how innovators interact and engage people, as Roshi explained:

> I am extremely proud of the records that we've made … I initially found the process challenging, standing back and listening to the record … I defer to the producer to help me with the mix of elements … I listen to my fans … I know the market … I keep developing my skills and putting new technologies to work … I assert a different cultural interpretation and bring a different cultural voice to the mix.
>
> (Roshi, musician)

Each of Roshi's albums has been successful, but one in particular, *The Sky and the Caspian Sea* (2009), has been recently applauded for 'refusing to be categorised' and for having 'an entrancing otherworldliness and admirable disregard of conventional song form' (Burnard 2012: 95). This uniqueness is Roshi making her mark, winning recognition, establishing a distinctive identity and developing her career.

Kenneth, who works in a games company, reflected that as a graduate with little career preview, he needed to learn how to negotiate the field:

> I knew that I wasn't particularly employable when I finished my undergraduate degree. I didn't have any experience of sound to picture. That's why I did the Masters degree in sound design. I spent a year just learning all that side of things, as well as investing most of my free time finding out as much as I could about interactive audio, the collaborative process of making games, and researching the games industry itself and getting my finger on the pulse of the job market. I was lucky enough to get a job with Sony's London game development studio, pretty much straight out of that Masters degree. It was a junior position … it was an apprenticeship. I was very lucky to work with those people. It was a kind of baptism by fire, but a really great opportunity to just sort of get on and do it. You've got to pick the right company to work for.
>
> (Kenneth, sound engineer)

As a new graduate, Kenneth had little awareness of what the field looked like and what skills and capacities he might need to establish his career. The creative and business needs identified by the 181 survey respondents suggest that Kenneth's concerns are shared by many new graduates, who would benefit from knowing what their intended industry sector looks like, how it works and how they might begin to position themselves within and beyond it. Much of this might be achieved through industry placements, industry-aware educators and curricula that involve students in developing their disposition and capacity to engage as professionals.

Inspiration-forming creativity acts as thematised capital

Inspiration-forming creativity emerges as another important dimension of professional capital creatives because it involves role models, inspirational figures and supporters: significant others who have played a role in creative and business choices. For Simon, one of the most transformative moments of his DJ career was a mashup produced by an admired, established DJ:

> The crowd just went absolutely ballistic because they were hearing these two incredibly well known pieces of music, mashed up and new. This was a really big turning point for me. Since then, I have moved back and forth between taking risks with new ideas and building on existing traditions.
>
> (Simon, DJ)

Roshi is, likewise, known for her ability to move and influence a crowd, but in different ways. Roshi credits her original sound to her encounter with jazz musician Keith Tippett, who ran free improvisation sessions that Roshi described as some of the most 'significant and transforming experiences in … my musical life' (Roshi, musician). Roshi also articulated the significant impact of her family culture, in particular the heritage music of first-generation Iranian parents. These inspirational capitals were credited with uniquely defining her.

Working in the games industry, Kenneth addressed inspirational capital in terms of innovators who had acted as role models and influenced his professional identity:

> The innovation that comes from game developers is how we innovate in the use of technology. It's very exciting to be working with the best in the field, in terms of the hardware you get given. These people are risk takers, driven and inspirational in making interactive entertainment products built to positions that top the game industry. What I have learnt from working in this culture with the best is the back and forth between how to create a fair amount of assets, set the bar, and then give the assets and creative tools to our community who build the games for themselves. It's quite a game.
>
> (Kenneth, sound engineer)

As can be seen, inspirational capital is enacted as drivers and strategies. Drivers play out as a powerful human resource, motivation, passion, direction and personal engagement with a profession. Strategies involve interaction in the networks and professional communities on which artists count to successfully drive these passions forward.

Inspirational capital offers a kind of nirvana for artists: being a professional artist will always have its abiding joys and frustrations, but, over time, the inspirational capital motivates and sustains the creative worker, enabling resilience and creativity to operate. This was clear from the survey responses:

> The number of people involved in theatre at any one time is enormous and encompasses people from all walks of life. The quality that unites us all is that every single one of us, almost without exception, has a passion for the performing arts.
>
> (Mario, theatre director/actor)

Four years ago, I was casting yet another 'corporate' film and the Italian actress put her hand on the script and said, 'Is this what you want to be doing for the rest of your life?' ... I decided I wanted to be more true to my 'vision' and have refocused on personal work.

(Reena, actor)

Bestowed creativity is thematised as a capital that is 'given away' in forms, such as mentorship, pro-bono work and shared knowledge. One established dance artist described how capital is bestowed in networked, reciprocal ways:

As an arts consultant I can assist more creatives/artists and arts orgs and arts groups through my self-employed work ... I offer pro bono or a barter system to assist artists/creative local government as I realise the potential that the [arts] community can bring to people.

(Bo, dance artist)

The DJ's relationship with the profession is distinguished by the particular sounds of 'disc culture' and communicated through dancing and the DJ's performance. The DJ lives in the social space of dancing and dance culture; within this scene, bestowed creativity as 'gift-giving' results from the interaction of music, DJ and crowd. This was evident in DJ Simon's account of his early career:

You spend a lot of time, especially in the first 15 years, going into the record stores several times to shop for imports ... But you have to spend a lot of time listening to a lot of music. This is where the DJs help each other out. We share stuff ... talk for hours about music and particular club cultures.

(Simon, DJ)

Roshi's relationship with Iranian music is 'very much a back and forth between performing individual songs in a different sound world and cultural meaning making' (Roshi, musician). She bestows a type of capital that enables creativity, endowed with cultural meanings and with valued practices, in a space of artistic possibility, where the performance emerges from the actions of all those in her band. As Roshi explains, 'I think the nucleus of what it represents is about creating space in relation to each other; what I'm singing and what we're playing unites us' (Roshi, musician).

Bestowed creativity emerged as a strategic practice that also offers opportunities and supports risks in the application of new technologies. For Kenneth, in the game industry this 'involves working on prototypes that you can show to a publisher and say, "Look, this is an idea, it's nowhere near finished yet, but here's the core concept. Please give us some money to go and make it"' (Kenneth, sound engineer). Here, bestowed creativity is a strategic practice that supports the introduction of new technologies, particularly with the integration of customer views and technological aspirations.

Conclusions and recommendations for future research

Creative industries graduates are known to face a period of identity uncertainty as they attempt, often multiple times, to establish their careers (Bennett and

Bridgstock 2015). This negotiation requires both persistence and resilience, which Buse *et al*. (2009) attribute to five characteristics: self-efficacy, optimism, hope, identity and relational culture. These characteristics are most often seen in workers who have identified their goals and outcomes, and who have explored their salient (personal and professional) identities. However, there is little understanding of how these are acquired.

Our research sought to understand the role of human capital career creativities in enabling creative work and how these might be operationalised within higher education. We identified: (1) the taken-for-granted internalised dispositions that operate in the personal histories (habitus) and social scripting/positioning (capital) of creative workers; (2) the plurality of practices and career-positioning in the subjective vocations they present; and (3) how workers' practices are manifested in the social institutions, industry markets and industry (field) spaces of potential and active forces of professional learning. The research provides important insights into the nature, role and momentum of workers' human capital career creativities and their role in defining successful industry practices.

For creative workers, community capital, in the form of community-building creativity, enables peer learning, shared resources and networked, collaborative forms of employment. Career-positioning capital is built by creating interest, recognition and reputation. It involves creating new markets and opportunities and learning the skills required to access them. Inspiration-forming capital includes role models, figures and supporters who variously endorse, model or directly support creative work. Finally, bestowed creativity, such as mentorship and pro-bono work, serves to strengthen community and career. While bestowed creativity is most often observed within the narratives of established creative workers, it is also evident in the work of early careerists and is an important aspect of graduate work.

The key features of creative workers' professional learning culture manifest in each worker's habitus, the group's habitus and the institutional habitus as the dispositive centres of musical creativities. These align with individual history and to different ways of playing, making, socialising, talking, eating, thinking, acting and knowing one's place, as well as the place of others operating within one's (potential) market. The key features of professional workers' practices are simultaneously positioned in multiple fields – with different capital and habitus – to include a plurality of differently valued and newly recognised, professional capital creativities.

The importance of human capital career creativities to creative workers signals the need for these creativities to be developed within higher education. Specifically, the findings suggest that higher education providers and career support programmes might: (1) visibly position human capital career creativities by exploring these concepts with students and graduates; (2) incentivise student participation in programmes infused with industry practice by working in partnership with industry; (3) provide opportunities for students to interact with sources of inspiration and motivation, including in on-campus and industry-based interaction; and (4) offer post-graduation support as graduates seek to establish their practice.

As evidenced in this volume, creative work is receiving increasing attention from researchers. However, the social practices through which different creativities are recognised and communicated (that is understood within the professional learning cultures) remain under-researched. Future research might consider the alignment between human capital career creativities and employability in terms of how educators might foster students' professional identities along cognitive dimensions with respect to their disposition and capacity to engage as professionals. It might also consider alliances that enable the synthesis of large-scale data sets with empirical studies of creative work, such that graduate work can be better illustrated for students and better understood by policy-makers. While higher education's current emphasis on the functional aspects of employability is a somewhat simplistic alignment with these research needs, it positions them at the forefront of higher education debate.

References

Bennett, D. (2013) 'Creativity beyond the notes: exploring future lives in music to develop self-concept and salient identity', in P. Burnard (ed.), *Developing Creativities in Higher Music Education*. London: Routledge, pp. 234–44.

Bennett, D. and Bridgstock, R. (2015) 'The urgent need for career preview: student expectations and graduate realities in music and dance', *International Journal of Music Education*, 33 (3): 263–77.

Bennett, D. and Robertson, R. (2015) 'Preparing students for diverse careers: developing career literacy with final-year writing students', *Journal of University Teaching and Learning Practice*, 12 (3). Available at: http://ro.uow.edu.au/jutlp/vol12/iss3/5.

Bennett, D., Coates, H., MacKinnon, P., Poronnik, P., Richardson, S., Schmidt, L. and Mahat, M. (2015) *Navigating Uncertainty and Complexity: Higher Education and the Dilemma of Employability*, 2015 Higher Education Research and Development Conference, Melbourne, July, pp. 1–10.

Bennett, D., Coffey, J, Fitzgerald, S, Petocz, P. and Rainnie, A. (2014) 'Beyond the creative: understanding the intersection of specialist and embedded work for creatives in metropolitan Perth', in G. Hearn, R. Bridgstock, B. Goldsmith and J. Rodgers (eds), *Creative Work Beyond the Creative Industries: Innovation, Employment, and Education*. Cheltenham: Edward Elgar, pp. 158–74.

Bourdieu, P. (1979) *La distinction: Critique sociale du jugement*. Paris: Editions de Minuit.

Bourdieu, P. (1986) 'The forms of capital', in J. Richardson (ed.), *Handbook of Theory and Research for the Sociology of Education*. New York: Greenwood, pp. 241–58.

Bourdieu, P. (1993) *The Field of Cultural Production*. Cambridge: Polity.

Bourdieu, P. and Wacquant, L. (1992) *An Invitation to Reflexive Sociology*. Chicago: University of Chicago Press.

Bowman, C. and Swart, J. (2007) 'Whose human capital? The challenge of value when capital is embedded', *Journal of Management Studies*, 44 (4): 488–505.

Burnard, P. (2012) *Musical Creativities in Practice*. Oxford: Oxford University Press.

Burnard, P. (2014) *Developing Creativities in Higher Music Education: International Perspectives and Practices*. London: Routledge.

Burnard, P. and Haddon, E. (2015) *Activating Diverse Musical Creativities, Teaching and Learning in Higher Education*. London: Bloomsbury.

Burnard, P., Hofvander Trulsson, Y. and Soderman, J. (2015) *Bourdieu and the Sociology of Music Education*. Aldershot: Ashgate.

Buse, K., Perelli, S. and Bilimoria, D. (2009) *Why They Stay: The Ideal Selves of Persistent Women Engineers*. Cleveland, OH: Cape Western Reserve University.

Commonwealth of Australia (2013) *A Plan for Australian Jobs: The Australian Government's Industry and Innovation Statement*. Canberra: Department of Industry, Innovation, Science, Research and Tertiary Education.

Cunningham, S. (2013) *Hidden Innovation: Policy, Industry and the Creative Sector*. St Lucia: University of Queensland Press.

Grenfell, M. and James, D. (1998) *Bourdieu and Education: Acts of Practical Theory*. Basingstoke: Falmer Press.

James, D., Biesta, G., Colley, H., Davies, J., Gleeson, D., Hodkinson, P., Maull, W., Postlethwaite, K. and Wahlberg, M. (2007) *Improving Learning Cultures in Further Education*. London: Routledge.

Moore, R. (2008) 'Capital', in M. Grenfell (ed.), *Pierre Bourdieu: Key Concepts*. Stocksfield: Acumen, pp. 101–17.

Oakley, K. (2009) *'Art Works' – Cultural Labour Markets: A Literature Review*. London: Creativity, Culture and Education.

Peck, J. (2005) 'Struggling with the creative class', *International Journal of Urban and Regional Research*, 29 (4): 740–70.

Ragin, C. C. (1994) *Constructing Social Research: The Unity and Diversity of Method*. Newbury Park, CA: Pine Forge Press.

Reay, D. (2015) 'Habitus and the psychosocial: Bourdieu with feelings', *Cambridge Journal of Education*, 45 (1): 9–23.

Reay, D., David, M. E. and Ball, S. J. (2005) *Degrees of Choice: Class, Gender and Race in the Higher Education Choice Process*. Stoke-on-Trent: Trentham Books.

Schmidt, P. (2015) 'The geography of music education: establishing fields of action', in P. Burnard, Y. Hofvander Trulsson and J. Soderman (eds), *Bourdieu and the Sociology of Music Education*. Aldershot: Ashgate, pp. 175–92.

Smith, C. and McKinlay, A. (2009) 'Creative industries and labour process analysis', in A. McKinlay and C. Smith (eds), *Creative Labour: Working in the Creative Industries*. Basingstoke: Palgrave Macmillan, pp. 3–28.

Thomson, P. (2008) 'Field', in M. Grenfell (ed.), *Pierre Bourdieu: Key Concepts*. Stocksfield: Acumen, pp. 67–81.

Part III

Connecting the dots

Arts schools and local art scenes

8 Support or competition? Assessing the role of HEIs in professional networks and local creative communities

The case of glass-making in Sunderland

Lauren England and Roberta Comunian

Introduction

There is a growing interest in the academic literature (Comunian and Gilmore 2015; Comunian *et al.* 2013; Roodhouse 2009) and policy field (DCMS 2006; Universities UK 2010) around the role played by higher education institutions (HEIs) in the creative economy. Within the broader area of investigation, we can find reflections on a range of issues from community and regeneration (Chatterton 1999) to knowledge transfer (Crossick 2006), impact and commercialisation (Hearn *et al.* 2004) to the role played by creative human capital, as highlighted also by Comunian *et al.*'s chapter in this book.

The creative economy (UNCTAD 2008) is an umbrella term which encompasses a range of very different organisations, from private corporations to public sector organisations and not-for-profit activities. It is a sector not only multi-faceted in relation to its needs and practices, but also in reference to the extreme range of sizes of the organisations that can be involved with HEI partnerships: from large private global conglomerates, to large public national institutions, to smaller creative charities, to individual creative sole traders. It is important, therefore, not to generalise the kind of collaborative practices in a sector so diverse. Therefore this chapter aims to reflect on the relationship between higher education and the creative and cultural industries (CCIs), focusing specifically on small cultural and creative producers in the craft sector.

The focus on small cultural and creative producers is particularly important. As Comunian and Gilmore (2015) highlight, there has been a lack of research on the effect of institutional powers on small, independent, creative organisations. Furthermore, because of the networked nature of CCIs (Comunian 2012), the range of networks involved – from social to professional – and their permeability and flexibility beyond institutional barriers, a better understanding of these dynamics is necessary. It also seems important to highlight another shortcoming in the literature – the specific role that HEIs can play in local creative and cultural clusters (Pratt 2004). While a lot of attention has been given to the relationship between places and CCIs (Drake 2003) and the importance of location, networks and collaboration in the development of creative clusters and cultural quarters

(Comunian *et al.* 2010; Comunian 2015), the role played by HEIs has been surprisingly under investigated (Sapsed and Mateos-Garcia 2011).

These issues are particularly relevant for the sector we focus on. Among the creative industries in the UK, the craft sector is one of the least represented and understood sectors because of its size and fragmented nature. This is demonstrated by the debate that took place in 2014 following the proposed exclusion of craft from future DCMS economic estimates (DCMS 2013, 2015) – because of the difficulty of capturing its value. A series of recent publications and research by the Crafts Council (Crafts Council 2014a, 2014b) has engaged with these difficulties and addressed some of these concerns, such as the high number of sole traders in creative occupations rather than standardised industry work (ibid.: 2014a). This not only makes craft occupations hard to measure, but also highlights the limited employment opportunities in the craft sector outside of individual creative practice. Makers in the study also highlighted the difficulty of being categorised as a craft maker or associated with a specialist practice or production style (e.g. glass-blowing), as this increased sector competition and hindered their ability to enter wider art markets. Looking at the craft sector, it is therefore particularly interesting to highlight the dynamics that are common to sole traders, and small creative and cultural practitioners, and their ability to engage with and take advantage of the opportunities that higher education knowledge and infrastructure can offer, both within specialised practice and the wider creative sector.

Using a regional case study – the University of Sunderland (UoS) and its connected infrastructure of the National Glass Centre (NGC) – the chapter explores, in detail, the range of opportunities and interactions that can involve HEIs and small creative producers, like the local glass-makers that cluster in Sunderland and the surrounding area. Within the North East region, there has also been an increased emphasis on the role that universities can play in the local economy (Universities for the North East 2001; Universities UK 2014), although not with particular emphasis on the creative economy.

The chapter builds on the data collected during the summer of 2015, but also on the long-term involvement of the researchers with the local context. It includes in-depth historical desk research, which highlighted the distinct trajectories of glass-making in Sunderland. Multiple visits to the locations relevant to Sunderland glass-making took place during the period of 2007–15 to collect ethnographic accounts during specific events, as well as visits to institutions and local studios. This analysis is mainly based on a collection of 17 interviews, undertaken during the summer of 2015 and conducted with local artists and glass-makers, working independently and in connection with UoS and NCG, as well as experts and students based at the university and gallery to provide a broader overview of the context and development of the sector. A thematic analysis was applied to the interviews to specifically consider the way interviews could articulate the local knowledge dynamics and their connection with higher education.

The chapter is organised in four parts. Firstly, in an overview of the literature, we consider two areas of research and bring them together. We provide a brief review on the role of place in the CCIs literature, with some reflections on networks and co-location (or clustering) dynamics. We then consider the extensive literature on the role of HEIs in the development of knowledge economies and try to bring the two sets of ideas together, introducing a framework to understand the relation between CCIs, HEIs and place. In the second part, we focus on the existing knowledge of crafts as part of the CCIs, and the (underexplored) connection with higher education. Here we also present the case study of the University of Sunderland and the methodology used for data collection. In the third part, we analyse the data using the framework and for each area – soft infrastructure, physical infrastructure, markers and governance – we highlight positive and negative dynamics emerging within the data. Finally, the conclusion presents the supporting and hindering capacities of HEIs within the creative economy, and the need for network inclusivity in order to generate and sustain sector growth. We further conclude that sustaining HEI interaction with creative producers requires a balancing of institutional agenda and policy with the needs of local creative producers, and the creation of open and engaged spaces for collaboration.

CCIs, higher education and localities: a literature review

Creative and cultural industries and place

Many authors have attempted to articulate the complex relationship between CCIs and their location. Here we concentrate specifically on CCIs and places of cultural production, rather than focusing on cultural quarters and museum quarters, usually identified more as places for consumption and entertainment (Mommaas 2004; Mould and Comunian 2015; van Aalst and Boogaarts 2002). Using the framework identified by Comunian *et al.* (2010), it is important to highlight the key connections between place and creative industries in terms of physical infrastructure, soft infrastructure, markets and governance. There are many external factors influencing CCI location and co-location in specific cities or regions. The infrastructure dimension refers to the role played by the built environment (Brown 2013) as well as the built heritage, but also the more generic role played by transport connections and connections with other industries (Harvey *et al.* 2012). Soft infrastructure refers to the role played by networks, sociality and knowledge in the context of creative clusters (Comunian 2012; Grabher 2004; Kong 2005). These soft infrastructures tend to be embedded and idiosyncratic to a specific location and, due to their complex nature, cannot be simply planned or engineered (Comunian 2011). The third key dimension is the role played by (local or connected) markets. While a lot of emphasis is placed on production in creative clusters, the importance of contacts, clients, and customers – as specialised and knowledgeable demand (à la Porter 1990) – plays a key role in helping creatives respond to fast-changing markets (Potts *et al.* 2008) and demand uncertainty (Caves 2000). While there is an acknowledgement that HEIs are part of the creative clusters infrastructure, this is still an area which remains under-investigated in the context of the creative economy; however, if we look at the broader literature on the connection of clusters and higher education – there is much more research looking at the connection between HEIs, clusters and localities in other fields.

Higher education, localities and connections

There is a growing body of literature on the role of universities in the development of regions (Charles 2006; Deiaco *et al.* 2012), and their connections with 'smart specialisation' (Kempton *et al.* 2013) and specialised industries and knowledge. The triple helix theory (Etzkowitz and Leydesdorff 1997), in particular, highlights the importance of the interconnections and exchanges taking place between industry, (local and national) policies, and higher education. This theory has been extensively applied to the study of university–industry relations in the case of science and technology disciplines (Lee 1996). The development of innovation and science parks connected to HEIs have also exemplified the power of clustering and co-location in relation to industry and university relations (Lee 1996; Vedovello 1997). With the growth of the knowledge economy, and the economic value generated by such knowledge, there has been a stronger alignment of universities with the neoliberal agenda (Olssen and Peters 2005) and, with it, the pressure to show the economic value generated via knowledge transfer and the importance of HEIs as drivers of new forms of entrepreneurialism (Etzkowitz 2004).

It is clear with the broader economic development arguments that HEIs play a key role in supporting both start-ups and existing industries, leading to wider externalities and benefits for the localities they are engaged with (Goddard and Vallance 2013). Recent research has looked at the application of the 'triple helix' theory to the CCIs and arts and humanities departments (Comunian *et al.* 2014; Powell 2007); however, it is clear – compared with the extensive research undertaken within the science and technology field – that more emphasis needs to be placed on understanding the connections between localities, HEIs and the CCIs.

A framework for HEIs' interconnection with CCIs

Going beyond the acknowledged connections between CCIs and HEIs in a given geographical context, it is important to explore in more detail what kind of dynamics, interdependencies and collaboration take place at the local level. It is important first of all to consider that while it seems obvious to think about the advantages that CCIs can derive from working with, or co-locating nearby, HEIs with specific specialised knowledge, there is also a strong interdependency taking place in the opposite direction. In particular, we know from Comunian and Faggian (2014) that the presence of local systems of cultural production (and the possible work opportunities they create in a specific locality) can attract students to specific courses and localities. We now use the framework of Comunian *et al.* (2010) introduced earlier to explore these dynamics in CCI and HEI connections in more detail (see Figure 8.1). If we focus on *physical infrastructure*, it is easy to see the interconnection between CCIs and HEIs. Especially for independent cultural producers

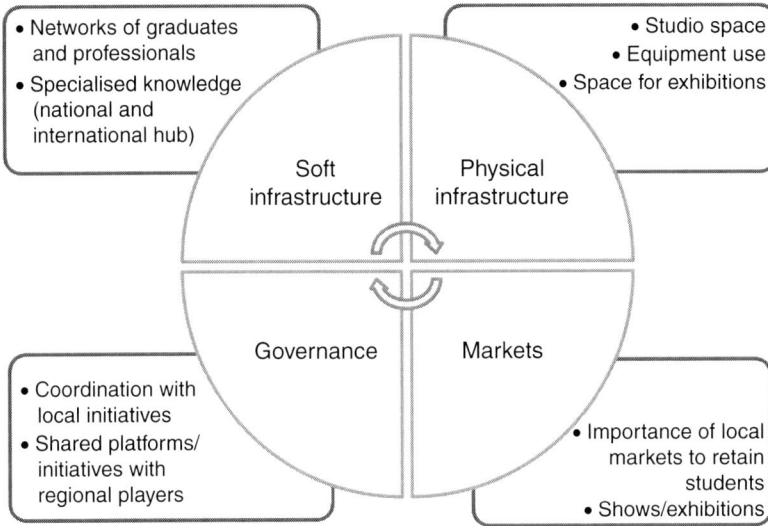

Figure 8.1 A framework for the interconnections between higher education institutions and creative and cultural industries

and small sole traders, HEIs offer many opportunities to access broader infrastructure. In particular, HEIs try to offer their graduates, or associated companies, opportunities for (cheap or free) studio space. For some, especially disciplines which require expensive and specialised equipment – for example, recording studios or laser-cutting equipment – the opportunity for external companies to rent spaces or share the costs of using these facilities can provide a lifeline. HEIs also can provide infrastructure in reference to space for exhibition or conferences. While HEIs tend to have more facilities and infrastructure-type of opportunities, in the case of small CCIs, sometimes clusters can also offer specialised infrastructure for the university to benefit from, as in the case of Bath Spa University space within 'Paintworks' in Bristol introduced by Ashton in this book.

Soft infrastructure covers a range of activities and opportunities, from networks and knowledge sharing to co-creation. These sometimes seem to be less valued within HEIs – apart from the increased emphasis on impact brought in by the last Research Excellence Framework (REF) – but are often of greater relevance when developed within the context of creative and cultural production, as this is deemed much more market and industry relevant. In reference to knowledge development, HEIs are benefiting from a range of opportunities to engage with CCIs, as in the case of the 'creative voucher' scheme described by Virani and Pratt in Chapter 3 of this book. However, CCIs also play a very important role by providing access to local professional networks to students or graduates. This is particularly important for the retention of graduates (Comunian and Faggian 2014) and for students to have access to placement, internships and other opportunities.

The importance of *markets* in the interconnection between CCIs and HEIs is probably less explored and less obvious. However, graduate retention and the opportunity to help develop and foster local clusters only becomes sustainable if HEIs remain aware of the role that the markets – with the sophisticated demand (à la Porter 1990) and specialised interests – can play in that specific sector. For example, support for fairs and exhibitions, or funding for alumni to attend international trade events, play a key role in supporting local start-ups, as well as HEI recognition within the sector. Similarly, universities, with their intention to give students experiences or engage with markets, might sometime hinder or discourage growth. This is the case where students offering free consultancy services, or able to work for free when they are still studying, might actually create dynamics of unfair competition within the local system.

Finally, the main role of HEIs in CCIs and creative cluster development seems to be about *governance* and coordination. HEIs often have the infrastructure and also the knowledge and connections to be able to establish connections between local policy for industry and urban development as well as industry, local communities and other third-sector players (for example, galleries, museums, festivals, etc.). HEIs, despite the recent neoliberal turn (Canaan and Shumar 2008), still seem to be considered by many local policy-makers, industry stakeholders and alumni as neutral agents or intermediaries, not driven by private interest but the greater (local) good and, therefore, are looked to as the ideal intermediaries and brokers of local development. While this is an important role that can be played by HEIs, it is also one that is often ignored in favour of focusing on specific HE issues, rather than the broader local and community development agenda (Benneworth and Jongbloed 2010). The result is that while investments and opportunities within universities might look like they could have broader positive externalities for local contexts, the disconnectedness and weak networks limit the reach and impact of these effects (Comunian and Mould 2014). Continuous student recruitment – led by a neoliberal model that follows demand – can lead to the ongoing production of creative graduates destined for oversubscribed (Banks and Hesmondhalgh 2009) or precarious (Gill and Pratt 2008) labour markets. This might also evidence a lack of market awareness and local engagement, as highlighted in the case of Australia in Chapter 13 by Brook in this book.

Researching the craft sector and the role of higher education

While there has been a growing interest recently in better understanding the role of craft in the creative industries and its connection with the broader economy, the role played by HEIs in the sector is under-researched. Research on craft in the UK has tended to focus on mapping and estimating contribution to local and regional economies, while emphasising the difficulties in doing so due to the size and fragmented nature of the sector (Crafts Council 2014a). This instigated a lively debate at the policy level, after initial suggestion in a DCMS consultation document that Craft should be dropped by the current economic estimate exercise.[1] This triggered broader research from the Crafts Council on the value of the craft sector, but very little research is available on the role of clustering for the sector in the UK, apart from an acknowledgement of its link with rural and regional economies (Bell and Jayne 2010; Gibson *et al.* 2002). Specific emphasis is also placed in the literature on the role that craft producers have in bridging local economies with potential international and global links, because of their highly independent and unique nature (Fillis 2004). Linked to the development and potential of craft, there has also been an interest in better understanding the development of craft careers and their relation to livelihoods (Blackwell and Harvey 1999; McAuley and Fillis 2005). While the role of clustering is acknowledged in the literature on craft industries and small producers (Thomas *et al.* 2013), with specific concentrations in the South West of England[2] (Harvey *et al.* 2012), very little is known about their connection with education and specialised higher education provision. However, interestingly, Comunian *et al.* (2011) found the highest concentration of craft graduates, as well as craft courses, to be in the South West regions, suggesting a certain degree of co-location and connection between the two spheres.

Within craft, in this chapter, we focus specifically on glass-making. As with many other sectors within craft, in glass-making there is recognition of how the value of craft labour is depicted often against the creative potential of artistic labour (Banks 2010: 312), with the craft person often reduced to 'a mere producer who inhabits only a mundane world of tools and technique'. These issues are very much present in the glass sector, with a range of perspectives from glass-makers to glass artists inhabiting the landscape of work in a fluid manner. Glass-making, both as an industry sector and as a creative and artistic practice of production, is under-researched, but it is definitely acknowledged that historically it has always been a highly clustered activity across Europe (Godfrey 1975; Segre and Russo 2005). The specific development of glass-making in Sunderland exemplifies perfectly a mix of raw materials, access to transport and labour possibility to distribute the products internationally (see a more historical analysis in the next section). As with many manufacturing processes, the opening up of new markets internationally offering cheaper labour and manufacturing conditions (especially in Eastern Europe and later in East Asia) meant a slow but constant collapse of UK production from the 1970s to the end of the twentieth century. The development of clusters of artistic production in Sunderland highlights a shift towards a post-industrial symbolic and artistic production of glass, as part of a specialised, flexible production development (Storper and Scott 1990).

Glass-making in Sunderland: networks and education

Glass-making in Sunderland dates back to the seventh century and formed the 'basis of the explosion of high quality glass produced in the region from the start of the Industrial Revolution to the latter part of the twenty-first century' (Swan 2002: 3). This success was attributed to three main factors: coal, sand and exports, enabling cheap access to furnace fuel, raw materials and exportation (NGC 2015). However, the factors that enabled the growth and success of the region's glass industry also led to its demise at the end of the nineteenth century. The end of glass manufacturing in Sunderland was marked by the closure of James A. Jobling & Co. in 2007.

A lack of regional professional craft activity in the 1970s inspired the development of support networks for craft makers, resulting in the creation of the first specialist undergraduate degree in glass in 1982 (Davies 2007) at Sunderland Polytechnic, now UoS, and the establishment of the International Institute for Research in Glass in 1988 (Swan 2002). Today, UoS is the largest of its kind in Europe (Davies 2007), hosting the largest number of academic researchers in glass in the UK (Petrova 2010). It is also one of the few remaining providers of higher education programmes in glass in the UK following a spate of closures in 2010 due to high running costs (ibid.). Alongside the UoS campus, the National Glass Centre (NGC) opened to the public in 1998, built to 'showcase the city's link to the creation and production of glass over the centuries' (Short and Tetlow 2012: 283).

Outside of UoS, formal artist groupings, such as Cohesion, Lime Street (Newcastle) and Designed & Made (Newcastle), have been influential in maintaining the glass-making community by assisting and supporting business and practitioners (ibid.). The Cohesion Glass Network, which was founded in 2000 as a City of Sunderland initiative, was unique to the region as a specialist glass group. Cohesion was a network of practising artists from across the UK for and through which exhibitions, workshops and career development opportunities were organised. A once thriving network, it folded in 2010–11, continuing as Creative Cohesion studios that house a variety of visual arts, although the national element of the network has been lost. Despite the efforts of remaining members of Creative Cohesion, lack of available funding and their geographical location have proved significant barriers to the regeneration of the network.

Today, the North East is home to the largest number of glass-makers in the UK, nearly all of whom have a connection with UoS (Davies 2007). However, Sunderland's local economy has shifted to the automotive and software industries (Sunderland City Council 2010) and glass-making activity outside of UoS is limited. Nevertheless, UoS has seen an increase in student numbers on their glass and ceramics programmes. In particular, there has been a significant increase in independent artists applying for PhD grants as an alternative method of funding their practice. This suggests that in the current economic climate, the university plays a crucial role in continuing glass-making in Sunderland and the North East as the largest provider of educational and professional opportunities in the region.

Higher education and local CCIs: support or competition?

The analysis of our data was organised using the framework identified in Figure 8.1 to facilitate the understanding of the multiple (sometimes overlapping) issues in a structured way. Within each dimension, we identify the positive and reinforcing relations between higher education and the local glass-makers, as well as the difficulties or contradictions that interviewees highlighted.

Soft infrastructure: knowledge networks and exclusive networks

As mentioned, HEIs can act as network hubs bringing students, academics, practising artists and curators together under one roof, particularly through conferences and links with wider network associations, drawing both from their own connections and the wider international networks of resident artists/academics. The addition of the gallery setting also facilitates network connections between staff, students and academics and exhibition artists on an international scale.

Access to specialist knowledge and potential knowledge transfer (within and outside of the university) is also a key feature of HEI networks. In this context, knowledge is stored, in particular, within the artist/academics, research students and technical staff at the university, who are often experts within their field. Visiting artists and residency programmes also enable the flow of new knowledge in and out of the institution. Access to this knowledge is especially important for students: during education, the HEI enables the transfer of skills from staff to student; post-graduation the connections made with staff and visiting artists are used for support and access to opportunities – exhibitions, residencies etc. – and knowledge, both technical and business. The skills transfer, therefore, encourages the continuation of specialist practices and perpetuates the generation of creative human capital within graduates.

In the case of UoS and NGC, specialised industrial knowledge is also found in the resident lampworking company and NGC hot-shop team, many of whom trained in Sunderland's now extinct glass-making factories. The ability of the university to employ or house people with these technical skills enables the continuation of practices and the retention of tacit and/or embodied knowledge that may otherwise disappear. However, in addition to traditional and industrial glass-making skills (glass-blowing factory, scientific and artistic skills and kiln casting), modern technology capabilities are also stored within HEIs (for example, water-jet cutting and CAD/CAM processes).

> Without that history, none of this would probably be here and therefore glass-making probably wouldn't have been continued. Most of the skills probably would have been lost. At least you know within this building people are still learning these skills and they are still within the country.
>
> (Interview with glass artist)

In contrast to the potential support offered by HEI network inclusion, limitations and issues of exclusivity were highlighted. Firstly, as a national centre, the need for recognition within the wider glass and visual arts community is integral to the future development and success of the institution, in order to avoid organisational irrelevance or stagnation (Visser and Boschma 2004). However, this can cause tensions particularly between the institution and local (non-institutionally based) artists regarding the distribution of resources and opportunities, in that the institution is seen as 'inward looking'.

> It's a bit of a balance, supporting the people who've come up through the system the traditional way through glass and ceramic courses but also ensuring that glass

has its wider place in the visual arts and that there's different influences coming into glass … and that's not to say in any way that I think the glass scene is stagnated … but for a number of reasons it's quite important to keep networks wide.

(Interview with curator)

It has also been noted that the knowledge held by the university in its academics and staff is increasingly institutionalised. This influences the type of knowledge produced and disseminated and limits their ability to inform graduates of the skills needed to develop businesses as independent practising artists due to a lack of relevant knowledge and the institutionalisation of graduates' networks. This is in a sense mitigated by residency programmes bringing practising artists into the university and the presence of artist/academics that also run their own creative businesses. However, the degree of interaction and knowledge exchange in this area of specialty is currently undetermined.

HEIs and (physical) infrastructure for creative producers

The physical infrastructure of HEIs – studio and exhibition spaces, equipment and material resources, and their availability for hire – provides a support mechanism for creative producers in a challenging economic environment. This is further encouraged by the access to expert technicians within the institution that enables a wider scope of non-specialist creative production. As HEI departments operate on a large scale and have access to different funding sources than independent makers and arts organisations, their ability to support creative production, train students, employ artists and exhibit their work is significantly greater than the capabilities of sole traders, micro businesses or small-scale charities (e.g. Creative Cohesion) in the creative sector.

Access to technologically advanced (and expensive) equipment is also a key benefit of HEI physical infrastructure for creative producers. In addition to equipment like the water-jet cutter, universities, including UoS, are becoming more involved in the development of a FabLabs, piloted by MIT, designed to facilitate creative entrepreneurship.

> […] the accessibility to other students, like the MAs and PhD students, their programme of visiting artists and their connection with the Glass Centre. Following its refurbishment with the, you know, the gallery they've got now and the rolling programme of exhibitions was just um, was great really to have on your doorstep.
>
> (Interview with glass student)

> I think the direction of the glass industry has been undecided. I think it probably, because of the expense of glassblowing and kiln casting, probably sits a lot more alongside modern technology, the water-jet cutter and 3D printing and that sort of thing is probably the direction it will have to end up going in, maybe. So actually having access to that kind of machinery will be fundamental.
>
> (Interview with glass artist)

On the other hand, the rising commercialisation of HEIs (Slaughter and Rhoades 2004) has had a detrimental impact on local creative producers. Although low rental rates for the institution's incubator spaces are available to recent graduates, other makers have been 'priced out' following the amalgamation of UoS and NGC in 2010, resulting in perpetually empty and unused units. The rise in studio rental can be seen as an impact of increased market pressures exerted on both HEIs and cultural organisations. Furthermore, it appears that once outside of the protection of the institution, graduates are seemingly unable to sustain their creative practice due to a lack of resources or local infrastructure.

> Look at the graduate retention. How many glass-makers stay in Sunderland to run their businesses? I know that the NGC has some incubator units. I also know that when the university took over, those, the tenants in those incubator units then had to move out.
>
> (Interview with glass artist)

The lack of local or regional infrastructure (soft and physical) outside of HEIs can be closely linked to geographical location: Sunderland has a low tourist economy (which often drives the craft in specific localities) and only 1.6 per cent of the UK's crafts makers are located within the North East (Crafts Council, Creative Scotland and Craft Northern Ireland 2012). Craft markets, domestic and tourist, are heavily influenced by the value of 'place' and local authenticity (Brown 2014; Morris Hargreaves McIntyre 2010), and many makers associated the lack of funding and support initiatives, or the limited activity of those in action (Creative Cohesion), with a lack of public and national interest in the locality. However, it was stated that the institution also feels this keenly, linking back to their concerted effort to improve their status within the national and international field to the detriment of their local community. The lack of physical and soft infrastructure also has a negative impact on the maintenance and development of the local and regional creative economy, in that it limits the potential for local market visibility and development through the showcasing of local creative talent (Brown 2014).

> What we're trying to do or have tried to do with Creative Cohesion is all weakened by certain forces making it tricky to do anything, a lack of interest in where we're based and money, it's always money, and lack thereof.
>
> (Interview with glass artist)

Markets: cooperation or competition between HEIs and creative producers

Evidence suggests that the continued expansion of creative education programmes at undergraduate, postgraduate and research levels increases involvement in smaller creative industry sectors (e.g. craft) and can, to an extent, drive the regional creative economy (Davies 2007). In particular, the role of the UoS in producing glass graduates is increasingly significant today, in light of continued course closures and the loss of specialist glass programmes across the country. This high-lights the importance of those HEIs with specialist facilities in the training of creative practitioners, the continuation of professional practices within niche areas of creative production and the maintenance of local market structures. Furthermore, through investment in modernised equipment, new technologies and creative human capital the institution is able to support sector innovation and the market-place competitiveness of practitioners by facilitating the development and diver-sification of their practice, a capacity that is vital in order to maintain craft as a professional occupation (CC Skills and Crafts Council 2009; Brown 2014).

On the other hand, it can be argued that continually generating graduates from these programmes does not support growth within the (local) creative economy, as many graduates turn to portfolio working or full-time non-creative employ-ment in order to support their practice on a part-time/casual basis (Ball *et al.* 2010) rather than forming sustainable creative businesses. This highlights the need to make sure the universities educate and employ people who have 'market awareness' (Ball 2003).

It was suggested that the lack of necessary soft and hard infrastructure to support creative producers, particularly early graduates and emerging artists, outside of the institution results in a reduction of the creative economy through loss of practitioners. In these circumstances, many creatives struggling to main-tain their practice post-graduation have moved to other regional cities or further afield where more support for creative businesses is available, rather than compete with the institution for the already limited pool of local opportunities and commercial contracts. The lack of infrastructure and loss of practitioners creates a self-perpetuating dampening of the local glass economy, but also reinforces the position of the university.

> What I now observe is that a lot of students graduate and in order to keep a roof over their head and feed themselves, they get a job. And then the glassmaking is just done purely part-time, maybe working at weekends and doing craft fairs … whether they ever move beyond that model or not, I don't know.
>
> (Interview with glass artist)

Although the institution does contribute to the local economy through employ-ment and infrastructure, the growing institutional dominance of an already limited market for glass drives a greater divide between HEIs and creative producers. Problems arise particularly when institutions 'undercut local makers', including graduates of the university, through their access to greater and cheaper resources. This is a growing issue compounded by the increasing cost of creative production materials, studio/facilities hire, energy and shipping costs, which is felt keenly in glass-making as an energy-intensive practice.

> How do I put this delicately? Um, every contract, big contract that comes in for a glass commission generally goes to the Glass Centre. And they have the resources to undercut prices and they have undercut local glass-makers in the

past to get contracts. So if you are a glass-maker working commercial work, um, you are working in competition with the National Glass Centre at the end of the day, and IKEA!

(Interview with glass artist)

Governance: importance of the 'triple helix' and balance of power

As with many other examples of collaboration and interaction between higher education and the creative economy, the role of the locality – including public policy at different geographical levels – is highly important. This is highlighted specifically by the 'triple helix' theory (Etzkowitz and Leydesdorff 1997) that considers the importance of a concerted dialogue between industry, policy and education.

The role of locality is particularly prominent in the case of glass-making in Sunderland and looking back, we can see signs of strong triple helix partnerships and dialogues between those in policy, industry and education. First and foremost, the region's glass-making heritage was key to the development of Sunderland's glass education programme and the reason public funding was made available for the construction of the NGC, showing a clear policy–industry dialogue. The educational link came later with the university's purchase of the NGC in 2010. Outside of that, the development of Cohesion Glass Network by the city council, originally intended as a regional project although it quickly went national, shows a clear link between policy and industry.

However, shifts in local council interest towards automotive manufacture and software, combined with higher public interest in cultural regeneration projects for Newcastle-Gateshead (2000) over Sunderland, have limited support for arts and culture in Sunderland. The recent economic recession has also caused local authorities to tighten their belts, further restricting publicly funded development opportunities in the creative economy. There has, however, been a recent move to develop Sunderland as a city of culture (Sunderland Cultural Partnership 2014), which may improve local support infrastructure outside of the university and encourage the retention of creative human capital.

The decision for the UoS to take over the NGC can be seen partly as a means of ensuring the continuation of the organisation and future of the glass industry in its new format of individual creative production. While the acquisition was followed by a £2.25 million capital investment from the Arts Council and Heritage Lottery in particular, indicating a continued policy dialogue with the HEI and industry representatives, it highlights the pre-existing issues with governance and dialogue in the local cluster that could be read as a failure of policy to support diminishing local glass production outside of the institution.

I sometimes think that that's where the NGC has fallen down, in that it has tried to be 'well we're going to do what we're going to do without regard to anybody else' and I think if there had been a bit more interaction and a bit more interconnection with what's going on in the region, and indeed elsewhere in Sunderland, they might have been shored up a bit against these financial difficulties they've had over the years.

(Interview, policy-maker Sunderland)

Although the dialogue is sustained between education and policy through Arts Council funding of the NGC and connections between UoS and the Crafts Council, the lack of engagement with external local industry (in its marginal existence) marks a disconnect between the three areas, particularly education and industry. This limits the development of triple helix collaboration which in turn has a negative knock-on effect on the already depleted creative economy for glass in the region.

Conclusions

This chapter has reflected on the role that HEIs play in supporting and enabling the development of local creative industries clusters. Using the case study of glass-making in Sunderland, we consider the advantages and disadvantages that emerge from the coming together of industry, policy and higher education in the local creative economy. Using the framework of Comunian *et al.* (2010), we highlighted how the connection between HEIs and local creative producers can be classified as linked to physical infrastructure, soft infrastructure, markets and governance. While there is some research on the connection of physical and soft infrastructure opportunities, less is acknowledged in reference to the importance of universities engaging with local markets and governance of local creative clusters.

In particular, our findings highlight that while co-location and collaboration might take place within a local creative cluster and HEIs can play an important role in supporting local independent creative producers, HEIs can also hinder this development or increase competition. In particular, while HEIs are not particularly engaging with local markets, they often have the power to weaken them when their students and facilities enter the market with unfair advantages. Furthermore, the fact that students and employees are sheltered by the reality of the glass-making industry via funding and free/supported infrastructure can create an even greater issue when those graduates need to face the reality of supporting their own practice within the real market. Furthermore, HEIs have a role to play in educating local communities and increasing the appreciation (and potential markets) for glass and the inclusion of NGC within the UoS should enable this gap to be bridged.

While HEIs do support local producers to an extent through graduate studio rates, gallery/shop sales and enterprise support centres, networks will often have an exclusive nature and benefit those who have established relations more than people who might come from the outside and could expand the knowledge and innovation stock of the locality. The university also endeavours to encourage Sunderland's craft economy through investment in large-scale exhibitions, national and international projects and the delivery of public glass-making workshops.

Currently, however, these efforts remain largely institutionalised and for the benefit of the university, although recent local council initiatives to improve engagement between the university and the city's cultural economy (Sunderland City Council 2010; Sunderland Cultural Partnership 2014) may influence future engagement and support mechanisms.

Finally, in terms of governance, locality is clearly a dominant influence on glass-making in Sunderland, holding both advantages and disadvantages for market actors (creative producers and HEIs). While regional industrial heritage may have kick-started the regeneration of Sunderland's glass and wider creative economy, its ability to be sustained and supported demands an acknowledgment of the needs of those creative producers working both within and outside the four walls of the institution. Following the merging of the NGC with the UoS, the potential healthy 'triple helix' that could have been developed locally across industry–policy and higher education is now very unbalanced, with local producers suffering from decreased public investment in the local and regional creative economy and a large and powerful pole within the UoS. The risk that the network and context might become strongly self-referential and subject to lock-ins (Visser and Boschma 2004) needs to be addressed, and building open and engaged spaces where creative practitioners, local communities and university staff can come together to discuss and share knowledge and expertise needs to remain a priority.

Notes

1. 'Most crafts businesses are too small to identify in business survey data, so while there has been a crafts section in the former classification, we've not been able to provide GVA data. [...] We believe that many crafts workers are very clearly in creative occupations. However, in the official classifications, many of these workers are spread across a range of occupational and industrial codes which contain vastly greater numbers of obviously non-creative workers' (DCMS 2013).
2. This concentration may be due to the extensive crafting history of the South West, ties to eminent figures such as Leach, Hepworth and Nicolson, and the founding of twentieth-century schools of crafting, and is supported today by craft centres (Dartington Hall/Totnes, Devon Guild of Craftsmen) and universities such as Falmouth with active R&D centres and cutting-edge craft education, although the closure of Falmouth's contemporary crafts programme, announced in 2014, may have a significant impact on future craft education in the region.

References

Ball, L. (2003) *Future Directions for Employability Research in the Creative Industries*. Available at: http://www.adm.heacademy.ac.uk/resources/resources-by-topic/employability/future-directions-for-employability-research-in-the-creative-industries (accessed 12 May 2009).

Ball, L., Pollard, E. and Stanley, N. (2010) *Creative Graduates, Creative Futures*. London: Creative Graduates Creative Futures Higher Education Partnership and the Institute for Employment Studies.

Banks, M. (2010) 'Craft labour and creative industries', *International Journal of Cultural Policy*, 16 (3): 305–21.

Banks, M. and Hesmondhalgh, D. (2009) 'Looking for work in the creative industries policy', *International Journal of Cultural Policy*, 15 (4): 415–30.

Bell, D. and Jayne, M. (2010) 'The creative countryside: policy and practice in the UK rural cultural economy', *Journal of Rural Studies*, 26 (3): 209–18.

Benneworth, P. and Jongbloed, B. W. (2010) 'Who matters to universities? A stakeholder perspective on humanities, arts and social sciences valorisation', *Higher Education*, 59 (5): 567–88.

Blackwell, A. and Harvey, L. (1999) *Destinations and Reflections: Careers of British Art, Craft and Design Graduates*. Birmingham: Centre for Research into Quality, UCE. Available at: http://www0.bcu.ac.uk/crq/publications/dr/drexec.html (last accessed 2 May 2009).

Brown, J. (2014) *Making It Local: What Does This Mean in the Context of Contemporary Craft?* London: Crafts Council.

Brown, R. (2013) *Creative Factories: Hackney Wick and Fish Island*. London: London Legacy Development Corporation.

Canaan, J. E. and Shumar, W. (2008) *Structure and Agency in the Neoliberal University*. New York: Routledge.

Caves, R. E. (2000) *Creative Industries, Contracts Between Art and Commerce*. Cambridge, MA: Harvard University Press.

Charles, D. (2006) 'Universities as key knowledge infrastructure in regional innovation systems', *Innovation*, 19 (1): 117–30.

Chatterton, P. (1999) 'The cultural role of universities in the community: reivisiting the university–community debate', *Environment and Planning A*, 32: 165–81.

Comunian, R. (2011) 'Rethinking the creative city: the role of complexity, networks and interactions in the urban creative economy', *Urban Studies*, 48 (6): 1157–79.

Comunian, R. (2012) 'Exploring the role of networks in the creative economy of North East England: economic and cultural dynamics', in B. Warf (ed.), *Encounters and Engagement Between Economic and Cultural Geography*. The Netherlands: Springer, pp. 143–57.

Comunian, R. and Faggian, A. (2014) 'Creative graduates and creative cities: exploring the geography of creative education in the UK', *International Journal of Cultural and Creative Industries*, 1 (2): 19–34.

Comunian, R. and Gilmore, A. (2015) *Beyond the Creative Campus: Reflections on the Evolving Relationship Between Higher Education and the Creative Economy*. London: King's College London. Available at: http://www.creative-campus.org.uk.

Comunian, R. and Mould, O. (2014) 'The weakest link: creative industries, flagship cultural projects and regeneration', *City, Culture and Society*, 5 (2): 65–74.

Comunian, R., Chapain, C. and Clifton, N. (2010) 'Location, location, location: exploring the complex relationship between creative industries and place', *Creative Industries Journal*, 3 (1): 5–10.

Comunian, R., Faggian, A. and Jewell, S. (2011) 'Winning and losing in the creative industries: an analysis of creative graduates' career opportunities across creative disciplines', *Cultural Trends*, 20 (3/4): 291–308.

Comunian, R., Taylor, C. and Smith, D. N. (2014) 'The role of universities in the regional creative economies of the UK: hidden protagonists and the challenge of knowledge transfer', *European Planning Studies*, 22 (12): 2456–76.

Crafts Council (2014a) *Measuring the Craft Economy: Defining and Measuring Craft*, Report 3. London: Crafts Council.

Crafts Council (2014b) *Studying Craft 2: Data Workbook 2*. London: Crafts Council.

Crafts Council Creative Scotland and Craft Northern Ireland (2012) *Craft in an Age of Change*. London: Crafts Council.

Creative and Cultural Skills and Crafts Council (2009) *The Craft Blueprint. A Workforce Development Plan for Craft in the UK*. London: Crafts Council.

Crossick, G. (2006) *Knowledge Transfer Without Widgets: The Challenge of the Creative Economy*. Paper presented at the Lecture, Royal Society of Arts, Goldsmiths University of London, London.

Davies, P. (2007) *Glass North East*. Sunderland: University of Sunderland Reg Vardy Gallery.

DCMS (2006) *Making the Case for Public Investment: Developing Entrepreneuriship for the Creative Industries – The Role of Higher Education*. London: DCMS.

DCMS (2013) *Classifying and Measuring the Creative Industries. Consultation on Proposed Changes*. London: Department for Culture, Media and Sport.

DCMS (2015) *Creative Industries Economic Estimates*. London: DCMS.

Deiaco, E., Hughes, A. and McKelvey, M. (2012) 'Universities as strategic actors in the knowledge economy', *Cambridge Journal of Economics*, 36 (3): 525–41.

Drake, G. (2003) '"This place gives me space": place and creativity in the creative industries', *Geoforum*, 34 (4): 511–24.

Etzkowitz, H. (2004) 'The evolution of the entrepreneurial university', *International Journal of Technology and Globalisation*, 1 (1): 64–77.

Etzkowitz, H. and Leydesdorff, L. (eds) (1997) *Universities and the Global Knowledge Economy: A Triple Helix of University–Industry–Government Relations*. London: Pinter.

Fillis, I. (2004) 'The internationalizing smaller craft firm: insights from the marketing/ entrepreneurship interface', *International Small Business Journal*, 22 (1): 57–82.

Gibson, C., Murphy, P. and Freestone, R. (2002) 'Employment and socio-spatial relationships in Australia's cultural economy', *Australian Geographer*, 33 (2): 173–89.

Gill, R. and Pratt, A. (2008) 'In the social factory? Immaterial labour, precariousness and cultural work', *Theory, Culture and Society*, 25 (7–8): 1–30.

Goddard, J. and Vallance, P. (2013) *The University and the City*. Abingdon: Routledge.

Godfrey, E. S. (1975) *The Development of English Glass-making 1560–1640*. Oxford: Clarendon Press.

Grabher, G. (2004) 'Learning in projects, remembering in networks? Communality, sociality and connectivity in project ecologies', *European Urban and Regional Studies*, 11 (2): 99–119.

Harvey, D. C., Hawkins, H. and Thomas, N. J. (2012) 'Thinking creative clusters beyond the city: people, places and networks', *Geoforum*, 43 (3): 529–39.

Hearn, G., Cunningham, S. and Ordoñez, D. (2004) 'Commercialisation of knowledge in universities: the case of the creative industries', *Prometheus*, 22 (2): 189–200.

Kempton, L., Goddard, J., Edwards, J., Hegyi, F. B. and Elena-Pérez, S. (2013) *Universities and Smart Specialisation*, S3 Policy Brief Series. Newcastle upon Tyne: Centre for Urban and Regional Development Studies (CURDS), Newcastle University.

Kong, L. (2005) 'The sociality of cultural industries', *International Journal of Cultural Policy*, 11: 61–76.

Lee, Y. S. (1996) '"Technology transfer" and the research university: a search for the boundaries of university–industry collaboration', *Research Policy*, 25 (6): 843–63.

McAuley, A. and Fillis, I. (2005) 'Careers and lifestyles of craft makers in the 21st century', *Cultural Trends*, 14 (2): 139–56.

Mommaas, H. (2004) 'Cultural clusters and post-industrial city: towards the remapping of urban cultural policy', *Urban Studies*, 41 (3): 507–32.

Morris Hargreaves McIntyre (2010) *Consuming Craft: The Contemporary Craft Market in a Changing Economy*. London: Crafts Council.

Mould, O. and Comunian, R. (2015) 'Hung, drawn and cultural quartered: rethinking cultural quarter development policy in the UK', *European Planning Studies*, 23 (12): 2356–69.

National Glass Centre (2015) *Stories of Glass in Sunderland: Exhibition Guide*. Sunderland: National Glass Centre.

Olssen, M. and Peters, M. A. (2005) 'Neoliberalism, higher education and the knowledge economy: from the free market to knowledge capitalism', *Journal of Education Policy*, 20 (3): 313–45.

Petrova, S. (2010) 'Context, content and relevance', in M. King, C. E. Greer and J. Hunt (eds), *British Glass Biennale 2010*. Stourbridge: International Festival of Glass, pp. 9–12.

Porter, M. E. (1990) 'The competitive advantage of nations', *Harvard Business Review*, 68 (2): 73–93.

Potts, J., Cunningham, S., Hartley, J. and Ormerod, P. (2008) 'Social network markets: a new definition of the creative industries', *Journal of Cultural Economics*, 32 (3): 167–85.

Powell, J. (2007) 'Creative universities and their creative city-regions', *Industry and Higher Education*, 21 (6): 323–35.

Pratt, A. C. (2004) 'Creative clusters: towards the governance of the creative industries production system?', *Media International Australia*, 112: 50–66.

Roodhouse, S. (2009) 'Universities and the creative industries', *Journal of Arts, Management, Law and Society*, 39 (3): 187–99.

Sapsed, J. and Mateos-Garcia, J. (2011) 'The role of universities in enhancing creative clustering', *Brighton Fuse: Enhancing the Creative, Digital and Information Technology Industries (CDIT) in Brighton*. CENTRIM, University of Brighton.

Segre, G. and Russo, A. P. (2005) 'Collective property rights for glass manufacturing in Murano: where culture makes or breaks local economic development', *Università di Torino*, Working Paper No. 5.

Short, M. and Tetlow, M. (2012) 'City profile: Sunderland', *Cities: The International Journal of Urban Policy and Planning*, 29 (4): 278–88.

Slaughter, S. and Rhoades, G. (2004) *Academic Capitalism and the New Economy: Markets, State, and Higher Education*. Baltimore, MD: JHU Press.

Storper, M. and Scott, A. J. (1990) 'Work organisation and local labour markets in an era of flexible production', *International Labour Review*, 129: 573.

Sunderland City Council (2010) *Smart and Sustainable: The Sunderland Economic Masterplan*. Sunderland: Sunderland City Council.

Sunderland Cultural Partnership (2014) *Sunderland Cultural Strategy*. Sunderland: Sunderland Cultural Partnership.

Swan, F. (2002) 'The development of studio glass at the University of Sunderland', In University of Sunderland (ed.), *Sunderland Glass Connections: 25 Years of Studio Glass Practice at the University of Sunderland*. Sunderland: University of Sunderland.

Thomas, N. J., Harvey, D. C. and Hawkins, H. (2013) 'Crafting the region: creative industries and practices of regional space', *Regional Studies*, 47 (1): 75–88.

UNCTAD (2008) *Creative Economy Report*. Geneva: UNCTAD.

Universities for the North East (2001) *The Regional Mission: The Regional Contribution of Higher Education – The North East*. Newcastle upon Tyne: Centre for Urban and Regional Development Studies (CURDS), University of Newcastle.

Universities UK (2010) *Creating Prosperity: The Role of Higher Education in Driving the UK's Creative Economy*. London: London Universities UK.

Universities UK (2014) *The Economic Impact of the North East Higher Education Sector*. London: London Universities UK.

van Aalst, I. and Boogaarts, I. (2002) 'From museum to mass entertainment: the evolution of the role of museums in cities', *European Urban and Regional Studies*, 9 (3): 195–209.

Vedovello, C. (1997) 'Science parks and university–industry interaction: geographical proximity between the agents as a driving force', *Technovation*, 17 (9): 491–531.

Visser, E.-J. and Boschma, R. (2004) 'Learning in districts: novelty and lock-in in a regional context', *European Planning Studies*, 12 (6): 793–808.

9 Staying and making it in regional creative cities – visual arts graduates and infrastructures for professional development

Abigail Gilmore, David Gledhill and Ivan Rajković

Introduction

This chapter investigates the experiences of creative graduates working in managed artist studio spaces in Manchester in the North West of England. It considers their trajectories and career development after art school and explores their professionalisation, recognition and success in relation to the opportunities provided by studio spaces and the broader arts infrastructure and creative economy in Manchester and beyond. It attempts to understand the relationship between training, teaching and learning within higher education and the strategies and realities of emerging and established visual artists in a regional city. In doing so, it critically examines how creative human capital, mediated by the community of practice offered by a managed studio space, moves through the structural relations of 'town' and 'gown', which impact on the careers and mobility of artist-practitioners and their opportunities for market entry and professional development.

The relationship between universities and creative economies can be understood as a variety of symbiotic activities, which reveal the character and prosperity of places and the people that live and work in and visit them. Research on higher education and its relationship to local creative economies has shown how universities contribute to the infrastructure for arts and cultural provision, for example through museums and performing arts spaces on campus and academic research on arts and cultural activities (Chatterton 1999; Chatterton and Goddard 2000; Powell 2007). They also contribute through the knowledge, training and skills development supported by academic research, teaching and learning that is transferred to places through the mobile human capital of students, graduates and staff (Florida *et al*. 2010; Comunian *et al*. 2015; Comunian and Gilmore 2015). The value of this capital to places has not gone unnoticed by policy-makers; indeed, there has been a growing pressure to understand and increase the impact of higher education in relation to the arts sector and the creative economy (Arts Council England (ACE) 2006; Universities UK 2010; Comunian and Gilmore 2014). Recent studies identify the geographic patterns and impact of attracting and retaining 'creative human capital' in specific places (Comunian *et al*. 2013; Comunian and Faggian 2014), in addition to a longer-term policy interest in the importance of the creative workforce (and its clustering) to local economic development (Pratt 2008; Florida 2014). In policy terms, the aspiration is that higher education can specifically benefit places through its role in producing the creative capital that, if retained, transforms these localities.

These policy expectations are riven, however, by difficulties, such as oversupply to and retention within local creative economies (Benhamou 2011; Jones 2011). At the same time, there is an expanding critical enquiry into the conditions for creative labour, including pay, entry points, skills and professional development, and the failure of local institutions in supporting and regulating appropriate infrastructure for progression and retention. So while there have been a number of initiatives aimed at enhancing knowledge transfer from higher education and improving skills for the creative economy at a national level, the conditions at a local level often present a fragmented and ill-equipped ecology for emerging visual artists who want to stay and work in places away from the centre of the arts world, the metropolitan capital.

This case study account explores the experiences and journeys of visual artists in a regional city. It draws on empirical research comprising qualitative interviews with emergent and established artists who are part of Rogue Studios, Manchester, whose number include graduates from the Manchester School of Art as well as from art schools elsewhere. We consider the contention that while Greater Manchester is an attractor to creative graduates, ranking second in the UK after London as a location for students taking creative programmes (Comunian and Faggian 2014), it does not yet have a strong enough indigenous infrastructure to retain them, particularly against the magnetic pull of London, to seek career development. It investigates the argument that this is in part due to the privileging by publicly funded institutions of established international artists in their programming (The Confidentials 2014), implicating the city's own cultural policy failure to encourage retention and professional development in the visual arts, despite its long-standing support for creative industries, in particular the music and digital sectors. Through insight into the lived experience of artists in their local creative economies, it explores what attracts and retains creative graduates to Manchester's visual arts world, and the ways in which they bridge their experiences between art school and their emerging futures as professional artists.

Mapping research on creative graduates: the geographies and pedagogies of the creative economy

Literature on the creative economy highlights the importance of understanding the economic geographies of creativity and the value of locating those who work in the creative industries, through 'creative cities' (Bianchini and Landry 1995) and 'creative class' approaches (Florida 2002; Markusen 2006). The role of higher education within these geographies is also investigated through the mapping of university students in the different creative disciplines (Comunian et al. 2011) and of skilled graduates and their retention and reward (or lack of reward) within local economies (Florida 2006; Comunian et al. 2010; Comunian *et al.* 2013). Furthermore, by identifying correlations between student location choice, graduate destination and the factors associated with creative cities (cultural consumption and production, employment and retention within creative industries) in relation to the spatial distribution of both creative higher education institutions and the creative job market, it is possible to show how universities intervene in local creative economies through their 'bohemian graduate' output (Comunian and Faggian 2014). The same research also confirms discourses of competitiveness between creative cities concerning the inequalities of this spatial distribution, most notably in the UK between the metropolitan capital and the regions, as well as disparities between supply and demand for creative occupations. In the case of Manchester, the attributes that attract creative students to come to, stay and work in the city are unmatched by the opportunities to work in the creative economy:

> Greater Manchester … ranks second for percentage of creative students trained, but third for percentage of creative graduates working in the local area and only fourth for the percentage of graduates working in creative occupations. This seems to suggest that the local labour market for creative jobs is not strong enough to retain all the creative graduates educated by the local universities.
>
> (Comunian and Faggian 2014: 30)

As the costs of the increasingly marketised education sector rise, questions are levelled at the private and public value of creative education and its responsibilities to properly equip graduates to realise their potential in the creative economy. The mass expansion of higher education, from 20,000 students at the beginning of the twentieth century to around 100,000 full-time students in English, Welsh and Scottish universities in 1958–9 and 1.9 million in UK higher education today (Willetts 2013: 24), further exacerbates these responsibilities, as does the changing profile of students, with a decline in those taking arts and humanities subjects, but a continuing under-representation from those of traditionally lower participating socio-economic groups (Willetts 2013). As both undergraduate and postgraduate education move to a model of private good and individual risk, through cuts in public funding and increases in student loans to cover rising fees, there is pressure to demonstrate the employability of graduates, their value to the economy and the value of their own investment in higher education.

Higher education is responding by publishing information on its performance in helping graduates achieve positive destinations and developing curricula to highlight their inclusion of relevant transferable 'employability' skills.[1] A pre-eminent focus on vocational skills training over critical pedagogies has been identified by some commentators who are concerned that this focus overturns the received conceptualisation of art schools as radical, anarchic spaces with permissive indulgence in experimental aesthetics and critical theory, particularly in post-war 1960s Britain (Frith and Horne 1987; Banks and Oakley 2016). The tensions between the practical and aesthetic obligations of arts schools to their graduates continue to be negotiated along lines of mobility and social class, as the increasing cost barriers to higher education present further challenges both to social mobility and workforce diversity.

Bridgstock and Cunningham (2016) refute the suggestion that there is an erosion of criticality in research into vocationally oriented curricula, emphasising how research that identifies the precariousness of creative work actually highlights the importance of providing appropriate pedagogies for a skilled and entrepreneurial workforce adept at navigating these conditions. However, they also identify a key problem for creative higher education that needs to deliver programmes which raise entrepreneurial capabilities for arts students – that many of those working as creative education lecturers may not have had enterprise training themselves, so may not feel confident or competent in developing these skills in others. In their research mapping the perceptions of creative graduates of their own career success following graduation, they suggest technical creative skills are valued equally in creative and non-creative work by graduates, supporting the thesis that creative occupations and transferrable creative skills are a valuable, embedded component of the broader economy, as proposed by the Creative Trident model (see Higgs *et al.* 2008). Interestingly, this seems a broader concern in arts education, as similar points are raised by Frenette and Tepper in their chapter in this book on arts graduates in the United States.

Bridgstock and Cunningham's research also suggests interesting distinctions in objective and subjective measures of career success following graduation which are highly tempered by discipline area. In terms of earning-related measures, design and digital graduates earned significantly more overall from creative work than graduates of visual and performing arts programmes; however, graduates of visual and performing arts programmes maintained high ratings on subjective (self-defined) career success, reflecting an identification with 'good work' and important non-economic value associated with creative work found in other studies (Banks and Hesmondhalgh 2009; Oakley *et al.* 2008). While this provides some comfort that visual arts graduates receive career satisfaction as a return on their investment in creative education, at the same time it supports the observations of others that this is a form of social economy that ultimately mitigates the precariousness of the creative economy. By complying with a 'star system' which rewards only the few (Throsby 2010), that demands continual portfolio and 'cross-over' working to cross-subsidise creative activity (Summerton 1999; Throsby and Hollister 2003; Volkerling 2012) and where the value of artists' work and art works is so contingent on an anomalous and exceptional pricing system (Abbing 2002), it can be argued visual artists are contributing to and reproducing the structural inequalities of their own creative economies.

Oakley *et al.* (2008) identify a number of common characteristics of visual arts graduates in their survey of the field which are relevant here. Firstly, they are loyal to their discipline with over 40 per cent of their sample remaining in the arts and cultural industries following graduation, and a further 20 per cent in the more broadly defined creative industries, albeit in portfolio and multiple-job circumstances as consistent with the archetype above (Oakley *et al.* 2008: 4). Secondly, they are lifelong learners, with 80 per cent continuing some kind of informal training (ibid.: 5); again, similar dynamics are also highlighted by Frenette and Tepper's chapter in relation to US-based arts graduates. This is conducive to the form of teaching and learning during art school – problem-solving, experimental/inductive and unstructured – which then continues into working life; however, it could also be interpreted as problematic, reflecting a poor initial education in key skill areas. Thirdly, artists clearly distinguish between symbolic work as production and utilitarian production, between arts as a creative activity and creative production as a means to a functional end. It is interesting to consider whether and how this distinction between 'good work' for aesthetic reasons and 'work' for instrumental reasons carries through into decision-making and directions for earned income and for artistic practice.

Research into the geographies of creative work has identified that a number of aspects of these relationships are potentially useful to both higher education and local cultural policy-makers. Understanding of the spatial distribution of creative networks and clusters of artists can illuminate their role in urban regeneration (see, for example, Jacobi's chapter in this book), and there is a growing body of evidence on the impact of artists on economic development (e.g. Markusen 2006; Markusen and King 2003). In terms of location choices of creative artists, they remain 'bound to place' (Oakley *et al.* 2008: 16), co-locating (sometimes perversely) in more expensive inner-city areas rather than working remotely in cheaper accommodation. This can be partly explained by the wealth of research from cultural and economic geographers identifying the added value of knowledge spill-overs, cluster effects (Knudsen, Florida and Stolarick 2005; Markusen and King 2003) and more informal exchanges of gossip and rumour (Pratt 2005) in localities, which reinforce both supply chain relationships and social ties (Oakley *et al.* 2008) and the conditions for maintaining communities of practice and knowledge exchange networks (Menger 1999; Wenger 1998).

The case study research presented here combines these critical questions and explores their implications in relation to the experiences of artists in the context of Manchester, a city with a global reputation for popular culture, in particular music and football (Brown *et al.*, 2000). Manchester's cultural strategy has continually emphasised the aim of becoming a leading global creative city in all areas of artistic and cultural production, and these aspirations have been polarised by recent debates about the unequal distribution of arts funding (Stark *et al.* 2013) and the twinned prospects of devolution and a cultural 'Northern Powerhouse' announced within the Autumn Statement that included central government investment in Manchester's arts infrastructure ahead of the General Election in 2015 (HM Treasury 2014).

In the next section we look at the context and recent history of visual arts in the city, before considering the empirical experiences of the Rogue artists in the final section.

The Manchester context

Further and higher education in art and design in Greater Manchester is based at three higher education institutions (the University of Bolton, Manchester

Metropolitan University and the University of Salford) and over twenty further education colleges. Graduates from these programmes tend to gravitate towards Manchester and Salford city centres and away from the regional towns within the Greater Manchester area, stimulating further demand for studio space (Slater *et al.* 2013). The growth of the studio network in Manchester during the 1980s and 1990s has not been matched, however, by a comparable growth in infrastructure for artist development, despite significant public investment in the two cities' major cultural institutions over the same period.

Routes to commercial success for individual artists are constrained locally in part because of the absence of a significant regional market for contemporary art in the North West, but also due to the lack of opportunity for local representation, exhibition and hence critical endorsement. At the same time there has been a decrease in local authority investment in arts development that might provide the networks for business support (Slater *et al.* 2013: 12). There is also a tendency to programme in favour of artists from outside the region within the public subsidised institutions and in large-scale, high-profile events such as the Manchester International Festival (Slater *et al.* 2013: 28; Chavez-Dawson 2005). Although the growth of horizontal 'peer-to-peer' activities and networked 'collectivist' strategies (Gordon-Nesbitt 2012: 8) for professional development have helped to mitigate this comparative lack of investment, the number of artists achieving higher career goals at the national or international level is limited (Slater *et al.* 2013). This has resulted in the perception of a 'glass ceiling' effect within the region, encouraging the migration of artists towards the South East and exacerbating the tension between the attraction of affordable production space (in the North) and the concentration of commercial opportunities in London.

A number of key organisations established in the 1980s and 1990s form the basis for the current contemporary arts infrastructure. Prior to this, opportunities for Manchester-based artists to exhibit in the city were scarce. Castlefield Gallery was established by members of Manchester Artists' Studios Association (MASA) in 1984 and alternated shows by high-profile established painters and sculptors with North West graduate and postgraduate artists. Buoyed by an international revival of interest in painting in the 1980s at Manchester School of Art at Manchester Metropolitan University (MMU), MASA and Castlefield provided a platform for artists from Greater Manchester that raised standards and extended creative horizons beyond the region. The opening of Cornerhouse (a cross-art form venue with gallery space) in 1985 also brought a wider range of contemporary practice to the city, and meant that artists could start to build networks beyond the confines of the studio groups and exhibit in a professionally curated context. MASA itself opened in 1982, providing a model for other studios in the city, including the Sculptors in Greater Manchester Association (SIGMA), the Cultural Utility Building Ancoats (CUBA) and Bankley Studios and Gallery in Levenshulme – and a former member of MASA went on to set up Rogue Artists' Studios in 1995. While MASA is constituted as a limited company and has charitable status and Bankley Studios became a cooperative in 1998, since 2000 Rogue has been run by a small team of artist administrators on a 'payment in kind' basis, together with voluntary steering and selection committees, and is constituted as a 'not-for-profit partnership'.

During these decades, the availability of underused light industrial building stock in both outlying and city centre locations meant that genuinely affordable studio space was ample. Studio membership was principally drawn from the fine art programme at MMU, but by the time Rogue opened, the North West was beginning to draw graduate and postgraduate artists from other parts of the UK, attracted by the availability of space and the lower cost of living. At its inception, Rogue absorbed members from a number of smaller studio groups that had either proved difficult to sustain or who had lost their premises to fire (as was the case for CUBA) or termination of lease due to redevelopment, a continual threat to the longevity of Manchester studio groups. Between 1995 and 2000, Rogue and MASA occupied separate floors of Hanover Mill adjacent to Piccadilly Railway Station, creating a critical mass of artists in the city centre. In 2000, the studio group moved to the nearby Crusader Mill, which was mainly occupied by clothing manufacturers at that time. As the recession started to drive these companies out of business, Rogue expanded in response to demand and currently provides studio space for 97 artists over three floors.

These studio groups help make up for the lack of exhibition opportunities available in the city. Rogue hosts annual 'Open Studios' weekend events, during which members can sell directly to the public on a commission-free basis or curate displays of work by students or non-studio members. In turn, local arts schools, their curricula and the practices and research interests of their staff influence local contemporary scenes and approaches. While the fine art department at MMU was a driver for the growing studio network in the 1980s, the introduction of the interactive arts course in 1993 produced a second wave of graduates exploring research-driven, collaborative and interdisciplinary approaches. Enterprising collectives such as the Annual Programme (1995–2000), some of whom were MMU graduates, began to attract wider attention, and visiting lecturers helped to evolve a critical theoretical discourse at MMU previously missing from the creative ecology of the city (Simpson 2001). The professional networks they mobilised set a precedent for the regional infrastructure, where written contextualisation was seen to be as important as production. The use of their own homes as temporary venues extended the DIY spirit of Manchester's music scene into the visual arts. By contrast, independent commercial galleries, such as Comme Ça Art and Philips Art Gallery, supported the promotion of both younger emerging and unrepresented mid-career artists. By the end of the 1990s, some of these factions began to work together with curators and artists from other cities in the North to organise large-scale group shows, taking advantage of the continued availability of disused shops, offices and mills for multi-venue projects, such as artranspennine98, MART 1999 and LMN in 2000 (Shillingford and Lee 2001).

Other artist- and network-led activities have helped to build DIY infrastructure for promotion and professional development, outside of the larger publicly funded institutions, particularly in the early twentieth century. In 2003, the Comme Ça Art Prize and Comme Ça New York broadened the reach of Manchester artists and attracted media attention, and a new wave of independent dealers and small independents, such as Bureau and Untitled Gallery (now Object / A), offered exhibiting and selling opportunities for represented artists. Studio spaces begin to exploit digital technologies to promote and map their present, and magazines, such as *Flux*, included regional and international arts coverage alongside fashion features and national distribution. However, other than local coverage in listings magazine *City Life* (Birch *et al*. 2001) and occasional features in *Art Review* (Simpson 2001) and *Flash Art* (Mulholland 2001), the city still lacked outlets for critical art journalism.

Alongside the increase in the number of galleries after 2000, a rapid diversification of artist-led activity took advantage of the new clubs, bars and cafes based in Manchester's regenerated Northern Quarter to mount one-off themed projects and exhibitions. At the same time, artists were opening self-funded galleries in short-lived alternative spaces including a living room (Bert and Ganddie Gallery), a porch (Porch Gallery), a plan chest (Floating ip) and a coat pocket (La Galerie Dans Ma Poche). Apartment, the most durable of these ad hoc spaces, combined international guest exhibitors with artists drawn from MMU's postgraduate programme and the studio network. Based in a council flat, Apartment brokered international exposure for its artists and, like many other artist-led projects, subsisted on occasional support from the Arts Council England (ACE) Grants for the Arts scheme. The introduction of more professional development content on university fine art courses and increased arts funding through schemes like Grants for Arts supported the growth of a wider constellation of artist-led studio and gallery associations throughout the Greater Manchester conurbation, for example in Bolton where *neo*: provides studios and print facilities, an annual open exhibition and an art prize.

The recession of 2008 and cuts to ACE budgets brought about the contraction of the visual arts ecology in Manchester, with venue closures and widespread gallery downsizing or relocation. The cohesion, plurality and enterprise of the early millennium yielded to the reinforcement of divisions between artist-led, commercial and public-funded sectors. Excepting Castlefield Gallery, which has regained its National Portfolio Organisation status and remains active in facilitating grass-roots curatorial and artistic activity (Clayton 2015), the basis for a local ecology capable of sustaining diversity and facilitating upward mobility has somewhat receded. In 2014, the reduction of the commercial sector, compounded by the lack of access to exhibition opportunities in public galleries, gave rise to an Open Letter calling for more support for artists working in the region in exhibition programming and promotion (The Confidentials 2014), meriting a response from the City Council's Strategic Lead for Culture. While the issue of local representation in public galleries is perceived to be a problem throughout the UK (McGregor 2014), tensions between policies which support and represent local artists versus the commissioning of external/international artists remain far from resolved and run parallel to concerns about London-centric commissioning and arts funding, for example in the publication of the ROCC report (Stark *et al*. 2013; Gledhill 2014).

In 2015, there is a growing recognition within local cultural policy of the value in retaining home-grown creative communities and investment for nurturing conditions for artistic production and distribution locally. However, networking opportunities leading to exposure of work as a means of career progression (Air and a-n The Artists Information Company 2011) are restricted as a result of an oversupply of graduates to the existing infrastructure (Slater *et al*. 2013). In the meantime, artist-led galleries, project spaces and agencies have stepped into the breach, combining often self-taught social media marketing skills and residency programmes to promote emerging talent and provide a much-needed bridge between graduation and establishment.

In terms of artistic diversity, previous distinctions between traditional and expanded practice (Williams 2001) have been ameliorated by larger studio spaces, such as Rogue and Islington Mill in Salford which accommodate a broad range of activity. There is a more consolidated local platform for critical writing than a decade previously, through online journal *Corridor8*. Contemporary Visual Arts Manchester (CVAM), an ACE-funded association involving both artists and curators, is part of a national network of organisations intended to promote visual art in the regions and also makes a significant contribution to artists' career development prospects. Manchester Contemporary Art Fair provides a market-facing profile for independent galleries. However, the strengthening of the local creative economy has not yet reached the individual artist and entrenched economic precariousness continues to prevail. Of the artists in Greater Manchester who responded to a recent survey, 73.5 per cent do not make a living from their work (Slater *et al*. 2013: 20) and incomes in fine art are stuck at half the UK national average (Spriggens 2012). As a consequence, artists are often working part-time in service and retail jobs, as attendants in public galleries, or as lecturers in further or higher education in order to subsidise their artistic income (Slater and Lee 2014).

Rogue artists' experiences

The following sections consider the conditions and factors impacting on artists' professional development and experience post-art school, from the perspective of individual artists based at Rogue studios. The project used an explorative qualitative research methodology, conducting semi-structured interviews with resident artists at Rogue Studios. Questions focused on their trajectories during and after art school, strategies for career and professional practice development and their plans for the future. We also asked about their perceptions of and connections to Manchester, their relationship to the broader arts ecology of the UK and the international arts market, and their attitudes towards art education and cultural policies.[2]

During art school

Although most of the interviewees recognise the creative skills they developed in their art schools, the majority felt they did not have enough training on what it means to be a 'practising' artist during their degree programmes. Specifically, the artists felt unprepared for the promotion of their work, as something distinctive in a competitive arts world, and for the practical social aspects of 'networking' with others. Perceptions differed across the sample, however, and some praised the practical education they received at art school, particularly in terms of writing artist statements, grant applications and the use of studio and technical equipment and photography for profiling work. It was artists who graduated before the mid-2000s who were more likely to report having little or no instruction on how to apply for competitions, get funding or organise their first exhibitions, suggesting that changes to art schools curricula may be taking effect.

Professional practice skills training was also accompanied by implicit knowledge on career development, which was crucial to graduates' career expectations. The artists who finished their degrees with little knowledge of the implicit rules of the arts market tended to have an expectation that their work is going to be valued on its own merit, without requiring further action, for example lobbying gallery representatives for exhibitions or making grant applications to research and develop their practice. These graduates were more prone to report feelings of initial disappointment after graduation and to doubt themselves after early rejections. On the other hand, artists who were pushed by their schools to develop strong professional profiles – for example, by putting on external exhibitions as an assessed task before graduating – had a clearer sense of how to approach their development early on, and were generally quicker in gaining wider recognition. Early experiences prior and post-graduation were the optimum formative learning stages for emerging artists for building personal confidence and early success in the art world.

Establishing oneself as an artist: trajectories in creative economies

Regardless of their education experiences, all of our interviewees reported intense feelings of crisis and disorientation after finishing art school. Usually, this is a time when they stopped being financed through scholarships, loans and grants and had to suddenly become financially accountable. This presents a common pattern of vulnerability, where going back to live with family, taking jobs unrelated to art and relying on a partner's income are all frequent occurrences. Post-graduation precariousness also influences one's ability to produce art: art-making happens less frequently, often in improvised circumstances (such as in one's living room, which affects the potential scale of work) or at weekends. Unless progressing immediately to a Master's programme, the first couple of years after Bachelor's study marked a much lower volume of making and displaying one's art.

There are many different routes on leaving art school, often with little signposting or prior guidance, and options include postgraduate education, internships, lecturing or teaching, part-time work in other related areas (such as galleries or in consultancy), or leaving the arts completely (Francis 2013). Only a tiny fraction of graduates gain gallery representation immediately after their degree show. For our sample, in many cases the first response was to find a temporary job in a minimum paid position in a service or trade industry, such as a non-art related office job or (less frequently) in arts-related media industries. Bar work is especially common; this is seen as convenient work for the artist as it is often flexible, leaving enough time for one's art, but is also feared as a 'trap job' (leaving one complacent and less ambitious). Preferred work includes part-time work in art supplies shops, visitor services and other roles in galleries, and art-teaching jobs, in other words arts-related income, broadly following patterns of cross-subsidy seen in other studies (e.g. Oakley *et al.* 2008; Oakley 2009; Throsby and Hollister 2003).

It is possible to differentiate long-term strategies of graduates by examining the relative proportions of their creative and arts-related income to non-creative work (Throsby 2010). For the majority of our informants, the ultimate aim was to become and stay a 'full-time artist', who exclusively earns income by producing original artistic work – the 'good work' as described in the literature above. This is often not immediately possible, however, and requires careful planning and gradual phasing out of 'non-creative' as well as arts-based income, saving and sometimes claiming benefits until an opportunity emerges to switch to being a full-time artist. For those of our interviewees who considered themselves to be in full-time status (four out of seven), this was the main strategy. As Sophie, a sculptor and installation artist, puts it:

> I think artists should be very ambitious. I don't think we can rely on other people to hand us things. I've gone out and I've searched for opportunities, exhibitions, commissions. And I tried to be savvy as much as I can about how I make money as an artist, without having to go into employment, to maintain being a full-time artist. Because I know that if I had a part time job, it would destroy any creative cells. You need to be focused full-time.
>
> (Sophie)

Being 'full-time' allows a full commitment to art, both practically and symbolically, and this commitment has a value in itself, even if it comes at the expense of sacrificing some comfort. At the same time, full-time status is seen as precarious in the longer term, as one depends on the steady flow of grants, commissioned work or art sales. Not knowing whether and when money will come often means intermittent periods of getting a grant and becoming really 'thin', while trying to bridge sporadic income by frugal living. As a response to this uncertainty, the preferred alternative long-term strategy is to develop a 'part-time' grounding, backing up one's dedication to producing art with a stable, usually art-related part-time job, such as a teaching position in an art school. This also offers the advantage of continued involvement in art networks and, in the latter case access to resources such as university studio space and technicians.

However, there are fears and constraints attached to continuing relationships between artistic practice, economic necessity and the academy related to the need for doctoral qualifications to gain lectureship tenure, a growing strategy of young artists for financial security. This was viewed by some informants as potentially limiting, distorting one's freedom and inducing a lot of unnecessary stress.

One interviewee suggested that the pressure to continue into postgraduate education was raising the bar too high for other developing artists and leading to 'over-qualification' of the sector. However, despite these difficulties, it was recognised that postgraduate research can benefit artists by introducing 'the right ideas' of critical theory to articulate their art, with the PhD qualification seen as a guarantor of academic propriety.

In terms of exhibition strategies, our informants differed greatly in planning their first shows. First exhibitions were primarily graduate shows and DIY projects with other emerging artists, but beyond this their pathways become very contingent. It is usually with first shows that one recognises, after art school, the need to stay in an art community in order to be 'displayable' and the importance of networks for getting recognised. As one interviewee put it, 'you need somebody else to confirm your value.' Some managed to sidestep those obstacles by applying 'cold' to group shows under specific themes (usually set in the North West). Some were discovered at Rogue Studios' Open Weekend and invited to contribute to high-profile group exhibitions because they worked with a specific medium or theme (such as paper). Some also used postgraduate study explicitly for professional development, both in terms of developing the distinctiveness of their artistic practice and to gain relevant contacts. One of the more established artists, Mark, founded a group of artists working in film, and was invited to exhibit by a curator of a local gallery who got to know his work during his Master's programme in Manchester.

All of the 'full-time' artists we interviewed had secured public funding for their work at least once, most often from Arts Council England. Several of them had their work commissioned, usually by local or regional galleries or by galleries abroad. Selling work varied depending on the medium used and types of artistic practice, with figurative paintings most likely to be sold to private collectors (and conceptual and experimental art sculpture less likely). The medium and materials used also influences the format of representation and recognition more broadly, sometimes influencing the choice of artistic practice and introducing an economic instrumentalism into artistic and career direction. For example, one conceptual artist who works with temporary materials is considering switching to more durable materials and bigger formats for her next project in order to secure a museum commission.

By contrast, there was a sense that utilitarian approaches should be taken cautiously, and that what was most valuable was original creativity; most of our interviewees believed that they had to develop a distinctive style or perspective, often in critical dialogue with others' ideas, in order to be recognised by curators and funding bodies. Hence most of them narrated their emerging pathways as periods when they were still perfecting the originality of their contribution, and worked hard to create and retain a consistent set of themes and styles with which they wanted to become publicly associated. Conversely, the more established artists report the discouragement they faced when trying to change the approach they became known for, and the pressure to do what they describe as repetition of similar work, at the expense of their own creativity. They describe a need to walk a fine line between being recognised for a distinctive style and being a brand, or a 'factory', that reproduces things, because galleries will only show what is already recognised as one's personal work.

Finally, some of our informants employed a range of tactics to diversify their profile, by broadening their collaboration with various unorthodox partners and the scope of spaces in which they display their work. John (a conceptual sculptor), for example, had decided early on to exhibit 'wherever' possible and joined a group of similar artists on a long-term group project. The nature of their work (a blend of sculpture, electronic music and science) has enabled them to broaden the scope of spaces where they exhibit, from conventional traditional galleries to disused spaces, from publicly funded regional venues to electronic music gigs and popular science shows. He remains deeply assured that it is possible to find a niche for oneself outside of the conventionally recognised art world. Similarly, Sophie plans to branch out from her successful installation activities to commercial sectors of the music industry and architecture. But as these examples show, the creation of more 'lateral' pathways for display and recognition might be more open to those working in conceptual forms and multimedia, with the more traditional art forms (such as figurative painting) remaining limited to the conventional gallery-based venues as pathways to recognition.

Artists' mobility in relation to London, Manchester and other places

All the artists interviewed, and the majority of other Rogue residents, can be roughly grouped into two categories in relation to their trajectories of mobility. The first group grew up in Manchester or other places in the North West, finished a BA at MMU or one of the many art schools in Greater Manchester, and embarked on employment and their artistic development in the city. The second grouping is made up mainly of those from other regions, such as Wales and Scotland, who finished their Bachelor degrees in other regional cities and subsequently moved to Manchester. They were attracted by a sense of a cultural 'buzz' and the rapid artistic development that occurred in Manchester in the mid-2000s. Additionally, some moved to Manchester as a result of other links to the city, such as the presence of extended family or artistic partnerships, or a partner's migration to the North for work. This reflects observations by Comunian *et al.* in this book about the role of mobility (or lack of) as a strategy to enable career progression or to strengthen existing networks and opportunities.

All agreed that London was still a privileged place in the UK art industry. They described it as having the most galleries and museums and, hence, exhibition opportunities, the majority of collectors and commissioning bodies, and the largest networks of tutors and curators that act as crucial gatekeepers for recognition in the art world. Conversely, Manchester was criticised for having too small an artistic scene, that it can become 'cliquey', with a relatively small number of galleries, artistic spaces and collectors, which determines the 'ceiling' for the prices of artistic work. Artists also noted the gap between the well-known reputation of Manchester as a music centre and the lesser known visual arts profile of the city, reproducing a sentiment about Manchester and the 'North' as on the periphery of the national visual art ecology.

The interviewees shared a common perception of the disadvantages of living in London post-graduation. With the average wage of fine artists in the UK being around £10,000 p.a. (Kretschmer *et al.* 2011: 3) and the prices of housing and studio rent in London being unbearably high, most of their time is dedicated to non-art related employment just to pay the bills. In addition, the art scene is seen as overwhelming, so that even when located in the city, it is hard to find the time and resources to build enduring contacts with galleries and representatives that one can actually capitalise on. Interviewees who aspired to becoming full-time artists preferred to devote more time to actually making art by living outside of London, inventing new ways to achieve recognition that did not revolve around the capital.

Manchester is therefore appreciated as a better site for emerging artists to realise their ambitions to become 'full-time artists', through relatively cheap housing and studio rent (in comparison to the South) and the convenience of an accessible urban infrastructure, with a vibrant art scene of a size that allows for full engagement. Interviewees also highlighted the reputation of the city in the broader UK art scene, and its proximity to other cities with provincial contemporary galleries that can showcase their work. A number of key institutions within the city were also identified as important, including both smaller, independent 'project' or artist-led spaces and more enduring publicly funded galleries that have played a longer role in the city's history of artistic production and display. As discussed above, they appreciated the access to resources and networks provided through enduring relationships with local art schools, and recognised the developing collaborations between higher education and exhibition activities, particularly in relation to the partnership between Castlefield Gallery and MMU providing exhibition and project space at Federation House. However, there was a tacit recognition that the reputations of London art schools and their surrounding networks made a temporary move to London advantageous, particular at Master's level.

However, another characteristic was identified with Manchester: a greater freedom, not only from the financial worries associated with London, but also from the constraints of particular forms of artistic practice and direction that are said to prevail there. This echoes broader regional divides and symbolical geographies in the UK that present Manchester (especially its music scene) as more punk, oppositional and cutting-edge in comparison to the more developed, yet complacent, capital:

> I think that a good thing about being in Manchester is that a lot of the trends and a lot of the fashions that people get sucked into in London, because that's how it is orientated, you can kind of ignore it and do your own thing. You don't have to be swept by the tide of fashion. You can say 'well, I am not interested in doing that, just because everyone else is, I am just going to do my own thing'. And I think that has something to do with the North–South divide. I think that is just a bit like 'Fuck you London, we do our own thing' – which was always a big thing in Manchester.
>
> (Anna, conceptual artist)

This DIY regionalism is not just in spite of, but because of, Manchester's disconnection from London's central core of artistic circles and it repositions London: for our interviewees, it is no longer the exclusive centre of their art worlds and residence there is not necessary for career development. They identified the crucial role of the Internet as a platform for developing reputations beyond national borders and increasing opportunities to build careers by sidestepping London. New strategies involved developing stronger bases laterally in smaller Northern towns, which may have specific allocated budgets for regional arts development, and also by developing international presence through thematic shows abroad or touring work or through overseas artists' residencies, particularly in Western Europe, East Asia and the United States.

Within this transcendence of spatial ties, Manchester is positioned more as a production 'base' than as a centre of display and recognition. Particularly for the more established younger artists, there is a consistent gap between these two functions, with the desire to live and make art in Manchester but to exhibit elsewhere: 'You can be in Manchester and be an artist anywhere in the world. I have no interest in exhibiting in Manchester anymore. It's like preaching to the converted' (Sophie).

Rogue as a collectivist strategy for professional development

All the interviewees were recommended to Rogue by people they know, whether lecturers they met at local art school or their peers and collaborators. Once in the studio, spaces are usually rented for several years, a residency in Rogue often marking the beginning of a full-time career. Having a dedicated studio space is a further commitment to arts practice, not just because of its functional value but also through the social learning opportunities it provides, which the isolation of home-based work lacks. Rogue's mixture of artists at various career stages and working in different art forms facilitates these roles along with the affordability of its spaces.

Since it is home to some ninety artists of various ages and practices, Rogue often does not act as a single community, and it is unlikely that every artist knows all of their fellow studio members, although most have a sense of sociality with the fellow residents. Close to the circles of art display and critique, networked with local art schools through the relationships with their staff and the professional skills learned while studying, Rogue acts as an alternative 'third space' (Soja 1996) that permits artists to reflect on their shared aspirations and uncertainties. While related to the individual undergraduate and postgraduate experiences and competencies of artists-as-graduates, Rogue allows them to mediate the deadends of other institutional spaces and to mitigate collectively for their shortcomings. Interviewees mentioned the valuable advice they got from more experienced fellow residents along with other collective activities, such as a monthly support group with a number of residents who comment on one another's pieces of work and plans for future projects.

There were other signs that while mutual support is on offer, the experience of an emerging artist is distinctly individual rather than uniform, and that certain qualities of individual entrepreneurialism are strategies for survival. This was manifest in the different views about public funding, which revealed some broader meritocratic appraisals of hard work and individual perpetration. Some, such as Dean, a painter in his late twenties who had not yet achieved commercial success or professional recognition and was without gallery representation, narrated their sense of disappointment in the city curators of the public institutions who failed to support local artists more, in relation to their own personal goals and motivation: 'I am not show driven, I do this for me' (Dean).

Others such as Sophie, who had experienced success early on in the two years since graduation, took a more hard-line approach to self-reliance:

> I can only answer it from my perspective … for me that comes down to teaching yourself how to apply for it, or if you can't do it, find someone who can help you. And ambition and drive. And altogether those things, eventually, if you work hard enough, you'll do it. So don't complain about it, just do it. Just keep going.
>
> (Sophie)

This demonisation of dependency in the contemporary UK can be a strategy for self-preservation, creating a sense of control over the future, and 'a sense of security in an insecure world' (Valentine and Harris 2014: 91). Rogue's place within these individual narratives was predominantly articulated in terms of its visibility and uniqueness in the regional art ecology of the region, and the benefits of being part of a wider community which it offers. These benefits include intelligence on forthcoming career development opportunities, as Rogue residents receive updates on calls for commissions, competitions and grants, get invited to openings of new shows, and generally, gain recognition from the city's wider network of art curators and collectors. In this sense, Rogue residents often feel that Rogue is not just a 'production' space, but also an incubation, promotion and exhibition space that, through the association with membership of a large body of artists, offers more effective routes into the art world, not just in Manchester but at an international level.

Conclusions

The experiences of the artists at Rogue studio demonstrate many of the qualities and affordances identified by other research on visual artists finding their way into the creative economy after graduation from arts school. The artists are vulnerable to precarious conditions and dependent on strategies that help them facilitate and subsidise their artistic practice. They benefit to some extent from the increasing inclusion of employability training within higher education curricula, although the application of skills learned during art school are highly contingent on other factors, including implicit knowledge available during art school, their own existing social and cultural capital and the opportunities to achieve early success and recognition. These are in turn dependent on access to particular elements of the visual arts ecology, to exhibition opportunities, and to the social networks and critical discourses of curators, gallery representatives, critics and dealers.

These experiences also reflect the specific affordances of the particular space within the local visual arts infrastructure that Rogue studios offer, through supporting both collectivist and individual strategies and opportunities for representation and recognition. They also provide some commentary, not only on Manchester's status as a creative city (relative to London), but also on aspects relevant to local cultural and higher education policy concerning artistic production for economic development. It seems the priorities here are not solely to subsidise local exhibition opportunities in Manchester, but also to find ways to support artists' own ambitions and individual drive to commit full-time to art-making, while drawing on the existing collectivist strategies and communities of practices which make Manchester a viable place and base for artistic production. The implications of the findings for higher education and its relationship to the creative economy, albeit from a small-scale study, suggest that curricula for professional development, as well as artistic development, would benefit from partnerships with broader artist communities, such as studio spaces like Rogue, during as well as after degree programmes.

Notes

1. See also Ashton's chapter in this book in relation to the possibilities of work-based learning within higher education settings.
2. Our sample consisted of seven emerging and early established visual artists between their late twenties and early forties. They worked in a variety of media, mostly painting, sculpture and film. Three informants were female and four male. All of their names have been changed to preserve anonymity. In addition we have undertaken an analysis of the curriculum vitae of Rogue's residents to provide some general context for these individual narratives.

References

Abbing, H. (2002) *Why Are Artists Poor: The Exceptional Economy of the Arts*. Amsterdam: Amsterdam University Press.

Air and a-n The Artists Information Company (2011) *The Big Artist Survey*. (Online) Retrieved from http://www.a-n.co.uk_big_artists_survey (accessed 10 June 2015).

Arts Council England (ACE) (2006) *Arts, Enterprise and Excellence: Strategy for Higher Education*. London: Arts Council England.

Banks, M. and Hesmondhalgh, D. (2009) 'Looking for work in creative industries policy', *International Journal of Cultural Policy* (Special Issue): 'After the Creative Industries', 15 (4): 415–30.

Banks, M. and Oakley, K. (2016) 'The dance goes on forever? Art schools, class and UK higher education', *International Journal of Cultural Policy*, 22 (1): 47–57.

Benhamou, F. (2011) 'Artists' labour markets', in R. Towse (ed.), *A Handbook of Cultural Economics*, 2nd edn. Cheltenham: Edward Elgar.

Bianchini, F. and Landry, C. (1995) *The Creative City*. London: Demos.

Birch, T., Black, K., Griffin, K. and Vincent, M. (2001) 'Artful lodgers: Manchester studios exposed, *City Life*, 444, 16–28.

Bridgstock, R. and Cunningham, S. (2016) 'Creative labour and graduate outcomes: implications for higher education and cultural policy', *International Journal of Cultural Policy*, 22 (1): 10–26.

Brown, A., O'Connor, J. and Cohen, S. (2000) Local music policies within a global music industry: cultural quarters in Manchester and Sheffield', *Geoforum*, 31 (4): 437–51.

Chatterton, P. (1999) 'The cultural role of universities in the community: reivisiting the university – community debate', *Environment and Planning A*, 32: 165–81.

Chatterton, P. and Goddard, J. (2000) 'The response of higher education institutions to regional needs', *European Journal of Education*, 35 (4): 475–96.

Chavez-Dawson, J. (2005) *Manchester: Naturally Proactive and Curatorially Inquisitive.* NYARTS (Online) Retrieved from: http://www.nyartsmagazine.com/?p=3431 (accessed 10 June 2015).

Clayton, E. (2015) 'Postcard from Manchester', *Frieze*, 171: 25–6.

Comunian, R. and Faggian, A. (2014) 'Creative graduates and creative cities: exploring the geography of creative education in the UK', *International Journal of Cultural and Creative Industries*, 1 (2): 19–34.

Comunian, R. and Gilmore, A. (2014) 'From knowledge sharing to co-creation: paths and spaces for engagement between higher education and the creative and cultural industries', in A. Schramme, G. Hagoort and R. Kooyman (eds), *Beyond Frames*. Antwerp: University of Antwerp Press, pp. 141–7.

Comunian, R. and Gilmore, A. (2015) 'Beyond the creative campus: reflections on the evolving relationship between higher education and the creative economy', King's College London, London. Available at: http://www.creative-campus.org.uk.

Comunian, R., Faggian, A. and Jewell, S. (2011) 'Winning and losing in the creative industries: an analysis of creative graduates' career opportunities across creative disciplines', *Cultural Trends*, 20 (3/4): 291–308.

Comunian, R., Faggian, A. and Li, Q. C. (2010) 'Unrewarded careers in the creative class: the strange case of bohemian graduates', *Papers in Regional Science*, 89 (2): 389–410.

Comunian, R., Gilmore, A. and Jacobi, S. (2015) 'Higher education and the creative economy: creative graduates, knowledge transfer and regional impact debates', *Geography Compass*, 9 (7): 371–83

Comunian, R., Taylor, C. and Smith, D. N. (2013) 'The role of universities in the regional creative economies of the UK: hidden protagonists and the challenge of knowledge transfer', *European Planning Studies*, 22 (12): 2456–76.

Confidentials, The (2014) 'Open Letter to City Curators and Exhibition Programmers', *Manchester Confidential*, 24 June. Available from: http://www.manchesterconfidential. co.uk/culture/open-letter-to-city-curators-and-exhibition-programmers (accessed 18 September 2015).

Florida, R. (2002) *The Rise of the Creative Class*. New York: Basic Books.

Florida, R. (2006) 'Regions and universities together can foster a creative economy', *Chronicle for Higher Education*, 15 September.

Florida, R. (2014) *The Rise of the Creative Class – Revisited*. New York: Basic Books.

Florida, R., Gates, G., Knudsen, B. and Stolarick, K (2010) 'The university and the creative economy', in D. Araya and M. Peters (eds), *Education in the Creative Economy: Knowledge and Learning in the Age of Innovation*. New York: Peter Lang.

Francis, A. (2013) *Signpost: Stepping Out as a New Artist - What You Need to Know and Where to Find It*. Carlisle: Susan Jones/a-n: the Artist Information Company.

Frith, S. and Horne, H. (1987) *Art into Pop*. London: Methuen.

Gledhill, D. (2014) *Looking North: The Arts Ecology in Manchester*. Miriad. Retrieved from http://news.miriadonline.info/looking-north-the-arts-ecology-in-manchester/.

Gordon-Nesbitt, R. (2012) *Value, Measure, Sustainability: Ideas Towards the Future of the Small-scale Visual Arts Sector, December 2012, Common Practice*. Retrieved from: http://www.commonpractice.org.uk/wp-content/uploads/2014/11/Common-Practice_Value_Measure_Sustainability.pdf.

Higgs, P., Cunningham, S. and Bakshi, H (2008) *Beyond the Creative Industries: Mapping the Creative Economy in the United Kingdom*. London: Nesta.

HM Treasury (2014) *Autumn Statement*. London: HMT. Retrieved from: https://www.gov.uk/government/publications/autumn-statement-documents (accessed 24 July 2015).

Jones, S. (2011) '"Too many artists?" Transcript 1 from Too Many Artists: A Public Debate'. Available from: http://marketproject.org.uk/too-many-artists-transcript-part-i/.

Knudsen, B., Florida, R. and Stolarick, K. (2005) *Beyond Spillovers: The Effects of Creative Density on Innovation*. Retrieved from: http://www.creativeclassgroup.com/rfcgdb/articles/Beyond_Spillovers.pdf.

Kretschmer, M., Singh, S. Bently, L. and Cooper, E. (2011) *Copyright Contracts and Earnings of Visual Creators: A Survey of 5,800 British Designers, Fine Artists, Illustrators and Photographers*. University of Cambridge and Bournemouth University. Full report available from: https://microsites.bournemouth.ac.uk/cippm/files/2011/05/DACS-Report-Final1.pdf.

McGregor, S. (2014) *Homegrown Talent: Who Cares?* Axis. (Online) Retrieved from: http://www.axisweb.org/features/news-and-views/the-rant/rant-85/ (accessed 10 June 2015).

Markusen, A. (2006) 'Urban development and the politics of a creative class: evidence from the case study of artists', *Environment and Planning A*, 38 (10): 1921–40.

Markusen, A. and King, D. (2003) *The Artistic Dividend: The Arts' Hidden Contributions to Regional Development Minnesota*. Project on Regional and Industrial Economics, Humphrey Institute of Public Affairs, University of Minnesota.

Menger, P. (1999) 'Artistic labor markets and careers', *Annual Review Sociology*, 25: 541–74.

Mulholland, N. (2001) 'Aperto Manchester', *Flash Art*, 36 (232): 69–71.

Oakley, K. (2009) 'From Bohemian to Britart – art students over 50 years', *Cultural Trends*, 18 (4): 281–94.

Oakley, K., Pratt, A. and Sperry, B. (2008) *The Art of Innovation*. London: Nesta.

Powell, J. (2007) 'Creative universities and their creative city-regions', *Industry and Higher Education*, 21 (6): 323–35.

Pratt, A. (2005) 'Digitisation and Face-to-Face Interactions: The Example of the Film Industry in London'. Unpublished.

Pratt, A. C. (2008) 'Creative cities: the cultural industries and the creative class', *Geografiska Annaler Series B – Human Geography*, 90B (2): 107–17.

Shillingford, F. and Lee, K. (eds) (2001) *Monitor*. Manchester: Monitor.

Simpson, R. (2001) 'Life is good in Manchester', *Art Review*, LII: 34–7.

Slater, A. and Lee, K. (2014) *Artists in Greater Manchester*. Manchester: Castlefield Gallery Publications.

Slater, A., Ravetz, A. and Lee, K. (2013) *Analysing Artists Continual Professional Development in Greater Manchester: Towards an Integrated Approach for Talent Development*. Manchester: Castlefield Gallery Publications.

Soja, E. W. (1996) *Thirdspace: Journeys to Los Angeles and Other Real-and-Imagined Places*. Cambridge, MA: Blackwell.

Spriggens, T. (2012) *Artist Salary Research* (Online) Available from: http://www.dacs.org.uk/latest-news/artist-salary-research?category=For+Artistsandtitle=N (accessed 10 June 2015).

Stark, P., Gordon, C. and Powell, D. (2013) *Rebalancing Our Cultural Capital*. Independent report available from: http://www.theroccreport.com.

Summerton, J. (1999) *Artists at Work: A Study of Patterns and Conditions of Work in the Southern Region*. Winchester: Southern Arts Board.

Throsby, D. (2010) *The Economics of Cultural Policy*. Cambridge: Cambridge University Press.

Throsby, D. and Hollister, V. (2003) *Don't Give Up Your Day Job. An Economic Study of Professional Artists in Australia*. Strawberry Hills, NSW: Australia Council for the Arts.

Towse, R. (1995) *Economics of Artist's Labour Markets*. London: Arts Council of England.

Universities UK (2010): *Creating Prosperity: The Role of Higher Education in Driving the UK's Creative Economy*. London: Universities UK.

Valentine, G. and Harris, C. (2014) 'Strivers vs skivers: class prejudice and the demonisation of dependency in everyday life, *Geoforum*, 53: 84–92.

Volkerling, M. (2012) *Assessing the Value of Cultural Investment: Towards a New Policy Model*, in VII International Conference on Cultural Policy Research, Barcelona, 9–12 July.

Wenger, E. (1998) *Communities of Practice*. Cambridge: Cambridge University Press.

Willetts, D. (2013) *Robbins Revisited: Bigger and Better Higher Education*. London: Social Market Foundation.

Williams, R. J. (2001) 'Anything is possible: the Annual Programme 1995–2000', in S. Grennan (ed.) *Life Is Good in Manchester*. Salford: Trice Publications, pp. 7–15.

10 Beyond the art school

Pedagogic networks in the visual arts and their engagement with the city of Leipzig

Silvie Jacobi

Introduction

This chapter investigates how artists bond with a city during their time in higher education, by illustrating the significance of art schools and their pedagogic networks for the development of a resilient creative city – both in terms of cultural distinctiveness and socio-economic longevity. While this is situated within the field of cultural and creative industries research, I employ economic geography theory and complexity thinking as an interconnected framework to analyse the factors influencing the relationships and processes between institutions, people and place (IPP). On the basis of this, empirical data from qualitative research on the visual arts economy in Leipzig (Germany) will be applied to this framework, as a way to meaningfully structure the data. This will allow for a linear analysis of links between IPP.

Due to the city's recent re-urbanisation and hype around its cultural scene attracting many young people from other parts of Germany and Europe (frequently encountered with scepticism by locals), Leipzig serves as a timely case study for understanding how the visual arts sector and its institutions strongly influence the city. Leipzig is not just of interest from an urban studies perspective, due to its recent growth after long-term urban shrinkage after German Reunification, the cultural economy provides a rich basis for a critical discussion around artistic practice as livelihood at the intersection between commercial and autonomous goals. To understand the in-depth relationship between higher education institutions (HEIs) and the formation of a creative city, the following sub-questions and themes informed the qualitative data collection process:

- How do visual arts institutions, networks and their pedagogies and practices shape Leipzig's urban and cultural identity?
- How does the local art school contribute to the attraction and retention of artistic talent to Leipzig? What effect does this have on local cultural repertoire as mediated in communities of practice (Wenger 1998)?
- How does embedding cultural workers in a city reconcile with creative city development?

These questions are intended to determine the extent to which there is a link between the local art school 'Hochschule für Grafik und Buchkunst' ('Leipzig Academy of Visual Art'), (HGB) and whether and how this influences the development of Leipzig's renowned visual arts economy and associated urban spaces. For this purpose, I have conducted semi-structured interviews with art students and visual artists, as well as with professionals working with them as either career advisors, curators or lecturers. The pathways of visual arts that most participants engaged in were based on the two dominant streams of teaching at HGB, which were 'Medienkunst' (Media arts) and 'Malerei/Grafik' (Painting/Graphic Arts). Participants were recruited through the webpages of 'off-spaces' (the German term for artist-led spaces), HGB tutor groups and social media and the recommendation of gatekeepers and participants. To understand group dynamics and shared meanings within networks, I have conducted participant observation as a platform to gather shared meanings within artist communities during a participatory exhibition project developed by HGB students (Rödel *et al.* 2014), generating new actor-centred insight and research questions. Additionally, my own identity as a visual artist helped to establish an in-depth dialogue and trust.

The challenge of describing creative city complexities

While there has been in the past strong interest in creative city development as a toolkit for innovative urban problem-solving (Landry 2008) and human capital centred economic regeneration (Florida 2005a) especially within the context of re-urbanising cities (Champion 2001), there has been little mention of the role that HEIs play in shaping urban creativity – in particular as a vital part of the local creative economy[1] (Comunian and Faggian 2014). The lack of existing creative city theory and policy for understanding how to make cities culturally active (Vickery 2011) goes along with many of the recent academic contributions in this field questioning the current relevance of creative city strategy for bottom-up urban problem-solving (Harris and Moreno 2010; O'Connor and Shaw 2014). This again clearly indicates the importance of developing a differentiated perspective between the creative economy value chain embedded in cities and, on the other hand, aspirations for 'good city' development. These two streams intersect at the point at which cultural and social capital shapes the culture of a place (Lefebvre 1991).

Hence, developing in-depth local knowledge through empirical research on cities that are already culturally active is an important case to explore in order to understand how actual 'creative' cities can be developed and/or sustained. This ensures more inclusive and regionally specific policy development beyond the mere instrumentalisation of culture, which requires a theoretical framework within which the importance of IPP (including the relationships and processes between them) can be considered as interconnected parts of urban and cultural complexities. This is an approach adapted by Comunian (2010) who envisions the creative city as 'complex adaptive system' to determine how infrastructure, networks and agents engage in a city's cultural development. Exploring culture-led urban regeneration in Newcastle and Gateshead, Comunian's paper exemplifies how the creative city is an open system that has to deal with a variety of external influences and interactions between IPP that are constantly changing and cannot be planned. While managing adaptive change has become the recent focus of resilience research in the creative economy (Robinson 2010), complexity thinking (even if not being a universally accepted framework) is also embedded in economic geography theory, stretching across evolutionary and relational thinking. Whereas the evolutionary approach discerns how geographic-economic space both shapes and is shaped by the growth and transformation of knowledge (Martin and Sunley 2007), the relational approach sees space as a field of contextual economic relations consisting of actors and their socio-economic practices (Bathelt and Glückler 2003). In order to describe dualisms closest to their empirical reality, such as I aim to investigate between IPP, Sunley (2008) suggests placing research around actors and networks in evolutionary theory as a two-level approach. This is key to avoiding bias around the exclusivity of certain actors and networks, and allows for an integrated study of emergence and adaptation alongside the development of IPP.

Additionally, Wenger's (1998) communities of practice concept holds strong relevance for structuring the internal social processes of learning not directly related to place but indirectly, assuming that communities are co-habited through mutual engagement, joint enterprise and a shared repertoire of local knowledge and meaning. As will become evident later during this chapter, I will refer to place attachment as a dominant process within this empirical research. Scannell and Gifford (2010) offer a clear tripartite model for place attachment, which interconnects person, place and process for developing of a sense of place, as well as person–place bonds. One could criticise that the addressed concepts are overlapping and incomplete; however, as I have illustrated in Figure 10.1, they provide a valuable structure for identifying and describing key elements through which place-based phenomena materialise.

Leipzig's urban and cultural scene: a pioneer playground and talent hot spot

The city of Leipzig is located in the German state of Saxony, which was part of socialist East Germany until 1990. Leipzig was originally built for a capacity of 700,000 inhabitants (Bontje 2005). According to recent census information, the city has a current population of roughly 540,000 inhabitants (Stadt Leipzig 2013) with a strong population growth tendency. However, during the socialist regime up to 1989, Leipzig had lost its prominent role as one of Germany's core commercial centres, causing severe decay, especially of the inner-city, pre-war housing stock (*Gründerzeithäuser*) that was considered too bourgeois and, therefore, not meeting socialist ideals. Spared from heavy bombing during the Second World (Bontje 2005), they are a unique and numerous feature of Leipzig's urban fabric, and are currently very attractive to cultural workers and what could be considered members of a creative class (Florida 2002). After Reunification, Leipzig's population

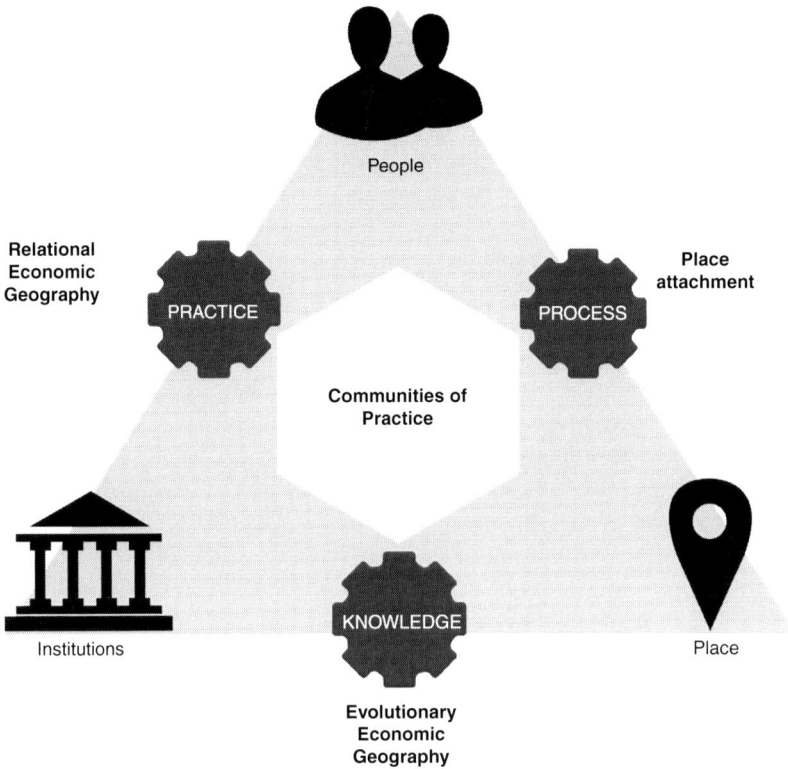

Figure 10.1 Complexity framework IPP
Source: Author.

declined to a dramatic low of 437,000 by 1998, in line with the loss of approximately 90,000 manufacturing jobs (Plöger 2007). The rapid social and economical transformation triggered by the integration of East Germany into the social market economy system of the BRD (Bundesrepublik Deutschland[2]), led to a wave of outmigration, primarily to West Germany, and on the other side to a process of sub-urbanisation as inner-city housing stock was in severe disrepair. As part of a vast economic and urban transformation process, primarily financed by West Germany (Wießner 1999), a large percentage of Leipzig's inner-city building stock was able to be refurbished despite vacancy rates reaching a peak of 65,500 units in 2000 (Plöger 2007). From 2003 onwards, the city regained population (Stadt Leipzig 2009, 2013) as primarily young demographics in educational or transitional living stages migrated into inner-city neighbourhoods (Haase *et al*. 2012). In fact, a comparatively high population gain suggests that West Leipzig's neighbourhoods Plagwitz and Lindenau are attracting new residents, as well as the East Leipzig regeneration area Leipziger Osten becoming a new area of interest. This shows how the west of the city, which until the mid-2000s had a comparatively high percentage of buildings in disrepair, attracts a community served by afford-able space and an existing diverse cultural infrastructure (Stadt Leipzig 2010).

Most remarkable are the many bottom up urban initiatives founded in the city within the last 10–15 years, such as many neighbourhood gardens, off-spaces and the guardian house (*Wächsterhäuser*) initiatives set up by the association HausHalten e.V. This has become a locally prominent model of pioneer regen-eration (or even pioneer gentrification, as some critics suggest), widely accepted and promoted by locals and the city government as a counter strategy to urban decay and long-term shrinkage. The mostly voluntary run association provides local expertise for connecting property owners with tenants – a mix of artists, activists and students, among others, often living in a communal setting. They can live rent-free in vacant, non- or semi-refurbished dwellings in exchange for basic maintenance work, such as protecting the building from intruders and covering the basic upkeep and utility fees (Bernet 2011; Plöger 2007).

Furthermore, the embeddedness of a network of cultural workers and social entrepreneurs, especially in the West of the city, formed the basis of recent creative-city policies, such as Projekt Creative City that is an EU-funded initiative to develop and sustain West Leipzig's cultural infrastructure (Stadt Leipzig 2012). Such initiatives were aimed at strengthening the creative and cultural industries (CCIs), particularly in the Lindenau-Plagwitz creative cluster (Stadt Leipzig 2010), which unavoidably resulted in the marketing of production venues and subcultural developments. This stands in critical juxtaposition to the preferred self-management principles of many of the local communities, among them artists who express fear of over-marketing and the commodification of open space (Bernet 2011; Treppenhauer 2013). Although Leipzig offers its communities the ability to shape an authentic urban living through the previously mentioned house projects as a prominent example, there is a consensus that the timeframe of using such opportunities will be closing in soon as pressure for the displacement of cultural uses grows due to property speculation, rising population numbers and increasing awareness of Leipzig's lively cultural sector (Treppenhauer 2013; Raabe and Waltz 2014). In line with much of the hype around Leipzig's urbanness and cultural milieu, the subcultural scene and, most importantly, the visual arts economy in Leipzig have become marketing instruments for the city – not just in attracting art world elites and the educated middle classes (*Bildungsbürgertum*), but also German and international students wishing to explore the city and become part of its developing scene. This can be seen as a form of regeneration of the city image, which is in fact accelerated by online travel blogging and marketing of the city's unique character, described as 'Berlin 10 years ago' (New York Times 2010) or more recently through the emergence of the term 'Hypezig' (Herrmann 2014).

Alongside this, the success of the so-called New Leipzig School (NLS) was a highly important player in the hype process. NSL is a post-Reunification move-ment in postmodern German painting, connected to a group of artists trained at the HGB in the late 1980s. Most of the painters, among them Neo Rauch, Matthias Weischer and David Schnell, are currently based at Spinnerei, a former cotton mill and now commercially successful visual arts hub located at the edge between Plagwitz and Lindenau in West Leipzig. The NLS artists were all educated at the HGB during the 1980s and early 1990s, when conceptual and new media practices gained huge popularity. Then, the traditional figurative principles trained at HGB were considered backward looking (Modes 2007; Rehberg and Schmidt 2009). After Reunification, however, the skill-based education model dramatically distinguished the school from its West German and international counterparts, hence attracting a large amount of West German students who favoured traditional teaching over a studio-led experimental approach (Gerlach 2008). This quality of teaching strongly reflects the technical capacity and figurative style of NLS work[3] which was considered highly desirable, not only because of its skill-based aesthetics but due to its novelty status on the art market. Looking further back into the East German art school education reveals that the HGB was one of only four official art schools in East Germany. Arts education opportunities then were kept to a minimum, as the CCIs were institutionalised and only served by the socialist state (Bismarck and Koch 2005) However, due to a continuity of strong HGB leadership that supported the teaching of a critical and independent voice in artists, students were allowed to develop politically challenging work within the boundary of the academy (Rehberg and Schmidt 2009).

Although the success of the NLS as a poster child for Leipzig's blossoming cultural economy has secured markets for key cultural institutions, selected gallerists and artists, Leipzig's cultural economy became stigmatised by these trends. The supposed members of the NLS did not support the branding of their identity as a movement, as they believed the media hype constituted a devaluation of their artistic content (Modes 2007). This balancing problem reflects the strife between artistic and commercial goals, which in essence builds on Adorno's (2001) critique of the conceptual ambivalence of culture and economy. Whether or not the NLS is a good example of a community of practice (Wenger 1998) is not readily determinable, as the definition of the movement and its members is intangible. Nevertheless a strong linkage between values and skills gained at the school suggests a distinct cultural repertoire is being shaped among visual artists in the city, even today.

To counteract the NLS stigma, Koch (2006) argues that the diversity of the different artistic fields – from the corporate art market to socially engaged art, for example – cannot be reconciled, unless we allow for a compromise to take place at the interface between each field to build common opportunities. While securing a historic continuity of skill-based training at the HGB, critical engagement with the current state of artistic training engages with some of Koch's contextual questions. This was manifested through recent events and exhibitions at the HGB including an artist-centred inquiry into cultural work that culminated with a publication on artistic livelihoods beyond art school education (Bismarck and Koch 2005) and, most recently, a student-led committee and exhibition project that discusses new student-led possibilities for artistic training (Rödel *et al.* 2014).

One cannot deny that Leipzig's cultural diversity and its unique urban setting contribute hugely to its attractiveness, both in terms of quality of life and its capacity for cultural emancipation. However, due to a relatively weak economy and lack of employment opportunities for young demographics, the attraction and retention of cultural workers is limited to the city's economic capacities, i.e. through the fulfilment of employment perspectives and/or the development of alternative economies (Burdack *et al.* 2009). Despite the creative class being considered highly mobile (Florida 2005b), Burdack *et al.* (2009) found that cultural workers were unlikely to move away once settled in Leipzig, as they were generally satisfied with the quality of life in the city. Soft factors such as cultural diversity, personal relationships and the friendliness of the city were considered key retaining factors for creative talent in Leipzig. But most importantly, the affordability of space serves as a crucial element for the decision to stay in Leipzig to balance out the weakness of the local job market. Leipzig's urban planning department (Stadt Leipzig 2010) followed this up with a study on reasons for settlement and place attachment in Leipzig's West, underlining the findings above. In this way the actors reinforce the importance of pioneer-potential in the above areas through the quality and affordability of dwellings, the existing creative networks and the unique cultural and urban atmosphere. Whereas the relaxed spatial market through the availability of industrial architecture and open spaces (participants stressed the need for rawness in the build environment) was a concurrent reason for settlement, the importance of existing networks increased between 2000 and 2010 with the growth of the creative network and changing image of the neighbourhoods. Steets' (2007) extensive qualitative study entitled 'We Are the City' investigates Leipzig's cultural networks and the development of open spaces through a biographically induced qualitative angle. This research carefully considers connected processes that lead to place attachment of cultural workers, assigning significance to strong networks as a prerequisite for place attachment rather than to the character of the city itself. It is also argued that social networks were crucial for the realisation of specific projects, which generated a feeling of buzz and momentum.

The art school as interface for practices at the intersection between artistic autonomy and commercial activity

This section outlines the findings of this chapter, putting the theoretic framework in Figure 10.1 into practice by investigating the links and processes between IPP. I will start the discussion by highlighting the importance of the local art school for the development of artistic positions and networks. The HGB, as similarly outlined in the literature, was perceived as a highly attractive and distinguished place to study, due to its traditional teaching framework that is unique within the national and international context. In fact 13 out of the total 17 participants for this research have or have had close connections with HGB, through either studying or working at the institution:

> Without the HGB, there would be nothing here. This art school was and still is a major hub. I am not there anymore, but everything I do is connected with people from the HGB.
>
> *(Curator)*

The notion of the institution as the interface for Leipzig's visual arts economy was addressed many times by the respondents, who also acknowledged the importance of the traditional teaching system consisting of a two-year foundation and three-year Master's-level diploma. Foundation studies at the HGB, considered extremely beneficial to the attractiveness of the HGB, include solid training in drawing and conceptual skills, while going through all the workshops that the academy has to offer, e.g. woodwork, photography and print-making, among others. The diploma can be topped by a two-year master class (*Meisterschüler*) study, which is a system by which selected students can intensify their practice through working closely with a specific tutor, who either works similarly technically or conceptually. While this is considered unique within the current Western art school context, it is felt that the system is not as open to accommodate new forms of artistic training independent from the agenda of tutors. Nevertheless, due to the continued skill-based distinctiveness, the school is a renowned place for emerging artists to aspire to. This also aligns with the NLS movement, which was considered by some participants a strong driver of the hype around the school and its graduates, especially since the mid-2000s. This again had a lasting effect on the perception of the city as an attractive and unique place, as a number of participants have noted:

> The good thing about this school is that you have solid foundation studies, which is really important. That is also one of the reasons why so many apply to us.
>
> *(Lecturer 1)*

> I believe that the HGB had an important role [in attracting talent], on the one hand due to the NLS hype, which brought many people to the city and to the HGB.
>
> *(Arts professional)*

> I always thought that as a painter you are flexible, that you can work wherever you want [...] But I actually realised that the time I spent here [at art school] has done some unconscious bonding with place, where you teach yourself how to understand it and how to use it for your work.
>
> *(Meisterschüler student)*

The school does not just attract young people to the city; it is also an important element in the process of artists bonding with Leipzig. As the above student has illustrated, it becomes clear that the time art students spend at the school offers a unique setting for one's personal and professional development. This clearly highlights the importance of having a formal structure – in this case, the pedagogic network of the HGB – within which one has time for experimentation around the development of an artistic livelihood and an independent artistic practice away from market pressure. There are a number of students who stretch their time at the institution even longer than the regular 5–7 year frame, as they fear the difficulty of entering the cultural labour market, as well as the loss of backup structure the institution provides. Many of the school's mature students also have childcare responsibilities because of which they are forced to pause their studies.

While the school is considered to be a large part of the success story behind the hype around NSL, and part of the city's attractiveness, there are a lot more differentiated and critical views on this phenomenon. This has already trickled through in Modes' (2007) argument that artists – especially those directly associated with NSL – felt instrumentalised by the hype around the movement. A lecturer at HGB notes on a connected issue that he perceived that the aspirations of the school and its prospective students fade as they enter the system:

> People are engaged for as long as they are not enrolled yet. As they arrive, they often tick the boxes and remove themselves from what the school has to offer.
>
> *(Lecturer)*

> I have the feeling that there's a strong inside–outside notion. Although I had many friends at HGB, there still was a strong sentiment of belonging or not belonging to the HGB.
>
> *(Arts educator)*

While the exclusivity of the HGB is criticised by some outside actors that were interviewed, one can also perceive increasing fragmentation within the student body of the institution itself. There are those students who are critically engaged around the context of their education, wishing to be autonomous and not aligned with the commercial ambitions of the school, while others go along with the system and are critical only within the parameters of their own artistic practice. The more autonomous ambitions again reflect the conscience that the school needs to open up to new forms of teaching around new media and contextual studies (Rödel *et al.* 2014), while at the same time, many students aspire to develop new models for integrating autonomous artistic ambitions with institutional structures:

> There are very few places that are not as fragmented. Places where you can go, where many different interest groups can come together and explore similarities. But those places are weakened. Those places are famished through autonomy.
>
> *(Lecturer)*

While fragmentation can prevent certain economic activities from happening simply because there is often not enough common ground for conversation, there was a perception that these tensions are also needed in order to develop new opportunities outside the institutional context – whether that is through setting up off-spaces or through developing alternative economic models, such as around improving cultural work conditions and creating alternative markets for visual artists. The tension between autonomy and commercial thinking becomes particularly clear when investigating the evolution of key cultural stakeholders in Leipzig.

Lindenow, as a prime example of autonomy in the arts, is a network of independent art spaces in Leipzig with a core focus to showcase visual art outside the commercial setting, and testing new artistic formats and experimental ideas not just within the parameters of cultural practice itself, but also in terms of its urban context. The core team curates a yearly festival in collaboration with off-space initiatives and more permanent independent galleries. Lindenow also facilitates exchange and residency activities for visual artists, similar to many other actors in Leipzig who run initiatives within the autonomy context in Leipzig. The network, while representing a range of artists and off-spaces, is linked with social activists and guardian house initiatives in order to access joint opportunities and sustain affordable space. Initiatives like these are linked to an alternative economy that is based on bypassing the monetary system of exchange, and building collective forms of exchange and ownership with a long-term vision. People with these ambitions have often either bought property collectively within the timeframe of the last 5–10 years when it was still reasonably cheap to buy underused period-style houses, or maintained them by participating in a guardian house project:

> First of all, we have just paid bills but no rent at all. Then we decided as a collective to dare the experiment and live together. Hence, we decided to buy this house, because we already invested time in it. We knew the house very well. We knew its weaknesses. That's why we could estimate what needed to be done. You have many expenses with a house. The other side to it is that it takes a long time and energy to refurbish a place bit by bit.
>
> *(Artist)*

This statement also hints at the bonding work that is done while investing time and energy in such a large collective effort. It shows dedication to a place and a community. However, while this is an aspirational context for selected artists to be engaged in (not exclusively linked to an artistic practice), for others this seems a distraction from a more conventional professional artistic career:

> There are many here in Leipzig who turned their off-space projects into a career, so to speak their main professional focus, and they are idealistic about clamping onto it while putting aside other professional aspirations. Then with 30 they live a lefty existence in an occupied house and only complain about gentrification. I find that tragic.
>
> *(Curator)*

This to some degree also reflects on the level of self-exploitation that is expected of artists in order to develop an independent artistic practice that does not necessarily bring financial return. It instead offers the freedom for self-realisation and emancipation at the cost of stability and self-sustainability. Often actors are engaged in such endeavours over a long period of time – starting with when they are still in HE – but find themselves lacking mechanisms to make projects financially sustainable. Similar actors also rely on public subsidy, or the sole support of a network of volunteers within a shared economy, within which ideals such as solidarity and collectiveness are inevitable. While it is necessary for the visual arts to have enough space for autonomous practices embedded in a context of sustaining cultural production space over a long term, it is also very important to engage in an economically viable vision for extracting some financial return from artistic practice or from the contexts in which it operates. Along this line, there has been a consensus that autonomous thinking needs to balance with commercial thinking in order to support the continued growth of individual and collective practices. This means coming to terms with financial systems and commercial interests, and mediating them carefully, in order to enable economic activities without disabling independent artistic vision.

Some key stakeholders within Leipzig's visual arts economy were classified by a number of participants as post-institutional spaces, as they perceived them as a direct extension of the HGB, providing transition space from pedagogic to professional structures. The most important player within this context is Spinnerei, the arts hub in Plagwitz, that hosts several internationally acclaimed galleries and artists, especially many of those considered to be part of the NLS. Due to the commercial orientation of many of the galleries and studio spaces at Spinnerei, the hub is considered a direct counter model to Lindenow. Spinnerei serves many (mostly commercially successful) artists not just with studio and exhibition space, but also with workshop facilities and networking opportunities within a rather exclusively perceived network that is occasionally open to wider audiences on open days and educational events. Similarly as with the HGB, Spinnerei functions as a hub/interface for the visual arts economy. This goes along with some artists' perception of having found exactly what they were looking for at Spinnerei, in terms of a workshop and networking environment:

> Artist A was in Rome for one year, but he actually has his centre of life here in Leipzig. He has a studio here [Spinnerei] and a silk screen workshop, similarly as Artist B who manages a publishing house here and exhibits in London and Paris. His centre is Leipzig too, where his publishing business is and his print workshops are. That's the same as with Artist C who works on this campus too.
>
> *(Artist)*

Others again have stated that the availability of open, non-institutionalised space in connection with the more formal institutional frameworks, e.g. HGB, Spinnerei and off-spaces, makes the city so attractive and diverse. The tension between formal and informal (unfinished, crude, imperfect) is perceived as something very valuable for the development of new opportunities and ideas. One student, who is practising from a shared studio space in the East of the city, has expressed this sentiment in the following way:

> You need this dirt to stimulate, there's this need to be in such makeshift circumstances in order for you to have an engine, to have this friction, that

makes you do the work. Everything still breathes here. You have the feeling you can move things with very little means. You don't need to have millions in your bank account to own property or to develop a project. And that's where subculture starts: With little and no money, creativity, and, just, passion to engage with a city that is open for that.

*(*Meisterschüler *Student)*

This clearly highlights the important interconnection between the identity and form of the city in relation to the development of cultural institutions and networks. There are inevitably many links between artists and urban change in Leipzig, due to their pioneer activities and transformation of unused property into living and work space. However, while their urban impact and engagement with gentrification is an important process, it is not the main focus of this chapter. Instead, I will highlight more closely some concluding dynamics aligned with the community of practice concept, in order to outline how evolution within networks enables urban pioneering activities.

As previously outlined, there is a strong notion around collectiveness embedded in Leipzig's creative economy, and beyond that across the city's subcultural environment, that is coined by a vast student population and a historically acknowledged sense of solidarity, i.e. Leipzig as the site of peaceful revolution in 1989. However, this solidarity seems to take place within rather small fragmented groups/networks, within which similar interests and ambitions are shared. One of the participants, who has an inside and an outside view by virtue of the position of lecturer at the HGB, has stressed that these scenes are 'a world within a world' (Lecturer) and, hence, difficult to understand for outsiders. As activities evolve within small groups, a number of participants recalled that their economic opportunities became more tangible. However, as interests and activities intensify and/or diversify, there is a risk of (1) fragmented interests within the group which might lead to members leaving and (2) less tolerance of outside actors wishing to join:

The spirit of cooperation can only be carried by an idea of departure, that you will create something new and something proper. But when the first excitement is over, then it becomes difficult as people develop different interests [...] That's why our team broke apart. There are changing collaborations, but also those that intensify.

(Curator)

Groups or networks within which innovation takes place were perceived to often protect their distinct knowledge through developing exclusive internal support structures. Also, for artistic practice as a mode of work, such support structures were considered highly important to overcome isolation and risks associated with financial uncertainty and instability (Banks *et al.* 2000). Here we can draw a line between the exclusivity of the HGB on the one hand and, on the other, the small, differentiated networks that either break away from the school or develop completely independently as a counter-argument to the commercial art market.

	HGB	Spinnerei	Lindenow, off-spaces
Actors	Students, gradutes, lecturers, staff, NLS visual artists as honorary staff	Students, gradutes, professional artists, gallerists, curators, non-for-profit arts institutions	Students, emerging artists, social activists, local community etc.
Organisational structure	Institutional	Post-institutional	Self-organised, non-institutional
Economic alignment	Art market, publicly funded	Art market, publicly funded	Alternative economy (shared economy, non-monetary, collective finance)
Ideology	Commercial vs Autonomy	Commercial	Autonomy
Network composition	Exclusivity, inside-outside notion, fragmentation of student body due to different ideologied	Exclusivity occasional community enga gement events	Fragmentation and diversification of networks and interests, small exclusive groups

Figure 10.2 Structure of Leipzig's visual art economy
Source: Author.

It can thus be argued that the art school is the interface/key institution that brings artistic talent to the city and, through providing an open yet structured pedagogic framework, shapes a lot of the cultural repertoire through which engagement at the intersection between the art market and autonomy takes place. To provide a clearer orientation around the role of key actors and institutions that were discussed in the findings, I have developed a framework aligning them within a spectrum between the art market and autonomy (Figure 10.2).

Conclusion

In conclusion I will provide a short discussion on how the findings link with the theoretical framework outlined in the beginning of this chapter. This serves firstly as a way to highlight the relevance of complexity thinking for creative cities research, and secondly it will illustrate the importance of the local art school as an element within the development of Leipzig as a creative city. Therefore, I have adapted the introductory framework (see Figure 10.1) to the specific Leipzig context by replacing the theoretical elements with actual actors (people), institutions and processes identified in the findings and the literature about Leipzig (Figure 10.3).

While Figure 10.2 clearly shows how the art school is an interface for the emergence of communities of practice between the art market and autonomy, Figure 10.3 highlights the close relationship between knowledge, practice and (place attachment) processes evolving within communities of practice and between IPP. According to this framework, the art school links both relational

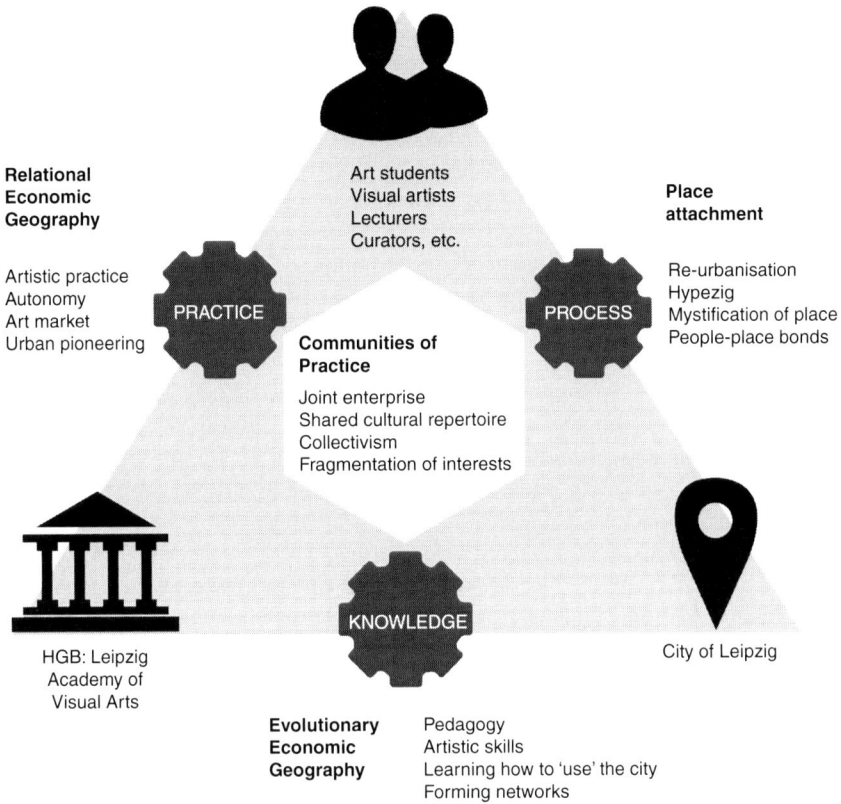

Figure 10.3 Complexity framework IPP applied to the Leipzig context
Source: Author.

aspects with evolutionary economic geography approaches. This indicates how embedded the emergence of local knowledge (evolutionary aspects) is with the development of network embedded practices, such as through professional artistic development or urban pioneering, as an alternative to this (relational aspects). This again holds relevance for understanding the structure of communities of practice, which is a concept that is situated at the heart of this complexity analysis. This is because it provides insight into the internal processes of networks, such as through shared cultural repertoire, which in the Leipzig context is coined by the ambivalence between the art market and autonomy, as well as through joint and co-located enterprise, mediated within small fragmented groups and exclusive networks, to protect the local cultural repertoire. Here again the role of place attachment is key, as is noting its important interconnection with local knowledge and practice. Aligned with the knowledge development, through the distinguished skill-based pedagogies at the HGB, is the emergence of informal knowledge on how artists can engage with the city – both as space in which an artistic livelihood is negotiated and as a realm for inspiration through the city's crudeness and cultural tensions. Precisely because Leipzig has such an open character (unfinished built environment, affordability, culturally active, diverse, etc.), it allows for the materialisation of a diversity of commercial or autonomous opportunities for artists that are practices piloted already during an artist's time at the HGB. At the same time as professional artists require access to local infrastructure and networks (e.g. workshops and studios at Spinnerei), more autonomous groups also have strong infrastructural ties and responsibilities, such as maintaining a collective house or artist-led space. This often means long-term investment of time and manpower, which binds people with place.

While this has served for an in-depth understanding of the different types of economic activities from commercial orientation towards alternative economic models outside monetary markets, there is space for debating how and whether the visual arts sector can be further developed. Until now, Leipzig held the unique position of a city with enough affordable space to accommodate artists at different stages of their careers. I would argue it is crucial to a city's cultural distinctiveness, and cultural productivity, to understand this economic diversity (i.e. to accommodate different economies or different development stages within an economy) as an asset for enabling creative city development.

However, with the vastly increasing population and rent increases to follow, the hierarchy of these spaces may no longer be sustainable. This could be an incentive for art students to engage more with the art market, as a way to balance out autonomy thinking, which seems to starve the institutional spirit of the school. The growth of the city might attract more economic and financial capital, which could lead to increasing public and private investment in the visual arts sector. It could, however, also mean further displacement of visual arts production spaces and less room for experimentation. It is yet to be determined whether the city's growth has the potential to strengthen the economic viability of the sector and provide employment for arts graduates, rather than exposing them to more voluntary and self-exploitative activity under the umbrella of social engagement and urban pioneering.

Notes

1. For clarification the creative economy includes both the creative industries commonly aligned with digital technologies as well as the broader often publicly funded cultural sector (UNESCO 2013; UNCTAD 2008).
2. Translates as Federal Republic of Germany. The term was used during the Cold War to refer to West Germany.
3. For examples of work of the so-called New Leipzig School (Neue Leipziger Schule) and a detailed discussion on its emergence see: https://www.youtube.com/watch?v=0bBBq4sZ89I (in German only).

References

Adorno, T. W. (2001) *The Culture Industry: Selected Essays on Mass Culture*, 2nd edn. London and New York: Psychology Press.

Banks, M., Lovatt, A., O'Connor, J. and Raffo, C. (2000) 'Risk and trust in the cultural industries', *Geoforum*, 31 (4): 453–64.

Bathelt, H. and Glückler, J. (2003) 'Toward a relational economic geography', *Journal of Economic Geography*, 3 (2): 117–44.

Bernet, T. (2011) *Bunte Grauzone: eine Ethnographie lokaler Akteure der Stadtentwicklung in Leipzig-Lindenau*, Lizenziatsarbeit der Philosophischen Fakultät edn. Zurich: Universität Zürich.

Bismarck, B. v., and Koch, A. (eds) (2005) *Beyond Education. Kunst, Ausbildung, Arbeit und Ökonomie*. Leipzig: Revolver-Archiv für aktuelle Kunst.

Bontje, M. (2005) 'Facing the challenge of shrinking cities in East Germany: the case of Leipzig', *GeoJournal*, 61 (1): 13–21.

Burdack, J., Lange, B. and Ehrlich, K. (2009) *Creative Leipzig? The Views of High-skilled Employees, Managers and Transnational Migrants*. Amsterdam: AMIDSt, University of Amsterdam.

Champion, T. (2001) 'Urbanization, suburbanization, counterurbanization and reurbanization', in R. Paddinson (ed.), *Handbook of Urban Studies*. London: Sage, pp. 143–61.

Comunian, R. (2010) 'Rethinking the creative city: the role of complexity, networks and interactions in the urban creative economy', *Urban Studies*, 48: 1157–79.

Comunian, R. and Faggian, A. (2014) 'Creative graduates and creative cities: exploring the geography of creative education in the UK', *International Journal of Cultural and Creative Industries*, 1 (2): 19–34.

Florida, R. (2002) *The Rise of the Creative Class*. New York: Basic Books.

Florida, R. (2005a) *Cities and the Creative Class*. New York: Routledge.

Florida, R. (2005b) *The Flight of the Creative Class: The New Global Competition for Talent*. New York: Harper Business.

Gerlach, S. (2008) 'From famed to shame – the transition of a former East German arts academy to the talent hotbed of a contemporary painters' school, Hochschule für Grafik und Buchkunst, Leipzig', in M. Jordan and E. Miles (eds), *Art and Theory After Socialism*. Bristol: Intellect.

Haase, A., Herfert, G., Kabisch, S. and Steinführer, A. (2012) 'Reurbanizing Leipzig (Germany): context conditions and residential actors (2000–2007)', *European Planning Studies*, 20 (7): 1173–96.

Harris, A. and Moreno, L. (2010) *Creative City Limits: Urban Cultural Economy in a New Era of Austerity*. London: UCL Urban Lab.

Herrmann, A. (2014) *Hypezig Tumblr*. Retrieved from: http://hypezig.tumblr.com/ (accessed on 10 April 2015).

Koch, A. (2006) *Künstlerische Grenzverschiebungen? Sind die ostdeutschen Transformationserfahrungen von Kulturbetrieb und Gesellschaft Sinnbild für ein neues Verhältnis von Kunst, Institutionen und Politik?*, Referat zur 5. Kulturwerkstatt des Gesprächskreises. Berlin: Kultur und Politik des Forum Ostdeutschland der Sozialdemokratie e.V.

Landry, C. (2008) *The Creative City: A Toolkit for Urban Innovators*, 2nd edn. London: Earthscan.

Lefebvre, H. (1991) *The Production of Space*. Oxford: Oxford Blackwell.

Martin, R. and Sunley, P. (2007) 'Complexity thinking and evolutionary economic geography', *Journal of Economic Geography*, 7 (5): 573–601.

Modes, C. (2007) *Die Neue Leipziger Schule: Eine akteurzentrierte Diskursanalyse*, Magisterarbeit am Institut für Kulturwissenschaften der Universität Leipzig. Munich: GRIN.

New York Times (2010) *The 31 Places to Go in 2010* (Homepage of New York Times). (Online) Retrieved from: http://www.nytimes.com/2010/01/10/travel/10places. html?pagewanted=alland_r=1 and (accessed on 10 April 2015).

O'Connor, J. and Shaw, K. (2014) 'What next for the creative city?', *City, Culture and Society*, 5 (3): 165–70.

Plöger, J. (2007) *Leipzig City Report*, CASEreport No. 42. London: London School of Economics and Political Science.

Raabe, M. and Waltz, M. (2014) *Swinging Leipzig: Subkulturelles Image und Marketing.* (Homepage of Deutschlandfunk). Retrieved from: http://www.deutschlandfunk.de/ swinging-leipzig-subkulturelles-image-und-marketing.1170.de.html?dram:article_ id=275496 (accessed on 22 April 20140.

Rehberg, K. and Schmidt, H. (2009) *60/40/20 Kunst in Leipzig seit 1949*. Leipzig: Seemann.

Robinson, M. (2010) *Making Adaptive Resilience Real*. London: Arts Council England.

Rödel, P., Czarnecki, C. and Ruske, L. (2014) *AG zeitgenössische künstlerische Lehre* (Homepage of Hochschule für Grafik und Buchkunst). Retrieved from: http://www. hgb-leipzig.de/agzkl/ (accessed 15 April 2015).

Scannell, L. and Gifford, R. (2010) 'Defining place attachment: a tripartite organizing framework', *Journal of Environmental Psychology*, 30 (1): 1–10.

Stadt Leipzig (2009) *Leipzig 2020: Integriertes Stadtentwicklungskonzept (SEKo)*. Leipzig: Stadt Leipzig Dezernat Stadtentwicklung und Bau.

Stadt Leipzig (2010) *Die 'Kreative Szene' im Leipziger Westen: Eine Untersuchung über den Einfluss der Kreativen in Plagwitz/Lindenau auf die Stadtteilentwicklung, Wechselwirkungen zwischen Gebietsstrukturen und Szene sowie potenzielle Ansätze zur Entwicklungsverstätigung.* Leipzig: Stadtplanungsamt Leipzig Abteilung West.

Stadt Leipzig (2012) *Kreative Zukunft: Werkstatt zur Entwicklung des Leipzier Westens. Projekt Creative Cities (INTERREG IV B)*. Leipzig: Stadt Leipzig, Amt für Stadterneuerung und Wohnungsbauförderung.

Stadt Leipzig (2013) *Statistischer Quartalsbericht 4/2013*. Leipzig: Stadt Leipzig, Amt für Statistik und Wahlen.

Steets, S. (2007) *Wir sind die Stadt! Kulturelle Netzwerke und die Konstitution städtischer Räume in Leipzig*. Frankfurt: Campus-Verlag.

Sunley, P. (2008) 'Relational economic geography: a partial understanding or a new paradigm?', *Economic Geography*, 84 (1): 1–26.

Treppenhauer, P. (2013) *Gastbeitrag: Gentrifizierung und die 'kreative Stadt'.* (Homepage of Kreatives Leipzig). Retrieved from: http://www.kreatives-leipzig.de/leipzig/gastbeitrag-gentrifizierung-und-die-kreative-stadt.html (accessed on 26 November 2013).

UNCTAD (2008) *Creative Economy Report*. Geneva: United Nations Conference on Trade and Development.

UNESCO (2013) *United Nations Creative Economy Report*. New York and Paris: UNESCO.

Vickery, J. (2011) *Beyond the Creative City – Cultural Policy in an Age of Scarcity*. Birmingham: MADE Centre for Place-making.

Wenger, E. (1998) *Communities of Practice: Learning, Meaning, and Identity*. Cambridge: Cambridge University Press.

Wießner, R. (1999) 'Urban development in East Germany   specific features of urban transformation processes', *GeoJournal*, 49 (1): 43–51.

11 Cultural policy, creative economy and arts higher education in renaissance Singapore

Venka Purushothaman[1]

Introduction

Since the tail end of the twentieth century, postcolonial Singapore has seen an astonishing investment, development, and growth in the cultural and creative industries aimed at creating a renaissance city-state. The opening of the National Gallery, on the fiftieth year of independence in 2015, ushers in a symbolically central place for the arts in ensuring Singapore remains a distinctive global city in a rapidly shape-shifting geopolitical environment in Southeast Asia. This global city remains small, nimble, and directed: a city-state of 718 square kilometers, with a population size of 5.5 million, boasting a literacy rate of 97 percent, a near perfect employment economy, and a per capita GDP that is the envy of even first-world nations.[2] Central to the unprecedented development for a city-state that gained independence in 1965 are principles of economic pragmatism and nationalism based on multiculturalism and Asian values, which direct social and political life in Singapore. These principles have provided Singapore with world-class transport, public housing, financial, and industrial systems.

Singapore also boasts a world-class educational system. The 2015 OECD global ranking places Singapore at the pole position above most developed economies in the Western world for its quality education and high literacy rate among its citizens.[3] OECD research shows a clear correlation between investment in education and economic growth; this is underscored by Singapore's annual budget where education is the second largest recipient of allocation following defence.[4] Unlike many governments where economic downturn sees budget cuts in education, in Singapore the education sector thrives, receiving serious injection of resources. This is a clear directed belief that a nimble economic system must rely on continuous self-reflection, restructuring, and repurposing of the skills of the workforce. This has augured well for Singapore to allow it to tide over economic challenges. In 2015, the government established the Skills Future Council in a national effort to 'develop skills for the future and help Singaporeans develop a future based on skills mastery.'[5] This generous support for all citizens proposes to help Singaporeans compete in the marketplace through skills mapping, planning for career progression, and developing a culture of lifelong learning. This is championed by the top brass of the government, notably the Deputy Prime Minister and Minister of Finance, Tharman Shanmugaratnam.

Since the 1990s, Singapore has invested in the arts in the way it knows best: anchored in the economy. The ultimate aim is to generate a creative economy that will develop alternative modes of economic output as traditional modes, such as manufacturing and electronics, face increasing global competition from emerging market economies in Asia. From arts centres and museums to musicals and circuses, from arts festivals to Formula One races, and from food festivals to design and media festivals – Singapore has opened up to the possibilities of the creative world in ways that were deemed fictitious in a city known for its tough economic pragmatism. The arts have become one of the drivers of economic inno-vation and growth (besides education, science, and technology), as well as making Singapore a liveable city attractive to international investment and maintaining its competitive advantage in the global economy. Singapore takes this seriously and clearly sees the benefits of a creative and vibrant culture, benchmarking itself against cities such as Hong Kong, Glasgow, and Melbourne, aspiring to becoming the London or New York of Asia.

The competition to be a global city is on the rise in Asia. Other Asian cities, such as Seoul, Hong Kong, and Abu Dhabi, demonstrate similar aspirations to become global cities through the arts, flagging an existential jump into the global league. Unfazed by geopolitical shifts, changes in critical political leaderships – in particular China, India, and Indonesia, where such investments in the arts and culture are part of a larger socio-political-culture agenda – Singapore's proposi-tion remains focused on the economy. While a multi-billion dollar investment in the arts in Singapore has helped the development of artist communities and increased economic multipliers (STB Report 1998), the arts and culture are relevant, insofar as their nexus to the economy, making it increasingly difficult to articulate a culture outside of its economic conditions.

To support the creative economy, art and design education was fortified, gaps were identified, and new areas developed through input from industry. Since the 1990s, the National Arts Council has invested in arts enrichment programs, while the Ministry of Education (MOE) has introduced a range of elective arts educa-tion programs to permeate every stage of a student's learning journey. From 2009, MOE rolled out an Arts Syllabus for primary school education (ages 6–12 years) to systematically and methodically introduce art to young learners. The Ministry of Information, Communications, and the Arts (MICA) established a pre-tertiary (ages 13–18 years) School of the Arts (SOTA) in 2008 in the International Baccalaureate (IB) curriculum for secondary arts education. Yet there are also community-based arts organizations providing hobbyist and/or skills-based train-ing. Schools such as the Theatre Practice, Intercultural Theatre Institute, Singapore Indian Fine Arts Society, and Sri Warisan provide self-validated certificate programs in niche areas. In addition, Singapore's business develop-ment arm, the Economic Development Board, courted educational investment in a short lived enterprise called the Global Schoolhouse project.

If the entrenched link between higher education and economic output needs a creative boost, arts higher education in Singapore became a major pipeline for the creative economy. The university sector introduced western classical music

(Yong Siew Toh Conservatory) at the National University of Singapore and the School of Art, Design and Media (ADM) at the Nanyang Technological University. The Singapore University of Technology and Design was established in 2010 to bridge design and engineering education to develop a new generation of design thinkers who can effect change in various sectors of Singapore society. Singapore's renowned and established arts schools – Lasalle College of the Arts (1984) and the Nanyang Academy of Fine Arts (1938) – remain central to the creative economy as producers of art, artists, and designers, even as local universities and polytechnics jump into the fray to supply much needed manpower to fuel the creative economy. Both schools remain important counterpoints to an instrumentalized economic model of developing the arts by continuously providing a critical opportunity for Singaporeans to express their identity and sense of place and as a citizenry focused on the arts' role in nation-building. This chapter first maps the development of the creative economy through key cultural policies and locates the place of arts higher education in Singapore. It demonstrates that the weighted hand of cultural policy, while critical to the establishment of a creative economy, is largely passive on the place of artist education within the world-class conventional educational system.

Decolonization and emerging cultural community

A segue is necessary. The founding of Singapore as a trading port in 1819 did not present itself as a site of inspiration to draw artists, artisans, and craftsman. Key developments in the arts emerged through personal interests and grass-roots community manifestations found in expatriate/colonial and migrant worker communities who engaged with arts and heritage from their country of origin in order to entertain themselves, as well as assert a sense of belonging within their community. History demonstrates that the British presence in Asia saw the introduction of arts education in the late 1800s. For example, immediately after the English language was made the language of the law courts and administration in 1835 in British India, arts schools (Madras in 1854, Calcutta in 1854, Bombay in 1857, and Lahore in 1878) emerged to help revive industries, train professional craftsmen, and improve public taste (Purohit 1988: 639). In 1923, British educator Richard Walker arrived in Singapore to assume the appointment of Art Master of Government English Schools. He oversaw incidental art activities within the formal educational system and the preparedness of a few students for art papers in the Cambridge junior and senior examinations (Kwok 2000). An avid painter trained at the Royal College of Art, he became a key artist of the emerging colonial enterprise of the early 1900s:

> From 1937, Walker's designation was changed to Art Superintendent Singapore Schools. He organised and taught art classes at the Raffles Institution for art teachers and interested students. That year, the Saint Andrew's School Sketching Club was formed, its establishment no doubt influenced by the school principal, Francis Thomas, who was also active in art

education. In 1938, Walker taught art to non-English speakers (mainly Malay teachers) for the first time.

(Kwok 2000: para. 5)

Around the same time, a number of European artists worked out of Singapore during the 1930s and 1940s, such as Russian artists Anatole Schister and Dora Gordine, British painters Margaret Felkin and Eleanor Watkins, Austrian sculptor Karl Duldig and the Belgium artist Adrien-Jean Le Mayeur, who brought classicism to post-impressionism into the language of their art work (Kwok 2000). This formed a small nucleus to inspire and influence an emerging group of Asian artist-migrants within a safe creative learning environment.

Art historian T. K. Sabapathy (1987) pegs the possibility for a modern art history in the making in 1937, when a few China-born artists and enthusiasts sought to establish an arts school. The Nanyang Academy of Fine Arts (NAFA), under the stewardship of artist, educator, and administrator Lim Hak Tai, commenced in 1938 and modelled itself after the art schools in Shanghai. It became the first art school in Singapore/Malaya during British colonial rule and was a hothouse for many self-exiled artists before the World War II, particularly the affectionately known Nanyang artists Cheong Soo Pieng, Chen Chong Swee, Chen Wen Hsi, Liu Kang, and Georgette Chen. Drawing from Chinese painting and School of Paris traditions, these artists were comfortable in both traditions. They were very much part of the regenerative art movement of the 1920s and 1930s in China, particularly in major cities like Shanghai and Guangdong where artists engaged aggressively in 'reinvesting Chinese art with fresh scope and new dimension' (Sabapathy 1987: unpaginated). Caught between a growing nationalism in China and an anti-colonial regionalism in Southeast Asia, tradition, nativity, and modernity framed the works emerging from artist-migrants in a new-found homeland. That the idea of home was in a situatedness rather than a place of birth and was integral to the development of an artistic language and that of an identity through visual culture. This informed the development of various other art societies, notably the Equator Art Society (1956) and the Modern Art Society (1964); the former delved into pictorial realism and the latter into anti-realist, non-objective forms (Chia 2002: 164).

In his 1999 *The End of Empire and Making of Malayan Culture*, T. N. Harper shows that the investment of the British in culture was an explicit promotion of citizenship, a civilising mission of late colonialism to enrich Southeast Asia with a colonial legacy and 'ideological resistance' to the festering problem of Communism that was on the rise in Asia. From the establishment of a National Museum and an Arts Council to research and publish the history and geography of the region, to blatant promotion of tourism by the Singapore Public Relations Office, 'Europeans took the lead in condemning the cultural starvation they felt in insular expatriate communities and the materialism of cities such as Singapore' (Harper 1999: 276). The British also deemed Malaya (of which Singapore was part) a 'cultural desert,' and sought to create a 'cultural renaissance' through British patronage of arts and culture. The formulation of a particular type of colloquial English was promoted through theater and film, while renowned academic I. A. Richard and civil servant Victor Purcell sought to entrench the English language as the first language of the post-colonial elite (ibid.). It was a period of cultural vibrancy with urban and artistic cultures sprouting around movie venues such as Shaw Theatres and Cathay Cinema and amusement parks such as the Great World and the Gay World which served as family and communitarian leisure centres in a poverished yet industrializing milieu (ibid.: 283). These cultural developments balanced artistic and entertainment endeavours with communal aspirations for a social identity. Furthermore, the British supported these developments, as they were part of the process of decolonization.

From 1965 to 1990, post-independence Singapore gained a reputation for its investment in education, industrialization, public housing, and tightly managing a complex group of migrants to become citizens of a nation. While the arts in this period support principles of nation-building, it did not have the cultural vibrancy that an emerging community of newly arrived economic migrants expressed in the 1950s. It is only in the 1990s, when the arts emerged as a constituent of an emerging creative economy, that a semblance of vibrancy was ignited.

Cultural policies for a global renaissance city

> What we are witnessing is an economic and cultural renaissance on a scale never before experienced in human history. Like the renaissance in Europe a few centuries ago, this East Asian renaissance will change the way humanity looks at itself, at human society and at the arts. The rise of cultural life in Singapore is part of an oceanic tidal flow that will wash onto every shore in the Pacific.
>
> (Yeo 1992, cited in Bereson 2003: 6)

As a global city with no natural resources, Singapore is only relevant insofar as it is connected to global economies and their capitalisms, thereby anchoring a nexus between the economy, national identity, and survival. In this regard, any planned cultural policy cannot ignore this imperative. Two cultural policies, the Report of the Advisory Council on Culture and the Arts (1989) and the Renaissance City Report (2000, 2005, 2009), foreground the ways in which they map cultural practice and the shape of the creative economy in Singapore.

The Report by the Advisory Council on Culture and the Arts (ACCA) (Ong 1989), marked a cultural turn for postcolonial Singapore. Not only did this document outline strategies to transform Singapore into a 'global city for the arts' by 2000 (MITA 1995), it drew a clear correlation between art, commerce, and national identity (Koh 1989; Chang and Lee 2003; Kong 2000; Kwok and Low 2002; Chong 2005; Ooi 2010). This policy, which has been extensively deliberated by scholars, reveals the government's use of the arts as a tool to flag its status as a developed country, while simultaneously reinforcing the centrality of economic imperatives within artistic discourse. Moreover, the policy remains the first strategic platform of Singaporean governmentality to have used the arts to signal a new political order and change in political leadership in the 1990s. The political agenda was premised on the need to build a cultural soul for Singapore and develop the arts as an economic asset (Chang 2000).

The ACCA report draws from the Economic Committee Report (1986), which sets the vision for Singapore to become a developed country by 1999. Signalling the ascent of a new Prime Minister, Goh Chok Tong, this formed the key engine for all major policy initiatives from 1990 onwards. The economic plan, which was benchmarked against the Swiss 1984 per capita GNP (MTI 1991), identified economic dynamism, national identity, quality of life, and the configuration of a global city to be central to this vision. This vision included the development of a cultivated society comprising 'well-informed, refined, gracious and thoughtful' individuals where ideas, art, literature, and music flourish (ibid.: 43). Goh's plan was to ensure Singapore sets out to:

> [...] match the quality of life of the best cities in the world if it is to retain its most talented people. By reaching for, and attaining, a high quality of life, Singapore can in turn attract talent ... to achieve economic growth. (Ibid.)

This economic imperative planted the embryonic development of a cultural and creative economy. The industry's function was to ensure Singapore's continued relevance as a centre for international corporate investment, to encourage Singaporeans to take greater ownership of their cultural and social life, and to imagine a sense of community and belonging in a group of migrants maturing to form a citizenry. This is informed by the need to cultivate a well-informed, creative, sensitive, and gracious society; to promote excellence in multi-lingual, multi-cultural collective art forms that make Singapore unique; and to make Singapore an international centre for world-class performing arts and exhibitions marketplace (ibid.: 5). Singaporeans were encouraged to develop an interest in the arts and culture through participation in a wide spread of cultural activities, as amateurs or professionals, which were provided through opportunities of extra-curricular activities at the workplace and at community centres, factories, social clubs, trade unions, clan associations, and religious institutions. This hegemonic system infiltrated layers of society to motivate the citizenry to move away from a third-world mindset and develop a first-world mindset, behaviour, and cultured self.

The strategies of the ACCA report yielded tangible benefits. The city saw the firm development in regulatory agencies, such as the National Arts Council, the National Heritage Board, the Media Development Authority, and the Singapore Design Council, who were tasked to discharge the strategies through expedient administration. A repertoire of works that reflected Singapore's multicultural traditions and artistic endeavours was developed, together with the establishment of a credible community of cultural workers (artists, arts administrators, and arts entrepreneurs) through the import of foreign talent to help nurture and develop them. The ACCA report's overemphasis on developing the city's cultural hardware (Kwok and Low 2002) brought about rapid infrastructural renovations of existing venues, the preservation of historical buildings with architectural and heritage value, and the construction of new venues. It also resulted in performance spaces, such as the Esplanade-Theatres on the Bay, new museums (the Asian Civilisations Museum, the Singapore Art Museum, the Singapore Tyler Print Institute, the Singapore History Museum and the Singapore Philatelic Museum), and highly technologized public libraries in major shopping malls island-wide. These developments provided Singaporeans with the opportunity to view and experience a wide range of performances, exhibitions, and art in public places in a mesmerising first-world, global-city aura.

The economic plans of the 1980s assumed that the vision of changing Singapore into a global city with Swiss living standards would weather conditions that may arise out of a range of natural and human calamities, including economic recession. However, calamities did surface, coupled with public criticism of the government's distribution of funds for arts infrastructure but reticence to provide for art and artist development. Building on the need to connect with disenfranchised Singaporeans, and the need to flag Singapore as a centre for a new renaissance to global investors (Wee 2003), the *Renaissance City Plan: Culture and the Arts in Renaissance Singapore* (MITA 2000) (hereafter RCP) emerged with the sole 'intention to chart Singapore cultural development into the twenty-first century' (Lee 2004: 289).

The concept of a cultural renaissance city is driven by two trajectories. As a remnant of the rising Asian Tiger economies of the 1990s, pundits predicted that the upward rise of these economies would naturally lead to a revisioning of culture. This was fervently developed and championed by then Arts Minister George Yeo in Singapore and then Deputy Prime Minister of Malaysia Anwar Ibrahim in his 1998 critical collection of writings and speeches titled *Asian Renaissance*. Yao Souchou (2000: 18) argues:

> The cultural resurgence in Southeast Asia is primarily a state project that celebrates the moral and utilitarian qualities of the 'Asian tradition' of which the contemporary states and their peoples are the proud inheritors.

Its rise, he asserts, cannot purely be accrued to state domination alone, but needs to take into account the 'active participation and tacit complicity of political subjects' (ibid.). Furthermore, the government saw the arts and culture as a viable economic sector as seen in first-world cities such as Venice, London, New York, Paris, and Milan, which had thriving economic and cultural sectors known as creative industries. Moreover, just as in the British colonial period, the government sought to invest in the arts and culture to mobilize and harness a citizenry that was increasingly desirous of greater social and civic space for socio-political discourse, and the arts and culture were adequate distractions.

With its perpetual penchant for reinvention, the government, in response to global economic changes, invested in the creativity, ingenuity, and imagination of Singaporeans as its next phase of development. This investment in the people as capital was to develop a connected society expressed through tangible links with their emotional and social capital. Just as the ACCA report found its engine in an economic plan, the RCP and the focus on a new cultural/creative economy was fuelled by the 2003 Report of the Economic Review Committee (ERC 2003). The report was published as a formal manifesto titled *New Challenges, Fresh Goals: Towards a Dynamic Global City* (ibid.), and, much like its predecessor, was centered primarily on trade and economy but, embedded within its folds, were critical developments that would design the shape of culture for Singapore. The ERC report envisions transforming Singapore into a twenty-first-century hub for creativity, innovation, and entrepreneurialism. It foregrounds the importance of 'creativity' and the need to build cultural capital as a way forward for Singapore. In so doing, it sought to build a 'creative and innovative society, always eager to try out new ideas and change for the better, with a culture that respects achievements in the sciences and the arts' (ERC 2003: 5). The ERC report notes that the growth of the creative industries was at 14 percent per annum in 2001, outstripping previous overall economic growth of 10.5 percent per annum from 1956 to 2000. The creative industries accounted for 3.2 percent of the country's gross domestic product and provided 3.8 percent employment. With the potential to garner financial gain from the creative industries, the Ministry of Information, Communication, and the Arts (MICA), tasked to build a creative economy, established Creative Industry Singapore, which oversaw the development of three cultural policies targeting specific sectors in the creative industries: *The Renaissance City Plan* (RCP), *Design Singapore*, and *Media 21*. I will focus on the RCP.

The RCP, bold in its expression of a twenty-first-century renaissance Singapore, came in three editions: *Renaissance City Report: Culture and the Arts in Renaissance Singapore* (2000), *Renaissance City Report 2.0* (2005), and *Renaissance City Plan 3* (2008). For the purposes of this chapter, I will refer to them collectively as the RCP and, where appropriate, refer to them as RCP I, RCP II, and RCP III.

The RCP articulates a clear business to 'integrate arts and cultural development more deeply and pervasively into the economic landscape of Singapore' (RCP 2005: 14) by harnessing the existing and new arts infrastructure and building bridges with the business sector. The RCP II is blunt that the government is less interested in the arts for its cultural and discursive value and significance. It starkly states:

> MICA agencies (National Arts Council, National Heritage Board, Media Development Authority, etc.) must shift away from the 'arts for arts' sake mindset, to look at the development of arts from a holistic perspective, to contribute to the development of the creative industries as well as our nation's social development. (Ibid.)

Policy-makers and bureaucrats got into immediate action and in the urgency to fulfill the ambitious economic goals, developed complex systems of funding and support leading to the bureaucratization of the arts and esthetics eschewing the purposiveness of art in Singapore (Chong 2014). This was discharged by developing hegemonic systems to embed arts, design, and media education within all levels of education in Singapore, and beautify the living environment through art and design. This reinforced past policy imperatives to establish Singapore as a global arts city that would be ideal to live, work, and play in (for both Singaporeans and expatriates) and conducive for a creative and knowledge-based economy, and provide cultural ballast to Singaporeans to strengthen national identity and, more importantly, a sense of belonging. A financial pledge of S$50 million over a period of five years, for 'software' development of the arts, aimed to transmogrify the harsh physical infrastructures into 'incubators for the arts' (Chang and Lee 2003: 133) and in the process 'strengthen the Singapore Heartbeat through the creation and sharing of Singapore stories, be it in film, theatre, dance, music, literature or the visual arts' (MITA 2000: 4). Terence Lee (2004: 289–90), in his critique of this policy, purports that this investment is a 'tacit admission of Singapore's "cultural lack" marked by Singaporeans' inability to understand or appreciate the fullness of the arts, as well as an attempt to further shore up the economic potential of the arts.'

I would assert that this laid the ground for the bureaucratization of art not dissimilar to the colonial imagining of arts' role to connect industry, citizenry, and life (Dutta 2006); the bureaucratization of the process of imagining the place of art in the economy (Chong 2014); and the financialization of the arts in Singapore, where principles of financial or esthetic deficit are countered through a key performance index (KPI) system to monitor funds granted to arts groups, the transactional impact of art on audiences, and the groups' abilities to develop business plans.

The tracking and measuring of the value of the arts to the economy and its contribution to national employment figures commenced in 2005, entrenching the place of the arts as a source of cultural consumption for domestic and international markets touring at the top global festivals, biennales and fairs, and art markets. Key statistics from the National Arts Council reveal that from 1996 to 2006/7 the number of performance and visual arts exhibition days rose from 6,000 to 27,000, the total nominal value-added to the economy rose from S$557m to S$978m, and contribution to employment rose from 16,000 to 21,000. With these astounding figures the arts were fast becoming financialized.

Arts higher education and arts schools

A financialised and transactional cultural environment is nurtured through a STEM (science, technology, engineering and mathematics) oriented educational system. Arts higher education, though vibrant at every level of post-secondary education, is still at a nascent stage. Post-secondary education in Singapore (after ten years of primary and secondary education) is a composite of institutes of technical education (ITEs), polytechnics, arts schools, and universities. ITEs and polytechnics are clearly geared towards skills training and industrial preparedness. These institutions have been globally lauded for their excellence and emulated by many aspiring third-world countries. Design and media education has been concentrated in these institutions to provide the battalion of workers needed for the creative economy, from film assistants and animators to fashion designers, interior designers, etc. The universities have historically been teaching institutions and, in the past 15 years, have transformed themselves into research universities, topping the league tables at annual Times Higher Education and QS rankings.

Lasalle College of the Arts (LASALLE) and Nanyang Academy of Fine Arts (NAFA) are Singapore's main arts schools at the tertiary level, dedicated to artist education in fine arts, performing arts, media, and design. If colonialism rendered art as an enculturing instrument for a migrant society, the two arts schools provided artists with a safe learning and working environment to hone their practice and build a body of work. The arts schools' survival, in a highly instrumentalized educational environment, came about through their ability to become cultural centres for an emerging arts ecology built around the professionalization of the artist's condition, their engagement with the global and local art market and industry, and their becoming purveyors of standards in the quality of artistic practice. Their pedagogies vary culturally and philosophically, differentiated by the artist studio and the preservation of heritage and artistic traditions (NAFA), as well as the interdisciplinary studio and promotion of experimentation and abstraction (LASALLE). NAFA, one of Southeast Asia's oldest art schools, draws from its rich traditional heritage and cultural lineage located in China, and maintains to date a bilingual (Mandarin-English) ethos, while LASALLE was a young Turk, founded in the 1980s as a response to established practices in keeping with Singapore's youthful contemporaneity as an English-language medium school. It should be noted that there was another institution, Singapore's first tertiary institution for the commercial and applied arts: Baharuddin Vocational Institute. Founded in 1965, it was focused on the craft of three-dimensional art (pottery and shell craft) and design (furniture-making, dress-making, and graphic design and illustration). Its aim was to upgrade the skills of the craftsman and apprentices who were part of the team that was building the fast industrializing Singapore. In 1990, the Institute was moved into the Singapore's polytechnic system and formed the Temasek Polytechnic's School of Design.

The curriculum offering in each arts school corresponds to their uniqueness, in that they relate to skills/vocational development, artistic practice/esthetics, professional development/industry needs, and/or applied/inquiry-based research. They are para-sites of openness, exploration, and critical innovation, which is alluring to the creative sector that is continuously seeking the unconventional, the next big thing. Both offer a portfolio of programs: diplomas for those who have attained an 'O' level equivalent education (16 years and above) and degrees for 'A' Level/International Baccalaureate equivalent education (18 years and above). Postgraduate programs are offered for artists working in the creative industry who seek to upgrade and upskill their practice. LASALLE, to date, offers the most comprehensive set of arts provision in Southeast Asia and continues to attract world-renowned artists, such as film director/producer Lord David Puttnam, theater director Robert Wilson, and artists Stelarc, Gilbert and George, and Thomas Heatherwick, to name a few. The graduates of these schools remain flag-bearers of Singaporean artistic temperament and remain the main artistic leaders for the city-state. These two schools have survived the tide of the conventional

STEM system and asserted their presence in an Asian environment, where the arts are often relegated to the fringes as a hobby or cultural celebration and not a possible career choice.

The importance of arts schools in the development of a creative economy was identified in the ACCA report, recommending the government to advance support. This led to the establishment of a high-level committee to study the upgrade of the two arts schools as centres of excellence. The report of the committee, released in 1998, was titled *Creative Singapore: A Renaissance Nation in the Knowledge Age*. As the two arts schools remain private, not-for-profit enterprises, the committee recommended to upgrade both arts schools into 'internationally renowned tertiary-level centres of artistic excellence which can contribute to the development of the arts in Singapore, enhance the competitiveness of the economy and extend the range of career options available to Singaporeans' (Tan 1998: 8). Following extensive consultation, which included visiting more than twenty arts schools around the world as well as manpower surveys and studies for graduate employment, the committee made the unprecedented recommendation for government to provide public funding to support diploma-level studies, degree-level funding within a five-year time frame with the local universities, and to consider moving the arts schools to the downtown civic district to sit alongside the Singapore Management University and the arts precinct. This new public-private partnership was not the only unprecedented recommendation. The committee also made other far-reaching recommendations to government, outside its terms of reference. It recommended the government consider expanding the range of arts education programs at the primary and secondary school levels, expand the pool of qualified and experienced visual and performing arts teachers, and establish an autonomous Institute of the Arts for degree programs in the performing arts.

The Arts Education Council was established, with representatives from the various ministries, to oversee this new public investment in the private sector to ensure accountability and realization of the vision for a knowledge-based economy. The Committee did maintain a key recommendation that both arts schools be preserved as private and autonomous institutions to deepen and preserve their strong character, heritage, and artistic expressions unique to them (ibid.: 25). With this recommendation, both arts schools came under the oversight of the Ministry of Education's (MOE) Division of Higher Education. Both schools continue to report to the MOE and, as part of the upgrade, were relocated to the civic district at the beginning of the twenty-first century. Ninety percent of the new campus development was funded by government. LASALLE and NAFA's move to the city centre placed them at the heart of the creative energy of the civic district. The civic district was transforming into a rich arts, education, and cultural district with a number of museums, performing arts venues, and educational institutions coalescing into a centre connected to Chinatown, Little India, and Kampong Glam heritage centres.

In addition, the arts schools came under the oversight of the Council of Private Education, a regulatory arm of the MOE governing private-sector provision of education. Clearly the relationship between the public and private value systems brings up challenges of independence and accountability. With regard to the arts schools, they demonstrably relate to the creative economy that is seeking to monetise their creative output, as they are centres of innovation, experimentation, and discovery. Ooi (2011) argues that creativity in this instance can lend itself to be exploited for wealth creation and organized with economic purpose, an intent contrary to the role of creativity, arts, and culture. This cautionary note remains key to tease out the co-optation of the arts into governmentality and economic viability that gets played out regularly, most often between the arts community and policy-makers, and less so between educators and policy-makers. With funding came a clear directive to align graduate output with manpower targets established by the Manpower Ministry, bringing the two arts schools within the ambit of the public-sector universities and polytechnics framework while maintaining their autonomy.

Ten years on, in 2011, both schools received public funding for degree provision. As neither arts school has their own degree-awarding powers, since 2011 LASALLE has teamed up with the world-renowned Goldsmiths College, University of London, to validate all its degree programs in art, design, media, and performing arts, providing graduates with Goldsmiths awards. NAFA, on the other hand, teamed up with the Royal College of Music in the UK to validate and top up its music programs. These partnerships with international universities are a unique proposition in Singapore. As a young society, the value of benchmarking against and learning from the best around the world has been a particular preoccupation of Singapore post independence. This leads to a continuously learning and reflexive environment at government and society levels, which has allowed Singapore to remain relevant and ride the tide of economic and geopolitical changes. Besides the two arts schools, public sector institutions have similarly teamed up with international partner universities to further this enterprise of benchmarking and learning. These include the National University of Singapore and Yale University (NUS-YALE College) to establish a liberal arts college; Nanyang Technological University and Imperial College (Lee Kong Chian School of Medicine) to establish a British-style medical school as an alternative offering to the Duke University-NUS medical school partnership; Singapore Management University and Wharton Business School, University of Pennsylvannia; Singapore University of Technology and Design partnership with Massachusetts Institute of Technology and Zhejiang University. The intent to set up an Institute of the Arts, offering undergraduate degree programs in the performing arts, proposed in the early policies found little traction, and in its place a narrow and focused undergraduate program in Western classical music was considered. The Yong Siew Toh Conservatory was established in 2003 at the National University of Singapore and its four-year Bachelor of Music curriculum was designed, developed, and accredited by the Peabody Institute, Johns Hopkins University. A School of Art, Design and Media (ADM), which was recommended under the then RCP, was established in 2005 at the engineering and science-focused institution, Nanyang Technological University. Though major international partnerships were not realised for the

ADM, it built its capacity through international and world-renowned faculty, such as Professor Ute Meta Bauer (formerly of the MIT and Royal College of Art) focusing on the interaction between art, design, and media, and the general humanities and social sciences. ADM offers four-year undergraduate degrees and postgraduate research degrees in digital animation, digital film-making, interactive media, photography and digital imaging, product design, and visual communication. Polytechnic graduates in design and media studies can enrol in the Glasgow School of Art Singapore (GSAS) programs, which has been in operation under the aegis of the Singapore Institute of Technology, a newly set-up university which provides franchised degree programs from the GSAS, Trinity College Dublin, Newcastle University, Manchester University, the German Institute of Science and Technology (TUM), the University of Glasgow, and others. These partnerships are intended not so much as a cultural importation, but are focused on rapid capacity-building within the educational sector for Singaporean institutions.

All these complemented the Economic Development Board's Global Schoolhouse Initiative, which sought to make Singapore an education hub for world-class education to capture some of the US$2.2 trillion global education market pie and transform Singapore into the 'Boston of the East' (Chan 2011: 24). Many world-class universities such as INSEAD, the University of Chicago Business School, Duke University, and arts institutions (such as the prestigious Tisch School of the Arts, New York University, Sotheby's Institute of Art, and DigiPen) arrived and helped to meet the rapidly growing demands for an education in the arts. But the financial imperatives made it difficult and many, including Tisch and Sotheby's, were unable to sustain their business, either shutting down or moving elsewhere in Asia where the market base was larger. Critics (Chan 2011; Olds 2007) have noted the complexity of the investment involved to transform Singapore into a knowledge economy. Long-term business strategy and the planning of sectoral needs by sector experts – instead of bureaucrats – is vital to ensure the success of these partnerships.

The RCP noted that while the public school system does have a full complement of arts-related extracurricular classes and activities, including the Arts and Music Elective Programs where top students are able to enrol in art or music at the ordinary and advanced level of the Cambridge high-school examinations, there was no clear pre-tertiary level education in the arts. In 2008, MICA established the School of the Arts (SOTA), a high school catering to those between the ages of 13 and 18 years. SOTA's vision is to 'develop creative leaders for the future – future artists, creative professionals and passionate supporters for the arts in all fields' (MICA 2008). SOTA embraces the International Baccalaureate diploma (IBDP). Graduates, while having a strong arts foundation, often go into mainstream tertiary education. Those keen on the arts continue their undergraduate studies at either overseas arts schools, or at LASALLE or NAFA. In recent years, SOTA has found that a number of its students do want to only pursue the arts and have adopted the International Baccalaureate's Career-related Diploma (IBCP). SOTA is a success story in Singapore with its students posting some of the top IB results in the world.

These examples show the rapid investment and development of the arts higher education (Comunian and Ooi 2015), in tandem with the rapid transformation of the creative sector. Inevitably, the question remains as to what kind of art and culture of representation would a financialized environment produce. Ute Meta Bauer, Director of the Centre of Contemporary Art at the Nanyang Technological University, in studying international practices argues that arts schools have increasingly been pulled into the art market:

> Art students have more knowledge of the market than ever before, and to 'create' successful artists – which largely suggests commercial success as a career artist – has become a standard promise read in almost every mission statement and call for application around the world.
>
> (Bauer 2009: 221)

This further compounds the situation in that, through the demands of graduate employment on arts schools, the 'route from art school to the gallery to the collector's wall' is very short (ibid.: 222). The creative economy's proliferation of biennales, art festivals, fairs, art markets, auctions, events, and mega celebrations continuously pressure institutions to produce quick fixes, and the allure of these remain a continuous threat to artistic development. There is little time for artistic deliberation or in-depth study of cultures and canons, of systems and processes, of modes of production and circulation, and of shifts in the esthetic and material. The quick-fix approach to appreciating the arts has become a key feature of a global city, a first-world nation, that is commodified, packaged, presented, and circulated.

Conclusion

The creative economy in Singapore remains an academic enterprise, measured purely by one mode of assessment: quantifiable dollars and cents, as an end in itself. As such, the Singaporean notion of culture, built on a communitarian ideology of multiculturalism and Asian values, was being replaced by a creative economy that was fast becoming institutionalized, formalized, and commoditized within the rubric of Lily Kong's (2000) 'hegemony of the economic.' Culture in twenty-first-century Singapore is markedly gluttonous and any form of existence seems to be acknowledged only through the deterministic processes of consumption (Yue 2006: 19), 'disneyfication' (Kwok and Low 2002) or 'renaissancification.' The economic shapes and legitimates the existence of culture in Singapore. A critical vigilance is necessary to admonish the creative economy's tacit commitment to lifestyle and consumption as the main mode of negotiation of culture, negating social histories and cultural specificities. As Yue (2006: 23) eloquently surmises, 'the good consumer is a good citizen.'

Sociologist Kwok Kian-Woon, in his article 'The Bonsai and the Rainforest: Reflections on Culture and Cultural Policy in Singapore' (2004), draws upon the apt metaphor of a bonsai tree. This bonsai is culturally debilitated through an arrest of its development to exude a structural esthetic. The bonsai self-regulates itself to remain muted, yet beautiful. Cultural development in Singapore is moving along this esthetic path. Kwok argues that the larger concern is less the economic but the depletion of Singaporean cultural capital (through the modes of regulation), which 'cannot be regenerated without cultural depth' (ibid.: 17). Cultural depth is achievable through the spirit of free enterprise (freedom of expression, transparent funding policies, and self-regulation), which is displaced by the superficial excitations of the creative industries. He calls on cultural policy-makers and arts administrators to recognize the inimitable qualities in artists and arts groups, and to foster and support their endeavour to deepen the esthetic environment that in turn engenders all kinds of creative effort (ibid.).

Noting the above concerns, I would like to return to some emerging concerns of artists in Singapore and Southeast Asia (and the arts schools that train and develop them). First, artists are constantly negotiating the traditional and global as a way of life and as a means of defining their 'locatedness.' For many, sustainability is not merely a reductive correlation between society, economy, and their lived environment, but rather a deep concept of preservation of ways of life (arts, practices, and language) in dialogue with globalisation (technology, virtuality, and travel). While critics and theorists have drawn important distinction between preservation and sustainability in Singapore and Southeast Asia, they are not really too far from each other's line of sight. The development of the arts continues to be plagued, well into the twenty-first century, by debates about preservation and promotion of the traditional arts against the development and promotion of contemporary arts, that are demonstrably having an alignment with economic development and an emerging affluent and mobile society. In another twist, as institutionalized world economies face the darkest hour, nation-states are increasingly closing ranks to support and protect their economies – through the embrace of community participation and engagement. For example, in Singapore the National Arts Council has implemented a five-year National Traditional Arts Plan, which sets aside S$23 million to support the traditional arts. This type of participatory politics in countries like Singapore has seen a resuscitation of the traditional arts, which serves as a compass of locatedness for a fast consumerizing society. With an increasingly well-educated and confident population asserting its presence on the global platform, artists are seeking new ways to express their sense of being by revisiting their history and tradition.

Second, in the instrumental nature of the development of the creative economy through cultural policies, there is a bureaucratization of art. One is reminded of Walter Benjamin's 'The Work of Art in the Age of Mechanical Reproduction' (1968), which was an ode to modernity's impact on the 'irreversible supplantation of craft by the mass-produced object' in the nineteenth century and thereby 'engendering a mythology of the original' (Dutta 2006: 189). This corollary has remained an axiom of twentieth- and twenty-first-century art, deepened and entrenched in not only visual and performing arts but, in particular, design and its extensions. The clutter of sameness cannot be ignored, as it supplants conceptual drought with an onslaught of visual culture, iconic valorism, and the estheticization of luxury as taste.

Finally, artists in Singapore and Southeast Asia are mining themes of a post-apocalyptic world where an unsettled public seem to reign. Art deals with the complex issues of outrage, disaffection, and social anxiety among the youth in a world which seems ordered and neat from a capitalist's binoculars. Lawrence Grossberg argues:

> […] youth have been condemned to a new modernity in which there can only be one kind of value, market value; one kind of success, profit; one kind of existence, commodities; one kind of social relationships, market.
>
> (Cited in Giroux 2012: 7)

In the commoditized creative environment in Singapore, it is about instrumental-ism and supporting a workforce. The resultant outcome is the danger of erosion for critical thinking. Henry Giroux starkly enforces this:

> The value of knowledge is now linked to crude instrumentalism, and the only mode of education that seems to matter is one that enthusiastically endorses learning marketable skills, embracing a survival-of-the-fittest ethic, and defining the good life solely through accumulation and disposing of the latest consumer goods. (Ibid.: 17)

He further argues that with the instrumental dictates of education and commodi-fication of all spheres of life, young people are no longer able to inhabit spheres of life that foster the opportunity for them to 'think critically, make informed judgments, and distinguish cogent arguments from mere opinions' (ibid.: 18). Therein lies the state of affairs.

What kind of esthetic environment does a young Singapore need? The answer potentially lies in the art, its maker, and the quiet arts school, where the idea of de-establishing frameworks and concepts and transforming individual capacities reigns paramount. The arts school is also a victim and perpetuator of the cycles of the economic factory, but within its ecology there is always space where culture breeds and the artist finds his/her voice. The commoditized creative economy is an institutionalized phenomenon across the world. The arts school environment thrives to appraise, resist, and support, to create parasitical opportu-nities and opportunities of engagement to innovate the new, the ephemeral and the process-oriented practice. While attracting new believers at each cultural turn, it is this constant reinvention that keeps the arts school ahead of the creative economy and the conventional in Singapore.

Notes

1. I thank the conference participants at the International Symposium on Theater Arts and Cultural Administration Conference, National Sun Yat Sen University, Taiwan (2010), and at Beyond the Camp/.us: Higher Education and the Creative Economy, King's College, London (2014), for their feedback when this was presented. In addition, I thank the peer-reviewers for their insightful comments on the various drafts of this

chapter. Aspects of this paper were documented in the Taiwan conference proceedings, and in my 2007 book, *Making Visible the Invisible: Three Decades of the Singapore Arts Festival, 1977–2007.*
2. Department of Statistics Singapore (2014) available at: http://www.singstats.gov.sg.
3. Organization for Economic Cooperation and Development (2015) available at: http://www.oecd.org.
4. Ministry of Finance, Singapore Budget 2015, available at: http://www.singaporebudget.gov.sg.
5. SkillsFuture Council Singapore – see http://www.skillsfuture.sg.

References

Baudrillard, J. (1988) 'The ecstasy of communication,' in H. Foster (ed.), *The Anti-Aesthetic*. New York: Bay Press.

Bauer, U. M. (2009) 'Under pressure,' in S. H. Madoff (ed.), *Art School: Propositions for the 21st Century*. Boston, MA: MIT Press, pp. 219–226.

Benjamin, W. (1968) 'Work of art in an age of mechanical reproduction,' in H. Arendt (ed.), *Illuminations*. New York: Schocken Books.

Bereson, R. (2003) 'Renaissance or regurgitation? Arts policy in Singapore 1957–2003,' *Asia-Pacific Journal of Arts and Cultural Management*, 1 (1): 1–14.

Bourdieu, P. (1993) *The Field of Cultural Production*. New York: Columbia University Press.

Chan, D. K. (2011) 'Internationalization of higher education as a major strategy for developing regional education hubs: a comparison of Hong Kong and Singapore,' in J. D. Palmer *et al.* (eds), *Internationalization of East Asian Higher Education: Globalizations Impact*. New York: Palgrave Macmillan, pp. 24–39.

Chang, T. C. (2000) 'Renaissance revisited: Singapore as a "Global City for the Arts"', *International Journal of Urban and Regional Research*, 24: 818–31.

Chang, T. C. and Lee, W. K. (2003) 'Renaissance city Singapore: a study of arts spaces,' *Area*, 35: 128–41.

Chia, W. H. (2002) 'Untitled canvas: the making of a visual art history,' in V. Purushothaman (ed.), *Narratives, Notes on a Cultural Journey: Cultural Medallion Recipients 1979–2001*. Singapore: National Arts Council, pp. 162–5.

Chong, T. (2005) 'Singapore's cultural policy and its consequences: from global to local,' *Critical Asian Studies*, 37: 553–68.

Chong, T. (2014) 'Bureaucratic imaginations in the global city: arts and culture in Singapore,' in H.-K. Lee and L. Lim (eds), *Cultural Policies in East Asia: Dynamics Between State, Arts and Creative Industries*. London: Palgrave Macmillan, pp. 17–34.

Comunian, R. and Ooi, C.-S. (2015) 'Global aspirations and local talent: the development of creative higher education in Singapore', *International Journal of Cultural Policy*, 1–22.

Devan, J. (1995) 'Is art necessary? In art vs art: conflict and convergence,' in W.-C. Lee (ed.), *The Substation Conference 1993 Publication*. Singapore: Substation Ltd, pp. 50–6.

Dutta, A. (2006) *The Bureaucracy of Beauty: Design in the Age of Global Reproducibility*. New York: Routledge.

ERC (2002) *Creative Industry Development Strategy: Propelling Singapore's Creative Economy*, Report of the Economic Review Committee Services Subcommittee.

ERC (2003) *New Challenges, Fresh Goals: Towards a Dynamic Global City*. Singapore: Economic Review Committee Report.

Giroux, H. (2012) *Disposable Youth, Racialized Memories, and the Culture of Cruelty*. New York: Routledge.

Harper, T. N. (1999) *The End of Empire and the Making of Malayan Culture*. Cambridge: Cambridge University Press.

Ibrahim, A. (1998) *Asian Renaissance*. Kuala Lumpur: Times Books.

Koh, T. C. (1989) 'Culture and the arts in Singapore,' in K. Singh and P. Wheatley (eds), *Management of Success: The Moulding of Modern Singapore*. Singapore: Institute of Southeast Asian Studies Publication, pp. 710–68.

Kong. L. (2000) 'Cultural policy in Singapore: negotiating economic and socio-cultural agendas,' *Geoforum*, 31: 409–24.

Kwok, K.-C. (2000) *Richard Walker, Colonial Art Education and Visiting European Artists Before World War II*, Singapore Art Museum and NUS University's Scholars Programme. Retrieved from: http://www.postcolonialweb.org/singapore/arts/painters/channel/9.html.

Kwok, K.-W. (2001) 'Singapore in 2000: a review,' in F. S. Luen (ed.), *Singapore 2001*. Singapore: Ministry of Information and the Arts, pp. 2–14.

Kwok, K.-W. (2004) 'The bonsai and the rainforest: reflections on culture and cultural policy in Singapore,' in C.-K. Tan and T. Ng (eds), *Ask Not: The Necessary Stage in Singapore Theatre*. Singapore: Times Editions, pp. 1–25.

Kwok, K.-W. and Low, K.-H. (2002) 'Cultural policy and the city-state: Singapore and the new Asian renaissance,' in D. Crane, N. Kawashima and K. Kawasaki (eds), *Global Culture: Media, Arts, Policy and Globalization*. New York: Routledge, pp. 149–68.

Lee, T. (2004) 'Creative shifts and directions: cultural policy in Singapore,' *International Journal of Cultural Policy*, 10 (3): 281–99.

MICA (2005) *Renaissance City Report 2.0*. Singapore: Ministry of Information, Communications, and the Arts.

MICA (2008) *Renaissance City Plan 3*. Singapore: Ministry of Information, Communications, and the Arts

MITA (1995) *Singapore: Global City for the Arts*. Singapore: Ministry of Information and the Arts.

MITA (2000) *Renaissance City Report: Culture and the Arts in Renaissance Singapore*. Singapore: Ministry of Information and the Arts

MITA (2002) *Singapore's Cultural Capital. Green Paper*. Singapore: Ministry of Information and the Arts.

MTI (1985) *Strategic Economic Plan*. Singapore: Ministry of Trade and Industry.

MTI (1991) *Strategic Economic Plan: Towards a Developed Nation*. Singapore: Ministry of Trade and Industry.

MTI (2002) *ImagiNation: A New Agenda for a Creative and Connected Nation. Investing in Singapore's Cultural Capital*. Singapore: Ministry of Trade and Industry Singapore.

Olds, K. (2007) 'Global assemblage: Singapore, foreign universities, and the construction of a "global education hub,"' *World Development*, 35 (65): 959–75.

Ong, T. C. (1989) *Report of the Advisory Council for Culture and the Arts*. Singapore: Advisory Council for Culture and the Arts.

Ooi, C.-S. (2010) 'Political pragmatism and the creative economy: Singapore as a city for the arts,' *International Journal of Cultural Policy*, 16: 403–17.

Ooi, C.-S. (2011) 'Subjugated in the creative industries: the fine arts in Singapore,' *Culture Unbound*, 3: 119–37.

Purohit, V. (1988) *Arts of Traditional India: Twentieth Century, 1905–1985*, Vol. 2. Bombay: Popular Press.

Purushothaman, V. (2007) *Making Visible the Invisible: Three Decades of the Singapore Arts Festival, 1977–2007*. Singapore: National Arts Council.

Sabapathy, T. K. (1987) 'Forty years and after: the Nanyang artists. Remarks on art and history,' in T. K. How *et al*. (eds), *New Direction: Modern Paintings in Singapore – 1980–1987*. Singapore: Horizon Publishing.

Souchou, Y. (ed.) (2000) *House of Glass: Culture, Modernity, and the State in Southeast Asia*. Singapore: Institute of Southeast Asian Studies.

STB (1998) *Singapore Annual Report on Tourism Statistics 1997*. Singapore: STB.

Tan, C. N. (1998) *Creative Singapore: A Renaissance Nation in the Knowledge Age*. Singapore: Committee to Upgrade LaSalle and NAFA.

Wee, C.-J. W.-L. (2003) 'Creating high culture in a globalized "cultural desert" of Singapore,' *Drama Review*, 47 (4): 84–97.

Yue, A. (2006) 'The regional culture of new Asia: cultural governance and creative industries in Singapore,' *International Journal of Cultural Policy*, 12 (1): 17–33.

Part IV

Higher education policy and the creative economy

12 Tensions in university–community engagement

Creative economy, urban regeneration and social justice

Paul Benneworth[1]

Introduction

There is an increasing expectation that universities, in return for their public funding, will make strong contributions to their host societies. This so-called third mission is seen as not just being something for technical disciplines, creating patents, licensing them to firms, launching spin-off firms and transferring their know-how to high-technology business. The social sciences and humanities, at least in part fearing being seen as less valid and useful than their technical counterparts, have recently taken great pains to politically mobilise and demonstrate the myriad ways in which their teaching and research creates concrete benefits for governments, businesses and civil society. Policy-makers, users and universities have raced to find ways to encourage and support those creating the benefits and place their full spectrum of university knowledge demonstrably at the service of society.

The creative industries, the subject of this book, have proven extremely useful for these groups in making these arguments that social sciences and the humanities are useful. The creative industries are highly valued by economic ministries in many countries as a means of both stimulating innovation and economic power more generally, but also for providing a platform to project 'soft' cultural power in the world (Belfiore 2015; O'Brien 2014). They provide comfort for arts and cultural representative organisations so that, even in an age of austerity, there are ways for arts and culture to make claims on the public purse in terms of the positive economic benefits they make. And of course for universities, they provide a very neat justification for the public value of their arts and humanities research in a way that gets beyond having a purely intrinsic value in preserving elite cultures.

The aim of this book (and its underlying research network) is to chart and map the diversity of ways in which higher education and creative industries are interacting in synergy to create value-added for society. And in a spirit of constructive criticism, I want to ask the question of whether – in the rush to create justifications for the value of creative industries – an overly optimistic view has been taken of these interactions' societal value. Using the idea of the 'dark side of the creative economy', where risk is passed from public institutions and the business sector to individuals and civil society groups, I want to ask whether these new higher education spaces have a dark side. Following Slater (2006), have shiny new cultural campuses been placed to obscure increasingly socially unjust political processes around urban regeneration, gentrification, and economic development? What I want to do to answer that question is to make four relatively straightforward sequential arguments. Firstly, that universities have always been useful, and that their spatial form reflects the kinds of demands that social sponsors and patrons place on them: the rise of the idea of the creative campus reflects a changing set of demands and pressures on universities to engage with the new creative economy. Secondly, in the absence of a sense of solidarity in their societal role, universities have a tendency to play a primarily individualistic role, which reinforces the risk, rather than the reward, elements of the creative economy. This can reinforce rather than address structural exclusion leading to universities playing a regressive rather than progressive role, a fact that is often overlooked in the extant literature (Penman and Ellis 2003; Kezar 2004; Benneworth and Humphrey 2013).

Thirdly, the wider contexts in which universities operate have effects on the kinds of roles they can play, and reveal the drivers and dynamics of their connections to the creative risk economy. This is explored in this chapter via the case study of a single university regeneration project that became entangled in a much larger and problematic regeneration regime, which, despite the best intentions of the university and its active approach, constrained and influenced its potential to play other developmental roles. Finally, the idea of the creative campus can be situated as a moment in urban regeneration struggles, highlighting a risk that these creative activities drive regressive exclusionary processes, as well as contributing to developing competitive societies. It is this struggle that requires further reflection to avoid uncritically reproducing happy family narratives of higher education, communities and cultural regeneration. I here seek to provide an additional dimension complementing and corroborating this volume's overall largely positive message of the potential of creative campuses to drive emerging creative economic activities.

Useful universities, creative campuses and the social compact

To take a critical look at the notion of creative campuses, I want to consider what the potential 'dark sides' might be of universities making themselves useful to society (cf. Bozeman *et al.* 2013). There is a growing recognition advocated by Bozeman *et al.* that some attempts to encourage more use of universities can reduce their overall value to society. This is a prima facie example of a public value failure (Bozeman 2002: 152), where market-efficient transactions together have highly sub-optimal public welfare effects, 'when core public values are not reflected … in market relations'. In the case of the university, public value failure is usually constructed around an argument that a focus on the immediately useful application distracts from studying the more generally applicable theory from which conceptual development and, hence, scientific progress can be made (Sauermann and Stephan 2013). However, in this chapter, I propose the idea that the creative campus is embedded within an increasingly risky, individualised version of societal relationships that ignores these wider public benefits, encouraging universities to promote private benefits even where there are clear examples of public failure (such as increasing land prices driving social inequality). To examine how this may happen, I take a broad view of the tension that is absolutely central to the idea of the university, namely balancing between immediate use and general value, and ask whether the pursuit of societal use in creative campuses can lead to public value failures.

The university as a profoundly useful institution

Although it is now quite common to evoke the idea of university as an 'ivory tower' where academics seek refuge from the pressures and demands of society, a study of the historical record reveals that this claim is a relatively modern phenomenon. Shapin (2012) traces the way that the metaphor of the ivory tower emerged from its Biblical roots with notions of purity to be adopted in the nineteenth century to describe the artistic creative process. There are a variety of reasons for the rise of the description of universities as ivory towers, but it is hard to see that it has ever represented a normative model describing what the university *should* be like. As Rüegg points out (1992), the University of Paris was created by a Papal decision to allow its teachers to hold prebendary stipends, effectively providing a Church subsidy for these first professors. But this was not done out of any desire to support the generation of new knowledge or indeed to create the secular equivalent of a monastic order aloof from society. Rather, these positions were created, embracing the idea of a university, because these teachers were able to educate an administrative clergy. Indeed, as Biggar (2010: 77) notes:

> Right from their medieval beginnings, [universities] have served private purposes and practical public purposes as well as the sheer amor scientiae ['knowledge for knowledge's sake'] … popes and bishops needed educated pastors and they and kings needed educated administrators and lawyers capable of developing and embedding national systems.

There has always been a relationship between universities and societal actors in which the support of those societal actors for the universities is in some way contingent on the services that those universities provide society, something Barnett (2000) refers to as a 'social compact'. The idea of a social compact is perhaps misleading, because it potentially conveys the sense that universities have to work exclusively on socially useful benefits, but I use it here to refer to the idea of universities experiencing societal demands. These societal demands create tensions for the universities, between the freedom to create and circulate general abstract knowledge, their internal desire, and the responsibility via the compact to create knowledge with immediate and particular applicability. Universities' long-term success as an institutional form relates to universities being effective in balancing these tensions, but at the same time, in balancing those tensions, universities are forced to choose between which interests to privilege, meaning that their societal benefits are always benefits for some stakeholders and exist by being withheld from others.

Ideal-type university forms, in various historical eras, adopted forms to balance these immediate societal needs with the longer-term needs to be able to curate, nurture and (latterly) develop corpuses of knowledge. One sees the great university of Leuven in Flanders being created to help develop the region beyond its wool trade, contributing to the creation of a Low Country elite (following mass professorial migration to Leiden after the fall of Antwerp in 1585). Likewise, Lund University was created to stimulate an elite Swedish culture in a remote outpost of the Kingdom passed to Swedish ownership following the 1660 Treaty of Roskilde. The industrial age saw universities adopting the role of training industrial, as well as political, elite. In the twentieth century, the role of educating a democratic elite emerged, exemplified most clearly with the creation of the Confessional Universities in the Netherlands for a range of societal groups (Calvinists, Catholics, etc.). Most latterly in the postwar expansion, universities evolved to create a democratically educated mass for Habermasian rationalist societies, with participation rates rising from single figures to, in some cases, half the population cohort.

In each of these societal shifts, there has been a parallel shift in the spatial form of the university as it evolved to provide the best spatial frame to deliver these social activities (see Table 12.1). The cloister of the eleventh-century university freed staff and students alike from material pressures of daily survival, while its move into the city increased the connectivity between scholarly communities. The post-Westfalian nation-building universities often had imposing physical forms, exuding cerebral authority in the same way that cathedrals and parliaments exuded spiritual and temporal authority. Leaping forward to the mid-twentieth

Table 12.1 The evolving nature of the university in response to changing societal conditions

Social change	Novel spatial form of university	Exemplar of a university
Agricultural revolution	Cloister (eleventh-century Italy)	Bologna (eleventh-century Italy)
Emergence of nobility	Independent ('free') cloister	Paris (twelfth-century France)
Urbanisation	The university as a marketplace at the city crossroads	Catholic University of Leuven (fifteenth century)
Sustaining national communities	The university as an expression of power	Lund University (seventeenth century)
Creating technical elite	The university as a factory	Humboldt University, Berlin
Promoting progress	The campus as a partner	Land Grant Universities (nineteenth–twentieth century USA)
Supporting democracy	The campus as a microcosm of democracy	Dutch Catholic Universities (twentieth-century NL)
Creating mass democratic societies	The campus as a model democratic society	UK 'Plateglass' universities of Robbin era.

Source: Benneworth (2014).

century, the term 'Plateglass' emerged in Anglophone discourses to describe a new form of university emerging at a time of expansion, seeking to produce a population educated for a mass democracy (Beloff 1968). The more recent rise of the 'third mission' for universities has seen universities' estates expand to create new entrepreneurial spaces where their knowledge resources can be valorised for societal benefits. On this basis, it therefore does not seem unreasonable to make the claim that creative campuses are a new form of university, reflecting the increasing importance of creative industries and the cultural class (Pratt 2008).

Creative campuses as a new spatial form of social compact

It is relatively uncontroversial to create a link between these new creative campuses and university attempts to best deliver their wider social mission. There is a recognition that post-industrialisation has placed an emphasis on creativity, design and affective relationships in the value creation process, the so-called rise of the creative economy (Florida 2002). Competitiveness in the creative economy is based on localities' capacities to apply cultural capital productively in their economic structure, adding value through innovation, as well as increasing place attractiveness (Ström and Nelson 2010). Universities have clearly responded to this, with a growing number of places developing territorial development strategies linking higher education to creative growth strategies. Indeed, Evans (2009) argues that one specific consequence of the rise of the creative economy has been the emergence of new spatial forms for universities in a range of creative campuses and districts.[2] These creative campuses contribute in various ways by supporting the emergence of creative clusters, which are in turn attractive to the creative classes associated with a cosmopolitan ambience, gentrification, and economic success (Comunian and Faggian 2011).

   With the creative sector being formed as a curious amalgam of public, private, and voluntary activities, creative campuses generate synergies between activities to realise the goals of a wide range of participating stakeholders. They become ways to leverage private value (economic activity) from public investments in cultural infrastructure, and, integrated into the urban fabric, they help contribute to the ambience and 'buzz' of city districts, increasing their attractiveness for further investors. New campus developments can represent a mid-phase in regeneration activities, taking place after artists move into districts attracted by low or zero rents, and bring life back into deserted old industrial areas (Kosmala and Sebastyanski 2013). Creative campuses involving universities can provide an additional stakeholder, an additional set of interests, and additional resources. These impulses can in turn stimulate further synergies, helping to cover the rent gap, further helping land prices to rise, and making them sufficiently attractive to private investors, who can complete the regeneration and realise the final added value. They can also become attractors for voluntary arts activities, providing financial support that can be difficult to come by when they are not offering these alluring promises of creative urban transformations (something that later features in this chapter).

These new campus developments are also attractive to universities feeling long-term financial pressures of expanding student numbers as well as the more immediate pressures of fiscal austerity. When public authorities choose to invest in these creative campuses, and allow universities to become anchor tenants, those campuses provide universities with additional public investments, supporting their teaching and research activities, enlivening the campus, enriching the educational experience and helping to further develop synergies between the various communities around universities. They can also become ways for universities to leverage value from their investments in research, to create activities of wider public value and thereby to create more tangible and demonstrable evidence of their returns on the public support they received. Just as the entrepreneurial university campus would not be complete without a high-technology hatchery or incubator for spin-off businesses, the creative campus (including the site mentioned in this chapter) has become a site for new experimental building forms to maximise creativity, support and mentoring in these non-traditional businesses in the creative and cultural sectors.

Universities, public value failure and the creativity campus

In this reading, the reason the creative campus has been so successful and mobile as an idea, as Evans (2009) highlights, is because it offers a win-win situation for a range of stakeholders who may otherwise have difficulties in making claims on the public purse, from the various cultural actors, cultural policy-makers, and also universities' arts and humanities faculties (Comunian and Gilmore 2014). There are clearly a huge number of ways that creative campuses can create complementary synergies between public bodies, universities and their host communities, and it is in no way the intention of this chapter to belittle these impacts. But in the context of those largely positive potential benefits, I nevertheless want to remind readers of the enduring tension at the heart of universities' societal compacts: these compacts are not simply win–win situations but the source of tension for universities in delivering these core missions, which lead universities to privilege some stakeholders over others (Baumunt 1997). Universities' patrons have urgent, context-dependent demands for particular knowledge, but, in the longer-term, those demands can only by met by creating and transmitting a stock of abstract-generalised knowledge through the slow, objective development of wider theoretical frameworks (Giddens 2009). Collini (2011) argues that this is precisely the reason why, despite governments wanting vocational higher education and creating technical colleges, over time these have had to evolve to be more autonomous higher education institutions in order to be able to deliver their mission.

Bozeman (2002) argued that in science there can be the risk of 'public value failure', when decisions which are in one version of the public interest (often restrictively defined) can act against the wider public interest more generally. An example of this is patent protection for life-saving drugs, which is in the public interest, allowing firms to benefit from their investments in R&D and hence sustaining R&D levels. But at the same time, that period of monopoly holds prices artificially high and can, indeed, deny access to those treatments, creating unnecessary mortality rates. In an age where universities are increasingly being held to account by their stakeholders (Jongbloed *et al.* 2008), there is a risk that this emergent process of defining the public interest for universities defaults to those needs that are most conveniently met, and this can lead to various kinds of public value failure. This is exemplified here by the idea of the university-industrial complex, where universities and pharmaceutical firms cosy up to each other to maximise public research subsidies and medicinal prices are hidden behind preferential contract research relationships (Kenney 1986; Nature 2001).

As creative campuses are real-estate development projects, there is the chance that these emergent considerations might lead 'good' publics to be defined in terms of those who can provide co-financing for these development projects. David Hewson (2007) charts the lengths to which one UK university went to take over a rural college as the site for a huge new urban development, something fervently resisted by the village's existing residents. Likewise, Columbia University in New York attracted criticism in 2011 for allowing its properties to become blighted, to allow powers of eminent domain (compulsory purchase powers) to force through gentrification in Harlem, to its private benefit (Hirokawa and Salkin 2010). So what I want to do here is to suggest a kind of equivalence – if universities' creative campuses can deliver synergy, growth and societal capacity then we have to acknowledge that they can also experience a kind of public value failure, delivering for particular strong groups and excluding weaker groups from accessing those benefits. The balance between those two strands is of course emergent, but there is a prima facie risk that public value failures may emerge in the creative campus, in terms of which publics benefit and which publics are excluded. And at the same time, these resources are being spent to promote the creative economy, one in which there are many new opportunities, but many concomitant risks, lacunae and exclusions, particularly for economically disadvantaged communities.

The sheer physical impressiveness of creative campuses can potentially offer tangibility to their supporters' claims that they are a 'good thing'. But one cannot help but feel that among those cleansed precincts (Slater 2006) the question of whose interests have not been served, as well as those that have, should be raised. Have they become a way of closing down wider societal debates about universities' purposes, defining universities' societal benefits against very partial (and often financially motivated) development projects? What are the conditions under which this putative public value failure can be addressed and how can the concept be harnessed to drive more inclusive versions of societal development and growth?

Liverpool, 'revanchist regeneration' and cornerstone campus

The case study methodology

To provide some insights on these questions, I explore the way that these tensions played out in a particular creative campus urban regeneration project, by looking at what happened with the 'university that went to Everton'. This chapter reports on a case study that was undertaken as part of the ESRC-funded project, Universities and Socially Excluded Communities, part of the ESRC Research Network, 'The Regional Economic Impact of Higher Education Institutions' (2007–9). The project as a whole aimed to understand whether universities were capable of contributing to socially excluded communities in ways that were valued in those communities' own terms, rather than as defined either by universities themselves or by other élites. The project involved two phases, an extensive phase mapping community engagement structures, activities and behaviours at all universities in three UK regions:[3] the North East, the North West and Scotland. The second phase involved intensive case studies exploring how three universities had embedded a number of engagement activities within their wider set of academic repertoires. These three case studies were chosen because they represented prima facie 'good practice' examples: higher education institutions (HEIs) where some progress had been made in addressing the barriers which otherwise undermine universities' well-meaning attempts to support these less successful communities.

The chapter reports findings from one of those three case studies, namely that of Liverpool Hope University (LHU).[4] LHU had invested heavily in developing a new campus, primarily for the Faculty of Arts, in the Liverpool district of Everton, to help drive community regeneration. As the campus project developed, its evolution assumed an increasing number of characteristics of a creative campus, suggesting it provides an interesting lens by which to reflect upon this chapter's research questions. The case study is presented as a stylised critical realist narrative attempting to reconstruct some of the key moments of a more extensive historical process. A number of key elements are highlighted in order to provide insights into the tensions that may exist in creative campuses more generally. The subject of the chapter should therefore be taken to be these general tensions and issues with the underlying concept rather than the particularities of what happened in Liverpool.

I therefore seek to provide the space – in the context of a broadly positive narrative about Hope's community benefits – to reflect on some of the tensions and negative issues that may emerge in developing a creative campus. The case study is not of conflict, rather of groups trying to work together to deliver a 'win–win' situation and yet finding that, in certain moments, they are pulled away from a more idealistic reading of the societal compact. My contention is that by studying good practice examples of community engagement that nevertheless have stress lines, tensions and even micro-injustices, we can point to problems that may also be present in other kinds of creative campus, where these excluded and subaltern communities are not necessarily immediately visible.

The deeper problematic of regeneration in Everton

It is instructive to study the case of Everton because the creative campus emerged in an extremely crowded and controversial local political economy of regeneration. The last fifty years of Liverpool's regeneration have been characterised by attempts to deal with a massive stock of unfit housing through slum clearance rather than expensive repairs, often moving the residents to new purpose-built communities that quickly reacquired the characteristics of the very slums they replaced (Batey 1998; Couch and Cocks 2013). More recently, there has been a desire to replace these slums with private rather than public housing, and in particular luxury housing investments that attract people to the city and arrest a long-standing population decline (the controversial Pathfinder approach to housing market improvement; cf. Allen 2008). The popular face of Liverpool's controversial regeneration scheme is endless rows of boarded-up terraces awaiting demolition and redevelopment, turning whole city districts, such as Edge Lane and Anfield, into ghost towns. It was not a specific single policy that has led to this situation, but a series of policies that since the 1960s have sought to manage and improve those communities in ways that have ultimately selectively destroyed them (Hatherley 2013). Huge amounts of public funding have been spent on these places, and yet regeneration has not been experienced positively – it has led to neither gentrification nor improved sustainability for these districts.

Everton was first settled in the eighteenth century as a suburb for the gentry, and from the early nineteenth century has gradually declined in its relative status. Early postwar regeneration efforts involved clearing some of the terraces and displacing residents to suburban estates, while building new tower blocks and maisonettes. Not all the land was cleared, and on the steep hill of Everton rise, former terraced housing was turned into a park, which formed the north-western boundary of the new Everton Campus of Liverpool Hope University. Despite the centrality and connectivity of places like Everton, the circuits of contemporary life in Liverpool flow around these places, leaving them disconnected and disempowered. The regeneration challenge is as much to reconnect them – physically, politically, socially – to the fabric of a city slowly recovering from the depths of its 1980s depression. Culture and the creative industries have played an important role in the rebirth of the city of Liverpool more generally, and featured as a central focal point in local regeneration efforts allied with the European Capital of Culture in Liverpool in 2008 (O'Brien 2011). Everton was at the time of the research the second most deprived ward in England and Wales, an impoverished and excluded community cut off from what little respite from decline the 2000s brought to more affluent parts of the city (for more detail on Liverpool, culture and regeneration, see Jones and Wilks-Heeg 2004; Harrison 2009; Cox and O'Brien 2012; Cohen 2013; Connolly 2013).

Liverpool Hope University and its Everton Campus

The basis of the case study was the creation of a creative campus in Everton by Liverpool Hope University (LHU), an institution that should be understood in terms of its place in a wider political economy of UK higher education since 1989. LHU was formed from the merger of three teacher training colleges from different denominational backgrounds and, at the time of the 1989 Act, its small size saw it restricted to acquiring higher education college status and its attempts to stylise itself as a university college were challenged by the Department for Education. At the time of its creation, it faced a perfect storm of challenges to its legitimacy and survival as an HEI: attracting students to a less prestigious institution, the need to upgrade its research capacity to a sufficient level to justify the title of university, to achieve research degree-awarding powers and to win local support for its presence. The Everton Campus was part of a 'charm offensive' to build strong local support for the HE college, to attract new students (often from non-traditional backgrounds), as well as to stake a claim for the more prestigious university status. It is worth noting at the outset that Hope was successful in achieving these goals, achieving taught degree awarding powers in 2002 and research degree awarding powers in 2009, and any negativity in the case study should be read against the background of this success.[5]

The volume *The Foundation of Hope* (2003) charts at some length the full breadth of activities initially undertaken towards that end, and in a later chapter, the volume's editor pointed to the work undertaken in initiating an urban development project (Elford 2003). The roots of that lay in LHU developing linkages with many local schools (including offering some degree teaching on school premises as part of attempts to attract non-traditional students). With its own confessional background and links to Church schools in the city, the university became aware of a derelict former Catholic school in Everton, a source of concern for residents as a focus for serious antisocial behaviour (prostitution and drugs). The university acquired the site for a nominal fee from the local diocese and began a decade of physical investment in the site that also attracted substantial public investments from regeneration and economic development agencies. A former Protestant seminary (adjacent to both school and church) had been acquired by property developers Urban Splash as the Collegiate, and there was other housing development financed by private capital starting up around the Hope site.

The development involved four sequential stages which resulted in a single coherent space stretching between Salisbury and Shaw Streets covering the full frontage of the school. The first phase was the development of student accommodation on the site (opened 1999), subsequently to be named Hopkins Halls in honour of the poet Gerard Manley Hopkins who had been curate at the adjacent church in the 1880s. Secondly came the development of the teaching and services facilities for the Deanery (faculty) of Arts and the Community, with all faculty activities being located at the main university on the Everton Site. At that point, the campus acquired the name of Cornerstone, a name with both biblical allusion but also reflecting the university's desire to be a foundation for the redevelopment and regeneration of the wider Everton community. The third phase was the development of the Great Hall as a performance and teaching space for not only students but also outside cultural users. The final phase was what later became called the Capstone Building, a mix of teaching space, performance space (including a self-styled International Arts Venue), studios, as well as business incubator units. A final addition to the site was the Angel Fields garden, linking the various buildings on a single site and providing a space of tranquillity in an otherwise busy suburb. At the time of writing, these various elements had been designated by LHU as their 'Creative Campus'.[6]

Community engagement at the Everton Campus

As documented by Elford, the university originally intended to use the Everton campus to drive regeneration of the community, both physically in terms of the new investments, but also to work with the existing residents to make the most positive contribution to their lives. From the outset, there was extensive consultation with the community to allow them to express their views on the new activities planned for their district, but also to ensure there would be a place there for their interests and activities. LHU created a forum for discussion and dialogue with the community that included representatives from the existing West Everton Community Council (WECC). WECC was at the heart of the community and had a good understanding of the particular issues facing local residents, as well as a degree of aloofness arising from having to resist and mobilise against the unintended negative consequences of policy-makers' decisions, particularly relating to the closure of schools and health centres as well as the further clearance of housing stock. The phase before the university really arrived in Everton was a period in which there was a great deal of optimism on both sides that the university would be able to create benefits for the community, as it sought to secure its survival and sustainability within a rather antipathetic local political economy.

As the Community campus developed, LHU sought to deliver on this promise in a wide variety of ways that can be categorised in three kinds of activity. Firstly, they sought to integrate the new campus physically into the existing community and contribute to an improvement in the quality of the urban space at the edge of the city centre. The campus was a vital, maintained place in a district where public bodies appeared to scrimp and economise on maintenance, allowing potentially attractive facilities to fall into disrepair. Everton Park was a prime example of this, the location of Prince Rupert's tower, made famous on the badge of the local Everton football club, had been abandoned to the less salubrious elements in society. But LHU had come to Everton and tastefully restored a shabby set of buildings to their once-impressive state, and were investing substantial sums of money in sustaining a high-quality built environment. In the early 2000s, their Urban Hope subsidiary built six community centres around Liverpool that they handed over to local trusts. They did this entirely on the basis of bidding for a range of different subsidies and built them using the skills acquired internally when developing the Cornerstone Campus. The Cornerstone Campus (as it was then called) went beyond this by establishing a creative venue in Everton, including performance and studio spaces, where creative workers could help to re-profile the Everton community and drive up the appreciation of and investment in the physical infrastructure of the district.

Secondly, they opened up the campus to a range of organisations that had what might broadly be considered a community orientation and who would contribute to improving the social capital of the local community, particularly through bridging social capital, for example connecting the very well organised WECC or the Parents Association of the local primary school into wider decision-making networks. The Liverpool branch of the Simon Bolivar Orchestra project 'In Harmony' had its pedagogical hub in the Cornerstone Campus, working very closely with the nearby Faith Primary School, with music students doing placements in the school to help improve learning outcomes for pupils from often very challenging and disrupted backgrounds. During selected weekends, in the academic year 2008–9, coinciding partly with the European Capital of Culture year, the Cornerstone hosted the 'Weekend Arts College' (WAC). The WAC offered one-off arts activities in drama, dance, music and graphic/plastic arts for students in return for a small fee, making arts education accessible to school-age students from poor backgrounds with little access to these activities in their schools and whose families could not pay for longer courses. Finally, Cornerstone was the birthplace of the Collective Encounters Theatre of the Oppressed group, run by a part-time lecturer within the Deanery. Embracing the philosophy of Paolo Freire, Collective Encounters ran youth and third-age groups where they devised plays to express their views on the issues that mattered to them. Collective Encounters' success would warrant a chapter to itself but, during the research, they were to perform at the Edinburgh Fringe festival, together with a parallel local theatre group, in *Barry, Radge and Minging*, an absurdist challenge to the lack of opportunities for innocent play they faced in growing up.

Thirdly, they ensured that through the activities of the faculty, then entitled the Dean of Arts and the Community, staff and students went out beyond the confines of the campus and contributed to Everton's vitality. There were both one-off events and festivals hosted in the Cornerstone site, where the community presence provided learning moments for students, provided more institutional contact with local residents, and contributed to local vitality (albeit in a relatively minor way). A number of courses involved students having placements in local community groups: in the course of the research I interviewed music students who had worked in the local first school as part of the In Harmony project (delivered jointly with the Liverpool Philharmonic Orchestra), where music was used to create a more enriching learning environment for pupils whose learning difficulties stemmed from their difficult life situations. Staff at LHU undertook research in Everton, collecting oral histories and attempting to co-create understandings of the local identity of a community under extreme pressures, where the researcher developed quite close links and empathy with the individuals concerned. A Kite Festival was organised in Everton Park, bringing local people into interaction with university actors, and at the same time bringing people back into the park to help reclaim a space that was perceived by both the university and the community as potentially dangerous because of (semi-) criminal activities that took place following the withdrawal of policing activity from the district. The university made efforts to recruit people locally, such as the porters and catering staff, but also worked with the construction firms to ensure that local people were either employed or provided training through the construction activities.

Although this chapter may seem to take a negative turn, my argument is not that LHU at any stage behaved disrespectfully towards the community. Certainly, in the earlier stages of the project, there was an impressive creative community ethos for the campus, involving local groups as ways of bringing local communities onto campus and thus sending out the benefits into the immediate Everton community. All the evidence suggested that people employed by the university were entirely sincere in their desire to engage with the local community and to find ways to benefit Everton. There was likewise a degree of affection in the community for their efforts and indeed there were employees of the WECC interviewed who had benefited from LHU's alternative education pathways (although they had studied at the suburban campus). But there was a more systematic problem in the pressures derived from LHU's other stakeholders. These pressures meant that when West Everton proved unruly and difficult to enrol as a 'stakeholder' the university retreated into its shell, figuratively but also literally, by enclosing the formerly open space of Cornerstone around Angel Field.

The mismatch of the university and the community

Although LHU was committed to being a good neighbour to Everton, it was clear that the university sat uneasily with the community in various ways. Part of this was community suspicion fuelled because of the way a long series of public funding decisions (about schools, local clinics, the park) saw official promises translate into unfavourable decisions. The fraught nature of the relationship dated back to the very early steps taken by the university after acquiring the campus, and in particular their notion for 'bringing Hope to Everton'. Community interviewees retorted that they had never lost their hope, reporting that there was a sense that the university was initially extremely patronising and regarded its intervention as being entirely positive, even where it created problems. One example cited was of the additional parking in streets not designed for heavy traffic creating traffic problems for buses, and on one occasion blocking a funeral procession. Such incidents were memorable and fuelled community resentments. Another complaint was that a local social club on the site of the church had been demolished during Cornerstone's construction, and although the university had promised to replace it, this had not happened. When the university had applied for community development funding, the funder's evaluation noted that LHU in this initial phase had done little to go outside its campus. Community interviewees reported that in fact this funding decision had led to the second engagement phase, which attempted to create infrastructures within Everton to engage with the community. The university created a Community Forum, but did so at a rather untimely moment when there was a split within the WECC over the approach to dealing with prostitution that had migrated to Everton Park in response to a push from local government and the police to drive anti-social behaviour out of the city centre.[7] One group adopted a very militant approach, seeking to drive the prostitutes away from the area, an approach that a more moderate group in the WECC disagreed with. But it was this militant group that was first in contact with LHU as they were creating the Community Forum: this group were much more open to the university and was reportedly less sceptical about the university's intentions, in contrast to the WECC which, in the context of its own role as a community conduit, had often made complaints to LHU (for example over traffic problems). But as the more militant group lost their links to the community infrastructure around the WECC, and their legitimacy as community interlocutors, so the real representative value of LHU's Community Forum dwindled. LHU re-engaged with the WECC, and indeed worked on a number of activities together, particularly on a set of issues where there were problems that both the university and the community wanted to solve, such as physical safety, drugs and the presence of police.

Even in this period of collaboration, there were tensions between the university and the community, illustrated neatly by the example of the In Harmony project. From LHU's perspective, the Liverpool Philharmonic Orchestra (LPO) was a long-standing strategic partner of theirs and, therefore, LHU were central in terms of creating the In Harmony project, and all the publicity relating to the project presented LHU as a core project partner. However, the WECC had previously been working with the LPO on ensuring that a closed church building near to the community centre was converted into a practice and education space for the LPO, the Friary. That collaboration had resulted in the idea for the LPO to work with the local Faith Primary School on being awarded a franchise of the In Harmony programme, and LHU had been invited in at the later stages of the programme. It was not possible to determine the truth through the research, but there was clearly a tension between the university, the community and the status and primacy of stakeholder relationships, despite the fact that they were collaborating on a highly successful education project that had benefits for both university and school pupils.

Ultimately, engaging with the community was not able to solve one of the main problems that Everton posed for LHU, that of physical safety. Various interviewees had expressed the hope that the Liverpool Capital of Culture year would stimulate a massive investment in Everton and trigger a wave of regeneration and gentrification, which from the university's perspective would have had the advantage of also making the locality more secure for its staff and students. However, a wall was erected around Angel Field, stemming the inflow and access of local community interests onto the site, but concurrently promoting the emergence of a more conventional creative leitmotif – creative industries rather than creative communities – on the campus. This final issue prompts a return to reflection on the overall research question of whether shiny new cultural campuses were placed to obscure increasingly socially unjust political processes around urban regeneration and economic development.

Creative campuses and social justice in the risk society

The case of Everton and Liverpool Hope University provides a means to explore some tensions and pressures that play out when those sincerely committed to social justice engage with the allures of the creative economy and find themselves drawn away from truly open and inclusive versions of creative campuses. I reiterate that what makes Liverpool Hope University so interesting is precisely because of their sincerity and strenuous efforts in delivering a creative campus true to their ethos of inclusion and social justice. There were clearly community benefits, even if the community felt those benefits fell short of initial promises. And if a sincere institution with a strong ethos of social justice nevertheless ends up enacting exclusionary practices, then what hope is there for creative campuses developed by more mercenary universities to build inclusive economies (Hewson 2007; Engelen *et al.* 2014)?

I therefore want situate the idea of the creative campus as partly reflecting a moment in struggles about urban regeneration and highlight the risk that these creative activities drive regressive exclusionary processes, as well as contributing to developing competitive societies. The new creative campus meant that Hope was brought into a relationship with an excluded community enmeshed in an existing rather corrosive political economy and, perhaps slightly surprisingly, the university found itself playing a role with which it was not entirely comfortable. It faced opposition from a community already focused on trying to elicit fairness and social justice from a set of local political-economic arrangements that had for a long time systematically disadvantaged that community.

More generally, creative campuses function within university systems to reflect a diversity of interests and values, not always oriented towards social justice. When local communities are not readily disciplined and conditioned to fit with the particular vision of 'creative people' embodied within creative campuses, then it is not just that there is a mismatch between the community and the creative campus. Rather, that emerging mismatch is itself a political act, further marginalising an already marginalised community, framing them as unworthy losers on the wrong side of a fault line in a creative economy which prioritises 'worthy' creative types. Creative campuses in poorer areas are navigating a rocky course between being a social justice solution and actually working against these communities' own efforts to improve their own situation in local political economies. If they then challenge the forces of revanchist gentrification that seek to remake the city – and its campuses – as spaces available for rentier exploitation, then they may challenge the potential financial viability of these projects. The mismatch, therefore, constitutes these communities as part of the problem, working against the solution (campus development), rather than thinking about the ways that these dynamic new activities and new urban topologies can create new changes and opportunities for formerly excluded communities.

I am acutely aware of the dangers of drawing such an eye-catching conclusion from a case study of a reasonably successful creative campus project. I merely want to foreground some niggling doubts in my mind when I see occasional inexplicable events in the course of an undoubtedly successful project. For me and in the wider context of this volume, this serves as a warning to those who see creative campuses as an uncritically positive force in creating connected communities. More consideration is clearly required for their effects, not just on the 'benefits' they give to their community, but on the aggregate local political-economies that actively construct and sustain these communities' marginal and disempowered positions within local urban political economies.

Notes

1. The author would like to thank the editors and two anonymous referees for their extensive and thoughtful comments on earlier versions of the proposal and manuscript. This chapter draws on the Economic and Social Research Council-funded project 'Universities and Excluded Communities', part of the Regional Impacts of Higher Education Initiative (co-funded by the Higher Education Funding Councils for England and Wales, the Scottish Funding Council and the Department for Education and Learning Northern Ireland). An earlier version of this paper was presented at the 'Higher Education, Communities and Cultural Regeneration' seminar, part of the Beyond the Campus AHRC Connected Communities Research Network. Many thanks to all the interviewees and participants who gave their time and insights in supporting the research, particularly the inestimable West Everton Community Council and Collective Encounters, as well as to Liverpool Hope University who greatly inspired the case study on my initial visit. Any errors or omissions remain the responsibility of the author.
2. The spaces listed by Evans include: Museum Quarter, Vienna; Arabianranta, Helsinki; Vancouver's Downtown Eastside; QUT's Creative Precinct, Brisbane; Barcelona's €80 million digital media campus @22; University of the Arts King's Cross/St Pancras development London; Eagle Yard Adlershof, Berlin (Humboldt University); Örestad & DTU Broadcasting Centre, Copenhagen; and Creative Toronto/MaRS Centre.
3. Scotland has claims to be a nation as well as a region; it was just a region from the perspective of the research project and the funder.
4. In the first phase research, there were nine interviews of between 20 minutes and two hours with academics, senior managers, engagement professionals responsible for engagement at Liverpool Hope University, as well as a community theatre group located at the Cornerstone Campus and a former university senior manager who provided a further three hours of insight into the management decisions taken in making LHU an engaged institution. In phase two a total of 19 further 'elite' interviews were undertaken, as well as a further 17 shorter (15–30 minutes) interviews undertaken during site visits and five non-participant observation sessions. The interviews were written up on the basis of contemporaneous notes while the non-participant observation sessions were written up retrospectively (within 24 hours of the sessions) as field notebooks. More detail on the case study is available in the project working paper (Benneworth 2010).
5. At the time of writing (summer 2015) Liverpool Hope had come in 35th (out of 160) place in overall student satisfaction rankings (89 per cent), and experienced the largest increase in that year, from 825 the previous year.
6. https://www.hope.ac.uk/lifeathope/campuses/creativecampus/ (accessed 19 August 2015).
7. This section is reconstructed on the basis of the interviews that contained opinions and as such is therefore hard to corroborate; at the time of the research it had passed into the collective memory, both of the community and the university and is presented in that sense.

References

Allen, C. (2008) *Housing Market Renewal and Social Class*. London: Routledge.

Barnett, R. (2000) 'Realising a compact for higher education', in K. Moti Gokulsing and C. DaCosta (eds), *A Compact for Higher Education*. Aldershot: Ashgate.

Batey, P. (1998) 'Merseyside', in P. Roberts, K. Thomas and G. Williams (eds), *Metropolitan Planning in Britain: A Comparative Study*. London: Jessica Kingsley.

Baumunt, Z. (1997) 'Universities: old, new and different', in A. Smith and F. Webster (eds), *The Post-modern University? Contested Visions of Higher Education in Society*. Milton Keynes: Open University Press.

Belfiore, E. (2015) '"Impact", "value" and "bad economics": making sense of the problem of value in the arts and humanities', *Arts and Humanities in Higher Education*, 14 (1): 95–110.

Bellof, M. (1968) *The Plateglass University*. London: Secker & Warburg.

Benneworth, P. (2010) *University-Community Engagement at Liverpool Hope University: Building Social Capital in the Inner City?*, Working Paper No. 4, 'University Learning with Excluded Communities' project. Newcastle: Centre for Knowledge, Innovation, Technology and Enterprise. Available online at: http://www.esrc.ac.uk/my-esrc/grants/RES-171-25-0028/outputs/Read/8251b5e7-7a00-466b-ad70-f2804fe7edfd (accessed 16 April 2015).

Benneworth, P. (2014) 'Decoding university ideals by reading campuses', in P. Temple (ed.), *The Physical University*. London: Routledge.

Benneworth, P. and Humphrey, L. (2013) 'Universities' perspectives on community engagement', in P. Benneworth (ed.), *University Engagement with Socially Excluded Communities*. Dordrecht: Springer.

Benneworth, P. and Osborne, M. (2014) 'Knowledge, engagement and higher education in Europe', in GUNi Series, *Higher Education in the World 5: Knowledge Engagement and Higher Education Contributing to Social Change*. London: Palgrave.

Biggar, N. (2010) 'What are universities for', *Standpoint*, 24: 76–9.

Bozeman, B. (2002) 'Public-value failure: when efficient markets may not do', *Public Administration Review*, 62 (2): 145–61.

Bozeman, B., Fay, D. and Slade, C. P. (2013) 'Research collaboration in universities and academic entrepreneurship: the-state-of-the-art', *Journal of Technology Transfer*, 38 (1): 1–67.

Bullen, E., Fahey, J. and Kenway, J. (2006) 'The knowledge economy and innovation: certain uncertainty and the risk economy', *Discourse: Studies in the Cultural Politics of Education*, 27 (1): 52–68.

Cohen, S. (2013) 'Musical memory, heritage and local identity: remembering the popular music past in a European Capital of Culture', *International Journal of Cultural Policy*, 19 (5): 576–94.

Collini, S. (2011) *What Are Universities For?* London, Penguin.

Comunian, R. and Faggian, A. (2011) 'Higher education and the creative city', in D. E. Anderssen, A. Anderssen and C. Mellander (eds), *Handbook of Creative Cities*. Cheltenham: Edward Elgar, pp. 187–207.

Comunian, R. and Gilmore, A. (2014) 'From knowledge sharing to co-creation: paths and spaces for engagement between higher education and the creative and cultural industries', in A. Schramme, R. Kooyman and G. Hagoort (eds), *Beyond Frames: Dynamics Between the Creative Industries, Knowledge Institutions and the Urban Context*. Delft: Eburon Academic Press.

Connolly, M. G. (2013) 'The "Liverpool model(s)": cultural planning, Liverpool and Capital of Culture 2008', *International Journal of Cultural Policy*, 19 (2): 162–81.

Couch, C. and Cocks, M. (2013) 'Housing vacancy and the shrinking city: trends and policies in the UK and the City of Liverpool', *Housing Studies*, 28 (3): 499–519.

Cox, T. and O'Brien, D. (2012) 'The "scouse wedding" and other myths: reflections on the evolution of a "Liverpool model" for culture-led urban regeneration', *Cultural Trends*, 21 (2): 93–101.

Elford, J. (2003) 'From urban beginnings …', in J. Elford (ed.) *The Foundations of Hope: Turning Dreams into Reality*. Liverpool: Liverpool University Press.

Engelen, E., Fernandez, R. and Hendrikse, R. (2014) 'How finance penetrates its other: a cautionary tale on the financialization of a Dutch university', *Antipode*, 46 (4): 1072–91.

Evans, G. (2009) 'Creative cities, creative spaces and urban policy', *Urban Studies*, 46 (5–6): 1003–40.

Ferruolo, S. C. (1988) 'Parisius-Paradisus: the city, its schools, and the origins of the University of Paris', in T. Bender (ed.), *The University and the City. From Medieval Origins to the Present*. New York and Oxford: Oxford University Press, pp. 22–43.

Florida, R. (2002) *The Rise of the Creative Class: And How It's Transforming Work, Leisure, Community and Everyday Life*. New York: Perseus Book Group.

Giddens, A. (2009) *Sociology*, 6th edn. London: Polity Press.

Harrison, J. (2009) 'Breaking down the barriers to growth: economic development, culture, and old industrial regions', in P. S. Benneworth and G. J. Hospers (eds), *The Role of Culture in the Development of Old Industrial Regions*. Münster: Lit Verlag, pp. 3–16.

Hatherley, O. (2013) 'Liverpool's rotting, shocking "housing renewal": how did it come to this?', *The Guardian*, 27 March. Retrieved from: http://www.theguardian.com/commentisfree/2013/mar/27/liverpool-rotting-housing-renewal-pathfinder (accessed 21 April 2015).

Hewson, D. (2007) *How an English Village Fought for Its Future ... and Won*. London: Matador.

Hirokawa, K. H. and Salkin, P. (2010) 'Can urban university expansion and sustainable development co-exist? A case study in progress on Columbia University', *Fordham Urban Law Journal*, 37: 637.

Jones, P. and Wilks-Heeg, S. (2004) 'Capitalising culture: Liverpool 2008', *Local Economy*, 19 (4): 341–60.

Jongbloed, B., Enders, J. and Salerno, C. (2008) 'Higher education and its communities: interconnections, interdependencies and a research agenda', *Higher Education*, 56: 303–24.

Kenney, M. (1986) *Biotechnology: The University Industrial Complex*. New Haven, CT: Yale University Press.

Kezar, A. J. (2004) 'Obtaining integrity? Reviewing and examining the charter between higher education and society', *Review of Higher Education*, 27 (4): 429–59.

Kosmala, K. and Sebastyanski, R. (2013) 'The roles of artists' collective in the Gdansk Shipyard's heritage protection', *Journal of Cultural Heritage Management and Sustainable Development*, 3 (2): 116–29.

Nature (2001) 'Is the university-industrial complex out of control?' [editorial], *Nature*, 409 (6817): 11 January, p. 119.

O'Brien, D. (2011) 'Who is in charge? Liverpool, European Capital of Culture 2008 and the governance of cultural planning', *Town Planning Review*, 82 (1): 45–59.

O'Brien, D. (2015) 'Cultural value, measurement and policy-making', *Arts and Humanities in Higher Education*, 41 (1): 79–94.

Penman, J. and Ellis, B. (2003) 'Mutualism in Australian regional university–community links: the Whyalla experience', *Queensland Journal of Education Research*, 19 (2): 119–36.

Pratt, A. C. (2008) 'Creative cities: the cultural industries and the creative class', *Geografiska Annaler: Series B, Human Geography*, 90 (2): 107–17.

Rüegg, W. (1992) 'Themes', in H. de Ridder-Symoens (ed.), *A History of the University in Europe*. Cambridge: Cambridge University Press, pp. 3–34.

Sauermann, H. and Stephan, P. (2013) 'Conflicting logics? A multidimensional view of industrial and academic science', *Organization Science*, 24 (3): 889–909.

Shapin, S. (2012) 'The ivory tower: the history of a figure of speech and its cultural uses', *British Journal for the History of Science*, 45 (1): 1–27.

Slater, T. (2006) 'The eviction of critical perspectives from gentrification research', *International Journal of Urban and Regional Research*, 30 (4): 737–57.

Ström, P. and Nelson, R. (2010) 'Dynamic regional competitiveness in the creative economy: can peripheral communities have a place?', *Service Industries Journal*, 30 (4): 497–511.

13 The creative turn in Australian higher education

Scott Brook

Introduction

The emergent field of creative labour studies is partly catalysed by a concern that Creative Industries policies have exacerbated problems within a labour market that is already oversupplied. There are different levels of implied culpability here relating to different moments of policy development: from the heady days after the 1997 UK election when New Labour images of 'cool jobs' and a 'thin air' economy failed to manage young people's expectations (McRobbie 2002), to the complete neglect of the topic of work in subsequent policy development (Banks and Hesmondhalgh 2009). While it's fair to note that cultural policy has never shown much interest in the employment conditions of artists and cultural workers, the implications of this critique are acute in the context of the ongoing marketisation of higher education. Evidence from both the UK and Australia suggests poor labour market returns and significant skills mismatching for graduates of creative industries-oriented courses seeking work in the sector (Comunian *et al*. 2011; Haukka 2011), with a recent cost-benefit analysis of the career returns to Australian graduates showing that some creative degrees, such as those in the visual and performing arts, are poor financial decisions (Daly *et al*. 2015). Such concerns can quickly spill into the media, as in Australia where broadsheet journalists have claimed creative writing courses (a bellwether discipline for popular anxieties about arts degrees) constitute a 'racket' in student fees and a 'pyramid selling scheme' for subsidising the creative practice of commercially unviable authors working in education (Pryor 2010; see Brook 2012). Creative Industries researchers have recently acknowledged the notion of an oversupply of creative labour (Goldsmith and Bridgstock 2015: 377–8) and broadened their focus to make a case for the value of 'embedded creativity' – i.e. graduates of creative courses who work outside the creative industries – with evidence suggesting that education is indeed a major employer.

As this brief summary suggests, the moral stakes of debate can become relatively high. Without denying the significance of the issues at stake, this chapter seeks to both lower and broaden the focus of critical discussion. Firstly, it seeks to *lower* attention by turning away from principled accounts of how best to defend *or* contest the value of creative arts courses (regardless of whether these principles concern aesthetic, social *or* economic value), in order to focus on the

specific institutional conditions that have supported the new significance of creativity in HE. The reason for this is simply that both critics and advocates of
Creative Industries thinking tend to appeal to what Meaghan Morris has labelled
'blockbuster' narratives of historical change ('the knowledge economy', 'neoliberalism', etc.), but fail to capture the mundane and incremental processes of institutional reform in which such a debate would be meaningful (Morris 1998: 2).
It is only by attention to the latter that we can reorient discussion towards a more
productive engagement with issues of student demand, course planning and
graduate outcomes.

Secondly, the chapter seeks to broaden attention beyond a focus on the
Creative Industries policy push, by suggesting that the importation of the latter
into HE was itself part of a broader 'creative turn' in HE that was already well
underway. It offers a somewhat parochial account – Australia from the mid-1970s
through to the late 1990s – of the institutional preconditions for the emergence of
a Creative Industries agenda both *within* and *for* HE. While the emergence of
these two agendas is related, they are not therefore aligned. Although the former
has supported a striking research agenda focused on national innovation policy,
the latter has increasingly had the unenviable job of redressing the implications
of this agenda for the somewhat less glamorous objects of graduate outcomes and
curriculum development. Unlike the UK, the Australian context for the promotion
of the Creative Industries was not a government ministry, but rather a massively
restructured university sector in which course planning and research were forced
to adapt to a newly competitive funding environment. It is the premise of this
chapter that if we are to describe the forms of governmental rationality that
enabled the spread of creative arts education in this period, we must look away
from the notion of a new economy considered as *either* the prescriptive target of
government policy whose neoliberal political rationality we might contest *or* an
emergent phenomenon of post-industrial economies whose reality we might
dispute, and focus instead on the advanced liberal reforms of the Australian
university system initiated by the Hawke-Keating government in the late 1980s.
As has scarcely been acknowledged, during the 1990s the 'creative turn' pressed
against the Australian arts faculty from *within*. Attention to the emergence of the
creative arts enables a critical understanding of not only the rhetorical strategies
of Creative Industries proposals for teaching and research, but more significantly
the broader institutional context in which creative graduate outcomes might later
emerge as a problem.

Often referred to as the rise of the 'enterprise' or 'entrepreneurial' university
(Marginson and Considine 2000; Gallagher 2000), the key developments in
Australia for the rise and spread of creative arts courses were: (1) a series of
institutional mergers that saw a number of colleges and technical institutes merge
with the university sector and (2) the creation of a quasi-market in domestic
student places designed to foster a demand-driven model of course provision. The
drivers for these changes did not concern any intellectual or policy project in
relation to a knowledge economy, but rather a new approach to public sector
management focused on sector accountability and efficiencies through the

construction of market-*like* mechanisms for allocating government funding (on New Public Management, see Minson 1998). The growth of the creative arts in Australian HE was an entirely unanticipated outcome of these changes, and produced an available space for a discourse that might plausibly articulate the relations between converging lines of interest; namely student demand for the creative arts, government agendas focused on quantifying the economic value of tertiary education and inculcating graduate employability, and a new cohort of creative arts lecturers who themselves constituted a source of demand for higher research degrees and therefore a discourse on the 'knowledge value' of creative practice. Synchronous with these developments was the construction of a nationally competitive field of research funding, in which government research priorities would increasingly guide the attention of academics towards a normative engagement with questions of economic development. It was the creation of this field of contestable research funding available to a new tier of universities with a shared background in vocational training (i.e. 'the polytechnics' – see Marginson and Considine 2000) that materially resourced a revival of a postwar discourse on the economic value of creativity.[1]

An institutional prehistory of the Creative Industries moment in Australia also enables us to understand the intelligibility of current critiques, whether these concern the experiences of cultural sector workers subject to poor labour market conditions or the adequacy of national data sources for describing the work arrangements of 'creatives' considered as a unique class of workers. Given that cultural economists have long demonstrated that there is no direct human capital argument for investing in creative arts education (Filer 1990; Towse 2006), the fact that the labour market value of creative education might *now* emerge as a problem reveals less about the impact of Creative Industries advocates and more about a present mode of governmental action that increasingly *problematises* HE. The work of course planning in a massified HE sector increasingly lies in managing the 'contact point' between student demand and labour market outcomes (Foucault 1997: 81; see Burchell 1996). Each of these phenomena are influenced by factors outside the scope of universities, such as, on the one hand, the educational values, ambitions and expectations of high-school students, their families and the school system, and, on the other hand, the state of national economies (as significantly impacted by the actions of governments that claim to manage labour markets in the interests of national economy). Each of these is 'represented' to the sector by different sets of metrics that increasingly impact on HE funding at the institutional level, such as (in Australia) data on student course enrolments, completions, experience and labour market outcomes. Furthermore, neither of these elements necessarily act according to the market logic implicit in the Human Capital Theory that has provided the main intellectual plank for their implementation. Given the intellectual history of aesthetic practices and their relation to *Bildung*, it is not surprising to find this 'contact point' under pressure. Pressure to articulate the vocational logics of HE have increased as western developed nations make the transition from what Mitchell and Muyksen (2008) describe as employment policies to *employability* policies. It is useful to recall this much broader and slow-moving policy transition, as it is highly likely that the massification of tertiary systems, in conjunction with the deregulation of labour markets and increased tolerance of high levels of underemployment (in several dimensions, including skills underutilisation), are – along with skills-biased technological change – the most likely drivers for the growth in cultural work that has taken place since the 1970s (Brook 2015). In any case – and regardless of how we interpret these changes at the level of political economy – the claim of this chapter is that it is in relation to the historically recent and slow-moving process of managing this 'contact point' that our appraisal of the creative turn in HE should be based.

The chapter commences with a review of the process of HE restructuring that enabled the creative arts to flourish in the Australian university sector, and then turns to the specific funding arrangements that have sought to forge stronger links between university course provision and student demand, and student demand and labour markets. It then considers how the Creative Industries movement sought to articulate the recently emerged field of creative arts programmes into a new mission for the Australian arts faculty.

The Dawkins moment

In the late 1980s and early 1990s, there was a profound discussion in Australia about the instrumental value of culture. This discussion effected a major reorientation of cultural critique along reformist lines, and arguably produced the first major post-Foucauldian account of the 'culture' idea (Hunter 1988). Coinciding with the end of the Cold War, this account would turn away from thinking about culture in terms of representations that index class struggles, such as those inspired by the work of Gramsci, Bakhtin and Althusser, and toward those historically sparse practices and institutions for *training* variable forms of 'the person', as documented in the writings of a diverse set of social thinkers such as Max Weber, Marcel Mauss and Michel Foucault. Part of the significance of the 'culture and government thesis' for Australian cultural studies during the 1990s was its orientation towards questions of cultural policy, and its appeal to an emergent reformist ethos that might not simply critique but actively engage 'the available arts of government' (Hunter 1992: 367).

The first half of the 1990s seemed opportune for this kind of intellectual orientation. Under the late Labour government of Paul Keating, this period saw the expansion of 1980s-era Cultural Industries agendas beyond film and television to embrace the arts and cultural sector, as evidenced by the watershed Creative Nation policy of 1994. A signature gesture of the new policy was the Commonwealth Arts Ministry's initiation and direct sponsorship of a national youth media programme ('LOUD') that supported the professional development of young cultural producers in Australia's media industries (Hunter 1999). While such a programme made policy sense in the wake of high youth unemployment rates produced by the early 1990s recession, the focus on early career artists was continued under the incumbent Liberal government from 1996, which both administered the programme and repurposed the new federally funded arts awards created by Labour (known as 'the Keatings') into a career and audience development scheme targeted at 'Young and Emerging Artists' (Gardiner-Garden 2009: 46).

However, behind the 'cultural policy turn' was an event of far greater significance for academics, one that appeared to underscore the new reformist ethos with the force of history. The numerous expositions and critiques of the instrumental value of culture appeared at the onset of the largest restructuring of Australian tertiary education ever undertaken. Often referred to as 'the Dawkins Reforms' after John Dawkins – Minister for Finance and then Trade (1983–7), subsequently Minister for Employment, Education and Training (1987–91) – these reforms directly challenged both liberal humanist and critical Marxian assumptions concerning the value of publicly funded tertiary education in the face of what was often descried as bureaucratic interference. Chief among these was the dissolution of the binary system of universities and technical colleges through the creation of a unified national HE sector and a massive increase in Commonwealth-supported student places to be funded, in part, through the reintroduction of student fees via an income-contingent loan system administered by the Australian Tax Office (the Higher Education Contribution Scheme, or 'HECS'). The Dawkins reforms also created a uniform research funding regime that would support areas of national priority (such as business, computer and Asian studies), and encourage universities to become more 'enterprising' through incentives to develop non-governmental sources of revenue (such as international education markets and research commissions from both public and private sectors). The creation of a state-supported market in domestic student places was also part of a major policy effort to embed vocational considerations in both students and course planners that also included the national reform of career advice services, the promotion of graduate destination survey data as a source of 'consumer information' and the reintroduction of student fees via the HECS. All of these developments had intended, as well as unintended, effects. Perhaps the most counterintuitive consequence was the migration of creative arts courses both horizontally across the university sector as well as vertically into undergraduate and postgraduate degrees.

The creative arts and Australian higher education

With the exception of music, which had been taught in university music conservatoria that existed in some Australian capital cities, prior to the Dawkins reforms tertiary programmes in applied arts, such as design, textiles, craft, creative writing and the visual and performing arts, were primarily based in the Institutes for Technical and Further Education (TAFEs), and Colleges of Advanced Education (CAEs), many of which were dedicated fine art schools (Strand 1998: 14; see also Polesel and Teese 1997: 9; Baker *et al.* 2009: 1). In addition to the CAEs and TAFEs were a handful of small prestigious national institutes, such as the National Institute for the Dramatic Arts (NIDA) and the Australian Film and Radio School (AFTRS). In 1984, five years before the Dawkins reform, 78 per cent of all tertiary enrolments in applied arts courses were located in the TAFEs, CAEs, NIDA and AFTRS (Botsman 1985: Table 3.52), with only 12 per cent of enrolments being in the universities.

The CAEs were established in the late 1960s and early 1970s by federal government, following the recommendations of the Martin Report which sought to significantly expand tertiary educational opportunities, partly in response to the postwar baby boom (Davies 1989). According to the committee charged with the responsibility for developing the CAEs, it was proposed that courses would be conducted with 'a greater applied emphasis' where 'the vocational purpose would be more direct and obvious' (cited in Davies 1989: 145). It was the creation of this second tier of colleges to supplement the universities that produced the binary system of Australian HE that lasted until 1988. Although the CAEs were intended to be distinguished from universities through their vocational curricula, they would accommodate liberal disciplines, such as the arts and humanities, as these would raise the status of the sector in the eyes of the public, as well as support the professional education of students (Polesel and Teese 1997: 7–8). Although the CAEs were intended to offer an 'equal but different' mode of professional education to the universities, 'the bulk of student demand was for courses in the humanities, business studies, and social sciences, not in the technologies,' and funding arrangements, in fact, encouraged CAEs to 'create arts courses resembling those offered by universities' (Meek and Goedegebuure 1989: 18–19). In 1973, the state-managed Teachers Colleges were merged with the CAEs, and this led to a much larger and multidisciplinary CAE sector with a significant focus on teacher training (41 per cent of CAE enrolments being in teacher education by the mid-1970s – see Meek and Goedegebuure 1989: 22). The CAEs were similarly motivated by funding arrangements to upgrade their diploma offerings to degrees, and in many areas teaching staff achieved salary parity with university academics. As the curricula of CAE courses increasingly resembled many university courses, the field of 'technical' and 'vocational' education was increasingly pushed down into a de facto *third* sector, the Institutes of Technical and Further Education (TAFEs), that remained outside the CAEs and which would form the distinct field of Vocational Education and Training (VET) after the 1988 amalgamations (ibid.: 19).

By the mid-1980s, the binary system was widely perceived as inefficient and overly bureaucratic, due to the overlap between sectors and the separate approaches to course regulation and accreditation by state governments (for the CAEs), as well as the federal government Commonwealth Tertiary Education Commission (CTEC) (for universities). With the Dawkins reforms, new funding settings and incentives for campus development had the calculated effect of encouraging a wave of amalgamations: local art colleges and TAFE schools were annexed, often reluctantly, by the older established universities seeking to enhance their size and disciplinary scope; formerly prestigious metropolitan TAFEs would now seek to develop university courses for the international student market; and many of the smaller and geographically less-well positioned CAEs would amalgamate in order to establish themselves as viable multi-campus universities. Between 1987 and 1994, Australia's 51 CAEs and 19 universities had merged into 36 universities (Marginson 1997a: 224).

Student demand

A key enabling condition for the rise of the enterprise university was the creation of a quasi-market in domestic student enrolments. This development needs to be analysed along two lines of policy reform: firstly, the use of student load-based funding mechanisms by government as regulatory tools in order to encourage universities to expand capacity by *meeting* student demand; and secondly, the reforms to student financing that sought to recoup some of the costs of this expansion through the HECS. Both sets of reforms used new economic relations not only to shift the balance of financial responsibility between government and students, but simultaneously to *create* a market-like relation between universities and students through the inculcation of market-responsive forms of calculation and conduct (Marginson 1997b). In addition to reduced costs to government, the anticipated benefits of a state-backed market in domestic student places were a closer alignment between student demand and university provision, as well as a more vocationally and investment-oriented approach to course enrolments and, therefore, (it was assumed) a more responsive relationship between course provision and the labour market.

In 1988 the Commonwealth Tertiary Education Commission (CTEC) was abolished and the newly formed Department of Employment, Education, and Training (DEET) initiated a direct funding relationship with individual universities. Since its establishment under the Whitlam government, CTEC had acted as the central administrative agency in disbursing government funding, monitoring standards and setting enrolment targets by field of study. With the abolition of CTEC, Australian universities were ostensibly free to develop their own corporate missions, yet such missions were tied to a funding environment based on a more immediate client–supplier relation to DEET. While universities were no longer presented with enrolment targets by field of study, DEET did, however, police general enrolment targets negotiated with each institution as a condition of funding (Karmel 1998: 56–7). Dawkins sought to increase the number of graduating students from 80,257 per annum in 1987 to 125,000 per annum by 2001 (Marginson 1993: 123), and the new funding arrangements responded to these ambitions: between 1987 and 1992 university enrolments would jump by 42 per cent and were distributed widely across the sector (Marginson 1997a: 220). This growth was accompanied by a significant increase in revenue from student fees: between 1992 and 1999 federal government grants to the sector would increase by 21 per cent, whereas university revenue from domestic student fees would increase by 84 per cent and for international students by 145 per cent. In absolute terms, by 1999, annual revenue from domestic and international student markets had risen to be worth over half the value of recurrent government funding (see Gallagher 2000: 13, Table 1).

The Relative Funding Model introduced by DEET in 1990 classified student load into five discipline-based funding categories designed to reflect the different costs associated with teaching, and was used to calculate recurrent government funding for universities. This funding formula was also made public for the first time, with the result that it started to be used by university management for allocating funding at faculty and sub-faculty level. This process enabled universities to make economic calculations about student load in the allocation of internal funding, and encouraged departments and schools to make increasingly strategic calculations about the kinds of units and courses they offered. The field of competition between universities for student enrolments would now be internalised within faculties as a competition between departments and schools. During this period, creative arts disciplines were represented in HE statistics by the Major Discipline Group 'Visual and Performing Arts' which included graphic design, fashion, craft and all the visual and performing arts (drama, music and dance). The Relative Funding Model grouped the Visual and Performing Arts in the third band with languages, computing and nursing. This weighting was disputed by creative arts programmes, which claimed that it did not reflect the true costs of teaching that required small class sizes and specialist infrastructure, and would lead to under-resourcing (SERCARC 1995: 148–51). Meanwhile, from 1997, the Department of Education, Training and Youth Affairs (formerly DEET) implemented a differential cost structure for HECS repayments designed to reflect the variable career returns to graduates. Unsurprisingly, the Visual and Performing Arts were grouped at the bottom of three relative cost bands, making it the least expensive area of university study so far as domestic students were concerned.

A comparison of student demand (measured in Equivalent Full-Time Student Units, or 'EFTSU'[2]) with the two major arts faculty discipline groups for the period 1991–2000 is revealing. Table 13.1 shows that not only did the Visual and Performing Arts commence the period with a healthy level of demand, but increased at a significantly faster rate than demand for the Humanities.

It was during this period that doctoral programmes in the visual and performing arts would expand from Professional Doctorates to PhDs and spread across the sector, from a total of 12 tertiary institutions offering doctoral programmes in the creative arts in 1987 to 30 universities in 2007. Between 1989 and 2007 enrolments

Table 13.1 Increases in domestic Equivalent Full-Time Student Units (EFTSU) by Discipline Group (1991–2000)

Discipline Group	Year		% change
	1991	*2000*	
Humanities	44,894	50,775	13.09
Social Studies	48,485	55,942	15.38
Visual and Performing Arts	21,089	24,293	15.19
Total all disciplines	396,046	464,227	17.21

Source: Department of Education, Science and Training (2002: 96).

Table 13.2 Increases in domestic Equivalent Full-Time Student Load (EFTSL) by Broad Field of Education (2001–13)

Broad Field of Education	Year		% change
	2001	*2013*	
Society and Culture	139,376	186,801	34
Creative Arts	37,199	63,997	72
Total all Fields of Education	477,976	693,377	45

Source: Department of Education and Training (n.d.) *uCube – Higher Education DataCube*.

would increase by 1,105 per cent (from 102 to 1,230 candidates) (Baker *et al.* 2009: 22). A significant source of demand for postgraduate degrees in the creative arts came from academics themselves; in 1992, only 6.3 per cent of visual and performing arts academics held doctorates, but within four years (and under significant pressure from university managers) this had increased to 18.8 per cent (Strand 1998: 27).

Of major importance to the visibility and prominence of the creative arts was the introduction in 2000 of the Australian Standard Classification of Education (ABS 2001) to replace the ABS Classification of Qualifications. The Field of Education classifications were developed to permit a more detailed analysis of individual areas of study whether these are grouped around potential vocational outcomes (Field of Education) or similarity of content (Discipline Group).[3] Significantly, the Broad Field of Education classification 'Creative Arts' emerged as a far more comprehensive classification than the earlier 'Visual and Performing Arts'. This now included five Narrow Fields of Education – 'Performing Arts', 'Visual Arts and Crafts', 'Graphic and Design Studies' and 'Communication and Media Studies' – each of which included numerous detailed fields of education. The detailed fields included *occupation*-specific titles, such as 'Floristry' and 'Journalism' while the inclusion of Media and Communications, Journalism, Written Communication (e.g. creative and professional writing) and Audio Visual Studies significantly boosted the size of the field coded to 'Creative Arts'. The most significant change here was the inclusion of Media and Communications, a fast-growing area of study that had previously been coded to the Humanities. A comparison of Equivalent Full-Time Student Load (EFTSL) for 2001 and 2013 (see Table 13.2) shows both this increase in absolute terms, as well as the significant increase in size of this sector compared to the Broad Field 'Society and Culture'.

The new classification 'Creative Arts', although still a smaller grouping compared to cognate areas, shows a dramatic rate of growth as measured by student load.

Administering employability

The Dawkins reforms sought to embed vocational considerations in HE through a raft of mechanisms, including the development of an innovative mechanism for student fee collection, the review and reform of student careers advisory services (Anderson *et al.* 1994) and funding for the development of curriculum statements concerning the 'graduate attributes' that reflected the needs of graduates and employers, which became mandatory from 1998 (Gallagher 2000). A raft of government career information services for students were accompanied by commercial initiatives such as the Australian edition of the *Good Universities Guide* that has been published annually since 1991 by Hobsons as an international university information service whose five-star rankings of Australian universities are regularly referenced in university advertising. Hobsons supplies prospective students with a range of subscription-based and free information services, often sponsored by government, on graduate careers and occupational pathways. Through its publications and websites, Hobsons also sells advertising to universities and graduate recruiters.

While the creation of a unified national HE sector clearly sought to install enterprising behaviours in organisations, it was the introduction of the Higher Education Contribution Scheme (HECS) that revealed the ways in which these reforms sought to embed vocational and investment-oriented considerations in students. Between 1974 and 1988, federal government funding had ensured that Australian HE was free of tuition fees for Australian citizens; however, from 1989, domestic students would be required to finance a portion of their studies (initially between 20 and 25 per cent of the calculated real cost) through an income-contingent loan scheme that for most students had led to deferred repayments through the taxation system. To date HECS liabilities have been interest-free but are adjusted annually in line with consumer price indices in order to maintain their original value (Papadopolous 2005: 40). This debt is monitored by the Australian Taxation Office and is automatically collected by employers when graduates achieve a nominated income level, as shown on their tax return. The income thresholds that trigger compulsory repayments are structured progressively so that higher incomes attract higher repayments proportional to income. Students have always had the option of paying their HECS liability at the point of enrolment or making voluntary contributions during the life of the debt and been incentivised to do so by discounts.

One of the claimed successes of the HECS is that it has been able to shift some of the costs of HE onto those who benefit from it, students, without deterring participation. The HECS has been further praised for the manner in which it links a student's obligation to pay for university to their capacity to appropriate its value as personal income. While both of these claims have been used to bolster the scheme's social-democratic credentials – claims that were essential political conditions for its introduction under a Labour government – they also represented the application of Human Capital Theory to public policy. Directly influenced by Milton Friedman's work on state-backed education loans, the HECS was designed to resolve the problem of the inherently uncertain relation between investments in human capital and economic returns (Papadopolous 2005: 63–7). For Simon Marginson, the HECS has been in line with neoliberal reforms in education, in so far as it 'tend[s] to produce the student as the *investor in the self* conceived by human capital theory' (Marginson 1997b: 22; see also Papadopolous 2005: 61).

Despite these intentions, Papadopolous found in her 2005 study of HECS debtors that the most prevalent relation to the experience of possessing a HECS liability was one of 'deferrence', where this neologism was used to signal both submission to the fact of the liability and the ability to *defer* thinking about it. Papadopolous's study demonstrated that the normative HECS experience was one of acquiescence to a debt that was no more freely chosen than any other tax liability. It is therefore open to question how successful this system has been in installing a more investment-oriented approach to study.

In relation to demand for creative arts study, evidence is mixed. A major review of career services in the early 1990s found that across all universities, students enrolled in courses in the Visual and Performing Arts (including graphic design, fashion, etc.) were one of the three most likely course cohorts to seek career advice (Anderson *et al.* 1994: Table 7.52). More recent data is available from the Australian Bureau of Statistics Survey of Education and Training, a cross-sectional survey based on a representative sample of the working age population, and which, until 2009, included questions related to motivation to study. Nick Fredman's analysis of the 2009 results shows that creative arts students are on average slightly *less* motivated by rationales related to employment across several measures (e.g. 'get a job', 'job requirement', 'extra skills for job' and 'promotion') and significantly *more* motivated by non-vocational rationales such as 'interest/enjoyment', 'confidence/self-esteem', 'education skills' and 'further study' when compared to students enrolling for a first qualification across all other fields of study (see Figure 13.1). Significantly, however, a much higher proportion of creative arts students (13.6 per cent) cited 'start a business' as a

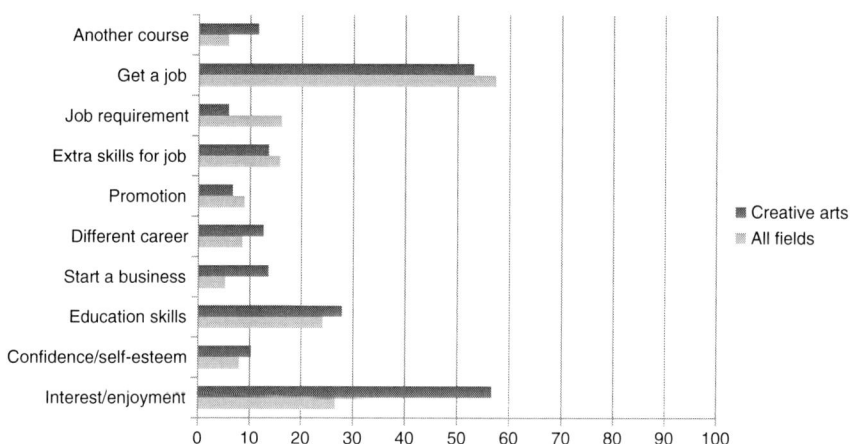

Figure 13.1 Percentage of respondents giving selected reasons for study for a first qualification in creative arts and for all first qualifications

Source: Fredman (2014: 10).

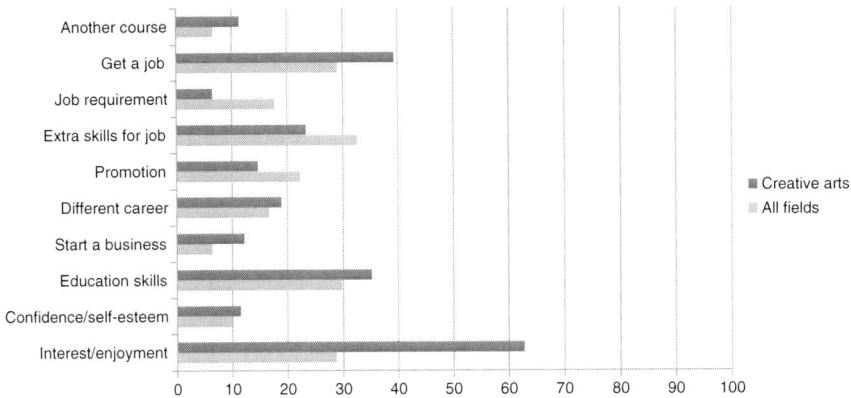

Figure 13.2 Percentage of respondents giving selected reasons for study for a second qualification in creative arts and for all second qualifications

Source: Fredman (2014: 15).

reason for their first qualification relative to an average of 5.3 per cent for all fields of study.

This survey's findings in relation to motivation to undertake a *second* qualification further complicates the picture (see Figure 13.2). While vocational reasons appeared less significant across all fields of study for those returning to study, among creative arts students this decline was far less pronounced, so that a higher proportion of graduates returning to study in the creative arts cited 'get a job' as a reason for their study compared to all fields of education. While the range of motivations for creative arts study are broader still, it is clear 'vocational considerations' are a significant part of this range.

Problems in the creative arts after Dawkins

While the new funding system enabled the sector to expand capacity, creative arts academics were mostly critical of the changes. The mid-1990s saw the emergence of several national professional associations that sought to actively represent the interests of the sector to government, notably, the Australian Council of University Arts and Design Schools (ACUADS), the National Council of Heads of Tertiary Music Schools (NACTMUS) and the Australian Association of Writing Programs (AAWP). Sector concerns resulted in two major government-funded reviews. In 1994/5 the Senate Environment, Recreation, Communications and the Arts References Committee (SERCARC) undertook a national review of creative arts education at all levels of the Australian education system. The inquiry received 131 written submissions and conducted 12 public hearings in major cities in all states and the Australian Capital Territory (SERCARC 1995). Unlike the new spirit of governmental thinking popular in Cultural Studies, the Senate Committee revealed a creative arts sector largely critical of the new focus on vocational training and the perceived economic instrumentalism of a focus on industry and employment outcomes. The report noted widespread concern about the extent to which the Key Competencies that were then being applied within the TAFE sector would recognise the non-instrumental values of the creative arts, with one of the recommendations being the inclusion of 'Aesthetic Awareness' as a Key Competency in the national training system (ibid.: 176).

The report concludes:

> The prime purpose of arts education for most students is to enrich their educational experience generally: to foster confident self-expression – the desire to *have a go*; to foster creative and innovative thinking that may have the benefit of carrying through into other school disciplines, other areas of life, both in and out of paid employment; to foster the habits of being self-directed and *involved* – habits which will be ever more important to the self-esteem of many in the future of insecure job prospects and periods of unemployment. (Ibid.: 22)

Although the report was sceptical of attempts to quantify the generic skills associated with the creative arts for the purposes of vocational training, it nevertheless made a clear case for the importance of *creativity* as a general and transferable skill. Quoting from a submission, the report notes:

> And creativity does not belong only to the arts – People can act creatively/ divergently in a great many ways and in a great many fields […] a footballer who makes a divergent play, a householder who decorates in a new way, a gardener who designs a new lay-out for the back yard, a surgeon who invents a better way of performing an operation, a shop keeper who devises a better selling strategy […] are all acting creatively. (Ibid.: 15)

References to the general value of 'creativity' are described in terms of 'innovation' and 'innovative thinking' where it is claimed: arts education 'nurtures' innovative thinking (ibid.: 15); 'innovative thinking is important in all fields of endeavour' (ibid.); and 'other graduates will go on to become teachers, or apply their skills to creative and innovative thinking in other fields of endeavour' (ibid.: 22).

It is in this context that the report's ambivalent relation to economic arguments concerning the growth of Australia's Cultural Industries can be located: while numerous submissions to the inquiry noted the economic importance of the Cultural Industries, and mustered statistical evidence of this, such attention was *not* to be read as support for an industry-focused approach to arts education in which 'vocational training' might supplant a focus on nurturing creativity:

> The Committee sensed that many witnesses raised the economic statistics because they felt obliged to talk the language of economics, but knew in their own hearts that this was not the real point […]. The consequences for

education of treating the arts as *no more than* an industry are an inability to recognise creative and innovative thinking. (Ibid.: 12–13)

The second major problem confronting creative arts lecturers, noted by the report, concerned research. During the 1990s, teachers in the creative arts were increasingly confronted with the problem of how to quantify the research output of staff and the new postgraduate degrees on offer. One of the new initiatives of the Dawkins reforms was the creation of a national field of competition for research funding through the establishment of the Australia Research Council (ARC) in 1987, and the use of research metrics that would increasingly link recurrent funding for research to success in competitive funding. In the 1990s, all universities created research offices and research managers to both motivate and train academics to compete in the new funding environment, while research indicators quickly became central to perceptions of the rank-ordering of universities and linked to the positional strategies of universities in competing for students. This period also saw the phasing-out of non-research academic positions: between 1988 and 1996 the number of teaching-only positions in Australian universities declined from 36 per cent to 4.3 per cent (Karmel 1998: 61). Given the dramatic reductions in federal funding from 1997 following a period of substantial institutional growth (the incumbent Liberal government reduced public funding for HE by 12–15 per cent over 1997–9 – see Marginson 2000: 65) with the result that the use of casual and short-term contract staff would become routine (Percy *et al*. 2008), academic concerns over research metrics were never far away from those of employment security.

The report made the case that the professional practice of creative arts lecturers may itself be understood as a form of research that could be recognised by a less discriminatory research funding system. The nascent strategy to emerge here, and supported in a subsequent dedicated report on research and the creative arts (Strand 1998), wasn't to join other arts faculty disciplines such as the humanities confronted with research funding metrics that devalued their objects and modes of inquiry, but rather the more radical proposal of arguing that *creative practice* was itself a mode of research.[4] This would lead to the promotion of 'practice-led research' as an innovative mode of knowledge production, with a dedicated conference ('Speculation and Innovation: Applying Practice-Led Research in the Creative Industries') taking place at Queensland University of Technology (QUT) in 2005. QUT was the flagship for Creative Industries teaching and research at that time, having established a Faculty of Creative Industries in 2000 and also in that year having been awarded major ARC funding to establish the ARC Centre of Excellence for Creative Industries and Innovation.

Apart from its popularity with creative arts academics in Australia, the notion of practice-led research has been modestly successful in broadening the remit of research metrics. The inaugural *Excellence in Research for Australia* exercise, conducted by the ARC in 2010 and designed to measure the research quality of Australian HE, included in its Submission Guidelines a section on the assessment of 'Non-Traditional Eligible Research Output Types' for selected disciplines.

The four forms of non-traditional research output universities may submit for assessment are 'Original Creative Works', 'Live Performance of Creative Works', 'Recorded/Rendered Creative Works' and 'Curated or Produced Substantial Public Exhibitions or Events' (ARC 2009: 41). Although clearly designed to include arts-based disciplines, the guidelines do not define the phrase 'creative work' beyond merely stating that such works are to be peer-assessed in terms of their contribution to 'innovation' and 'new knowledge'. The discipline matrices developed by the ARC show that non-traditional research outputs are valid not only for creative disciplines, but for a broad range of applied areas of research, including tourism, urban planning, marketing, accounting and education.

Conclusion

In a 2004 article on why the teaching and research of Australian arts faculties should be linked to the agendas of an innovation and knowledge economy, Stuart Cunningham noted this was not only because of the needs of a 'knowledge-based economy' but also 'because of the growth and integration of creative arts courses and staff into the university system over the last decade' (Cunningham 2004: 114).

Unlike general accounts of the promise and pitfalls of the new creative economy, this chapter has demonstrated how the 'creative turn' pressed against the Australian arts faculty from *within*. The rise to prominence of the creative arts in the post-Dawkins university was not the outcome of any new economic argument concerning the benefits of creativity; rather, it was a contingent and largely unanticipated consequence of a unified HE sector, the future development of which was determined by market-like structures for domestic student enrolments and research funding. It was *these* new institutional settings that necessitated a new set of arguments concerning the economic and vocational value of creativity. The debut of the Creative Industries idea in Australia worked to articulate the interests of a new cohort of HE students and lecturers to a normative policy discourse on the role of creativity for a knowledge economy (Hartley and Cunningham 2001). While innovation and knowledge economy agendas would clearly have been just as significant for HE had this not occurred, their articulation to a *creative* economy agenda was predicated on the local needs of HE providers. Such an account is fully in accord with Cunningham's claim that Creative Industries research 'reminds us that we are part of what we study (for example, the education industry)' (ibid.: 121–2).

By the early 2000s, a new caste of academics with backgrounds in professional creative practice was spread across an archipelago of institutions with a common history in mostly metropolitan technical schools and colleges. Even as this caste was itself a product of reforms designed to better link universities with the labour market, it largely eschewed the instrumentalism of such 'industry' and 'vocational' concerns. The problem confronting those seeking to craft a distinctive mission statement for a new tier of arts faculties was to articulate such dispositions – formed as they mostly were in the educational settings of the colleges rather than the Cultural Industries – to the ongoing processes of university massification and the embedding of national economic priorities in academic research. With hindsight, it is easy to see how the concept of 'creativity' was rhetorically well placed to address the convergence of vocational and liberal educational rationales in the aftermath of the Dawkins reforms, as well as respond to the increasing HE policy focus on employability. In place of a demonstration of the links between creative arts training, research and specific industries that trade in 'cultural' goods and services, creative industries researchers in Australia would promote the general and transferable value of arts-based training for a 'creative workforce'.

Such a history shouldn't be read as either a failure of course planning for creative sector employment or the success of a new educational mission aimed at embedding creativity in the university campus. The problematisation of creative employment *and* advocacy of creative education are themselves symptomatic of the new pressures on arts faculties to articulate creative arts practice to both student demand and graduate outcomes.

Depending on how we interpret the role of HE in the context of deregulated labour markets, such pressures may prove unresolvable. This would seem especially true in the case of the cultural sector. For instance, we might suggest that creative arts programmes cannot resolve the contradictions of rising demand for cultural work in a context of declining labour market returns in the cultural sector (Menger 2006), any more than the HE sector can act in a concerted way to prevent the process of increasing demand and declining returns for academic qualifications more broadly. Even as university courses become the site for such contradictions to manifest, such developments expose more fundamental problems with the theories of human capital that have been dominant in HE planning since the 1970s.

More practically, researchers on creative education might further *delink* arguments for the economic significance of any specific creative or cultural industry sector from educational accounts of the benefit of the creative arts for employability skills. Although less remarked, this more focused account of the relation between creativity and employability skills relating to 'enterprise' has accompanied the discourse of the Creative Industries since its debut under the early Blair government, and may well provide the most enduring economic argument for creative education going forward (Brook 2016). At the same time, we might question the extent to which the equation of creativity with enterprising behaviours is sufficient as a description of what creative arts education contributes to employability skills generally. A broader focus on the employability skills associated with capacities in working with various forms of symbolic, cultural and aesthetic value (highlighted by Bullen *et al.* 2004) would appear more plausible in terms of the goals of training in the creative arts, as well as the generic cognitive skills arts faculties provide more broadly. They would certainly seem relevant for those aspiring to make a vocation of the cultural field. Such an approach encourages a more mundane appreciation of the organisationally 'messy' space of the arts faculty in which a very limited set of pedagogic practices and rationales have produced a plethora of weakly differentiated cultural disciplines, and a healthy dose of scepticism in relation to the long-standing Modern belief that a unique caste of 'creatives' have a decisive role to play in resolving the socio-economic contradictions of the current historical period.

Notes

1. I'm thinking of the early American 'creative management' literature pioneered by the advertising executive Alex Osborn. Osborn's 1941 *Your Creative Power: How to Use Your Imagination to Brighten Life, Get Ahead* founded a genre of motivational guides and practical reference works for senior managers that would flourish through the 1950s and 1960s.
2. 'Equivalent Full-Time Student Load' (EFTSL) replaced the term 'Equivalent Full Time Units' from 2000.
3. For a comparison of the Field of Study classifications with Field of Education classifications, see Appendix 4, *Students 2001: Selected Higher Education Statistics* (DEST 2002).
4. Elizabeth Bullen, Simon Robb and Jane Kenway have discussed how Australian Creative Industries proposals for linking research to innovation policy effectively sidelined the contributions of traditional humanities disciplines (2004). Their article reminds readers of the extent to which the CI discourse displaced references to the economic importance of 'aesthetic', 'cultural' or 'symbolic' knowledges (as proclaimed in the 'culturalisation of the economy' thesis of the early 1990s), and hence just how institutionally targeted Australian CI proposals were. Thanks to Roberta Comunian for reminding me of their critique.

References

Anderson, D. S., Milligan, B., Caldwell, G. and Johnson, R. (1994) *Careers Advisory Services in Higher Education: the Influence of the 1990 NBEET/DEET Report.* Canberra: Department of Employment, Education and Training.

ARC (2009) *ERA 2010 Submission Guidelines.* Canberra: Australia Research Council, Commonwealth of Australia.

Australian Bureau of Statistics (ABS) (2001) *The Australian Standard Classification of Education.* Canberra: Australian Bureau of Statistics.

Baker, S., Buckley, B. and Kett, G. (2009) *Creative Arts PhD: Future-Proofing the Creative Arts in Higher Education.* Strawberry Hills, NSW: Australian Learning and Teaching Council.

Banks, M. and Hesmondhalgh, D. (2009) 'Looking for work in creative industries policy', *International Journal of Cultural Policy*, 15 (4): 415–30.

Botsman, P. B. (1985) *Review of Arts Education and Training.* Canberra: Commonwealth of Australia.

Brook, S. (2012) 'Creative writing, cultural capital and the labour market', *Australian Humanities Review*, 53. Retrieved from: http://www.australianhumanitiesreview.org/archive/Issue-November-2012/home.html.

Brook, S. (2015) 'Creative vocations and cultural value', in J. O'Connor and K. Oakley (eds), *Routledge Companion to the Cultural Industries.* London and New York: Routledge.

Brook, S. (2016 forthcoming) 'The exemplary economy: a Hunterian reading of the Creative Industries as educative project', *International Journal of Cultural Policy*, 22: 1.

Bullen, E., Robb, S. and Kenway, J. (2004) 'Creative destruction: knowledge economy policy and the future of the arts and humanities in the academy', *Journal of Education Policy*, 19 (1): 3–22.

Burchell, G. (1996) 'Liberal government and techniques of the self', in A. Barry, T. Osborne and N. Rose (eds), *Foucault and Political Reason: Liberalism, Neo-Liberalism and Rationalities of Government.* Chicago: University of Chicago Press.

Comunian, R., Faggian, A. and Jewel, S. (2011) 'Winning and losing in the Creative Industries: an analysis of creative graduates' career opportunities across creative disciplines', *Cultural Trends*, 20 (3–4): 291–308.

Cunningham, S. (2004) 'The humanities, creative arts, and the international innovation agendas', in J. Kenway, E. Bullen and S. Robb (eds), *Innovation and Tradition: The Arts, Humanities and the Knowledge Economy*. New York, Frankfurt am Main and Oxford: Peter Lang.

Daly, A., Lewis, P., Corliss, M. and Heaslip, T. (2015) 'The private rate of return to a university degree in Australia', *Australian Journal of Education*, 59 (1): 97–112.

Davies, S. (1989) *The Martin Committee and the Binary Policy of Higher Education in Australia*. Melbourne: Ashwood House.

Department of Education and Training (n.d.) 'uCube – Higher Education Data Cube'. Available from: http://www.highereductionstatistics.deewr.gov.au (viewed 29 June 2015.

Department of Education, Science and Training (2002) *Students 2001: Selected Higher Education Statistics*. Commonwealth of Australia, Canberra.

Filer, R. K. (1990) 'Arts and academe: the effect of education on earnings of artists', *Journal of Cultural Economics*, 14 (2): 15–40.

Foucault, M. (1997) [1980] 'Subjectivity and truth', in S. Lotringer (ed.), *The Politics of Truth*. New York: Semiotext(e)

Fredman, N. (2014) *Creative Arts Study in Australia: A Descriptive Quantitative Report*. Centre for Creative and Cultural Research, University of Canberra. Retrieved from: http://www.canberra.edu.au/research/faculty-research-centres/cccr/publications.

Gallagher, M. (2000) The Emergence of Entrepreneurial Public Universities in Australia. Canberra: Higher Education Division, Department of Education, Training and Youth Affairs.

Gardiner-Garden, J. (2009) *Commonwealth Arts Policy and Administration*, Background Note. Canberra: Parliamentary Library, Department of Parliamentary Services.

Goldsmith, B. and Bridgstock, R. (2015) 'Embedded creative workers and creative work in education', *Journal of Education and Work*, 28 (4): 369–87.

Hartley, J. and Cunningham, S. (2001) 'Creative Industries: from blue poles to fat pipes (case study 1)', in M. Gillies, M. Carroll and J. Dash (eds), *Humanities and Social Sciences Futures*. Canberra: Department of Employment, Education and Science.

Haukka, S. (2011) 'Education-to-work transitions of aspiring creatives', *Cultural Trends*, 20 (1): 41–64.

Hunter, I. (1988) *Culture and Government: The Emergence of Literary Education*. London: Macmillan.

Hunter, I. (1992) 'Aesthetics and cultural studies', in L. Grossberg, C. Nelson and P. Treichler (eds), *Cultural Studies*. New York and London: Routledge.

Hunter, M. A. (1999) 'Redefining "industry": young people and cultural policy in Australia', *Media International Australia*, 90: 123–38.

Karmel, P. (1998) 'Funding mechanisms, institutional autonomy and diversity', in L. Meek and F. Wood (eds), *Managing Higher Education Diversity in a Climate of Public Sector Reform*. Canberra: Department of Employment, Education, Training and Youth Affairs.

McRobbie, A. (2002) 'From Holloway to Hollywood: happiness at work in the new cultural economy?', in P. du Gay and M. Pryke (eds), *Cultural Economy*. London: Sage, pp. 97–114.

Marginson, S. (1993) *Education and Public Policy in Australia*. Cambridge, New York and Melbourne: Cambridge University Press.

Marginson, S. (1997a) *Markets in Education*. St Leonards, NSW: Allen & Unwin.

Marginson, S. (1997b) 'Investment in the self: the government of student financing in Australia', *Studies in Higher Education*, 22 (2): 119–31.

Marginson, S. (2000) 'Competition in Australian higher education since 1987: intended and unintended effects', in T. Seddon and L. Angus (eds), *Beyond Nostalgia: Reshaping Australian Education*. Camberwell, VIC: Australian Council for Educational Research.

Marginson, S. and Considine, M. (2000) *The Enterprise University: Power, Governance and Reinvention in Australia*. Cambridge, New York and Melbourne: Cambridge University Press.

Meek, L. and Goedegebuure, L. (1989) *Higher Education: A Report*. Armidale, NSW: Department of Administrative and Higher Education Studies, University of New England.

Menger, P.-M. (2006) 'Artistic labour markets: contingent work, excess supply and occupational risk management', in V. A. Ginsburgh and D. Throsby (eds), *Handbook of the Economics of Art and Culture*, Vol. 1. Amsterdam and Boston: Elsevier.

Minson, J. (1998) 'Ethics in the service of the state', in M. Dean and B. Hindess (eds), *Governing Australia: Studies in Contemporary Rationalities of Government*. Cambridge: Cambridge University Press.

Mitchell, W. and Muyksen, J. (2008) *Full Employment Abandoned: Shifting Sands and Policy Failures*. Cheltenham: Edward Elgar.

Morris, M. (1998) *Too Soon, Too Late: History in Popular Culture*. Bloomington, IN: Indiana University Press.

Osborn, A. (1991) [1941] *Your Creative Power: How to Use Your Imagination to Brighten Life, Get Ahead*. Schaumburg, IL: Motorola University Press.

Papadopoulos, A. (2005) '"Know Your Product": An Informational Analysis of the Higher Education Contribution Scheme in Australia'. PhD thesis. Melbourne: Faculty of Arts, University of Melbourne.

Percy, A., Scoufis, M., Parry, S., Goody, A. and Hicks, M. (2008) *The Red Report: The Contribution of Sessional Teachers to Higher Education*. Strawberry Hills, NSW: Australian Learning and Teaching Council.

Polesel, J. and Teese, R. (1997) *The 'Colleges': Growth and Diversity in the Non-University Tertiary Sector (1965–1974)*. Canberra: Department of Employment, Education, Training and Youth Affairs.

Pryor, L. (2010) 'A novel idea turns creative writing into an academic racket', *Sydney Morning Herald*, 27 February. Retrieved from: http://www.smh.com.au/opinion/society-and-culture/a-novel-idea-turns-creative-writing-into-an-academic-racket-20100226-p914.html (retrieved 29 June 2015).

SERCARC (1995) *Arts Education*. Canberra: Senate Environment, Recreation, Communications and the Arts References Committee, Commonwealth of Australia.

Strand, D. (1998) *Research in the Creative Arts*. Canberra: Department of Employment, Education, Training and Youth Affairs.

Towse, R. (2006) 'Human capital and artists' labour markets', in V. Ginsburgh and D. Throsby (eds), *Handbook of the Economics of Arts and Culture*. Amsterdam: Elsevier.

14 University as *Übungsraum*

Notes on the creative transformation of higher education

Sebastian Olma

Introduction: serendipity and the long shadow of Black Mountain

It is no accident that in the summer of 2015, the Deutsche Nationalgalerie in Berlin put on a show dedicated to Black Mountain College,[1] the legendary North Carolina art school that influenced the trajectory of Modernism in the second half of the twentieth century perhaps more than any other institution. The list of names of students or teachers populating this exceptional place between 1933 and 1957 reads like a Who's Who of twentieth century art and design and, perhaps to a lesser extent, of the natural and social sciences as well. And yet, the show doesn't focus much on the great names or the famous works they produced. It does not dwell on Buckminster Fuller's invention of the geodesic dome there, or the school's importance for the development of abstract expressionism, or the impact of the collaboration between Merce Cunningham and John Cage on contemporary art. Instead the exhibition demonstrates the institution's appeal, built on an ethos of radically democratic interdisciplinarity, experiment, and exploration. Initially, it was not even conceived as an art school per se, but rather as a free educational institution where young men and women could develop the knowledge and skills that suited them best in their quest to make a meaningful contribution to society. As the show's curators, Eugen and Gabriele Knapstein, write in the exhibition catalogue:

> Black Mountain College has remained an exemplary institution to the present day and, particularly in our time of higher education reforms, which posit principles of economic efficiency as the sole measure of success, it is a counter-example of direct democratic praxis.
>
> (Blume *et al*. 2015: 14)

Much like the Bauhaus, from which many members migrated, Black Mountain College presents something of an ideal type of higher education (HE) that in the early twenty-first century we seem to have completely lost touch with, one which operated at a small, intimate scale with few more than a hundred students enrolled at its peak. From the point of view of those involved in running massive educational machines today, this represents pure luxury. Yet, at a time when university administrations throughout the Western world make claims of their commitment to innovation and creativity, one wonders why these 'commitments' tend to have such detrimental effects on the material conditions of research and learning.

For France's most eminent philosopher, Michel Serres, the reasons are clear: universities are increasingly failing the young generations because of their clinging to obsolete disciplinary structures (Serres, 2012). What our institutions of HE fail to realise, Serres says, is the revolutionary potential inherent in digital technology that offers a great opportunity for a radical rethinking of the university. With all the knowledge of the world available at the tap of a finger, he argues, universities have an immense opportunity to reinvent themselves. They can become institutions of transversal adisciplinarity, shifting the function of education from knowledge transmission to teaching students skills to enable them to creatively explore the serendipitous connections between the bodies of knowledge previously confined to their disciplines, but which now are carried around in most pockets via smart phones and other devices. In other words, massive student populations are no excuse for their regulation via disciplinary structures and constraints; on the back of digital technology, it has become possible again to climb the Black Mountain – not just for future artists but for everyone.

This chapter takes Michel Serres' intervention as its point of departure for a reflection on the current challenges to HE in terms of providing a space where the younger generation is able to acquire the skills and capabilities they need in order to make a meaningful contribution to society. Universities are the infrastructural organs where society conceives of and develops important elements of its possible futures across the different academic disciplines. It is here that society's capacity to invent and innovate in the future is determined. Given the rapidly changing social environment, the question of the right skills and opportunities in today's HE presents a formidable challenge.

In order to do justice to the fundamental nature of this question, this chapter starts from a philosophical point of view and, for the most part, will also stay at this level of analysis. It does not aim, however, to be an exercise in detached philosophising. The reason why Serres' line of argument makes for an interesting point of departure is that it provides the philosophical analogue, which substantiates a developing recent strategy of university administrations across Europe. I refer here, of course, to the so-called creative industries programmes that form the thematic backbone of this book. The creative industries makeover within the disciplines considered relevant to this field (Arts and Humanities, some Social Sciences, as well as Design and parts of Technology Education) tries not only to overcome disciplinary boundaries within academia, but also to connect learning and research to the relevant professional fields beyond the university. Multi-, inter- and transdisciplinarity are important catchwords for these efforts but also, and perhaps even more importantly, serendipity. Creative industries programmes, collaborations and campuses are seen as platforms enabling disciplinary and institutional transgression that can reproduce, in a timely fashion, the serendipitous encounters that gave an institution like Black Mountain College its enormous creative and innovative edge.

Both for Serres and the proponents of creative industries education, serendipity has become a guiding reference with regard to the reorganisation of the university. The danger here is that these analytical and practical efforts are guided by a vague buzzword that can mean anything to anyone (we've seen the same thing occurring with creativity, innovation, social innovation, etc.). However, Serres' critique of the current state of HE can lead us into a closer exploration of the notion of serendipity. According to its inventor, Horace Walpole, this mid-eighteenth-century neologism signifies discoveries by accident and sagacity. While the *accidental* side of serendipity is a rather straightforward matter – i.e. the encounter of something unexpected – the question of *sagacity* is where the challenge lies. This challenge is not just an analytical one, but one that needs to be addressed in relation to the design of HE infrastructure. Within the creative industries discourse, sagacity tends to be strictly understood in terms of entrepreneurial agility: the accidental encounter with an idea, an artefact, a technology, a specific approach or a skill that is quickly transformed into a product or service. To be able to facilitate this sagacity is clearly of great value; however, one wonders if there aren't other rationales and logics of creativity that HE can cater to as well. To explore this question, I turn to Richard Sennett's (2008) analysis of the crafts(wo)man's virtuosity – which he understands in an immediately political sense in terms of the question of social participation and in the final analysis of citizenship.

While Sennett's reflection on the political implications of virtuosity helps widen our view on what it means to be 'creative', we need to bring this question back – rather literally – to the *space* of HE. Here, the work of German philosopher Peter Sloterdijk (2009) is instructive, as it turns the Foucauldian critique of discipline into a celebration of *Übung* (literally: exercise or training). According to Sloterdijk, who speaks with a clear Nietzschean accent here, human beings are an *Übungswesen*, i.e. a creature that needs exercise or training to grow into and beyond itself. *Übung*, of course, requires space and the task of providing such space, or indeed *Übungsraum*, is exactly that of HE. With reference to Sloterdijk, one might say that traditionally the challenge for HE has been to create a nexus where the relevant kind of *Übung* finds its appropriate *Raum*. Today, one of the areas in which this challenge needs to be readdressed is in the context of creative industries and HE: how to integrate the creative industries as a platform for serendipity in an *Übungsraum* that values vocational skill within a comprehensive ethos of *Bildung*?

Of thumbs and heads: damned to be intelligent?

Michel Serres' *Petite Poucette* (2012) is a strange little book. Written as a 'love letter to the networked generation' (the subtitle of the German translation) it celebrates the digital savviness of his grandchildren and their peers. *Petit Poucette* is the French name of the fairy tale character known in the English-speaking world as little Tom Thumb. The title is thus a pun on the agility with which the fingers of the younger generation of 'digital natives' dash over the touch screens of their mobile devices. For Serres, *Petite Poucette* does not just stand for a new generation but represents a new kind of human being. While the exact circumstances of her coming into being remain in the dark, whatever gave birth to her had something to do with digital technology. To illustrate what is going on, Serres refers to Jacques de Voragine's *Légende dorée*, that tells the story of St Dionysius, the first bishop of Paris who was captured by the Roman army and sentenced to death by beheading on top of what was later to be called Montmartre. Half way to the top, the lazy soldiers decide to avoid the strenuous ascent and cut off his head on the spot. The bishop's head drops to the ground. Miraculously, though, the decapitated St Dionysius raises, grabs his head and continues his ascent – head in hands. The soldiers flee in shock and horror. The point Serres is trying to make here is that today *Petite Poucette* is holding her head in her hands as well. She is decapitated in the sense of having her intellectual, cognitive capabilities externalised into devices whose memory is thousands of times more powerful than ours. Which leads Serres to the question:

> What then is it that we keep on carrying on our shoulders after being decapitated? Renewed and living intuition. Being 'canned' [in the computer, SO], pedagogy releases us to the pure pleasure of invention. Great: Are we damned to become intelligent?
>
> (Serres 2012: 55)

And here is where Serres sees the main problem with HE institutions: they are unable or unwilling to adjust to this new empty-headed yet 'agile-thumped' generation that does not need knowledge as stock anymore (as it always has it at hand anyway), but needs knowledge as process that feeds intuition, invention and innovation.

Serres goes on to present his ideas on what could be done to turn the university into a place that would be more accommodating to the evolutionary advances of Tom Thumb and *Petite Poucette*. He introduces another historical analogy, again from Paris, yet this time closer to the present. It concerns Boucicaut, founder of one of the world's first department stores, *Le Bon Marché*. Emile Zola made Boucicaut the template for Octave Mouret, the hero of his novel *Au Bonheur des Dames* (Zola 2008). At one point in the novel, Mouret, following a whim, abandons the well-ordered, classified structure of his department store, turning it into a labyrinth where the shopping-crazed *dames* find the latest silk-fashion (mid-nineteenth century we are talking about) next to fresh vegetables, etc. The resulting chaos that his move generated was an instant success: sales went through the roof. For Serres, this provides a great metaphor for what has to happen at universities. They can learn, he argues, from Boucicault's principle of serendipity, the principle of the unsought discovery through unexpected encounters. The university needs a reform that mobilises the disparate against classification. 'The disparate', as the author puts it, 'has advantages that reason cannot even dream of' (Serres 2012: 44).

The reference to serendipity is crucial here. On the face of it, it rearticulates, as a philosophical gesture, the call for disciplinary and institutional transgression that re-emerges on the back of the development of digital technology and creative industries. This is not wrong per se: it does make a lot of sense to think about disciplinary transgression for the sake of serendipity when it comes to keeping HE in sync with the development and requirements of its social environment. Where the arguments of both Serres and the proponents of the creative industries HE-makeover derail, however, is when they judge the significance of serendipity to HE only in terms defined by supply and demand, by the market rather than criteria based on innovation and by the intrinsic value of knowledge gleaned from serendipitous encounter and exchange. Isn't it curious that Serres believes the department store to be the apposite metaphor for his call for disciplinary transgression, rather than, say, the much richer and more relevant historical examples of institutions such as Black Mountain College or the Bauhaus? And doesn't his attempt to rethink HE on the template of the *Le Bon Marché* correspond to the fascination with the 'serendipitous' business models of Silicon Valley often held by the proponents of the creative industries approach to HE?

The point to be made here is that such an understanding of serendipity as disciplinary transgression for the sake of market success is an extremely narrow one. Whenever academic institutions in the past were *successfully* working on the principle of serendipity (as were those quoted above) they explicitly avoided such constraint. These institutions were serendipitous precisely because of their comprehensive practice of disciplinary transgression. Wouldn't it be rather nonsensical to argue for a disciplinary opening in order to then frame the opening in the narrow parameters of supply and demand? Even Silicon Valley, whose *current* business models function according to very impoverished interpretations of serendipity, the expected encounter between a great start-up idea and a willing investor (Hagel *et al*. 2010) would not exist without the serendipitous encounter of postwar cybernetic research and 1960s hippie culture (Turner 2006; Olma forthcoming), both of which were not exactly streamlined business cultures.

What this shows is that serendipity can and should be an important reference with regard to a timely reorganisation of HE but only if it is taken seriously in its own right, rather than preformatted by the logic of market exchange. The department store has obviously lost its power of attraction, but there is also more to serendipity than meets the Google-glassed eye. In order to fully comprehend what is at stake here, the next section looks briefly at the etymology of the notion of serendipity in order to then tease out conceptually what the notion might offer in terms of designing a creative and innovative system of HE.

The disparate against classification: the principle of serendipity

The notion of serendipity was originally conceived in the middle of the eighteenth century within literary circles, where it led its marginal existence until very recently. Horace Walpole, art historian and eccentric son of the first British Prime Minister, coined the term 'serendipity' in 1754. Walpole had come across the 'silly fairy tale' *Peregrinaggio di tre giovani figliuoli del re di Serendippo* that was the Italian translation of the ancient Persian parable of the three princes of Serendip, the ancient name of Sri Lanka. As the parable goes, the king had sent his sons on a punitive expedition for having refused to succeed him after their education. As Walpole writes, during their travels the smart royal kids constantly make 'discoveries, by accidents and sagacity, of things they were not in quest of' (Lewis 1937–83: 408). This became Walpole's definition of his newly coined term serendipity and, as such, it spread through the world of literates and biblio-philes. Scientists, of course, were always able to relate to the principle for which Walpole invented his neologism, as it describes an important logic of scientific discovery and invention (Merton and Barber 2004; Van Andel and Bourcier 2013; Johnson 2010); Louis Pasteur's often-cited adage about chance favouring only prepared minds is the most famous statement demonstrating serendipity's signif-icance for the world of science.

Serendipity is now becoming an important reference for those whose profes-sion it is to make economies more innovative, our industries and cities more creative and our future better (Muller and Becker 2012; Kingdon 2012; Johnson 2010). Within the creative industries with their co-working spaces, creative hubs and start-up centres, the notion has become a crucial reference for the new generation of freelancers and entrepreneurs for whom the principle of the valua-ble unexpected encounters (of new ideas for products and services, funding opportunities, contracts, business partners, etc.) is one of the foundations of economic survival (Johns and Gratton 2013).[2] For popular non-fiction authors and academics working within the field of the creative industries, serendipity is often instrumental for understanding the dynamics of 'creativity', for instance in the way in which scholars such as Richard Florida or Charles Landry conceptualise their vision of the creative city (Florida 2002; Landry 1995). It is via the discourse of the creative industries and innovation that the notion of serendipity is today re-entering the world of HE.

In Walpole's definition of serendipity, there are two important dimensions: acci-dent and sagacity. The first dimension, accident, implies the conjuncture of elements that, in the usual course of things, would not encounter each other. Contemporary philosophers refer to this dimension in terms of a multiplicity, where multiple, concurrent relations form a potential out of which the new may emerge. The second dimension, sagacity, is where this potential gets embodied, where it is actualised and enters into the world. Sagacity is where the depth of experience, expertise, crafts-manship and skill are applied, initiating the creative process by which unexpected encounters acquire efficacy. So serendipity needs both the multiplicity of encounters (accidents) and the creative act (sagacity) actualising the encounter. Without these, serendipity does not work and the act of creation does not occur. The next section takes a further, more critical look at these two dimensions in turn.

Understanding serendipity I: accident

The accident in serendipity refers to an unintended departure from the usual course of things. In the first instance, we might understand this swerve from the ordinary in the Lucretian sense of the clinamen: a deviation from the laminar movement of atoms causing a vortex out of which something new might emerge (Serres 2000). In the twentieth century, of course, Lucretius' Greco-Roman atomism has been popularised by the theory of complexity (Prigogine and Stenger 1984). Applying complexity theory's insights to the dimension of social life, we could say that the deviation is caused by an extraordinary conjuncture of ideas, objects, intuitions, knowledge fragments, etc. I would like to approach this dimension of serendipity in terms of what contemporary philosophers refer to as 'virtual multiplicity'.[3] These are relations forming a potential, prior to any subjective or objective embodiment. Multiplicity is the philosophical expression intended to mark an ontological network consisting of relations – forces, affects, desires – that don't yet have what we might call social efficacy. They have a latent meaning that still requires a creative (sagacious) act in order to become actualised (as something new, an innovation, etc.). Nonetheless, the virtual dimension of accidents is real; it represents the essential precondition for the new to emerge.

With regard to the accidental encounter, the diversity of elements encountering each other is crucial for the generation of novelty. Here, we find the inspiration for Serres' argument about the jumbling of university departments as a way of 'mobilising the disparate against classification' (2012: 43). What Serres might not appreciate is that universities all over Europe have for some time been investigating the creative industries as models for inspiration and 'best practice' in 'creating synergies' and facilitating unexpected encounters. It is true that interdisciplinarity had become an issue for HE long before the creative industries became a policy instrument (Kockelmans 1975; Gibbons 1998). However, the influence of the creative industries discourse, particularly on the academic management of the arts and humanities as well as some of the social sciences, has substantially modified the discussion of interdisciplinarity. An important source of inspiration for the creative reorganisation of HE is now found in those emphatically creative and innovative spaces, hubs and incubators that make up a crucial part of our so-called creative cities. The problem here is that often universities seem to strangely lack the critical faculties to properly assess these 'best practices' and their relationship to creative learning and entrepreneurship. As it turns out – and this goes very much against the grain of popular myth – in terms of their populations, these places often display the very homogeneity that the philosopher criticises with regard to the university. In Amsterdam, this has recently led to a debate on 'creative ghettos', questioning the sensibility of spatial policies where creative producers remain largely among themselves (Vonk 2014; Cnossen and Olma 2014). One might indeed wonder whether the spatialities of the creative industries, and the corresponding creative class, are the right source of inspiration (or even method) when it comes to reforming HE – even in terms of their supposed creative diversity (McCann 2007; Nathan 2005). Just think of the ubiquity of the demand of 'like-mindedness' as a precondition for collaboration in the creative industries scenes. And let us also not forget that there is a veritable army of coaches and experts that have besieged the creative class, streamlining their ability to creatively express themselves in the name of entrepreneurial success.[4] This is not to diminish the various impulses that have emerged from the sector in terms of urban development or new business models (Olma 2012; Cnossen and Olma 2014). However, the mobilisation of 'the disparate against classification' that we see in the creative city and business is of an entirely different order to what is needed in today's university. As I have argued above, what is at stake here is kind of inter-, multi- or transdisciplinarity that cannot be pressed into the straightjacket of the market.

Understanding serendipity II: sagacity

Which brings us to serendipity's second dimension: sagacity. This is where the potential that emerged within the virtual multiplicity gets embodied, where it is actualised and effectively enters into the world. Here is where the magic happens, except that it isn't magical at all. In fact, the creative act is essentially one of *resistance*. This is to say that the accident acquires social efficacy through the sagacious realisation that something potentially new is occurring, followed by an act of *resisting* the alignment of this occurrence with the existing vectors of knowledge and power. In other words, he or she resists the temptation of going down the path of least resistance in favour of a sagacious effort. In science, the responsibility for the sagacious act rest on the shoulders of the scientist who observes an anomalous datum and follows its lead, rather than trying to ignore it or force it into the edifice of an existing theory. However, this doesn't mean that sagacity is a question of an autonomous individual mind-set, as the scientist who recognises the relevance of the anomaly (potentially turning it into a discovery or invention) has been shaped by an ecology of scientific curiosity as well (Merton and Barber 2004). Rather, sagacity is the expression of what Lucretius (1995) defined as the joy of advancing our understanding in the 'nature of things' or, following Gilles Deleuze, the joy of accomplishing a moment of *le survol*, of being in synchronicity with the creative movement of becoming (Deleuze and Guattari 1994). Which is to say that we need to define sagacity as an act of joyous resistance that pushes the world forward. In this sense, sagacity could be understood as an antithesis to futurology and trend watching: instead of extrapolating the future as a linear progression of trends in the current 'system', sagacity is that which intervenes as a wilful disturbance, opening said 'system' to new and different possibilities.

When referring to sagacity in terms of resistance, I do not, of course, intend this in either the sense of pure defiance or as a romantic rejection of global change motivated by the dream of an ideal past. Rather, I would like to approach sagacity as an engagement with the potentially new in such a way as to open up ruling regimes of knowledge and power to the possibility of future deviation. Such an understanding of sagacity, in the context of serendipity, would allow us to broaden the creative industries approach to academic inter-, multi- and transdisciplinarity that today is overly focused on entrepreneurial and technological skills. These are important skills but need to be integrated within a pedagogic culture, encouraging the young to question the present for the sake of finding their own way to contribute to a desirable future as an act of self-determination.

Adopting a broader perspective on the purpose of HE is far from revolutionary. The ambition to educate not just disciplinary specialists but sovereign individuals capable of participating in and contributing to society as active citizens has always been part and parcel of the HE's ethos. It is only recently that the neoliberal disdain for anything public has gripped our institutions of HE to the extent that this important dimension of education has been wilfully left to rot (Davies 2014). If today our romantic gaze is going back to institutions such as Black Mountain College or the Bauhaus, this is because these institutions based their innovative capacity on a pedagogical ethos that treated creativity and citizenship as two sides of the same coin.

Serendipity has a role to play in our efforts to redesign our universities as places of creativity and innovation. However, it should be serendipity of the comprehensively sagacious kind, not the one of the quick buck. And this means that we have to rethink the relationship between creativity and citizenship for HE as well. I am aware this is a difficult question, particularly in a country like the UK, where HE has effectively become a question of supply and demand. Yet, while one cannot naively ignore the reality of the neoliberal university, it would be irresponsible to pragmatically accept the current dysfunctionality of HE. For those of us who disagree with the likes of Margret Thatcher and Bruno Latour (i.e. 'there is no such thing as society') and believe in education as a generational responsibility towards the young, the normative question of comprehensive *Bildung* needs to remain the ethical horizon (Stiegler 2014).[5]

Virtuosity: rethinking *Bildung* between creativity and citizenship

Recently, Richard Sennett has addressed the question of *Bildung* precisely in terms of the relationship between creativity (creative labour) and citizenship. In order to do this, Sennett engages in a historical analysis of craftsmanship as *virtuosity* (Sennett 2008). Virtuosity is relevant to this context because, as outlined below, it entertains an interesting relation to the notion of sagacity. It is in the contemporary mutations of the traditional practice of virtuosity that I hope to find the means for a further conceptual refinement of sagacity (and sagacious serendipity) that will allow us to creatively rethink HE without falling into the trap of ideological complicity.

Sennett's *The Craftsman* is an attack on the classical liberal conviction according to which craftsmanship is a mere economic matter. From the classical liberal point of view, the craftsman is the *bourgeois*, the economic citizen, and as such qualitatively different from the *citoyen*, the political citizen proper, so to speak. Sennett challenges this dichotomy by arguing that craftsmanship is an institutional practice connecting the worlds of *bourgeois* and *citoyen*. As he demonstrates, craftsmanship, as the result of a process of dedicated apprenticeship, provides a crucial training ground for faculties that are indispensible for a meaningful practice of citizenship. This is how he summarises his argument:

> The argument … is that the craft of making physical things provides insights into the techniques of experience that can shape our dealings with others. Both the difficulties and the possibilities of making things well apply to making human relationships. Material challenges like working with resistance or managing ambiguity are instructive in understanding the resistance people harbor to one another or the uncertain boundaries between people … [W]ho we are arises directly from what our bodies can do. Social consequences are built into the structure and the functioning of the human body, as in the workings of the human hand. I argue no more and no less than that the capacities our bodies have to shape physical things are the same capacities we draw on in social contacts.
>
> (Sennett 2008: 289–90)

Sennett's central concept here is *virtuosity*. The virtuosity of the craftsman, i.e. the purposeful application of one's body to the shaping of objects, Sennett understands as the precondition for the virtuosity of the citizen in shaping social relations to his fellow citizens. The experience of making a unique contribution through one's engagement with matter generates the self-consciousness necessary for a meaningful participation in society.[6] What Sennett describes here is a process of formation of individual sovereignty in the sense of professional virtuosity as being the path toward the ability for meaningful participation in society, i.e. political virtuosity. This conception of virtuosity necessitates a continuum that connects the professional skill of the craftsman to the political skill of the citizen. Of course, with regard to the challenges HE is facing today, Sennett's emphasis on the physical nature of education seems slightly outdated; in order to think through virtuosity in terms that resonate with our contemporary situation (in general, as well as HE in particular), the notion needs to be opened out.

This can be done with the help of German philosopher Peter Sloterdijk. His *Du musst Dein Leben ändern* (2009) approaches the question of education in terms of the Greek notion of *áskēsis*, the original meaning of which is 'exercise' or 'training'. Sloterdijk's exploration of *áskēsis* fundamentally builds on Foucault's excavation of the relation between discipline and citizenship, but rejects its reduction to a 'dark', manipulative and somewhat illegitimate force. Rather, he argues, discipline as asceticism should be understood as a dialectical process of self-formation in relation to the formative structures (the moulds) of a given society. As Sloterdijk puts it:

> Rather than the prisons and the places of repressive surveillance, it is the strict schools and universities as well as the craftsmen's workshops and the artistic studios that provide modernity with the space for the essential 'human orthopaedics,' i.e., the formation of the young according to the standards of Christian-humanist discipline. The actual destination of the journey into the age

of the arts and techniques is the active development of ever new generations
of virtuosi.

(Sloterdijk 2009: 497, author's translation)

The 'virtuosi' who Sloterdijk understands as the (never quite finished) products
of such orthopaedics are human beings able to lead their lives autonomously
precisely because they have gone through the formative process of asceticism.
What Sloterdijk's celebration of asceticism demonstrates is that virtuosity, as
the result of *Übung*, is not exclusively linked to the physicality of traditional
craftsmanship in Sennett's sense but applies generally to human beings, in so far
as they are *Übungswesen* (i.e. creatures that need exercise or training in order
to grow into themselves). And while 'the standards of Christian-humanist discipline' have run their course as exclusive ethical parameters of education, the
question should be exactly what kind of ethos should replace them.

 Sennett, unfortunately, is unable to address this question in a timely fashion.
The merit of his argument lies in having made explicit the connection between
craftsmanship and citizenship in terms of a continuum of virtuosity. Also, his
critique of the rapid devaluation of craftsmanship, as a result of neoliberal politics, cannot be easily dismissed.[7] However, Sennett's main problem is that his
argument is too romantic to offer any possible way out of this predicament,
yearning for pedagogical methods that are both unsustainable in the age of mass
education and largely useless for today's Tom Thumbs and *Petites Poucettes*. The
virtuosity that is necessary to manoeuvre in today's economic as well as social,
technological and political terrain is one totally different from the one Sennett has
in mind.[8] It cannot belong to the bygone era of crafting. Neither is it the virtuosity of the factory and the office – if such thing ever existed. It is a new kind of
virtuosity that necessarily entails the ability to reconstruct the continuum
connecting a professional ethos appropriate to the digital era with the social
responsibility of a sovereign political subject.

Virtuosity, sagacity and the need for *Übungsraum*

This new kind of virtuosity is not going to emerge by itself. Universities, as the
infrastructural organs where society conceives of and develops important elements
of its possible futures, are responsible for the construction of Sennett's continuum
between economic professionalism and social and political participation. Having
ignored this responsibility is as much an unforgivable omission of Serres' book as
it is the root cause for the crisis of the neoliberal university: HE is taken to be a
machine whose purpose is the commercial organisation of knowledge transfer (Ball
2012; Canaan and Shumar 2008). Since all 'the knowledge' today is canned in the
memory of the computer and digital networks, thumbs have become more important than heads. Yet, this kind of knowledge has very little to do with virtuosity or,
indeed, sagacity. Rather, it is close to what Bernard Stiegler calls *bêtise*, stupidity
(Stiegler 2014). Limiting the question of knowledge to that of technological savviness and entrepreneurial skill – as Serres and often the proponents of the creative

industries in the academy clearly do – reduces human beings to functional extensions of a technological system, ignoring the crucial importance of *savoir vivre*, knowledge of how to live and love. The question is: how can universities that are themselves in a state of profound disorientation become institutions of care, where Generation Y get the tools, skills and, indeed, the knowledge to leave their stupidity behind in order to become sagacious virtuosi of their own lives?

To even begin addressing this question, we need to move the notion of virtuosity even closer to the present, which, in our context, means closer to sagacity and serendipity. The work of the Italian philosopher Paolo Virno is instructive here, as it diagnoses the emergence of a new and very different kind of virtuosity that is linked to the immaterialisation of economy and society (Virno, 2004). Immaterialisation refers to a process by which the immaterial dimension of products, i.e. their symbolic, aesthetic and social value, has come to outweigh their classical material dimension. Images, knowledge, information, codes and affects as well as social relationships per se have become the predominant factors in determining the value a particular commodity has on the market (Hardt and Negri 2000; Lazzarato 2002; Potts 2011). In other words, for Virno, affiliated with the post-Marxist Italian left, immaterialisation stands for what policy-makers and economists refer to in terms of digitisation and creative industries.

In Virno's interpretation, this immaterialisation of economic practice leads to a development that seems to be the opposite of what Sennett describes: rather than virtuosity disappearing due to the growing distance between labour and politics, the virtuosity of labour and that of politics begin to converge. As commodities, as well as the ways in which they are produced, become increasingly cultural, communicational, semiotic, expressive and so on, the sphere of production takes on many of the characteristics that were traditionally assigned to the world of politics. Today, production, distribution and consumption are predicated on a techno-cultural infrastructure enabling constant multidimensional flows of communication. This is to say that today's regime of production runs on techno-cultural platforms sustaining publically organised spaces that in a strange manner resemble those of politics. The virtuosity required by this new spatiality is one that is immediately and radically social. It implies the permanent presence of others as co-producers, co-distributors and co-consumers. So the new virtuosity is intrinsically relational, even performative.

For Virno, this new kind of virtuosity marks a moment in the development of the human species in which our basic socio-linguistic faculties, the human ability to creatively communicate, have become productive. Robert Reich had already highlighted this fact more than twenty years ago, when writing about the growing importance of so-called 'symbolic analysts' within the economy (Reich 1992). Since then, the spectrum of activity that applies virtuosity for the sake of generating economic value has expanded massively. From the growing sector of services with (at least) a nod to the experience-creating creative industries, a kind of public space re-emerges, although one in which potentially emancipative, proto-political practice is perpetually transformed into intensified labour (Hochschild 1985; Head 2014).

And here, we encounter the point at which virtuosity, in the sense that both Sloterdijk and Sennett understand it, becomes utterly devoid of any political impetus. If the generation of economic value today takes place in a proto-political arena of instant communicative presence and connection, there is an increasing danger for the *citoyen* to collapse into the figure of a comprehensive *bourgeois* for whom the practice of citizenship is perverted into a mere marketing exercise. The creative industries are the great case in point here: just think about the ubiquity of vacuous references to 'community' when addressing customers and clients.

Seen in the light of Virno's critical socio-philosophy, the current attempt to 'modernise' the relevant parts of HE by putting them at the service of the creative industries appears to be an attempt to save a kind of virtuosity that no longer deserves saving. 'Let's look at the maker, hacker, and co-working spaces, the fablabs and creative hubs of the creative city,' says the innovation consultant to the university administrator, 'and see if we can transfer their timely creativity and innovativeness into the structure of the institution.' This is not entirely wrong, but it expresses a skewed perspective. The challenge for the university is not to make students more innovative and creative – whatever that might actually mean – but to enable them to manoeuvre the emergent social and economic topology as relatively sovereign individuals, i.e. not *just* as entrepreneurial *bourgeois* but also as critical *citoyen*. It seems to me that this model of the creative entrepreneur falls as short of this challenge as Serres' reference to Boucicaut's serendipitous department store in *Au Bonheur des Dames* does.

Conclusion: higher education as *Übungsraum* for social innovation

Instead, we have to understand, following Sloterdijk, that the human being as *Übungswesen* needs the university as *Übungsraum*, catering actively to the timely reconstruction of the continuum of virtuosity. *Übung macht den Meister* goes the German proverb, and the kind of *Übung* required today is that which not only 'makes the master craftsman' but also generates sagacity as a crucial prerequisite for the serendipitous disruption of current cultural and economic templates. To create the necessary *Übungsräume* or training spaces, we need a new wave of social innovation that liberates our educational institutions from their docility and opportunism. Here, the reference to social innovation is in no way intended as an endorsement of the homonymous policy discourse (Murray *et al.* 2010). This conceptually confused and ideologically preformatted field of 'social innovation' policy is part and parcel of the neoliberal charade of changeless change (Pol and Ville 2009; Olma 2014, 2016 forthcoming). What is meant here by the term 'social innovation' is a collective effort, in the present context requiring the collaboration of teachers, students, parents and everyone else concerned about the current state of HE to halt the purposeful neoliberal destruction of an essential pillar of our public infrastructure. Rather than mystifying the technological advances of 'the Internet' and expect the generation of 'digital natives' to somehow come to grips with its challenges, we need modes of education that enable young minds to not only performatively but also critically engage with today's rapid technological progress (Stiegler 2010b). Technological savviness and entrepreneurial skill should be part and parcel, but by no means the end of it. Our schools and universities need to become institutions where critical analytical capabilities for the digital age are cultivated as well.

The problem, of course, goes much deeper than the supposed lack of disciplinary transgression. There are blatant democratic and economic deficits at our institutions of HE (although they obviously vary between countries) that make even the most basic academic work increasingly impossible, let alone the creation of conditions for meaningful experiment and exploration, i.e. what in the past was referred to as academic freedom. As Johan Andrew Rice, founder of Black Mountain College, remarked (with a considerable dash of pathos) 'Students can be educated for freedom only by teachers who are themselves free' (Blume *et al.* 2015: back cover). Today, at a time of chronic underpay and short time contracts on the one hand and student indebtedness on the other, there is not much freedom left on either side of the equation.

Michel Serres' intervention, as should be clear by now, is unhelpful in this respect. In fact, with his mixture of euphoria for and ignorance of current developments in technology, he might fit well with those academic management bodies that helplessly embrace every digital fashion for the sake of appearing modern. Unfortunately, this is often the chief reason why the creative industries are invoked and, indeed, invited into the university: as another simulation of change, a fig leaf under which the 'market Stalinism' (Fisher 2009) of neoliberal management can proceed as planned. Much of what creative industries policies stand for amounts to little more than the celebration of apps and entrepreneurship,[9] which suggests that it is a programme leading the young generation straight into what Bernard Stiegler (2010a) calls 'digital proletarianisation', that is loss of *savoir vivre*, which also means loss of critical faculties and, in the final analysis, loss of individual sovereignty that is required for meaningful participation in society. No one is 'damned to become intelligent'. We cannot let ourselves off the hook so easily.

So perhaps, then, Serres is right about the younger generation holding their heads in their hands today. Good education means enabling our students to put their heads back on. However, it is unlikely that current university management will to take steps in this direction out of their own accord. The kind of social innovation needed lies with the university occupations and student protests that have spread from Amsterdam to universities all over Europe (Grey 2015). Here, we see the emergence of a timely *Übungsraum* for the skills that are necessary to liberate the university from the grip of managerial confusion, as the first step toward the construction of a new university. What this new university is going to look like remains to be seen. What is clear, however, is that academics have the responsibility to support this process of real social innovation by being part of it. By lending it the little bit of sagacity we have left, we might even turn the process into a serendipitous one: one, at whose end, we will have found something better than we seem to be able to hope for today.

Notes

1. Black Mountain: An Interdisciplinary Experiment, 1933–1957, 5 June to 27 September 2015, Hamburger Bahnhof – Museum for Contemporary Art, Berlin
2. Academics working in the areas of organisation und management studies as well as in the social sciences are slowly picking up on this phenomenon. The reason why I abstained from providing more than the one HBR reference here is that the 'proper' academic work on this issue tends to be of excruciating triviality. For those interested in an up-to-date (yet free of any critical reflection) picture of this world, I'd suggest going to the online magazine deskmag.com.
3. The reference is to philosophers working in the tradition of Friedrich Nietzsche, Henri Bergson and Gilles Deleuze. For an introductory account see Ansell-Pearson (2002).
4. Creative consultancy is indeed a blooming business, teaching aspiring entrepreneurs how to be different by doing exactly the same. Pamphlets are written as well for the sake of credibility but none of this is quotable. For an upmarket example of the structure of argument (with some pop-science thrown in) see Lehrer (2012).
5. And even for those of us who are of a more purely economic or business persuasion, it should be clear that the market can never generate the diversity of input necessary for truly path-breaking innovation. The history of Silicon Valley, already cited above, is only one example of this historical fact. Relevant in this context is also Mazzucato (2013).
6. This, of course, is John Dewey's (1938) pragmatist philosophy of education in a (very small) nut shell that also served as a guide to the experiment of Black Mountain College.
7. For the neoliberal university see also Mark Fisher's classic *Capitalist Realism* (2009). For the corporate context, refer to the excellent studies by Simon Head (2005, 2014).
8. For three different versions of this difference see Boltanski and Chiapello (1999), Friebe and Lobo (2006) and Stiegler (2014).
9. For a comprehensive treatment of the problem of 'social innovation' refer to the forthcoming book (Olma 2016). See also Olma (2014).

References

Ansell-Pearson, K. (2002) *Philosophy and the Adventure of the Virtual: Bergson and the Time of Life*. London: Routledge.
Ball, S. J. (2012) 'Performativity, commodification and commitment: an I-spy guide to the neoliberal university', *British Journal of Educational Studies*, 60 (1): 17–28.
Blume, E., Feli, M., Knapstein, G. and Nichols, C. (2015) *Black Mountain: An Interdisciplinary Experiment 1933–1957*. Leipzig: Spector Books.
Boltanski, L. and Chiapello, E. (2006) *Le Nouvel Esprit du Capitalisme*. Paris: Gallimard.
Canaan, J. E. and Shumar, W. (eds) (2008) *Structure and Agency in the Neoliberal University*. London: Routledge.
Cnossen, B. and Olma, S. (2014) *The Volkskrant Building: Manufacturing Difference in Amsterdam's Creative City*. Amsterdam: Amsterdam Creative Industries Publishing.
Davies, W. (2014) *The Limits of Neoliberalism: Authority, Sovereignty and the Logic of Competition*. London: Sage.
Debord, G. (2002) *The Society of the Spectacle*, trans. D. Nicholson-Smith. New York: Zone.
Deleuze, G. and Guattari, F. (1994) *What Is Philosophy?* trans. Hugh Tomlinson and Graham Burchill. London: Verso.
Fisher, M. (2009) *Capitalist Realism: Is There No Alternative?* London: Zero Books.
Florida, R. (2002) *The Rise of the Creative Class*. New York: Basic Books.
Friebe, H. and Lobo, S. (2006) *Wir nennen es Arbeit: die Digitale Bohème oder: Intelligentes Leben jenseits der Festanstellung*. München: Heyne.

Gibbons, M. (1998) *Higher Education Relevance in the 21st Century*. Washington, DC: World Bank.

Grey, J. (2015) 'Dutch student protests ignite movement against management of universities', *The Guardian*, 17 March. Retrieved from: http://www.theguardian.com/higher-education-network/2015/mar/17/dutch-student-protests-ignite-movement-against-management-of-universities.

Hagel, J., Seely Brown, J. and Davison, L. (2010) *The Power of Pull: How Small Moves, Smartly Made, Can Set Big Things in Motion*. New York: Basic Books.

Hardt, M. and Negri, A. (2000) *Empire*. Cambridge, MA: Harvard University Press.

Head, S. (2005) *The New Ruthless Economy: Work and Power in the Digital Age*. Oxford: Oxford University Press.

Head, S. (2014) *Mindless: Why Smarter Machines are Making Dumber Humans*. New York: Basic Books.

Hochschild, A. R. (1985) *The Managed Heart. Commercialization of Human Feeling*. Berkeley, CA: University of California Press.

Johns, T. and Gratton, L. (2013) 'The third wave of virtual work', *Harvard Business Review*, 91 (1/2): 66–73.

Johnson, S. (2010) *Where Good Ideas Come From: The Natural History of Innovation*. New York: Penguin Books.

Kingdon, M. (2012) *The Science of Serendipity: How to Unlock the Promise of Innovation*. Chichester: Wiley & Sons.

Kockelmans, J. (ed.) (1975) *Interdisciplinary and Higher Education*. University Park, PA: Pennsylvania State University Press.

Landry, C. (1995) *The Creative City: A Toolkit for Urban Innovators*. London: Routledge.

Lazzarato, M. (2002) *Puissances de l'Invention: La Psychologie Économique de Gabriel Tarde contre l'Économie Politique*. Paris: Les Empêcheurs de Penser en Rond.

Lehrer, J. (2012) *How Creativity Works*. Edinburgh: Canongate.

Lewis, W. S. (ed.) (1937–83) *The Yale Edition of Horace Walpole's Correspondence*. New Haven, CT: Yale University Press.

Lucretius (1995) *On the Nature of Things: De rerum natura*, trans. Anthony M. Esolen. Baltimore, MD: Johns Hopkins University Press.

McCann, E. J. (2007) 'Inequality and politics in the creative city-region: questions of livability and state strategy', *International Journal of Urban and Regional Research*, 31: 188–96.

Mazzucato, M. (2013) *The Entrepreneurial State: Debunking Public vs. Private Sector Myths*. London: Anthem Press.

Merton, R. and Barber, E. (2004) *The Travels and Adventures of Serendipity: A Study in Sociological Semantics and the Sociology of Science*. Princeton, NJ: Princeton University Press.

Muller, T. and Becker, L. (2012) *Get Lucky: How to Put Planned Serendipity to Work for You and Your Business*. San Francisco: Jossey-Bass.

Murray R., Caulier-Grice, J. and Mulgan, G. (2010) *The Open Book of Social Innovation*. London: Young Foundation and Nesta.

Nathan, M. (2005) *The Wrong Stuff: Creative Class Theory, Diversity and City Performance*, Centre for Cities Discussion Paper No. 1. London: IPPR, pp. 1–8.

Olma, S. (2012) *The Serendipity Machine*. Amersfoort: Lindonk & De Bres.

Olma, S. (2014) *Rethinking Social Innovation between Invention and Imitation*. Retrieved from: http://www.networkcultures.org/mycreativity/2014/08/18/rethinking-social-innovation-between-invention-and-imitation/.

Olma, S. (2016 forthcoming) *In Defence of Serendipity. Essays Toward A Radical Politics of Innovation*. London: Repeater Books.

Pol, E. and Ville, S. (2009) 'Social innovation: buzz word or enduring term?', *Journal of Socio-Economics*, 38 (6): 878–85.

Potts, J. (2011) *Creative Industries and Economic Evolution*. Cheltenham: Edward Elgar.

Prigogine, I., and Stengers, I. (1984) *Order out of Chaos*. New York: Bantam Books.

Reich, R. (1992) *The Work of Nations. Preparing Ourselves for 21st Century Capitalism*. New York: Vintage Books

Sennett, R. (2008) *The Craftsman*. London: Allen Lane.

Serres, M. (2000) *The Birth of Physics*, trans. Jack Hawkes. Manchester: Clinamen Press.

Serres, M. (2012) *Petite Poucette*. Paris: Éditions Le Pommier.

Sloterdijk, P. (2009) *Du mußt dein Leben ändern: Über Anthropotechnik*. Frankfurt am Main: Suhrkamp.

Stiegler, B. (2010a) *For a New Critique of Political Economy*, trans. Daniel Ross. Cambridge: Polity.

Stiegler, B. (2010b) *Taking Care of Youth and the Generations*, trans. Daniel Ross. Stanford, CA: Stanford University Press.

Stiegler, B. (2014) *States of Shock: Stupidity and Knowledge in the 21st Century*, trans. Daniel Ross. Cambridge: Polity.

Turner, F. (2006) *From Counterculture to Cyberculture: Stewart Brand, the Whole Earth Network, and the Rise of Digital Utopianism*. Chicago: Chicago University Press.

Van Andel, P. and Bourcier, D. (2013) *De la Sérendipité dans la Science, la Technique, l'Art et le Droit: Leçons de l'Inattendu*. Paris: Editions Hermann.

Virno, P. (1996) 'Virtuosity and revolution: the political theory of exodus', in P. Virno and M. Hardt (eds), *Radical Thought in Italy: A Potential Politics*. Minneapolis, MN: University of Minnesota Press, pp. 189–212.

Virno, P. (2004) *A Grammar of the Multitude: For an Analysis of Contemporary Forms of Life*, trans. J. Cascaito, I. Bertoletti and A. Casson. Los Angeles: Semiotext(e).

Vonk, O. (2014) 'Creatieve getto's', *Parool*, 26 March, PS5.

Zola, E. (2008) *The Ladies' Paradise*, trans. Brian Nelson. Oxford: Oxford World Classics.

Concluding remarks

15 Higher education and the creative economy

Closing remarks and future research and policy agendas

Roberta Comunian and Abigail Gilmore

The contributions to this book offer an interconnected set of reflections on the collaborations, synergies and interactions between higher education and the creative economy in a range of cities, regions and national landscapes. Read together, they highlight the limited research available that specifically addresses the opportunities and challenges in this area, and make the case for a better understanding of the practices, as well as theories, at the crossroads between academia, the creative economy and public policy. Furthermore, the book proposes a new understanding that goes beyond a recognition of the cultural impact of university presence in specific locations, to raise questions about how this presence – through shared communities of practice, learning spaces and intermediation – stimulates both creative human capital and the development of shared third spaces for research and innovation, as well as tensions and frictions resulting from varying levels of power, interest and influence. We believe this framework can be a useful tool through which to understand collaboration, and explore the challenges and future scenarios of creative engagement across and beyond academia in different geographical contexts. However, we believe that the findings from the chapters also highlight the need for this new research agenda to prioritise three key dimensions that need further investigation:

- the relationship to issues of power;
- the value of creative education and creative human capital;
- the broader societal mission of universities.

Firstly, **it is important to consider and acknowledge power relationships in the collaborations emerging between academia and the creative economy**. This is a key theme of chapters in Part I of the book but also arises in other areas, for example the connections between HE and the development of artistic scenes. While knowledge institutions are large structures with access to space, knowledge and funding, the creative economy is mostly made up of small organisations that lack funding and support infrastructures. The unilateral establishment of collaborations and the traditional 'injection' model – where knowledge inside academia is fed to outside organisations in the hope of broader impact – can become a source of contention, as small creative and cultural organisations might struggle to state their role and importance in cross-boundary collaborations. For knowledge to be relevant and have a real impact there is a need to establish common research goals and objectives, rather than simply feeding in results with the hope that they will be relevant or meaningful to the outside world. As Virani and Pratt demonstrate, intermediaries play a really important role here; however, institutional culture can also shape projects in very different ways, as Schramme shows in the case of deSingel art campus in Belgium. In addition, small creative organisations often struggle to be able to set or contribute to the initial research agenda because of the difficulties in committing time or other resources to long-term collaborations.

Where these relationships are between HEIs and large public and third-sector institutions – such as museums and galleries – the power relationships may be differently structured, as there is greater 'fit' and recognition of the dynamics and missions of these knowledge institutions. With large commercial organisations the dynamics alter again so that, for example, in knowledge exchange and teaching activities, individual degree programmes and student cohorts can function as small R&D spaces within the supply chain. However, since they are dependent on the relationships (and must fit with the commercial timescales) to provide relevant student employability and skills development, commercial mechanisms can cause friction with degree structures. In the case of Artswork Media and Bath Spa University presented by Ashton, we encounter another different model, where the university embeds its teaching and learning within the professional settings of a creative cluster. This also resonates with some of the discussion in Part III of the book. This model is advocated by Gilmore, Gledhill and Rajković within the findings of their research on emerging visual artists in Manchester. In contrast, while England and Comunian find that the role of clusters and networks facilitates equal exchanges and collaborations, HE can also affect and unbalance the market dynamics of the creative economy.

Power relations are also present when we discuss the characteristics of relationships associated with physical and social regeneration initiatives as a secondary aim but primary motivation for creative campus developments, as Benneworth's chapter in Part IV discusses. Here surrounding external communities are brought into the nexus of relations involved when universities engage in deprived and marginalised areas, and are sometimes unwitting parties to decisions that are taken in the name of arts-led regeneration but which bear little relation to the motivations of the university, their students or community partners.

Secondly, **we acknowledge that a better understanding of the value (economic and socio-cultural) of creative human capital is needed**. While creative arts degrees are growing in numbers and popularity in the UK and internationally, graduates face unstable working patterns and conditions and often low economic rewards after their training, as discussed by Frenette and Tepper in Part II. Also, as revealed by Comunian, Faggian and Jewell, this can result in diverse migration and location strategies to respond to unstable labour markets. As Bennett and Burnard's chapter highlights, there is a range of 'human capital creativities' that enable graduates to enter creative work and that the university can foster. Similarly, while universities encourage engaged academics and lecturers/practitioners in their courses, the traditional pathways for promotion and recognition can often prove difficult for this new breed of intellectuals across HE and the creative economy, which Virani and Pratt highlight in their description of the new intermediaries connecting HE and the creative economy. Furthermore, an increased investment of time in relationships and project management is required when working collaboratively outside the walls of academia (and similarly for practitioners negotiating with HE), and the competencies and skills required are not always costed or recognised sufficiently, as Schramme shows in the case of deSingel art campus in Belgium in Part I. This disjuncture is nowhere more apparent than in the financial systems of HEIs, which find it hard to accommodate temporary payment schedules and the requirements of freelance practitioners. As a result, other informal economies sometimes evolve based on skills exchange and social transactions to avoid the issue of slow requisitioning and payment. These are the informal and interconnected networks at the core of Part III of the book, discussed in relation to the cities of Sunderland, Manchester, Leipzig and Singapore. While social economies may help get collaborations working, there is a danger that both artist labour and academic labour are devalued. The terms and conditions for working together, therefore, require change and a shift in valuation, performance management and appraisal, in order to build new pathways for progression for both creative graduates and practitioner-academics in dialogue.

Finally, as universities in the UK face increased criticism over their marketisation and the effects of higher fees, there is a need for **timely reflection on how culture and creativity could help universities engage with local communities** and break down barriers to access for segments of the community that are left outside of the campus and excluded through lack of economic means as well as social and psychological barriers. Both Purushothaman in the case of Singapore and Brook in the case of Australia highlight how arts and creative disciplines are located within an instrumentalised agenda as drivers of economic growth, nation-building and social mobility. Brook's chapter argues that this agenda is not just driven by economic and skills policy, but rather by structural changes within HE institutions that have led to the need for disciplines to remould and revaluate themselves in order promote their market value and 'attractiveness' to students.

As the value of arts and creativity to instrumental policy agendas is increasingly recognised, so the citizenship and social responsibility initiatives of universities are increasingly turning towards new modes of creative engagement which draw on the capacity of academics and practitioners in the creative economy to collaborate and operate in the same civic spaces. However, as Benneworth's chapter suggests, even with the best intentions such development involves risk, and engaging with the broader community can be problematic and challenging. These examples and new spaces of intervention require negotiation – and potentially eradication – of old boundaries, whether disciplinary or practice-based, in order that exchange, co-location and co-production of knowledge can be realised, helped by the recognition that technological change has radically changed access to information and rendered the stewardship of knowledge within universities elitist and outdated.

This is also the argument of Olma's chapter, which reflects on constraints of disciplinary boundaries and managerial frameworks with HE. His conclusion – with which many of the authors in this book would agree – sets the new challenge to be addressed by HE and policy for the next generation: how to equip society with creative citizens, through education with virtuous intent, which provides the conditions for collaboration and serendipitous encounters across disciplines as well beyond the campus.

While the reflections in this book have tried to contribute to future research and practice, they also aim to stimulate debate on the challenges ahead. We signpost a wide range of shared interests that have arisen in the context of policy drivers for collaboration and engagement across universities and the creative economy, but which are also driven by the passions, enthusiasms and specialist expertise of the individuals involved to develop new, more appropriate methods for knowledge exchange and cross-sector working.

We believe the contributions in this book are a first powerful call for a new research agenda, which addresses the close connection of higher education with local communities and economies beyond the paradigm of science and technology. As both higher education and the creative economy shape places, contributing to their economic, social and cultural well-being, it is important that policy actions, as well as research activities, are built on shared understanding and continuous research.

Index